PRAISE FOR

## Cleveland Ethnic Eats . . .

"Dipping into Laura Taxel's book is like putting on a pair of magic glasses. Before, Northeast Ohio is meatloaf and peas. After, it's a colorful melting pot of Jamaican jerk wings and Hungarian stuffed cabbage, of reggae in the back room and curried goat in the kitchen. . . . " – *Akron Beacon Journal*

"A jewel. . . . Good research, fine writing and touches of genuine love make this truly special. . . . Anything you might want to know about this area's ethnic restaurants and markets."
· – Linda Griffith, *Currents*

"Good reading—and good eating, too." – *Northern Ohio Live*

"This lively and wide-ranging book is a welcome guide. . . . With tips on how to find anything from Asian basil to zucchini kugel, it could be as useful to serious cooks as serious eaters."
– *The Plain Dealer*

"An adventure in dining on every page."
– *The Morning Journal*

"If you are tired of going to the same places for dinner every Friday and Saturday night, you won't want to miss out on this fun and informative book." – *Call & Post*

"Taxel methodically covers nearly every corner of the Cleveland food world, helping readers find what they are looking for."
– *Sun Newspapers*

"Whatever type of exotic food your taste buds might demand on a particular day, chances are that *Cleveland Ethnic Eats* can steer you to a place to get it." – *West Side Leader*

"A well-planned guide for diners seeking authentic culinary cuisine from around the world and for diners who simply want to try something different from their usual fare." – *The Gazette*

# Cleveland Ethnic Eats™

## 8th EDITION

## Laura Taxel

GRAY & COMPANY, PUBLISHERS
CLEVELAND

*To Barney, my partner in eating and driving as in all else.*

This book is my way of expressing appreciation to all the members of the ethnic communities who so graciously opened their doors to me. It is dedicated to those people who generously shared their ideas, insights, suggestions, and stories, and to the restaurant owners, managers, merchants, chefs, and shopkeepers who were so hospitable and helpful. My thanks to each of you.

© 2009 by Laura Taxel

Illustrations © Richard J. Konisiewicz

Gray & Company, Publishers
www.grayco.com

This guide was prepared on the basis of the author's best knowledge at the time of publication. However, because of constantly changing conditions beyond the author's control, the author disclaims any responsibility for the accuracy and completeness of the information in this guide. Users of this guide are cautioned not to place undue reliance upon the validity of the information contained herein and to use this guide at their own risk.

Text design by Laurence J. Nozik

ISBN: 978-1-59851-053-9
Printed in the United States of America

# CONTENTS

# ACKNOWLEDGMENTS

If you've never done it, it's hard to imagine just what it takes to pull all the pieces of a book like this together. Trust me when I say that it requires hard work and a great deal of eating. No one has done more to make it possible than my husband Barney. Over the years he has never wavered in his willingness to get me wherever I needed to go, keep me company, and try almost anything. Our three sons, Ezra, Nathan, and Simon, have also provided an immeasurable quantity of enthusiastic and participatory support for my efforts. They are my loyal, fearless, and always hungry band of culinary explorers. Together these four men have traveled far and wide, sampled dishes that lesser folk might shrink from, and stuffed themselves beyond the call of duty.

# INTRODUCTION

In this detailed guide to the authentic ethnic restaurants, bakeries, butcher shops, and grocery stores of Greater Cleveland, you'll find out who still makes strudel dough and sausages by hand—the old-world way; where to buy basmati rice or loquats; and what restaurant is the only one in town serving choucroute garni, an Alsatian dish made with pork and sauerkraut. Researching the book, I spoke with a true United Nations of Clevelanders, individuals who have a strong sense of their own ethnic background. I asked them to tell me where they and other people from their "home" country eat and shop for authentic meals. Housewives and community leaders were my expert advisors. With their help I was able to uncover a vast multicultural food world in this little corner of Ohio. Even a quick flip though the pages of this book testifies to how interesting and varied a world it is.

More than a directory, *Cleveland Ethnic Eats* is a guide to eating as an adventurous experience. It's about where to go when you're looking for an alternative to typical American fare or have a yen for the taste of faraway places. It lets you know what to expect when you get there. It offers no guarantees that you'll like what you find, but every place I visited was in its own way worth the trip. Some offer the kinds of dishes your mother or your grandmother made. Others present foods you may never have seen or even imagined people eating. Almost everything—from pierogies to pakoras, linguine to lo mein—is available in Cleveland. It may surprise you to find out just how easy it is to get a bowl of real pad Thai noodles or Jamaican goat curry.

There are spots, hidden behind nondescript storefronts and tucked away in innocuous strip malls, where shopkeepers wear saris; menus, posted on the walls, are written in beautiful Oriental calligraphy; and friendly smiles rather than English may be the only common language. Without flying across an ocean, you can sample Ethiopian yebug alicha (lamb stew) under a thatched roof or sit at a Japanese sushi bar and watch a master slice and wrap raw fish. You can cross a threshold, and leave the sights and sounds of this city behind you as you enter stores filled with exotic smells and unfamiliar foods, close to home and yet as foreign to most of us as a Middle Eastern shouk (bazaar).

I know a couple who have made shopping in Cleveland's ethnic markets a lifelong hobby. They say it's exciting, like a visit to another country, and the foods they encounter always give them new ideas to use in their own kitchen. Eating in ethnic restaurants, they told me, is also a low-cost way to "travel," a chance to soak up the flavor of the people and the culture along with the sauce. After spending many years investigating more than 30 of the area's ethnic food communities, I have to agree with them.

Shopping was an outing, not a chore. Many of the markets, family-owned and -operated, offered the hospitality and personal service of an old-fashioned corner store. Eating out became more than just a meal in a restaurant; it was an opportunity to take a little trip into parts unknown, break away from the usual, and enlarge my view of what Cleveland is all about. I discovered that this is truly a "cosmopolis," a city inhabited by people from all parts of the world, and it's this variety that can make living here so much fun.

## Discovering Cleveland's Ethnic Communities

In addition to being a dining guide, this is also a chronicle of the unique mix of peoples and cultures that come together in Northeast Ohio. Immigrants, representing more than 50 different nations, have contributed to the growth of Cleveland from its earliest days, changing it from a pioneer backwater to a thriving, culturally rich urban center. They have come with strong backs, skilled hands, and great minds that have helped to build this city and its institutions. And even as they forged new American identities, they kept alive the spirit of their homelands. The shops and restaurants they opened represent the need that each immigrant group has always had for a taste of home. The fact that as a country we've developed an appreciation for many of their distinctive dishes shows what a profound influence their presence has had on our national consciousness.

Some, like the Puerto Ricans and the Vietnamese, are relative newcomers, arriving in this region in significant numbers only since the early 1980s. Others, like the Germans and the Irish, were among the earliest settlers. The census of 1890 showed that more than half of the city's population was foreign born. The Haymarket area southwest of Public Square was called "Baghdad on the Cuyahoga" because so many different languages were spoken there. When Cleveland celebrated its 150th anniversary in 1946, the theme was "One World." The Chinese, Czechs, English, Finns, French, Germans, Greeks, Hungarians, Irish, Jews, Italians, Lithuanians, Poles, Scots, Slovaks, Slovenians, Spanish, Swiss, and Ukrainians living here all made floats for the parade.

But we don't have it all. Guides to eating ethnic in other cities include restaurants that feature the foods of Afghanistan and Cuba, Argentina and Tunis. An active community interest in ethnic foods demonstrates that we're not just a meatloaf and mashed potatoes town, as some have said, and will encourage other nationality groups to open restaurants and share their foods with us.

Nowadays, most ethnic communities in Cleveland are defined not so much by geographic boundaries as by a shared heritage. But in years past, nationality groups clustered in specific neighborhoods. There was Big and Little Italy, Greek Town, the Cabbage Patch and Chicken Village (Czech), Warszawa (Polish), and Chinatown. Remnants of some of those neighborhoods exist, and often that's also where there are still many stores and little hole-in-the-wall restaurants that offer foods unlike anything to be found on the shelves of an ordinary supermarket or under a heat lamp at a drive-thru. But special shops and restaurants are located in newer suburbs and shopping malls, too.

That means this book is also a kind of road map, showing you how to escape from the confines of your usual stomping grounds and explore parts of the city and the surrounding communities you may know little about or rarely have occasion to visit.

## How the Restaurants and Markets Were Chosen

My criteria for choosing what to include were ethnicity, authenticity, and personal recommendations from those who know the food best. This is a book with a theme, not a Yellow Pages, and that means there are many restaurants that I didn't include. That's not to say they aren't very good, but they didn't fit my definition. If I've missed a place you feel should be included, my contact information is at the back of the book. Tell me about it so I can visit and possibly add it to the next edition.

There are no national chains in this guide, no places that offer only one or two ethnically inspired dishes, or places that feature what's lately been described as "fusion cuisine" (or, as I call it, blue corn pasta in peanut salsa with a side of herbed collard greens). I was looking for traditional food made with integrity and respect for the eating style of the culture from which it springs. I stretched my definition of ethnic as far as I could comfortably go, in an effort to include places that honor the foods, flavors, and preparation techniques of a particular geographic region or cultural group.

I didn't pass judgment on the restaurants I've included, or rate them with stars. That's for you to do, though I have to admit that many times I decided that there really was no reason for me to ever cook again. I wanted to offer information, not evaluations, and encourage readers to investigate and experiment. That's what I did, and I had a wonderful time. Along the way, I met many fine people who are proud of where they come from, determined to link the best from their past with the present, and eager to share their customs and traditions. Hearing their stories and tasting their distinctive cuisines has been a process of building bridges, making connections, and opening doors.

Many of these cuisines almost qualify as endangered species. The "Americanization" of eating, with its emphasis on fast foods, continues to make inroads into traditional practices and lifestyles in Cleveland and around the world. Recognizing the value of Cleveland's ethnic restaurants and markets and patronizing these establishments is a way to preserve them and insure that the unique contribution each makes to the community will continue to nourish us.

"Through its food," Salvador Gonzalez, who came to Cleveland from Mexico, told me, "you can come to know the culture of any country." *Cleveland Ethnic Eats* is an invitation to participate in that fascinating cultural exploration, a journey around the world that can begin and end in Northeast Ohio.

# USING THIS BOOK

## How This Book Is Organized

This book is divided into eight broad geographic regions. I've established areas that reflect physical proximity and kitchen commonalities rather than political affiliations or national borders. Within each of those chapters, ethnic groups are listed alphabetically. For each group, there is a section of restaurants and another of stores, introduced with information about the specific ingredients that define the cuisine of that country or culture. In her cookbook, *All Around the World*, author Sheila Lukins likens these staples and seasonings to a painter's palette, with each cuisine having its own collection of foods and flavorings that set it apart from all others. Of course, these tend to be general descriptions, and there are always distinctive regional differences within every country.

The listings themselves go beyond just names, addresses, and telephone numbers. They'll tell you about parking, identify landmarks that make places easier to locate, and let you know when to call ahead for reservations and special orders. The market information makes rare and hard-to-find ingredients accessible, and points the way to one-of-a-kind treats like homemade meat pies and handmade dumplings. The restaurant information lets you know what sort of dress is appropriate, whether or not it's a good spot to bring the kids, and explains what goes into some of the foods featured on the menu. Using the descriptions, you can pick out a fancy, sophisticated place that serves bouillabaisse (a Mediterranean fish soup), an inexpensive little neighborhood hangout that has huevos rancheros (Mexican eggs), or a bar *cum* restaurant that offers moussaka (a Greek meat-and-eggplant dish) along with late-night jazz.

Some of the stores are big, brightly lit, and modern. Some are quaint, with a charming old-world ambience. Others are irritatingly small, or inconveniently hidden away on back streets, but they're open seven days a week and you're sure to find that jar of kimchee (pickled cabbage) essential for the Korean meal you want to prepare.

The same is true of the restaurants. A few may be well known to the general public and even qualify as trendy, but many serve mostly their own countrymen and a group of loyal fans who think of them as their own special secret "find." There are places that seat 120 and others that squeeze seven tables and a kitchen into a space not much bigger than the average living room. At one end of the spectrum are down-and-dirty joints where the linoleum is cracked and pinball machines provide the only background music; at the other, elegant, stylish dining rooms with well-dressed servers who bring artfully arranged food to your linen-covered table. And there is every variation in between. Some restaurants are located in neighborhoods that diners who come from beyond its borders might not consider the best. Many are unpretentious places, where a dollar goes a long way and the food makes you feel well fed and satisfied. Whether you're looking for upscale or downscale, this book is meant to help you find what you want.

Use it to figure out just how far you'd have to go in order to sample Vietnamese bun ga sao (stir fried chicken) or see what's available, ethnically speaking, in South Euclid (how about conch fritters and fried plantains at Rachel's Caribbean Cuisine?). Whether you've a hankering for a cannoli and a loaf of crusty, fresh-from-the-oven Italian bread or need green bananas and hot Scotch bonnet peppers for a Caribbean dish, this book can help.

If you've not been much of an eating adventurer, preferring steak and an iceberg lettuce salad, the predictability of a food franchise, or the familiarity of your own part of town, let *Cleveland Ethnic Eats* get you started venturing out into the frontiers of new taste sensations. It's full of the kind of information that makes everybody an insider. And who knows, new places may soon become your old favorites.

### What to Wear? Atmosphere and Attire

By "atmosphere" I refer both to the style of dress that seems to be the general rule at a restaurant and to the decor and tone of the place. These are connected: how the patrons dress is part of every dining room's particular ambience. Tank tops and shorts set one kind of mood; suits and ties, another. And if you know how people dress when they go to a particular restaurant, you'll have some idea of what to expect from the surroundings.

There is no denying that we're becoming a dress-down society in general, but around Cleveland tradition still holds on. Here, "dressing up" usually means more than just a jacket with jeans.

My four-step scale reflects local attitudes and standards for attire: Relaxed, Casual, Dressy, and Formal. (You may notice below that I have tended to define attire in terms of men's clothing. Please don't read into this any statements about politics or power. It's just a simpler way to make things clear. Men have fewer options, so it's simpler to base guidelines on their clothes.

*Relaxed*, for the purposes of this book, means almost anything goes, short of being barefoot and shirtless. Neither the management nor the other diners have any expectations you must meet. On the night I visited one such eatery, the couple ahead of me were dressed in warm-up suits; the woman behind me was wrapped in an ankle-length fur coat. The criterion to go by is what makes you comfortable—knowing, in advance, that it's next to impossible to be underdressed.

*Casual* has expanded as a category since this book was first published. Comfort is still the aim and informality the norm, but nowadays it's how most restaurants choose to define themselves and includes everything from upscale play clothes—what folks in the trendy mail-order catalogs and magazine ads wear when they're having fun—to business attire. You can get away with wearing a T-shirt, but it shouldn't sport stains, brand names, or lewd remarks. Turtlenecks, sweaters, and jeans are all acceptable, but you'd still fit in if you chose to go with more of an office look: shirts with collars, pressed slacks, and sport jackets.

*Dressy* and *Formal* have merged. Very few venues continue to require coats and ties for men. Upscale restaurants are more tolerant than in the past, but there remains an unspoken expectation at places with this designation that patrons will be well dressed. In times past I think this look was described as "nice," as in your mother saying, "Why don't you change into something nice?" or "Don't you have anything nicer than that?" before you went out on a date.

## Spelling

Throughout the listings, you may notice many different spellings for the same word. That's the nature of transliteration. There's often more than one way to create the English equivalent of a foreign word. In general, I took my cues from the people I spoke with. So one store owner suggested I write "filo" dough while another spelled it out for me as "phyllo," and when I checked, I found both are used in other books. I also adopted a policy of matching my spellings to those that appear on the menu of each establishment I was writing about, except where there were obvious English misspellings.

## Prices

I've used a scale of one to five dollar signs to indicate the relative cost of an average meal at each of the restaurants:

| | |
|---|---|
| $$$$$ | much lower than average |
| $$$$$ | slightly lower than average |
| $$$$$ | about average |
| $$$$$ | slightly higher than average |
| $$$$$ | much higher than average |

Obviously, one person's "average meal" varies from another's—even at the same restaurant—depending on what and how much you order. To give a reasonable standard, though, I based my rating on the average dinner entrée price from each restaurant's standard menu. I also considered other factors, such as whether entrées come with appetizer, or whether it's the kind of place that's intended for a lavish multicourse meal rather than a simple sit-down dinner.

## Don't Forget to Call Ahead!

Keep in mind that although the information is as accurate and up-to-date as possible, things can and will change. Hours don't always stay the same, policies and practices are altered, businesses come and go, and new owners often have new ideas. Moreover, if it's a long drive to an unfamiliar location, it's *highly recommended* that you call ahead for directions to save you time and to avoid confusion.

It is *always* best to call first.

## Location

I've divided Greater Cleveland roughly into 10 geographic areas: Downtown, Near West Side, West Side, Farther West, Near East Side, East Side, Farther East, Southeast, Southwest, and Farther South. This is to help you tell from a glance at the listings approximately where a restaurant or market is located relative to where you live or plan to visit. The map on the next page shows how these areas are divided. An area is indicated directly below each restaurant's and market's name, followed by specific city and street address information. Phone numbers appear next to each listing's name so you can call for directions.

## Areas Covered in This Book

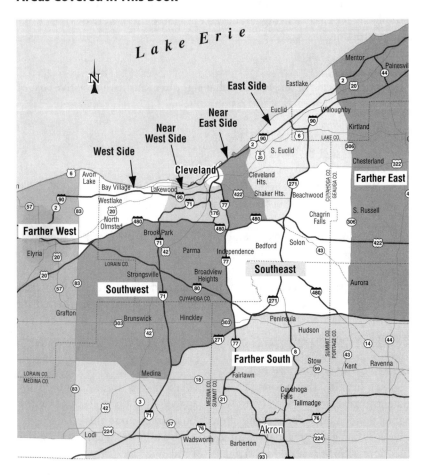

# Cleveland
# Ethnic
# Eats™

# PACIFIC RIM

The region known as the Pacific Rim includes the vast and varied terrain of more than 10 different Far Eastern countries. The Cleveland area is home to markets and restaurants from the Rim nations of Cambodia, China, Japan, Korea, the Philippines, Thailand, and Vietnam.

The Chinese were the first Asian group to come to Cleveland, and their numbers began to grow significantly in the late 1800s. In its early days, Cleveland's Chinese community was made up primarily of immigrants from the southern Cantonese province of Guangdong who came by way of the West Coast. Later it came to include people from northern and central China, Hong Kong, and Taiwan. Cleveland's Chinatown, along Rockwell Avenue between 24th and 21st streets, was once densely populated with immigrants. Though small by the standards of New York or San Francisco, it is nonetheless the historical heart of the community. Now Chinese live in all parts of Greater Cleveland, but the $2.3 million renovation of an old warehouse into Asia Plaza on Payne created a modern, bustling Asian shopping and dining center that is a new hub for the old neighborhood.

The Organization of Chinese Americans of Greater Cleveland, which networks with other local groups like the Asian Pacific Federation, is a tightly knit association active in cultural education. "We feel that our traditions are very rich," said Frances Namkoong, founding president, "and they are important to us. Most Chinese Americans live with a foot in both worlds. We continue to be close to our immigrant ancestors and a world view that comes very much from their past. But at the same time, we are Americans."

Ms. Namkoong's sentiments are echoed by others in the Asian community. "We teach our children that their roots are in Korea but their home is in Cleveland," says Dr. Sakoo Lee, former head of the Korean-American Association of Greater Cleveland. The organization now boasts more than 5,000 members.

Koreans did not become a visible presence here until the 1970s, when U.S. immigration quotas changed. According to Dr. Lee (and much to my surprise), one reason Koreans like Cleveland is our four-season climate, which is similar to, though slightly colder than, that of their homeland. But there's more to their attraction than weather.

"This city and the surrounding suburbs," said Dr. Lee, a physician with a family practice in Westlake, "are truly a multicultural melting pot. Every nationality group is unique with something to contribute. I've traveled in many other parts of the country, and Cleveland is one of those rare places where there's an understanding of that. Here, we can all live together, keeping what's best from our own heritage while becoming part of the community."

That receptivity and understanding were part of what helped the Japanese feel welcome in Cleveland after World War II. Forcibly removed from West Coast communities, they were encouraged to resettle here by the War Relocation Authority, and their numbers peaked in 1946. Filipinos, who settled here after 1950, make up another small subset of the Asian community. Like their Chinese and Japanese counterparts, many are professionals in the fields of medicine and technology. A large number of students from all three countries have come in recent years to take advantage of the area's colleges, medical schools and teaching hospitals, and industrial research facilities. According to Sunthorn Phetcharat, a Thai immigrant and former owner of the Thai Kitchen in Lakewood, there are not many people from Thailand living in Cleveland, and their stories would have to be told one by one, for they have come as individuals and not as a group.

Most Cambodians and Vietnamese began to arrive in Cleveland after 1970, driven to emigrate by war and its devastating aftermath. "My family is lucky," explained Liem Nguyen, a former South Vietnamese army captain (and prisoner of the North Vietnamese) now living on the city's West Side. "Once again we have a bright future. This is a chance to start a new life. We are willing to work very hard, night and day. We want to show our thanks and prove to Cleveland that we have much to give."

One of the things each of these ethnic groups has to give is its singular cuisine. Though influenced by geographic neighbors, each country possesses its own distinctive approach to food.

Chinese cooking represents one of the oldest continuing culinary traditions in the world. It is also the Asian cuisine most familiar to Americans. Won Kee opened Cleveland's first Chinese restaurant, on Ontario, before 1900; a second was added soon after on the west side of Public Square. Our taste for Chinese food has expanded in recent years beyond the now-familiar Cantonese and Mandarin to include the spicy styles of Szechuan and Hunan cooking. The Chinese New Year, celebrated in January or February, is a great opportunity to sample a wide variety of special traditional foods.

Korean food tends to be spicy, though not necessarily fiery hot. Kimchee appears on the table at every meal. It is a peppery, piquant condiment made primarily from pickled cabbage. Chili powder, vinegar, fermented bean pastes, and sesame seeds are important ingredients in the Korean kitchen. Bounded on three sides by water, Koreans have incorporated a wide variety of fish and seafood into their diet, though they also have a national enthusiasm for beef, an appreciation said to have been left behind by the invading Mongol hordes.

Japanese cooking, too, is dominated by seafood, much of it eaten raw and accompanied by varieties of pickles and pungent condiments like momiji oroshi, made from grated white radish with red chilies, or wasabi, a horseradish paste so strong that an overly large bite can bring on tears and provide instant cleansing of the sinuses. Classical Japanese cuisine shows virtually no signs of outside influences, perhaps because the country imposed a ban on foreigners from 1640 to 1868.

The same cannot be said for the cooking styles of Vietnam, Cambodia, and the Philippines. All bear the stamp of European colonial incursions into both their territory and their traditional ways of life. So Philippine food has a decidedly Spanish twist, and one of the most characteristic dishes, a chicken-and-pork stew called adobo, is reminiscent of Mexican cookery, which shares this Spanish influence.

From the French, who first arrived in the 16th century, the Vietnamese got a taste for sweetened milky coffee and also sausages, which they make from both meat and fish. Indian traders brought curry, used primarily by the southern Vietnamese, and the Buddhist influence means there are many vegetarian dishes. Traditional cooking uses raw greens, and food is often served on crisp lettuce leaves.

Thailand, though inspired by its culinary neighbors, China, India, Burma, and Laos, was never colonized, so its food has no Western leanings. Thai cooks make good use of all the tropical fruits and vegetables that grow in abundance throughout the country, and season them with fresh herbs like lemongrass, green coriander, lime leaves, mint, and Oriental basils. They make liberal use of coconut milk, chili peppers, peanuts, and sesame seeds. These same flavorings are used both by the Vietnamese and the Cambodians.

Soy is the salty condiment favored by the Chinese and Japanese; a similar effect is achieved by other Southeast Asian cooks through the use of a fermented fish sauce. Use of garlic, ginger, scallions, and hot capsicums (peppers) is universal, but cooks in each country, as well as in different regions, use them in quite different ways, and the results vary widely. Koreans, for example, often add the garlic at the end of cooking or eat it raw so that it keeps its bite.

Rice, of course, is an omnipresent staple. The Thai invitation to a meal translates as "Come and eat rice," while an age-old Chinese greeting is "Have you eaten rice yet?" All Asian cuisines rely on very fresh, seasonal foods and strive to retain rather than mask the natural flavors of each ingredient.

Eating styles throughout the Pacific Rim are very light and healthy. People eat few dairy products, meat in small quantities, and use only vegetable and bean oils. Rich desserts are the exception rather than the rule.

Technique and presentation are defining principles for all these Asian cuisines. Actual cooking methods tend to be quick and simple, reflecting the fact that food is eaten with chopsticks or spoons and so must be sliced and chopped into small pieces.

Delicate flavors come from painstaking preparation, with great attention to detail, and subtly seasoned sauces. The Chinese and the Japanese say that every dish must be made with four elements in mind: color, fragrance, flavor, and shape. Korean and Chinese cooks strive for balance and harmony among what they call the five basic flavors: sweet, sour, hot, tart, and salty. The equation for Thai cuisine is only slightly different: sweetness, sourness, saltiness, hotness, nuttiness, and bitterness.

We now have two Filipino restaurants and a few markets that carry ingredients for home cooking. There are a couple of Cambodian restaurants and a handful of Thai and Vietnamese ones. There are now a few Korean restaurants where Clevelanders can sample the food from "The Land of Morning Calm," and a few serving authentic Japanese cuisine. And although the list of Chinese restaurants is long, only a select few serve what the Chinese consider to be authentic, rather than American, Chinese food.

Frances Namkoong has some advice for those who want a true Asian eating experience. "Much of the best food is not on the English-language menus. But diners can ask for dishes they've heard about, enjoyed elsewhere, or things they notice other non-American people eating. A restaurant would feel honored if guests request recommendations from the kitchen."

# RESTAURANTS

## Asian mix

### Teahouse Noodles
☎ (216) 623-9131
CITY: **Cleveland**   AREA: **Downtown**
ATMOSPHERE: **Relaxed**   COST: $$$$$

**ADDRESS:** 1900 E. 6th St.
**HOURS:** Mon–Fri 10:30 a.m.–3:30 p.m.
**RESERVATIONS:** Not taken **PAYMENT:** MC, VS, AX,
DIS **BAR:** None **TAKEOUT:** Yes **ACCESS:** ♿ Limited
**OTHER ETHNIC:** Chinese, Filipino, Indonesian,
Japanese, Thai

Here is a very different kind of American fast-food restaurant, inspired by the noodle shops travelers can find on almost any city street corner in many Asian countries. And these meals really should make you happy because they're wholesome and flavorful.

To make everything "user friendly" and appealing to Cleveland diners, each dish begins with the same basic ingredients—rice noodles or steamed brown rice and fresh Oriental vegetables. Then comes the choice of sauce—Rica Rica (a Balinese sweet and hot sauce), a distinctive and very popular Thai peanut, a creamy Indonesian curry, or a pineapple-soy Hawaiian teriyaki—or, if the goal is a bowl of soup, either miso broth or a chicken broth seasoned with lemongrass and ginger to float them in. There's also the option of adding chicken and/or shrimp to the vegetarian combinations. Vegetable-filled, tofu and bean medley, steamed rice-flour-dough buns topped with the same selection of sauces are another possibility. Steam table specials change daily and include soups such as miso mushroom or coco ginger, along with steamed wontons and heartier entrées such as a Balinese-style chicken prepared in a sweet and tangy sauce; Thai curry chicken with sweet potatoes; or chicken and stir-fried vegetables made with coconut milk and mango. Salads can be dressed in a lemongrass vinaigrette, sesame ginger, or spicy peanut sauce.

Everything is made in-house and is relatively low fat, low salt, and very nutritious, but a feather icon on the menu marks those that are especially light and healthy. The wait for an order, which you place at the counter and pick up yourself, is usually not more than three minutes. There are no servers in this simple storefront space, and tables accommodate only 18. As to parking, walk if you can. Otherwise, good luck.

### Teahouse Noodles
☎ (216) 229-8599
CITY: **Cleveland**   AREA: **Near East Side**
ATMOSPHERE: **Relaxed**   COST: $$$$$

**ADDRESS:** 2218 Murray Hill Rd.
**HOURS:** Mon–Sat 11 a.m.–9 p.m. **RESERVATIONS:**
Not taken **PAYMENT:** MC, VS, AX, DIS **BAR:** None
**TAKEOUT:** Yes **ACCESS:** ♿ Limited **OTHER ETHNIC:**
Chinese, Filipino, Indonesian, Japanese, Thai

See listing for Teahouse Noodles on E. 6th St. in Cleveland for more information.

# Cambodian

## Phnom Penh Restaurant

☎ (216) 251-0210

CITY: **Cleveland**   AREA: **Near West Side**
ATMOSPHERE: **Casual**   COST: **$$$**$$

**ADDRESS:** 13124 Lorain Ave.
**HOURS:** Mon–Thu 11 a.m.–9:30 p.m., Fri 11
a.m.–10 p.m., Sat 11 a.m.–11 p.m., Sun 3–9
p.m. **RESERVATIONS:** Taken, recommended on
weekends for groups of 4+ **PAYMENT:** Cash
only **BAR:** BYOB **TAKEOUT:** Yes **ACCESS:** ♿ Full
access **OTHER ETHNIC:** Vietnamese

Owner Mono Bun is a native of Cambodia, and his cuisine is traditionally a strongly flavored one characterized by the use of coconut milk, fermented fish sauce, peanuts, and a variety of spices unfamiliar to Americans, such as galanga root (like ginger but milder), tangy Asian basil, lemongrass, aromatic mint, and kaffir lime leaves. The preparation and presentation are similar to the Chinese cooking Ohioans are more familiar with, but the sauces and seasonings render the taste quite different. The promise of "special sauce" here, unlike its burger-topping American counterpart, really delivers something special because sauces are made with spice-blend pastes similar to those of India, using turmeric, star anise, cloves, cinnamon, and nutmeg. Many dishes are made with noodles (wheat, rice, and potato based) that come soft and flat, round, crispy, stir-fried, sautéed, or pan-stirred. Plenty of options for the health conscious: vegetarian appetizers, soups, and entrées, a section of the menu devoted to "healthy traditional Cambodian dishes," and a flavorful low-fat dish called mikroolaa.

The pronunciation of most items is a mystery to the untrained tongue, but never fear—each item on the menu has a number so you won't have to struggle with trying to ask for loath chha (noodles with vegetables and egg) or banh sough (rice noodles with vegetables, whipped coconut milk, and crumbled spring rolls). For daily specials like the very unusual amok siemreap (spicy shrimp, scallops, crab, and catfish steamed in a banana leaf), just point. Servers, who are almost exclusively Cambodian, speak English and will help diners find their way around the nine-page menu, which also provides short English-language explanations of each of the 136 dishes. The menu offers even more options by allowing some food play: add their homemade tofu to any order; add seafood or noodles to soup; substitute vegetable fried rice for steamed rice; and personalize the heat in any spicy dish by ordering mild, medium, or hot. Loyal customers come back regularly from as far away as Toledo. One enthusiast insists their Khmer shrimp and seafood rice soup is better than "Jewish penicillin" (chicken soup).

The L-shaped space is small, plain, and simple. A mirror on one wall creates the illusion of space, as do the big storefront windows. There's seating for about 50 patrons. There are a couple of round tables that can accommodate groups of six or eight, but most are four- and two-tops. Phnom Penh is usually busy at lunchtime and caters to a dinner crowd of relaxed food adventurers who are willing to bring their own beer and wine. For those who want to quench their thirst without alcohol, there are some treats—a large variety of tropical fruit drinks, egg soda, soybean or coconut milk, and hot or cold French coffee. There is no waiting area to speak of, so you may find yourself standing in the entryway or outside until your table is ready, but I think it's worth it and apparently so do many other people who are willing to put up with the inconvenience. The restaurant's facade blends in so well with the other stores on the street that it's easy to miss when driving by. If you park in one of the few head-in spaces directly in front of it you're almost inside the dining room. Plenty of additional on-street parking in the neighborhood. Gift certificates are available.

## Phnom Penh Restaurant

☎ (216) 357-2951

CITY: **Cleveland**  AREA: **Near West Side**
ATMOSPHERE: **Relaxed**  COST: $$$$$

**ADDRESS:** 1929 W. 25th St.
**HOURS:** Mon–Thu 11 a.m.–9:30 p.m., Fri–Sat 11 a.m.–11 p.m., Sun 3–9 p.m. **RESERVATIONS:** Taken **PAYMENT:** Cash only **BAR:** BYOB
**TAKEOUT:** Yes **ACCESS:** ⅙ Full access **OTHER ETHNIC:** Vietnamese

If you have a hard time making decisions, consider this a warning: Like its sister spot on Lorain operated by the same family, this restaurant has an eight-page menu. But it makes things a bit easier once you realize that many items are actually just variations on a theme. Bay Chha Jee, for example, is a fiery version of fried rice. It comes eight ways: with vegetables, chicken, beef, shrimp, pork, seafood, a combination of these, or extra hot with chili-spiked beef and shrimp. There are many different curries: neak poan are made with coconut milk; bayon are a mix of zucchini, summer squash, eggplant, green beans, and snow peas; kuy teave chha kreoung tek trey phem are green vermicelli curries topped with crumbles of spring roll, chopped peanuts, and Asian basil; mee khmer dishes feature rice noodles and a topping of tofu, shredded bits of omelet,

bean sprouts, and crushed chilies. Kreoung means it's a stir-fry spiced up with a paste of lime leaves, garlic, turmeric and galanga roots, and lemongrass, and there are 15 of them.

Everything under the heading *taprom* has a sweet and sour sauce. Knowing all this, however, does not mean that ordering won't require focus and resolve. Soups alone pose a major challenge. There are 20 of them. Do you want potato noodles, rice noodles, or egg noodles? A small or large portion? You can add beef to some, seafood to others.

The only help I can offer is a few of my own personal recommendations. Among the appetizers I love the stuffed chicken wing, fish cakes, nating (ground coconut and pork with crispy rice), and fried home-made tofu. Some noteworthy entrées are mussels with ginger, Cambodian crepes, and chicken lemongrass, but I'd happily eat any of the noodle dishes any time. For a taste experience that's likely to take you into less common culinary territory try Amok Siemreap, seafood and coconut mil steamed in a banana leaf, or Samlaw Machou Phnom Penh, a tangy stew prepared with tamarind, tomato, and pineapple. The tropical fruit drinks are a treat. (For more information about the menu, see previous listing for Phnom Penh.)

This location, just a block from the West Side Market, opened in March 2006. The intimate space, with traditional carvings on the wall and nice lighting, is prettier than the older place. But don't forget—cash only at both restaurants.

# Chinese

## Bo Loong
☎ (216) 391-3113
CITY: **Cleveland**   AREA: **Near East Side**
ATMOSPHERE: **Casual**   COST: $$$$

**ADDRESS:** 3922 St. Clair Ave.
**HOURS:** Daily 10 a.m.–2 a.m.   **RESERVATIONS:**
Taken, recommended for groups of 6+
**PAYMENT:** MC, VS, AX, DIS, checks **BAR:** Beer,
wine, liquor **TAKEOUT:** Yes **ACCESS:** ఉ Full access

This place is big, seating 400, and the first impression is of something between a cafeteria and a university dining hall, with a funky red-and-gold Oriental motif. But the fact that the décor lacks a slick look (part of its unique charm) does not keep this restaurant from being a hands-down favorite among Cleveland's Chinese families, and their regular, visible presence is a measure of the authentic quality of the food.

Management is especially proud of the dim sum, a large selection of sweet and savory pastries, buns, and dumplings that can be ordered individually as an appetizer or in combination to create an entire meal. The number of choices is unequaled anywhere else in town, especially on the weekends. Some of the notable options include steamed or baked buns filled with barbecued pork; rice noodles stuffed with beef; sticky rice with pork; Chinese sausage, duck, and egg wrapped and steamed in a lotus leaf; fried dumplings stuffed with shrimp and vegetables; sesame seed pastry with a red bean paste filling; and an egg custard tart. They are also pleased to now offer patrons seafood so fresh that it's still swimming when you order it: lobster, eel, catfish, and tilapia are fished from the tank and immediately prepared.

While many of the other dishes on the menu will be familiar, reflecting a variety of regional cuisines and including shark's fin soup, chicken in black bean sauce, salt-baked shrimp, and beef with ginger and scallions, others cater to a more Asian palate and feature such unusual ingredients as chicken feet, beef tripe, and quail eggs. If you're feeling experimental, this is a great place to put the menu aside, point to what's being eaten at another table, and have a tasting adventure by saying, "I'll have some of that."

This is also a great place for a late-night visit. Your evening may include performance art—the restaurant offers karaoke, 10 p.m. to closing, seven nights a week. To make it even more interesting, the thousands of songs would-be lounge crooners and rock stars can choose from are available in English, Cantonese, Mandarin, Korean, Vietnamese, and Japanese. Banquet facilities available.

## Garden Cafe
☎ (216) 431-8518
CITY: **Cleveland**   AREA: **Near East Side**
ATMOSPHERE: **Relaxed**   COST: $$$$

**ADDRESS:** 3710 Payne Ave.
**HOURS:** Mon–Sun 11 a.m.–9 p.m.   **RESERVATIONS:**
Taken **PAYMENT:** MC, VS, AX, DIS **BAR:** BYOB
**TAKEOUT:** Yes **ACCESS:** ఉ Full access **OTHER ETHNIC:**
Thai

This is not your usual Chinese restaurant. Sure you can play it safe and stick with wonton soup, General Tso's chicken, and beef with broccoli, but that would be a shame because then you'd miss out on the Taiwanese-style delicacies that make this restaurant special. Fruit shrimp, sliced pork with preserved mustard, garlic grilled pomfret (a tender, sweet, flavored fish), and seafood steamed eggs are just a few of the dishes that will take most diners into new culinary territory. Orders of sliced stomach or intestine with sour mustard are likely to find takers only among those who grew up eating such things, Andrew Zimmern wannabes, and Tony Bourdain acolytes, but their presence on the menu is a sign that opportunities await those who go through life with both an open mind and an open mouth. "Business Meals," a nice way to get in and out quickly, are a great value. There are nine relatively simple and non-challenging entrées such as sesame chicken or braised pork, and the price includes salad, soup, rice, and dessert (no substitutions) served in a compartmentalized bento box. My favorite is the curry beef. Other bargain choices are the combo meals that let diners choose one dish from each of three categories. Two can share and feast on eggplant with hot garlic sauce, shredded pork with dry bean curd, and turnip beef.

The restaurant, a 2006 addition to the local dining scene, is part of Payne Commons, a short strip of shops that includes Koko Bakery (see listing in this chapter). It has seating for about 24 in a bright, modern room with blond wood tables and chairs.

## Golden Dragon
☎ (330) 929-1109
CITY: **Cuyahoga Falls**   AREA: **Farther South**
ATMOSPHERE: **Casual**   COST: **$$$**$$

ADDRESS: 1634 State Rd.
HOURS: Mon–Thu 11:30 a.m.–10 p.m.,
Fri–Sat 11 a.m.–11 p.m., Sun noon–10 p.m.
RESERVATIONS: Not taken   PAYMENT: MC, VS,
AX, DIS   BAR: Beer, wine, liquor   TAKEOUT: Yes
ACCESS: ♿ None   OTHER ETHNIC: Japanese

Both Chinese and Japanese food is served, and the many Chinese and Japanese people who choose to eat here attest to its quality and authenticity. You can choose from traditional floor seating or Western-height tabletops. The menu features the Japanese dishes favored in this country, such as tempura, teriyaki, yakitori (skewered pieces of broiled chicken or beef), and sukiyaki. But the real standout is the extensive selection of sushi and sashimi and the other fresh and raw fish creations served at the sushi bar. The chef, who enjoys entertaining his audience at the bar with his technique, works with flounder, salmon, red snapper, tuna, eel, octopus, sea urchin, and fish roe. Chunks, slices (30 different types), and rolls made with rice and seaweed are served on rectangular plates and small wooden cutting boards, garnished with paper-thin pieces of ginger and hillocks of sharp green wasabi. Japanese beer is available.

The Chinese menu offers 110 options. Some of the notable house specialties are five-spiced pork chop, crystal shrimp (prepared in a garlic sauce), Szechuan hot braised lobster, tachien chicken (made with green and red peppers in a spicy sauce), fire pots, abalone with black mushrooms, and happy family bird's nest (shrimp, pork, chicken, and beef with vegetables served in a noodle basket). Dishes can be prepared without salt or MSG on request, and with advance notice the chef will create a gourmet dinner of unique banquet dishes. Take special note of the fact that *only* Chinese food is available during the lunch hours. Japanese food service begins at 5 p.m. Also be aware that restaurants in Cuyahoga Falls are not licensed to serve liquor on Sundays.

## House of Hunan
☎ (330) 864-8215

CITY: **Fairlawn**   AREA: **Farther South**
ATMOSPHERE: **Casual**   COST: **$$$**$$

ADDRESS: 2717 W. Market St.
HOURS: Mon–Thu 11:30 a.m.–9:30 p.m., Fri–Sat
11:30 a.m.–10:30 p.m., Sun 11:30 a.m.–9:30
p.m. RESERVATIONS: Taken, recommended Fri,
Sat nights PAYMENT: MC, VS, AX, DIS BAR: Beer,
wine, liquor TAKEOUT: Yes ACCESS: ♿ Full access

An Akron favorite since 1983, this Chinese restaurant offers the familiar, dependable mix of Hunan, Mandarin, and Szechuan specialties. Yet, among the dishes most of us know and love are some surprises. Among the appetizers: steamed vegetable-and-shrimp dumplings, steamed meat buns, and the House Special Fire Pot soup. In the entrée department: prawns with walnuts and hot chili sauce, a whole steamed flounder, Tokyo Moon Land (a dish containing shrimp, pork, chicken, and vegetables in brown sauce), spicy hot pork, Hunan lobster with black mushrooms, boneless tung ting duck, rose beef (I guessed a flowery roast, but it turns out to be filet mignon in a tangy sauce that's a combination of sweet and hot), and a braised tofu. If you prefer the tried and true, you'll be choosing from the likes of egg rolls, wonton soup, the general's chicken, kung bao-ed beef (on other menus it's usually spelled Kung Pao), sizzling this and that, sweet-and-sour stuff, the moo shu mix (this is nondairy despite the name), shrimp and chicken the way the empress liked it, and those poems of the plate known as Dragon and Phoenix (lobster, vegetables, and chicken), Happy Family (shellfish, chicken, pork, and beef), and Lover's Dinner (a medley of meats, seafood, and vegetables for two—but you can just be friends). The menu even includes

what the owners delightfully refer to as Old Fashion dishes, which are actually those Americanized Chinese concoctions that were once, back in those benighted and less sophisticated days, all most of us knew when it came to Pacific Rim cookery—fried rice, chow mein, chop suey, lo mein, and egg foo young. Their presence on the menu makes it clear they still are the food of choice for plenty of folks. A Japanese-style sushi bar and some cooked Japanese dishes are a fairly recent addition.

The combination of old and new attracts a diverse crowd—gray hairs and green hairs, the baby carriers and the cell-phone set, the dressed for success and the dressed in sweats. It's a large, attractive place to eat. It doesn't seem sprawling because tables are on two levels. (If someone in your party has trouble with steps, make reservations and ask for a table on the lower level). There's some lovely traditional art on the walls, screens, a huge aquarium in the center, dragon statues, a burbling fountain, and lots of greenery. An eye-catching ceramic tile mural fills the back wall. The restaurant is located in Fairlawn Town Center, and it's easy to spot with its distinctive gold doors and bright red molding in classic Chinese style.

## House of Hunan
☎ (330) 253-1888

CITY: **Akron**   AREA: **Farther South**
ATMOSPHERE: **Casual**   COST: **$$$**$$

ADDRESS: 12 E. Exchange St.
HOURS: Mon–Thu 11 a.m.–9:30 p.m., Fri 11
a.m.–11 p.m., Sat noon–11 p.m.; closed Sun
RESERVATIONS: Taken, recommended Fri, Sat
nights PAYMENT: MC, VS, AX, DIS BAR: Beer,
wine, liquor TAKEOUT: Yes ACCESS: ♿ Full access

The menu here is similar to the one

at House of Hunan on W. Market St. (see above listing) but with more of a contemporary focus—no old-fashioned chop suey here.

## House of Hunan
☎ (330) 722-1899
CITY: **Medina**   AREA: **Southwest**
ATMOSPHERE: **Relaxed**   COST: **$$$**$$

ADDRESS: 118 Public Square
HOURS: Mon–Thu 11:30 a.m.–10 p.m., Fri 11:30 a.m.–11 p.m., Sat noon–11 p.m., Sun noon–10 p.m.; closed 3–4 p.m. Mon–Fri
RESERVATIONS: Taken PAYMENT: MC, VS, AX, DIS
BAR: Beer, wine, liquor TAKEOUT: Yes ACCESS: ♿ Full access

See Fairlawn listing for more information.

## Hunan by the Falls
☎ (440) 247-0808
CITY: **Chagrin Falls**   AREA: **Farther East**
ATMOSPHERE: **Casual**   COST: **$$$**$$

ADDRESS: 508 E. Washington St.
HOURS: Mon–Thu 11:30 a.m.–9:45 p.m., Fri–Sat 11:30 a.m.–10:45 p.m., Sun noon–8:45 p.m.
RESERVATIONS: Recommended, taken on Fri, Sat evenings only for groups of 6+ PAYMENT: MC, VS, AX, DIS, checks BAR: Beer, wine, liquor TAKEOUT: Yes ACCESS: ♿ Full access OTHER ETHNIC: Thai

This is innovative gourmet Chinese cuisine served in an equally modern and exceptional setting. Winner of numerous awards, including "Best"s from readers of *Northern Ohio Live, Cleveland* magazine, and the *Chagrin Valley Times*, this 80-seat restaurant has grown steadily in popularity since it opened in 1993. Part of the draw is surely the attractive, contemporary-looking dining area, decorated with paintings by local artist Kasumi, and an indoor waterfall. But the real attraction is the food that chef Kwan Kuen Chau prepares. It's a mix of traditional Chinese regional cuisine, featuring such well-known dishes as General Tso's chicken, Mongolian beef, Mandarin orange duck, shrimp in black bean sauce, and lo mein. Some less familiar dishes also emerge from his kitchen: fire pots (casserole-type combinations of vegetables with seafood, meat, or tofu); fu yong don (a lighter, more typically Asian version of egg foo yong, with oyster-flavored sauce); mala string beans, which are made with Chinese cabbage, chili peppers, and garlic; Singapore-style noodles (chow mai fun); and Asian taro basket, a weave of crisp fried strips of this tuber, made to hold vegetables and your choice of chicken, shrimp, or seafood. Chef Chau also produces some unique creations of his own: yau-tsoi (green leafy vegetables and portobello mushrooms sautéed in an oyster-flavored sauce), walnut prawns (prawns lightly floured, sautéed quickly in oil, and tossed in a walnut sauce), and red chili curry noodles (spicy rice noodles seasoned with cilantro, lemongrass, and basil). Some popular seasonal specials include tangerine roughy; a sautéed vegetable dish called dou mieu, made with pea pod plants and garlic sauce; and ginger lamb. The kitchen also prepares some Thai dishes, including red, yellow, and green curries; a sweet and spicy tamarind chicken; basil shrimp; and chili prawns. There are many menu items for vegetarians, a nice wine list, and rich desserts.

Service is attentive and personal, and kitchen staff will try to accommodate special requests and needs. Parking in front of the restaurant, and after 5 p.m. in back.

## Hunan Coventry

☎ (216) 371-0777

CITY: **Cleveland Heights**   AREA: **East Side**
ATMOSPHERE: **Casual**   COST: **$$$**$$

ADDRESS: 1800 Coventry Rd.
HOURS: Tue–Thu 11:30 a.m.–9:45 p.m., Fri
11:30 a.m.–10:45 p.m., Sat noon–10:45 p.m.,
Sun 4–8:45 p.m. RESERVATIONS: Taken, only for
groups of 6+ PAYMENT: MC, VS, AX, DIS BAR:
Beer, wine, liquor TAKEOUT: Yes ACCESS: ♿ Full
access

A wall of large windows lets in plenty
of light and opens out onto Coventry
Road. The décor is fashionably elegant,
though patrons—an eclectic crowd
of every age—are as likely to dress in
sweaters as suits. There are lovely details featured in the décor: framed Asian
flower prints, a glass wall sandblasted
in a flower motif to separate entrance
from dining area, and indirect light
from modern wall-mounted sconces.
Rich-looking, warm-colored wood,
gray carpeting, and polished brass accent white walls and table linens. The
food looks elegant, too, often garnished
with flowers or butterflies beautifully
sculpted from a simple radish or wedges
of tomato. The menu features a large
selection of classic dishes, both Hunan
spicy and not, and there are also some
unexpected offerings tucked among the
lo meins, kung paos, and moo shus:
mussels in spicy garlic sauce, Shanghai
chicken with honey walnuts, Mandarin noodles with sesame sauce, and
Beijing-style lamb with scallions. Plentiful options for vegetarian diners. Portions are generous, service is attentive,
and at the end of the meal you get not
only a fortune cookie but also a warm,
individually wrapped, disposable cloth
for freshening hands and face. A good
place to eat, visit, and celebrate. A mul-
tistory parking garage is located across
the street.

## Hunan East

☎ (216) 381-2266

CITY: **Richmond Heights**   AREA: **East Side**
ATMOSPHERE: **Relaxed**   COST: **$$**$$

ADDRESS: 724 Richmond Rd.
HOURS: Mon–Thu 11 a.m.–9:30 p.m., Fri–Sat 11
a.m.–10 p.m., Sun noon–9 p.m. RESERVATIONS:
Not taken PAYMENT: MC, VS, AX, DIS BAR: None
TAKEOUT: Yes ACCESS: ♿ Full access

This restaurant has been here for
years, but even I knew nothing about it
until May of 2001. It's as ordinary as can
be, outside and in, until you discover
"the secret." I was clued in by Bob P.,
a man who is a true good-food enthusiast. And now you, too, can be in the
know.

The place looks like a million other
little storefront Chinese restaurants,
the kind that do more carryout than
sit-down business. Its appearance has
nothing to recommend it. And the typical American-style Chinese food they
serve is nothing to write home about.
But you can't go by appearances, and
what you see is definitely not all you
can get. Because there's another menu.
That's the secret. It's in Chinese, so it's
generally not presented to those who
don't immediately appear likely to read
the language. This menu features many
of the same dishes that appear on the
English version, but they are prepared
in a completely different way aimed to
please a Chinese rather than an American palate. Fresh ginger, garlic, and
scallions are used more liberally. Uncommon Asian vegetables like Chinese
broccoli, pea pod leaves, black ear and
cloud mushrooms, baby choy, and miniature eggplants predominate.

Those who have eaten here without
knowing about this other menu may
have harbored some suspicions about
what was going on in the kitchen. The
food on their plates looked and smelled

quite different from what was being served to Chinese people at nearby tables—and every other table is nearby in this small room with only 60 seats. In fact, by pointing and asking if they can have "what those other people are eating," many diners discover "the secret." Once servers and management know you're interested in the Real Chinese Food, they'll do all they can to help, short of sitting down and translating every line on the multipage menu. You can tell them you want seafood, pork, or a noodle dish, something full of vegetables, or a dish that is highly spiced and laced with heat, and they'll make suggestions. Or you can choose something like kung pao chicken, crispy fish, or orange beef from the regular menu and ask them to prepare it Chinese style. But you have to make it clear you don't suffer from "fear of flavor." So "ask and ye shall receive." Once they understand that you are ready to go beyond pu-pu platters and chow mein, they'll take you there, into a world of taste that highlights regional specialties and intricately seasoned, complex dishes like Dragon Phoenix, Double Rainbow Delight, crispy Hunan fish, and Happy Family. Some authentic preparations require ingredients that are more costly, and the price will reflect this. If you don't want to be surprised by the bill, inquire about the cost of what you select from the Chinese menu up front.

Don't expect anything exotic in the locale or setting. What could be more mundane than an aging shopping strip across from Richmond Mall? Industrial-strength carpeting covers the floor, and those predictable Chinese horoscope placemats grace the tables. The room is decorated with fake plants and fish tanks. Booths line each wall, and there are three tables in the center, one for six and two with eight chairs each. There's parking in the small front lot and in another lot along the side.

## Li Wah
**☎ (216) 696-6556**

CITY: **Cleveland**   AREA: **Near East Side**
ATMOSPHERE: **Casual**   COST: **$$$**$$

ADDRESS: 2999 Payne Ave. (Asia Plaza)
HOURS: Daily 10 a.m.–midnight RESERVATIONS: Taken, recommended for groups of 10+
PAYMENT: MC, VS, AX BAR: Beer, wine, liquor
TAKEOUT: Yes ACCESS: ♿ Full access

Chinese people eat here because they can get dishes they aren't likely to find on any other local restaurant menu: duck eggs with ginger; shredded chicken with jellyfish; panfried noodles with abalone; and dim sum that includes beef tripe, chicken feet, sticky rice with lotus leaf, and turnip cakes. But the spacious restaurant, which can seat up to 400, attracts people of every ethnicity, because, in addition to an extensive selection of flavorful Chinese dishes, the setting is attractive, comfortable, and contemporary, and service is attentive and efficient. It's a place for dining out—not just chowing down—with an atmosphere that's conducive to good conversation, celebration, and gracious eating. Round tables for 10 or 12 with lazy Susans in the center are perfect for big groups. There's usually a sizable business lunch crowd. The location, in Asia Plaza, is convenient for folks who work downtown, and handy if you want to do some shopping at the other ethnic stores inside the mall. Dim sum, which translates roughly as "a little bit of whatever your heart desires," is available daily until 3 p.m., and the selection, made from carts wheeled up to your table, is sizable. On Saturday and Sunday, when the clientele is mostly Chinese, there are even more choices.

One small detail is noteworthy because it's so rare and so important if you happen to have a baby with you, and representative of an unusual level of consideration for patrons: there's a diaper-changing station in the ladies' room. (Of course, in a perfect world, there'd be one in the men's room, too.) In February, when the Chinese New Year is celebrated, there is a most unusual banquet menu; tickets for this event should be purchased in advance.

## Pearl of the Orient

☎ (216) 751-8181

CITY: **Shaker Heights**   AREA: **East Side**
ATMOSPHERE: **Casual**   COST: **$$$**$$

**ADDRESS:** 20121 Van Aken Blvd.
**HOURS:** Lunch Mon–Fri 11:30 a.m.–3 p.m.;
Dinner Sun–Thu 5–10 p.m., Fri–Sat 5–11
p.m.; no lunch Sat–Sun **RESERVATIONS:**
Recommended **PAYMENT:** MC, VS, AX, DIS **BAR:**
Beer, wine, liquor **TAKEOUT:** Yes **ACCESS:** ♿ Full
access **OTHER ETHNIC:** Thai

Readers of *Cleveland* magazine have voted Pearl of the Orient the best Chinese restaurant 12 times, and owner Rose Wong is well known in the community both for her culinary creativity and her volunteer work. Her original East Side location has been in operation since 1979, and the second, West Side one since 1987. (For information about Pearl of the Orient in Rocky River, see next listing). The two restaurants are fundamentally the same, serving a combination of traditional dishes and inventive variations in handsome, modern, upscale settings.

Wong believes she was the first area restaurateur to offer diners Szechuan-style dishes and a menu that did not include egg foo yong and chop suey. Though many offerings change seasonally, some of her customers' favorites that have a permanent place on the menu include the Pearl Wor Bar, a combination of shrimp, scallops, chicken, and vegetables on a bed of sizzling rice; Peking duck (24 hours' notice required);

shrimp and chicken with cashews; and filet mignon in ginger mushroom sauce. Hot and spicy dishes, which can be ordered at three levels of burn, include Szechuan scallops; string beans in garlic sauce; black pepper chicken; beef with tangerine peel; shredded spice pork; and Singapore rice noodles. Among the more unusual entrées the kitchen turns out are wok-seared salmon in black bean sauce; chicken with mangoes and honey walnuts; vegetables with roasted garlic cloves and toasted cashews; smoked duck breast with three types of mushrooms; a stir-fry of shrimp, melon, and strawberries; and calamari with black bean sauce. Brown rice can be substituted for white.

A few classic Thai dishes are also featured: pad Thai; red curry chicken; vegetables in peanut sauce; and prawns with basil. The wine list is extensive, with many available by the glass, and there's also a sizable selection of beers, including a number of microbrews. Each location seats about 110 and provides ample, convenient parking.

## Pearl of the Orient

☎ (440) 333-9902

CITY: **Rocky River**   AREA: **West Side**
ATMOSPHERE: **Casual**   COST: **$$$**$$

**ADDRESS:** 19300 Detroit Rd.
**HOURS:** Lunch Mon–Sat 11:30 a.m.–3 p.m.,
Sun 11:30 a.m.–3 p.m.; Dinner Mon–Thu
3:30–9:45 p.m., Fri–Sat 3:30–10:45 p.m., Sun
3:30–8:45 p.m. **RESERVATIONS:** Recommended
**PAYMENT:** MC, VS, AX, DIS **BAR:** Beer, wine,
liquor **TAKEOUT:** Yes **ACCESS:** ♿ Full access **OTHER
ETHNIC:** Japanese, Thai, Vietnamese

The Chinese menu here is much like that of its sister restaurant in Shaker Heights (see preceding listing), and reflects equally well the Wong family's accomplished style of preparation and presentation. But unlike its East Side counterpart, this location also has a full sushi bar, an inviting outdoor patio, and serves lunch on Saturdays and Sundays.

## Sun Luck Garden

☎ (216) 397-7676

CITY: **Cleveland Heights**  AREA: **East Side**
ATMOSPHERE: **Casual**  COST: **$$$**$$

**ADDRESS:** 1901 S. Taylor Rd.
**HOURS:** Lunch Tue–Fri 11:30 a.m.–2 p.m.; Dinner Tue–Fri 4–9:30 p.m., Sat 4–10 p.m., Sun 4–8:30 p.m.; closed Mon **RESERVATIONS:** Taken, recommended on weekends and for groups of 5+ **PAYMENT:** MC, VS, AX, DIS **BAR:** Beer, wine **TAKEOUT:** Yes **ACCESS:** ♿ Full access

Let go of all preconceptions about what a Chinese restaurant is supposed to be before you walk in the door. Owner Annie Chiu has created a brilliant fusion of East and West, old and new. Daily specials highlight traditional ingredients and techniques in unlikely contemporary combinations, such as mussels in a spicy red garlic-laced broth; grouper baked Continental style and served sizzling with stir-fried Oriental vegetables; puff pastry filled with sa cha beef (meat in a kind of barbecue sauce); shrimp and scallions layered with phyllo dough; and steamed chicken dumplings with spinach, a dish Chiu created to satisfy her customers' needs for something very low fat and low calorie but just as delicious as everything else that comes from her kitchen.

The décor reflects the blend of old and new. Original paintings by a local artist incorporate ancient Chinese mythological themes in a contemporary motif. Chiu serves special dishes rarely prepared in this country, never scrimping on rare or costly ingredients like baby ginger, dried Chinese scallops, Chinese chives, and saffron. Even familiar items like hot and sour soup

and governor's chicken take on a new and intriguing identity here. For those in search of the Chinese food they know and love, her spicy kung pao shrimp, and yu shan scallops are popular choices. She does amazing things with tofu: her dark tofu is so meaty and flavorful that if you don't tell the kids or those who've dedicated themselves to avoiding anything that smacks of health, they'll never know what they're eating. Her ma pau tofu, considered to be a kind of Chinese comfort food, is a favorite with her Asian guests.

Much of what she knows, Chiu learned by studying with master chefs in China, apprenticeships arranged by her mother's brother, who is a renowned chef and teacher there. And hers is among the few Chinese restaurants around that offer extraordinary desserts. There's plum cheesecake daily, and if you're lucky, you'll visit on a day she's had the urge to whip up something even more unusual like pistachio mousse, French pear tart with homemade pear ice cream, strawberry chocolate soufflé roll, or chocolate pecan tarts. For those with a taste—or doctor's orders—for something lighter, she creates her own sorbets from the likes of grapefruits, passion fruit, mangoes, and rose petals.

"People come here, before they know us," Chiu said, "expecting the Chinese food they've eaten elsewhere. They quickly realize this is a place where they can taste something quite different than the usual." Be sure to get on Chiu's mailing list. Guests can also sign up for a special mailing list to find out about the specials she's preparing for the week that take advantage of the best the markets have to offer and seasonal produce. Throughout the year she hosts special events, such as a unique Chinese English high tea. She's always on the lookout for unusual and outstanding wines from around the world that will complement her cooking; the selection is eclectic and ever changing. The restaurant is located at the end of Taylor Commons, a strip mall one-half mile north of Cedar Road; ample parking in front.

## Szechwan Garden
☎ (216) 226-1987

CITY: **Lakewood**   AREA: **West Side**
ATMOSPHERE: **Casual**   COST: $$$$

ADDRESS: 13800 Detroit Ave.
HOURS: Lunch Mon–Sat 11:30 a.m.–2:30 p.m.; Dinner Mon–Thu 4:30–9:30 p.m., Fri–Sat 4:30–10:30 p.m., Sun 4:30–9 p.m.; closed between lunch & dinner RESERVATIONS: Taken, recommended on weekends PAYMENT: MC, VS, AX, DIS BAR: Beer, wine, liquor TAKEOUT: Yes
ACCESS: ♿ Full access

Newcomers may be surprised to find that behind the unimpressive exterior of this little place located in an older neighborhood of small apartment buildings, single-family homes, and storefronts, is an exceptional restaurant. Once inside, patrons encounter booths and tables (seating about 60) set with peaked cloth napkins, expert service, and authentic regional Chinese dishes. The kitchen turns out Hunan lobster, orange chicken, and Szechwan duck; egg flower soup; a spicy pork dish with vegetables in a dark, pungent sauce; and Lake Tung Ting shrimp (made with beaten egg whites). Spiciness can be adjusted according to your preference for mild, medium, or hot. Meatless diners take note: Peking Gourmet, known for its vegetarian Buddhist menu, closed in 2008. But Ken Lam, the owner of that place, convinced his brother Hoa, the owner of this place, to add many of those dishes to the offerings here. The atmosphere is warm and hospitable, and there's a steady flow of patrons at all hours, both for eat-in and takeout. Plenty of parking available.

## Tom's Seafood Restaurant
☎ (216) 771-1928

CITY: **Cleveland**   AREA: **Downtown**
ATMOSPHERE: **Relaxed**   COST: $$$$

ADDRESS: 3048 St. Clair Ave.
HOURS: Mon–Fri 10:30 a.m.–midnight, Sat–Sun 10 a.m.–midnight RESERVATIONS: Taken
PAYMENT: MC, VS BAR: Beer, wine TAKEOUT: Yes
ACCESS: ♿ None

The food is done Hong Kong style, which means there's an emphasis on seafood. Hence the name, and there's plenty to lure your interest—especially if you're willing to look beyond crab Rangoon and shrimp chow mein. The menu's many intriguing offerings include fried oysters with spicy salt; grouper with sweet corn sauce; scallops in sweet walnut sauce; and a broiled frog hot pot. But there's much more than seafood served here, and it's not your usual ho-hum egg rolls and sweet and sour pork prepared American style. Hong Kong style also reflects a mixing of Cantonese, Chiu Chow, and Shanghainese cuisines with a dash of flavor from European colonizers. That translates into sautéed ong choi (a leafy green reminiscent of spinach) with preserved bean curd, a peppery beef short rib casserole, and braised duck. Another attraction is the large selection of dim sum. These appetizer-sized portions with the all-you-can-eat price are served daily from 11 a.m.–3 p.m. and draw a mostly Asian crowd on weekends. Among the 40 plus possibilities are an array of dumplings and buns, noodle rolls, turnip cake, sticky rice wrapped in a lotus leaf, congee (rice porridge) with pork, and the so-called thousand year egg (actually a duck egg that's been preserved in a crock for three to four months), steamed spare ribs, and stuffed eggplant. Carts laden with these delicacies are pushed around the room by ladies wearing something similar to old-fashioned soda jerk hats. Whenever you want something, just flag one of them down and point to your selection.

The restaurant consists of one big brightly lit room with the predictable red and gold color accents, a few dragons, and a laughing Buddha. A big-screen TV is always tuned to Chinese-language broadcasts.

## Wonton Gourmet & BBQ
☎ (216) 875-7000
CITY: **Cleveland**   AREA: **Near East Side**
ATMOSPHERE: **Relaxed**   COST: **$$**$$

ADDRESS: 3211 Payne Ave.
HOURS: Mon–Fri 11 a.m.–midnight, Sat–Sun 10 a.m.–midnight RESERVATIONS: Taken, only for large groups PAYMENT: MC, VS, DIS BAR: None TAKEOUT: Yes ACCESS: ♿ None

The clientele at this Asiatown destination is primarily Chinese, especially in the morning and the evenings, so tables are set with chopsticks, not silverware. The menu of Hong Kong–style specialties is printed in both Chinese and English, and it's rich with tantalizing options: shredded pork with pan-fried noodles, turnip cakes (a personal favorite), beef chow fun (curry flavored noodles), salted chicken, shredded scallion and ginger lo mein, and Chinese sausage fried rice. But the true gastronomic adventurer will also find all kinds of uncommon combinations to explore, including congee (rice porridge) with frog, steamed beef rice rolls, sautéed ribs with bitter melon, and fried chicken wings with red bean curd paste. There's a big selection of soups, among them versions made with brisket, tripe, roast duck, or fish balls. I'm a big fan of one called Three Flavor Shrimp Dumpling. According to the menu, a number of options are served over spaghetti.

Don't expect Italian pasta—something is definitely lost in the translation. Additional specials are posted in Chinese with English translations and photos on yellow signs hung around the room. According to May Tam, whose mother and father operate the restaurant, these are more traditional dishes, unfamiliar to Americans. But if you would like to give something a try, just point and take your chances. Nobody will refuse the request. But be warned, even if you ask and receive an explanation of what you're ordering, given the challenges of both languages and the lack of any English equivalent, any verbal description you get will leave you in the dark until the food arrives at the table. Even then, what's in the bowl or on the plate may still be a mystery. And if you're not up to Thousand Year Egg Pork, a separate menu geared to American tastes features the kinds of Chinese dishes favored by Westerners.

The tidy cream-colored little dining room is light, bright, and pleasant in a simple, unadorned kind of way. Seating is available for just 28, and every chair is within earshot of the kitchen where Tom Tam does his magic. On-street parking is available, as well as in a lot next to the building.

# Filipino

## New Kainan
☎ (216) 741-1332
CITY: **Parma**   AREA: **Southwest**
ATMOSPHERE: **Relaxed**   COST: **$$$**$$

ADDRESS: 5382 State Rd.
HOURS: Thu noon–4 p.m., Fri–Sat 11 a.m.–7 p.m. RESERVATIONS: Not taken PAYMENT: MC, VS BAR: None TAKEOUT: Yes ACCESS: ♿ Full access

Although there are a few tables here,

they're more for waiting than dining. This is a spare and simple takeout place, and the food you bring home provides a real taste of what eating Philippine style is all about. The cuisine of the archipelago nation of 7,000 islands is an expression of geography, the tropical climate, the presence of more than 100 ethnic groups, and the long history of trade and colonization. It's easy to spot the influence of Spain in dishes such as calderetta (a spicy beef stew), chicken adobo, menudo (pork and vegetables in a tomato-based sauce), meat-filled empanadas, and leche flan. The culinary heritage of China and other Asian nations is found in rice noodles with shrimp (pancit palabak), sweet and sour fish, rice porridge flecked with bits of chicken, egg rolls, stir-fried vegetables wrapped in a crepe and topped with peanut sauce (lumpiang sariea), and string beans and squash in coconut milk. In an effort to cater to health-conscious patrons and those with special dietary needs, the kitchen will make low-fat or low-salt versions of most dishes on request, and can sweeten many of their desserts with a sugar substitute if given advance notice. The menu is longer than you might expect for such a small and simple establishment, but not everything is available every day. You can check out what's cooking by calling or going to www.kainanexpress.com. Fax orders in to (440) 582-2094.

## Nipa Hut

☎ (440) 842-7333

CITY: **Parma Heights**   AREA: **Southwest**
ATMOSPHERE: **Relaxed**   COST: $$$$$

ADDRESS: 6775 W. 130th St.
HOURS: Mon–Sat 8:30 a.m.–7:30 p.m.; closed Sun RESERVATIONS: Taken, recommended for groups of 5+ PAYMENT: MC, VS, DIS, checks
BAR: None TAKEOUT: Yes ACCESS: ♿ Full access

Since 1985, Poli Ignacio and his wife, Mercy, have been making delicacies from their homeland, many of which require time-consuming preparation and slow cooking. This remains one of only two places in the region where you can get freshly prepared Filipino food. Although Filipino chefs use many of the same ingredients found in Chinese, Japanese, Korean, and Thai cooking, the spicing is quite different, the Spanish influence is apparent, and the end result is food unlike any other in the Pacific Rim. This means that even though Nipa Hut is more market than restaurant—with only four tables and some folding chairs, disposable plates and utensils, and a self-serve counter—it offers a not-to-be-missed dining experience.

Not every dish on their menu is available every day, but you can call ahead to place a special order.

The best selection is found on Saturdays, when they do their weekly buffet. It will likely include lumpia (egg rolls), marinated fried bangus (milkfish, the most popular fish in the Philippines), menudo (pork in a sauce made with garlic, tomatoes, and onions), pancit (rice stick noodles), barbecued chicken or pork, and sweets such as cassava cake, leche plan (flan), and purple rice cake.

The daily menu requires some knowledge of the language and the cuisine, because most items are listed only by their Filipino name. Here's an abbreviated glossary—but don't hesitate to ask the folks behind the counter for help. Chicken afritada and beef mechado are both meat-and-vegetable stews. Dinuguan is also a stew, but few Americans like it, according to Poli, as it is made with beef or pork blood. Empanadas are a cross between a pierogi and an egg roll—a fried pastry with a meat-and-vegetable filling. Pakbet is a mix of vegetables including long beans, Oriental eggplant, and okra. Kare-kare is oxtail soup. Ukoy is made with squash, onion, and fried shrimp. Pata is a dish of pork hocks that are boiled in a seasoned broth, dried, and then fried until crispy. Anything with palabok comes in a sauce of ground pork and oysters, clams, or mussels. In the dessert department, turon are fried bananas, puto is a sweet rice cake, bibingka is a confection of sticky rice and coconut milk, and hopia is a kind of cake.

Kids under 12 get a bargain rate on the buffet, and those three and under eat free. Tables are actually opposite shelves filled with products from all the Asian nations. (For more information about the grocery store, see listing under same name in the market section of this chapter). Most of the restaurant business is actually carryout, which is a good thing because there's only seating for 50. A large green-and-white sign near the road makes the place easy to find.

# Japanese

## Akira Hibachi & Sushi
☎ (440) 349-6850
CITY: **Solon**   AREA: **Farther East**
ATMOSPHERE: **Casual**   COST: **$$$$**$

**ADDRESS:** 6025 Kruse Dr.
**HOURS:** Lunch Sun–Fri 11:30 a.m.–2:30 p.m.;
Dinner Mon–Thu 5–10 p.m., Fri–Sat 5–10:30 p.m., Sun 5–9 p.m. **RESERVATIONS:** Taken, recommended on weekends **PAYMENT:** MC, VS, AX, DIS **BAR:** Beer, wine, liquor **TAKEOUT:** Yes
**ACCESS:** ♿ Full access

A jewel of a place set in the ever-expanding mall district of this southeastern suburb and one where diners are sure to find something wonderfully unique amid the overabundance of national chains and name-brand merchandise. Owners Anna and Hank

Saito, who came here from New York City, are determined to set themselves apart from other Japanese restaurants. They've crafted a menu that blends classic dishes with some of their own inspired creations, designed a space that is thoroughly contemporary but that subtly references traditional elements, and created an atmosphere that both welcomes children and appeals to adults.

Look for a mix of eating possibilities with presentation always treated as art. Some will challenge your palate to explore unusual textures and tastes, like edamame (steamed soybeans), nabe yaki udon (noodles, tempura, and fish cakes in broth), and the raw fish selections. Sushi and sashimi are impeccably fresh, varied, and expertly prepared.

Fish connoisseurs take note: This is the only restaurant in the Midwest, according to Anna Saito, to serve that infamous delicacy blowfish (fugu), when it is in season and available. They're also the only ones offering a cold summer version of a dish called shabu shabu, which they bring in a bowl made of ice. Generally served hot and named for the sound the ingredients make when they hit the steaming broth, it features slices of tender, shaved beef, noodles, and sculpted vegetables. Other entrées are comfortingly familiar—teriyaki steak, shrimp tempura, and grilled swordfish.

Dishes prepared tableside on the built-in hibachi grills offer eating-as-entertainment. Diners get a show that's sure to be a kid pleaser when the chef goes into action. He wheels a three-tiered cart over, laden with ingredients, and then masterfully plays with your food, flipping, swirling, and tossing everything including his utensils. A few surprising cross-cultural combinations, which too often produce a muddle of flavors, are culinary achievements here. Look for Latin American ceviche-style

New Millennium sashimi; tuna carpaccio; and a deep-fried, Italian-influenced crispy roll, made with smoked salmon, asparagus, and mozzarella cheese. This last offering and their popular Volcano Roll, made with shrimp tempura and conch, feature fully cooked fish, perfect for those who cringe at the thought of eating seafood that hasn't seen a stove.

For those who enjoy a drink with dinner, I recommend trying the chilled semi-dry sake. If you like the food, take note: not only do they do off-site catering, but they have a portable sushi bar that they can bring to you.

The décor is attractive and sleek, all earthy tones and natural wood. There's a 12-seat sushi bar. The spacious dining room is divided into discrete sections by half walls and sculptural semisolid partitions. Anna, who serves as hostess and one-woman welcoming committee, organizes the seating so that the front portion of the space is reserved for adults dining without children, creating a sort of intimate bistro within the larger room. She also chooses the background music, and we have the same taste in tunes—Norah Jones, Ella Fitzgerald, the Temptations. Although the surroundings are stylish, many diners dress very casually.

---

## Aoeshi

☎ (440) 716-0988

CITY: **North Olmsted**   AREA: **West Side**
ATMOSPHERE: **Casual**   COST: **$$$**$$

ADDRESS: 24539 Lorain Rd.
HOURS: Mon–Thu 5 p.m.–10:00 p.m., Fri 5 p.m.–10:30 p.m., Sat noon–10:00 p.m.; closed Sun RESERVATIONS: Taken, recommended on weekends PAYMENT: MC, VS, AX, DIS BAR: BYOB
TAKEOUT: Yes ACCESS: ♿ Full access

· · · · · · · · · · · · · · · · · · · · · · · · ·

Cleveland's own Joe Crea, food and restaurant editor at the *Plain Dealer* and

a man with the experience and expertise to know fine food when he tastes it, described this restaurant as "a surprising little gem" and wrote that he had three of the best maki rolls here that he ever had anywhere. Local celebrity chef Michael Symon, another guy who knows his way around the table, tipped him off, suggesting that the sushi was as good as that at Nobu, a famous and pricey NYC eatery. That's high praise for a small mom-and-pop restaurant located in an out-of-the-way strip mall in North Olmsted, an area not exactly known as a hotbed of culinary innovation.

Young Kim welcomes diners, and her husband, Chong, is the sushi master and chef. The selection is large and creative: there are 10 different seaweed-wrapped vegetarian maki; 22 nigiri sushi featuring such delicacies as smelt fish roe, quail egg, sweet shrimp, and river eel atop little mounds of rice; and cleverly named and conceived rolls—Three Amigo, Pink Lady, Dragon, and Rainbow. Sit at the sushi bar in one of the six seats and you'll have a great view of an artist at work as Chong Kim expertly slices whole fish and assembles his beautiful little packages and arranges his platters. The regular menu is just as enticing and eclectic. Look for steamed dumplings, salmon skin salad (don't be put off by the name), tempura, noodle dishes, and breaded and fried cutlets. The setting is modern and minimalist with a clean bright look. Seating for just 50, but there's enough parking in the strip mall's lot out front for an entire regiment.

## Aoeshi Café

☎ (216) 321-3700

CITY: **Cleveland Heights**  AREA: **East Side**
ATMOSPHERE: **Relaxed**  COST: **$$$**$$

ADDRESS: 2175 Lee Rd.
HOURS: Mon–Thu noon–10 p.m., Fri–Sat noon–10:30 p.m.; closed Sun RESERVATIONS: Not taken PAYMENT: MC, VS BAR: None TAKEOUT: Yes ACCESS: ♿ Full access

Fast food sushi style. Place orders at the counter. There are only 10 tables, making it clear that this place is more about takeout than dining in. In good weather more seating is added outside in the adjacent pocket park. Located just a few doors from the Cedar Lee Theatre, it's handy for a quick pit stop before or after a movie. The menu lists the usual line-up of rolls and nigiri sushi. The fish is fresh, handled with skill, and artfully presented. A plate featuring six pieces of eel roll, for example, comes "painted" with red and yellow fish roe, streaks of orange pepper mayo, dabs of green wasabi, swirls of thick, sweet soy glaze, and a dusting of nori flakes. Salads offer some interesting options thanks to the addition of squid, octopus, salmon skin, seared tuna, and either soy vinegar dressing or one called lanchi made with sesame paste.

Those in the mood for something other than raw mackerel and salmon roe can choose from a small selection of non-Japanese wraps, panini sandwiches, and a few hot entrées such as tempura and teriyaki.

## Ariyoshi

☎ (216) 321-1020

CITY: **Cleveland Heights**  AREA: **East Side**
ATMOSPHERE: **Casual**  COST: **$$$**$$

ADDRESS: 2206 Lee Rd.
HOURS: Lunch Mon–Fri 11:30 a.m.–2 p.m.; Dinner Mon–Thu 5–10 p.m., Fri 5–10:30 p.m., Sat 4:30–10:30 p.m., Sun 4–9:30 p.m. RESERVATIONS: Taken, recommended on weekends PAYMENT: MC, VS, AX, DIS BAR: Beer, wine, liquor TAKEOUT: Yes ACCESS: ♿ Full access OTHER ETHNIC: Korean

The former owner of Daishin in North Olmsted has been serving dumplings, spider rolls, vegetable tempura, and yaki soba here since early 2008. The décor of the spacious and comfortable dining room combines traditional Japanese and contemporary Western elements to good effect. Additional seating is available on the front sidewalk in good weather: It's not pretty, but it does let you savor sunny days and balmy nights. Staff seems remarkably tolerant of what dining out with young children can entail, making this a family-friendly dining destination.

The menu is everything we've come to expect for this type of cuisine along with a few tantalizing additions. A good way to get your greens is with an oshitashi appetizer of steamed spinach in a mild soy sauce. The aged dashi tofu is deliciously different, as are the broiled miso scallops. Plant yourself at the 12-seat sushi bar to watch the chefs wrap crab, cucumber, and pickled vegetables in seaweed for the futo-maki, or see them deftly slice raw fish and fan the pieces out on a bed of vinegared rice in a preparation called chirashi. Shabu Shabu (beef in broth) is one of four special dinners for two prepared tableside on an electric burner. Out of sight, kitchen staff cooks up light, greaseless tempura, skewers of broiled chicken, and deep-fried pork with katsu sauce. They turn out a few a Korean dishes, too, among them marinated short ribs called kalbi in a traditional barbecue sauce and beef with kimchee and noodles. On the beverage side, expect a limited selection of beer, wine, and sake, as well as some playful cocktails.

## Daishin Hibachi Steak House
☎ (440) 979-1337
CITY: **North Olmsted**    AREA: **West Side**
ATMOSPHERE: **Casual**    COST: **$$$**$$

**ADDRESS:** 26092 Brookpark Rd.
**HOURS:** Lunch Wed–Fri 11:30 a.m.–2:30 p.m., Sat–Sun 12:30 p.m.–3:00 p.m.; Dinner Mon–Tue 4 p.m.–10 p.m., Wed–Thu 4:30 p.m.–10 p.m., Fri–3 p.m.–10:30 p.m., Sat 3 p.m.–9 p.m.
**RESERVATIONS:** Recommended **PAYMENT:** MC, VS, AX, DIS **BAR:** Beer, wine, liquor **TAKEOUT:** Yes
**ACCESS:** & Full access

This very large space can accommodate 200 diners, but it's nicely divided into sections, each with a discrete function and atmosphere. Up front is the sushi bar, a room with six tables and 10 counter seats. Here you can watch as the chef slices, rolls, and wraps, creating classic and novel combinations of fish, rice, and seaweed. His cooler is typically stocked with tuna, salmon, mackerel, squid, eel, shrimp, crab, and yellowtail.

There's a cozy room on the opposite side of the entryway, perfect for a private gathering. At the back of the restaurant is an area offering what appears to be traditional on-the-floor seating. In a concession to Western habits, the area under the low tables is designed so diners' legs can hang down comfortably as they would in a full-size chair, and floor cushions are actually seats equipped with rigid backs. Twelve grill tables dominate the main dining area, and each one seats eight. If your party doesn't fill all the spots, don't be surprised if strangers are seated with you, European style. This could easily turn a meal into a party. It's a good way to make new friends—after all, you already know that you share a taste for hibachi-style shrimp, lobster, chicken, and steak.

Performance is part of the package. You watch as chefs prepare food with virtuoso knife, spoon, and spatula displays. The fancy flipping, tossing, and saucing typically earn applause from the audience. You can also catch the action from adjacent tables two steps up and opposite to the bar, which also provides views of the two big TVs positioned at either end of the room, sound off and generally tuned to sports. The décor is tastefully simple—wood furnishings, some rice-paper lanterns, mirrors, and hanging scrolls on white walls.

The menu offers plenty of options, and most dishes are pictured, helpful for those unfamiliar with this cuisine. There are 21 different appetizers and salads, including goma-ae (cold spinach in sesame sauce), shumai (steamed dumplings), and deep-fried tofu. In addition to the hibachi dinners, there are 17 other cooked entrées, among them pan-broiled cod, vegetable tempura, and marinated short ribs with Korean barbecue sauce, plus four bento box dinners. Child-sized hibachi portions are available for kids under 10.

The bar pours a variety of beers, a few wines (by the glass only), and hot and cold sake, and mixes up cocktails with silly names like Karate Punch and The Bomb. The restaurant is located deep in mall-land, on the northern strip of Great Northern nearest Brookpark Road.

## Ginza Sushi House
☎ (216) 589-8503
CITY: **Cleveland** AREA: **Downtown**
ATMOSPHERE: **Casual** COST: **$$$**$$

**ADDRESS:** 1105 Carnegie Ave.
**HOURS:** Lunch Mon–Fri 11 a.m.–2:30 p.m.;
Dinner Mon–Thu 5–9:30 p.m., Fri–Sat 5–10:30
p.m.; closed Sun; kitchen closed between
lunch & dinner **RESERVATIONS:** Taken, evenings
only **PAYMENT:** MC, VS, DIS **BAR:** Beer, wine
**TAKEOUT:** Yes **ACCESS:** ♿ Limited

Sonny Garcia, who is half Japanese and hails from the Philippines, is owner and chef here, and his mother, Virginia, is hostess and general PR person. To say that this family-run business is friendly is an understatement—it's not unusual to see "regulars" chat with "Mom" when they arrive and hug her when they leave. Sonny had 17 years of experience, much of it as a chef in local Japanese restaurants and the rest in Japan and Los Angeles, before bringing it all to bear in his own place in his preparation of nigiri sushi (small "fingers" of pressed rice and either raw or cooked seafood, mushroom, daikon, or egg); maki sushi (raw or cooked seafood or vegetables and rice hand-rolled in paper-thin sheets of seaweed); futomaki (extra-large maki); and sashimi (raw fish with sides of rice and vegetable). Sonny's signature creation is the Ginza roll, a futomaki made with three different fishes, avocado, and egg (tamago) arranged in eye-catching red, yellow, and green stripes.

The fish, flown in daily, is always very fresh. Ordering is simple: a list is provided; the numbered Japanese name is accompanied by a brief description of the contents. All you have to do is check off your choices. Sonny often prepares sushi creations that are not on the list, so be sure to ask about the chef's specials. Everyone in the family is glad to discourse on the healthful benefits of sushi and will happily provide advice about how to eat it properly. One of their tips is to use the decorative ginger pickles on the serving bowl as a palette cleanser between each selection.

For those who suffer from fear of fish, especially the raw variety, a visit to Ginza could be the beginning of a new era. There are, however, ample alternatives for the hard-core carnivores and those who want to sample other Japanese dishes. A separate menu offers hot entrées such as hibachi-prepared chicken or steak, tempura, noodle-filled hot pots, and teriyaki. A bowl of miso soup and a side of seaweed salad are a light and flavorful accompaniment to any entrée. Though it may not sound appetizing to most Americans, my eating troopers found green-tea or red-bean ice cream, imported from Japan, surprisingly refreshing as a finish to their meal. Japanese beers and both hot and cold sake are also available.

Located just one block from Progressive Field and the Quicken Loans Arena, Ginza offers boxed sushi-sashimi meals to go, and they have named one creation Gateway Maki.

Clever use of wooden latticework dividers and an area raised a few steps above the rest maintain a sense of intimacy, even though the seating capacity has doubled to about 90. The old place had a very casual East-meets-West décor; here the two cultures still combine forces, but the effect is much more elegant. A traditional motif that employs rice-paper screens and muted colors and some floor seating with cushions (there are also conventional tables and chairs) creates that impression of quiet calm associated with Japanese interiors. The restaurant Web site, www. ginzasushi.com, provides directions, a menu, and an option for making large-group reservations (six or more) online, 24 hours in advance.

## Otani

☎ (440) 442-7098

CITY: **Mayfield Heights**   AREA: **East Side**
ATMOSPHERE: **Dressy**   COST: **$$$**$$

**ADDRESS:** 6420 Mayfield Rd. (1625 Golden Gate Plaza)
**HOURS:** Lunch Mon–Fri 11:30 a.m.–2 p.m., Sat noon–2:30 p.m.; Dinner Mon–Thu 5–10 p.m., Fri 5–10:30 p.m., Sat 5–11 p.m., Sun 4:30–9 p.m.; closed between lunch & dinner
**RESERVATIONS:** Taken, recommended on weekends **PAYMENT:** MC, VS, AX, DIS **BAR:** Beer, wine, liquor **TAKEOUT:** Yes **ACCESS:** ♿ Full access

Two dining areas are handsomely decorated with a mixture of traditional and contemporary Japanese artwork, plants, and lantern lights. The large rooms are divided into intimate spaces by partitions and subdued lighting, and guests can choose to be seated at regular tables or on low tables surrounded by cushions. There's also counter service at the sushi bar. Other "raw" choices include sashimi (fish without rice) and maki (rice and fish or vegetables wrapped in seaweed); the restaurant has a large selection of all three. The presentation is a feast for the eyes. If you're not in the mood for raw fish (or never will be), you can still eat here; choose teriyaki steak, tempura vegetables (batter dipped and deep fried), or ginger chicken. For special occasions, tableside cooking is popular; Shabu Shabu is a beef and vegetable dish diners cook themselves, one bite at a time. In addition to Japanese beer, hot sake, plum wine, and sakura (a noncarbonated Japanese soft drink) are available. A nice setting for a celebration.

## Pacific East

☎ (216) 320-2302

CITY: **Cleveland Heights**   AREA: **East Side**
ATMOSPHERE: **Casual**   COST: **$$$**$$

**ADDRESS:** 1763 Coventry Rd.
**HOURS:** Lunch Mon–Fri 11 a.m.–3 p.m., Sat noon–3 p.m.; Dinner Mon–Thu 5–10 p.m., Fri–Sat 5–11 p.m., Sun 3–10 p.m.
**RESERVATIONS:** Taken, recommended on weekends **PAYMENT:** MC, VS, AX, DIS **BAR:** Beer, wine **TAKEOUT:** Yes **ACCESS:** ♿ Full access **OTHER ETHNIC:** Malaysian

Pacific East is the only source of Japanese food in the Coventry Village neighborhood. The selection is extensive and interesting, and it shows that chef Freeman Ngo wants to stake out new culinary territory. In addition to the standard miso soup, diners can choose from seven others, including one made with shiitake mushrooms and another that features crabmeat. The list of appetizers and salads is even longer and equally innovative, and two or three of the 50 possibilities make a fine meal on their own. There's ankimo, a paste made from monkfish liver; poached bean curd in seaweed broth; broiled eggplant with sweet miso sauce; oshitashi, a spinach dish; grilled squid with daikon radish and ginger; and shrimp with asparagus in spicy dressing.

The menu also includes a tempting array of noodle dishes (udon), rice bowls (don buri), tempura, teriyaki, yakitori (skewered, grilled meat, poultry, or fish), and bento box meals. And then there are the sushi bar entrées: generously cut slices of fish, artfully rolled and assembled into a multitude of combinations, and beautifully presented. The palate of special ingredients the chefs work with includes plum paste, pickled radish, fermented soybeans, fish roe, eel sauce, egg custard, and fish powder. Not to be missed is chirashi, made with vividly colored slices of fresh fish atop a bed of seasoned rice. Groups can take advantage of the house's sushi and sashimi combos for a special treat—The Bridge serves two, The Boat is for three (and is indeed served in a ship), and the glorious King and Queen feeds four royally.

Chef Ngo is also bringing us the tastes of Malaysia. That makes him the only restaurateur in the entire region to be serving this multicultural and astonishingly tasty cuisine. Some dishes feature peanut sauce, lemongrass, and coconut milk as in Thai cooking; others, such as curry puffs, roti (griddle fried bread), or mee goreng, a combination of noodles, potatoes, eggs, tofu, and shrimp, are more Indian style. There are Vietnamese-style meal-sized soups, and Chinese-inspired stir fries and ribs. But everything has a unique twist, and many dishes made with mango, taro, and spicy shrimp paste are unlike anything tasted anywhere else.

The most striking feature of the space at the corner of Coventry and Mayfield is the color blue, so intense and pervasive that it's easy to imagine oneself underwater, hanging with the octopus, tuna, giant clams, and sea urchins that show up on the menu. Once you recover from the initial shock, it's quite pleasant and peaceful. Service is always attentive and friendly. Parking meters on the street and down the block in a public garage.

## Pacific East
☎ (216) 765-1305
CITY: **Woodmere**   AREA: **Southeast**
ATMOSPHERE: **Casual**   COST: **$$$**$$

**ADDRESS:** 28601 Chagrin Blvd.
**HOURS:** Lunch Mon–Thu 11 a.m.–3 p.m., Fri 11 a.m.–3 p.m., Sat noon–3 p.m.; Dinner Mon–Thu 5–10 p.m., Fri–Sat 5–11 p.m., Sun 3–10 p.m. **RESERVATIONS:** Taken, for groups of 7+ **PAYMENT:** MC, VS, AX, DIS **BAR:** Beer, wine **TAKEOUT:** Yes **ACCESS:** &. Full access

The original Pacific East is in Cleveland Heights. This second, more easterly location in the Eton Collection shopping mall opened in January 2008. A sushi bar snakes through the diminutive L-shaped room where closely packed tables provide seating for 40. The owners Freeman and Jack Ngo, who are brothers, and their partner Ben Wu take pride in using only the freshest fish and the best quality ingredients. In addition to an outstanding collection of made-to-order sushi, sashimi, and maki options, the kitchen team prepares teriyaki, tempura, and agemono (breaded and fried meats and seafood) dishes, and udon noodle bowls.

For more information about the menu, see previous listing. But take note: Unlike the Coventry Road restaurant, Malaysian food is not served here. While reservations are only accepted for groups of more than six, you can take advantage of call-ahead seating to get your name on a waiting list before you head over there.

## Sapporo Sushi
☎ (216) 579-7000
CITY: **Cleveland**   AREA: **Downtown**
ATMOSPHERE: **Relaxed**   COST: **$$**$$

**ADDRESS:** 1906 E. 6th St.
**HOURS:** Lunch Mon–Fri 11 a.m.–3 p.m.; Dinner Mon–Fri 5 p.m.–8 p.m.; closed Sat–Sun
**RESERVATIONS:** Not taken **PAYMENT:** MC, VS **BAR:** BYOB **TAKEOUT:** Yes **ACCESS:** &. Limited

You'll find 25 seats in this handkerchief-sized space (since few carry handkerchiefs anymore, I'm wondering if the metaphor means much), plus five at the butcher block–style counter. Sushi chefs are stationed on the other side of that counter, scooping up rice from the steamer, shaping it into little mounds, and decking it out with jewel-colored slices of tuna, mackerel, red snapper, and yellowtail. It's the perfect perch from which to watch them make a Pretty Woman, Green Dragon, or Yum Yum—three of the house special rolls. They also works with some uncommon and delicious vegetables—kampyo (squash), yamagobo (mountain carrot), and oshinko (pickled radish). In all there are 62 choices of sushi, sashimi, maki, and variations on the theme, plus three noodle dishes, five vegetable salads, miso soup, tempura, and teriyaki—and everything is beautifully presented. Not bad for so diminutive a spot. If watching someone slice octopus tentacles isn't your idea of entertainment, you can always fix your gaze on the big flat-screen TV that hangs overhead.

## SASA Izakaya & Asian Bistro

☎ (216) 767-1111

CITY: **Cleveland** AREA: **East Side**

ATMOSPHERE: **Casual** COST: **$$$$$**

**ADDRESS:** 13120 Shaker Square
**HOURS:** Mon–Sat 5 p.m.–midnight, Sun 5–10 p.m. **RESERVATIONS:** Taken, recommended on weekends **PAYMENT:** MC, VS, AX, DIS **BAR:** Beer, wine, liquor **TAKEOUT:** Yes **ACCESS:** ♿ Full access

Chef Scott Kim is Korean by birth but an expert in Japanese cuisine, wisely making the decision not to compete with his mother when it comes to cooking the food he grew up eating. The menu at the Asian bistro he opened with his wife Brenda in late 2007 provides indisputable evidence that he's mastered the art.

Inspired by a trip to Japan, this restaurant is an izakaya, the country's version of a tapas bar. It features a selection of small sized portions and the operating principle is to sample many different dishes at a single sitting. The best approach is to swap plates and share everything with your tablemates. The result is that every visit is a taste fest. Expect both traditional selections and inventive, modern, and more playful creations. Among my personal favorites: a nutty clam and corn soup; the Daikon Wrap (paper-thin slices of marinated white radish wrapped around carrots, greens, shiitake mushrooms, and bits of seafood and egg); Whitefish Usuzukuri Duo (slices of uncooked fish flavored with two citrus-spiked sauces); soy and yuzu-glazed Kobe beef meatballs; and 5 Mushroom Tofu. (The soybean curd has an appealingly crisp crust and the woodsy flavor of shiitake, lion's mane, and other wild fungi.) The simple pickles and peppers is a beautiful looking arrangement of hot shitito peppers, tempura battered and fried, and brined yamagobo (burdock), takuwan (radishes), ajicuri (cucumbers), and plums.

SASA Fries are a great reinterpretation of an American staple. The spiced and crunchy potato fingers seasoned with shichimi pepper and sesame-roasted sun dried seaweed flakes, served with a wonderful dipping sauce, are addictive.

There are a handful of full-sized entrées on the menu, and one of the best is miso-marinated black cod. Also worth a shout out is Lamb Three Ways—a sesame-crusted loin, sweet barbecue-glazed ribs, and a braise with a tomato ginger sauce. Rounding out the menu options is a list of nigiri, sashimi, and specialty hand rolls. For a bit of excitement get the Fire Roll. It arrives in a flaming foil package. The flare-up adds a smoky note to the teriyaki sauce that flavors the lobster, crab, Chinese broccoli, and masago, bright orange fish roe inside.

The food is a good match for the more than 40 fine sipping sakes, served cold, and signature cocktails such as the

Lychee Cosmo, Fujii Apple Martini, and Tokyo Sangria.

The décor is understated and contemporary, featuring a black, white, and red color scheme with stainless steel accents. Outdoor seating on the Square is available in warm weather. Park at meters in front of the restaurant or free in the lot behind the building. Late night menu, happy hour deals, and out-of-the-ordinary, out-of-this-world desserts. This is a great place to start or end an evening.

## Shuhei Restaurant of Japan

☎ (216) 464-1720

CITY: **Beachwood**    AREA: **East Side**
ATMOSPHERE: **Casual**   COST: **$$$$**$

ADDRESS: 23360 Chagrin Blvd.
HOURS: Lunch Mon–Fri 11:30 a.m.–2:30 p.m., Sat 11:30 a.m.–2 p.m.; Dinner Mon–Thu 5:30–10 p.m., Fri–Sat 5:30–11 p.m., Sun 5–9 p.m. RESERVATIONS: Recommended PAYMENT: MC, VS, AX, DIS BAR: Beer, wine, liquor TAKEOUT: Yes ACCESS: ♿ Limited

At this address since 1993, Shuhei has only gotten better with time. Both atmosphere and food here are consistently true to a traditionally Japanese aesthetic. The first thing you see when walking in the door is a stunning, intricately embroidered wedding kimono mounted behind glass. It's only one of the numerous pieces of beautiful museum-quality art that are scattered throughout the restaurant. Among the most special is a large section of an exquisite 400-year-old paper screen. Female servers wear kimonos and obis. They watch over diners with great care and attention, quickly removing empty plates and supplying the chopstick-challenged with silverware.

The serene setting provides a calm and relaxing backdrop for enjoying expertly prepared raw fish from the sushi bar or a traditional nabe mono (a hot pot of noodles and vegetables, with optional meat or fish, in a seasoned broth). Owners Hiroshi Tsuji and his wife Sonya Bassett divide the culinary responsibilities. She's in the kitchen, overseeing the preparation of aged dashi tou, gyoza, crunchy panko-breaded tiger shrimp with a zesty wasabi cocktail sauce, roasted duck in plum wine, and other hot appetizers and entrées. Her shumai—deep fried dumplings—are not to be missed. The tori karaage, a stir-fry of marinated chicken, mushrooms, and green beans, is light, simple, and very satisfying. Hiroshi can usually be found behind the sushi bar slicing eel, flounder, and yellowtail, rolling scallops in nori, and assembling orders of sashimi. He's created numerous original and outstanding combinations, among them the Anniversary Roll made with crab salad, tempura shrimp, eel, and avocado topped with a dab of spicy mayo and fish roe; a sushi torte featuring blue crab or salmon over rice with tomato and avocado coriander salsa; and Tiger's Eye, a truly sublime marriage of smoked salmon and squid.

The extensive menu offers descriptions of every dish, so those less experienced with this cuisine need not feel intimidated. Portions are ample, and dinner entrées come with miso soup (a richly flavored broth made from fermented soybeans) and a choice of either a Western or a Japanese salad. The house stocks a small selection of good wines and a large variety of of sipping sakes. Guests of all ages will be appropriately dressed in anything from jeans to a business suit. The restaurant is located at the rear of an office building. A large sign near the road makes it easy to find. Turn into the parking lot and follow the driveway around to the rear. The kitchen offers full-service catering with a menu that is not limited to Japanese food.

## Sushi 86

☎ (216) 621-8686

CITY: **Cleveland**   AREA: **Downtown**
ATMOSPHERE: **Relaxed**   COST: **$$**$$

ADDRESS: 2013 Ontario St.
HOURS: Mon–Fri 11 a.m.–6 p.m.; closed
Sat–Sun RESERVATIONS: Not taken PAYMENT:
MC, VS, AX, DIS BAR: None TAKEOUT: Yes
ACCESS: & Full access

At last, fast futo maki. Who knew the world was waiting? Apparently Rachel and Mike Hsu did. That's why they opened their little sushi takeout place on Public Square. If you need food on the go and you prefer flying fish roe, smoked salmon, or red clam to McFat, McSalty, and McGreasy, think Sushi 86. Designed with convenience and speed in mind, the operation is meant to have you in, out, and eating in double-quick time. Call in your order ahead of time and you can probably get away with parking where you shouldn't and running in to pick it up.

There is room for eight bodies at the sushi bar if you don't want to take your eel-and-cucumber roll, seaweed salad, and miso soup with you. They also offer delivery service to a limited area downtown. It's free if your order totals $20 or more. Although they are closed on Saturday and Sunday, they will prepare party trays seven days a week, one day's notice required.

## Sushi Rock

☎ (216) 623-1212

CITY: **Cleveland**   AREA: **Downtown**
ATMOSPHERE: **Dressy**   COST: **$$$$**$

ADDRESS: 1276 W. 6th St.
HOURS: Lunch Mon–Fri 11:30 a.m.–2:30 p.m.;
Dinner Mon–Thu 5–11 p.m., Fri–Sat 5 p.m.–
midnight, Sun 5–10 p.m. RESERVATIONS: Taken,
recommended Thu–Sat PAYMENT: MC, VS,

AX, DIS BAR: Beer, wine, liquor TAKEOUT: Yes
ACCESS: & Full access

Sushi is hot, it's in, and it has suddenly become cutting-edge cuisine rather than mere ethnic fare. The hottest, "in"-est, "cutting"-est place to eat these bite-sized morsels of raw seafood, the place to see and be seen, is Sushi Rock in the Warehouse District, open since February 2000. The place aims to be cool—cooler than Cleveland is generally judged to be—and just to be sure you get the message, the walls feature large, backlit photos of New York City, the penultimate metaphor for urban chic. I thought I had the name figured out after I walked in, saw the DJ perched in a pulpit above the teeming, feasting throngs, and heard (or perhaps it would be more accurate to say felt) the throbbing, high-intensity music. Okay, I thought, I get it: rock, roll, and fish. But a chat with the manager revealed that I had sort of missed the boat. While the allusion to a certain chain of cafés that want you to associate music with food is undeniable, the name is actually meant to reflect the unique two-sided menu concept that lets diners choose from food of the sea or more earthbound offerings like free-range chicken, flank steak, or pork tenderloin. It's a water and land, sea and earth, marriage of opposites thing: hence Sushi Rock.

The watery side is Japanese style, which is where my interests lie. There's a long list of traditional sushi, sashimi (that's sushi without the rice), maki rolls, temaki (more of a cone), and the king-sized Big Rolls—each available by the piece so you can mix and match at will, and ordered by ticking off your choices on the printed form. The selection is vast and eclectic—tuna, salmon, eel, mackerel, octopus, snapper, sea urchin, clam, yellowtail, flying fish roe, and more. Combinations mix it up with cucumber, avocado, tofu, pickled radish, dried gourd, mountain carrot, and asparagus. Seaweed, baby octopus salad, and chirashi (a combination of vinegared rice, vegetables, and fish) round out the selection.

Sushi arrives at your table on a black marble slab brought by a server, male or female, who is dressed in black and sure to be young and well-proportioned, with great hair, and probably sporting a piercing or two. This description fits the clientele equally well, the main difference being that most of them have cell phones glued to their ears or at the ready, and leather jackets on their backs or the backs of their chairs. In contrast, the sushi chefs on a raised platform at the back of the restaurant who prepare your order look like . . . well . . . sushi chefs.

The lighting is carefully designed and dramatic, and the result is that the people and food all look appealing. Tables are packed tight on the first floor, and on weekends the crowd is also packed tight in the adjacent bar area, but there's a more expansive feel as well as room for larger groups upstairs. The bar serves martinis in "glam" glasses, some Japanese beers, and cold sake straight and flavored (a popular sip, in case you hadn't heard), nice wines by the glass, classy ports, and $3 bottles of water.

The entire place resonates with action and potential action, a spot where you can eat ethnic and rev your social engines. They have a party room for up to 50 people (book at least a month in advance). Be forewarned: parking in this neighborhood, especially on Friday and Saturday nights, is a complex and potentially expensive undertaking. There are lots, but the price tag is significant, and the search for an on-street spot can be long or leave you with a long walk. Valet parking available.

## Sushi Rock
☎ (216) 378-9595
CITY: **Beachwood**   AREA: **East Side**
ATMOSPHERE: **Dressy**   COST: $$$$$

**ADDRESS:** 2101 Richmond Rd.
**HOURS:** Lunch Mon–Fri 11 a.m.–4 p.m., Sat–Sun 11:30 a.m.–4 p.m.; Dinner Mon–Thu 5 p.m.–11 p.m., Fri–Sat 5 p.m.–12 a.m., Sun 5 p.m.–10 p.m. **RESERVATIONS:** Taken, recommended Thu–Sat **PAYMENT:** MC, VS, AX, DIS **BAR:** Beer, wine, liquor **TAKEOUT:** Yes **ACCESS:** ♿ Full access

See listing for Sushi Rock on W. 6th St. in Cleveland for more information.

## Tomo
☎ (440) 878-0760
CITY: **Strongsville**   AREA: **Southwest**
ATMOSPHERE: **Relaxed**   COST: $$$$$

**ADDRESS:** 15163 Pearl Rd.
**HOURS:** Lunch Mon–Fri 11 a.m.–2:30 p.m.; Dinner Mon–Thu 4:30 p.m.–10 p.m., Fri 4:30–10:30 p.m.; closed weekdays between lunch and dinner; open continuously Sat 11 a.m.–10:30 p.m., Sun noon–10 p.m. **RESERVATIONS:** Taken, recommended for grill tables, weekends **PAYMENT:** MC, VS, AX **BAR:** Beer, wine, liquor **TAKEOUT:** Yes **ACCESS:** ♿ Limited

Perched at the outer edges of a mall parking lot the stand-alone building is a chain restaurant makeover, and a well done one, too. Divided into two rooms, one with a sushi bar, the other with grill tables, the pleasant space is defined by its spare and understated Japanese look, featuring natural light-colored wood furniture, minimal table settings, discrete dining areas, and multiple levels. It's a quiet, easy-on-the-eye backdrop to some real culinary fireworks.

The menu offers a lot of choices, and for those in search of out-of-the ordinary taste experiences, there are some special rewards. Sumashi (clear broth with mushrooms) and hamaguri (clam soup) and a kani salad made with crabmeat offer a fresh take on the usual miso soup and seaweed salad. Things get even more interesting when it comes to appetizers: hiya yako (golden bean curd with bonito flakes); nasu dengaku (barbecued eggplant); oshinko (pickled vegetables); and usuzukuri (thin slices of fluke with chili and ponzu sauce). And beyond the familiar sushi, sashimi, and hand rolls are some very inventive and very good combinations: eel-lover maki with tempura shrimp, seaweed, and artful stripes of eel sauce; naruto roll featuring a choice of fish, plus masago (crunchy smelt roe), crabmeat, and avocado wrapped with thin cucumber slices; and volcano maki made with shrimp, crabmeat, kampyo (squash), salmon, and spicy sauce. Also worth noting for their rarity are bean curd skin (inari) sushi; egg custard (tamago) sushi; a sweet potato roll and another made with fried oysters. If you favor more familiar foods plus a chef show, sit hibachi-side and get a made-to-order dinner built around filet mignon, chicken, or lobster tails. Noodle and rice dishes, bento box meals, and tempura are also available.

Sake is a specialty here. The selection is large, and the list offers a beginner's education in the various types and styles. There are inexpensive California brands, midpriced imports, and costly bottles from Japanese microbreweries. All are meant to be sipped like wine, and the better ones are served chilled. Tomo means "friendly," and this family-run restaurant lives up to its name in every way, from the kimono-clad servers to the chatty sushi chefs behind the counter.

## Tree Country Bistro
☎ (216) 321-0644
CITY: **Cleveland Heights**   AREA: **East Side**
ATMOSPHERE: **Relaxed**   COST: $$$$$

ADDRESS: 1803 Coventry Rd.
HOURS: Mon–Thu 11:30 a.m.–3 p.m., 5–10 p.m., Fri–Sat 11:30 a.m.–3 p.m., 5 p.m.–1 a.m., Sun noon–10 p.m.; closed between lunch and dinner RESERVATIONS: Taken, recommended Fri, Sat nights PAYMENT: MC, VS, AX, DIS BAR: Beer, liquor TAKEOUT: Yes ACCESS: ప Full access OTHER ETHNIC: Korean, Thai

A more apt—and perhaps the intended—name for this multinational Asian eatery would be Three Country Bistro, as owner Preeha Suksomboon, who is from Thailand, gives favorites from his homeland equal billing with food from Japan and Korea. I did ask about the use of the word Tree and got a lengthy explanation. Unfortunately I couldn't understand more than a few words of what was said. But what's in a name anyway? It's what goes in the bowl and on the plate that really counts. And this little 50-seat place has a big menu that can satisfy a wide variety of cravings and preferences. The only problem is deciding what to eat. One approach is to make a southeast Asian smorgasbord of appetizers like chicken satay, scallion pancakes, tofu triangles, soft shell crab tempura, and ankimo (cooked monkfish liver with ponzu sauce). A large selection of sushi, sashimi, and makimono is the star attraction, and some of the more intriguing choices are Canadian maki-fried sweet potato, avocado, salmon and black pearl caviar; alligator maki; mutzu (black marlin); nd unasu—barbecued eel, flying fish roe, and avocado rolled in paper-thin slices of cucumber. The number of Korean specialties is small but noteworthy, among them a sizzling hot stone pot filled with bi bim bab (a mix of seasoned vegetables plus chicken or beef topped with a sunnyside egg); spicy pork bulgogi; or a noodle dish called japchae. Thai cuisine is well represented in more than thirty entrées, among them a lychee curry, mango fried rice, and sweet Bangkok duck. No matter what section of the menu you order from, presentations are beautiful. The carrots and radishes that have been carefully transformed into blossoms and butterflies are so pretty it's tempting to keep them, not eat them. In addition to tea, you can drink jasmine lemonade, coconut juice, or a fruit shake. A few beers and some sakes are available, or you can pay a small corkage fee and bring your own wine.

Imitation bamboo greens dress up the big front windows. The walls are painted in fruity shades of yellow and orange, and the furniture is light-colored natural wood. The overall impression is clean, uncomplicated, and easy on the eyes. The clientele looks like the neighborhood—a mix of college kids, families, and couples young and old. The space cannot easily accommodate large groups, but the kitchen will happily cater a meal that you can serve a crowd in your own home.

# Korean

## Ha-Ahn Korean Bistro
☎ (216) 664-1152
CITY: **Cleveland**   AREA: **Downtown**
ATMOSPHERE: **Relaxed**   COST: $$$$$

**ADDRESS:** 3030 Superior Ave.
**HOURS:** Mon–Sat 11 a.m.–9:30 p.m.
**RESERVATIONS:** Not taken **PAYMENT:** MC, VS, AX, DIS **BAR:** None **TAKEOUT:** Yes **ACCESS:** ♿ Full access

This modest eight-table eatery is tucked in what was formerly a Chi-

nese bakery. It's inside Golden Plaza, a blond brick building that houses multiple Asian businesses. It opened in 2008 and is offering gastronomic daytrippers a real taste of Korean cooking. The menu is small but the selections intriguing: kalgooksoo, thick noodles with house-made anchovy paste; la kalbi, grilled short ribs; and dwenjang jige, a seafood and tofu casserole spiked with soybean paste. The kitchen makes its own pickled condiments, and all offerings change regularly. Bibimbap features beef sizzling in a hot stone pot with rice, vegetables, and a fried egg. Soft tofu soup can be ordered mild, medium or hot, with dumplings, beef, vegetables, pork, seafood, or a combination of these ingredients.

Lunch-hour specials are good bargains. Street parking is plentiful and there is a lot at the rear entrance of building. Not much in the way of décor or atmosphere here, and not much conversational privacy either. This is a place to choose when food is the focus.

## Korea House
☎ (216) 431-0462
CITY: **Cleveland**   AREA: **Near East Side**
ATMOSPHERE: **Casual**   COST: $$$$$

**ADDRESS:** 3700 Superior Ave.
**HOURS:** Tue–Thu 11 a.m.–10 p.m., Fri–Sat 11 a.m.–11 p.m., Sun 11 a.m.–9 p.m.; closed Mon
**RESERVATIONS:** Taken, recommended for groups of 5+ **PAYMENT:** MC, VS, AX **BAR:** Beer, wine
**TAKEOUT:** Yes **ACCESS:** ♿ Full access

From the outside, this place used to look more like a factory than a restaurant. And in fact, it is a commercial building, surrounded by aging manufacturing and commercial spaces. When owner Housden Chong first opened this restaurant, she concentrated on remodeling the interior space. Enter from a side door that opens into the parking lot, and you'll find pristine white walls and table linens, standing rice-paper and latticework screens, stylized lanterns, silk flowers, and a quiet, spare atmosphere of Asian charm. Now the exterior of the building has been renovated, too, so that it is more inviting and attractive, with the addition of large front windows that will, as Ms. Chong explains, let you see from the outside how great it is on the inside.

And beyond the décor, what's great about the inside is the food. Korean food is not at all similar to Chinese food, so diners here should expect a very different eating experience. You'll encounter pot stews, ingredients like octopus, buckwheat noodles, and kimchee (a salty, fermented side dish made of cabbage). Many dishes are spicy, but the chef is happy to adjust the heat to your taste, so feel free to order mild, medium, or hot. Two of the most popular menu items for Americans are the Korean-style barbecued chicken, barbecue ribs, and bul gogi jung sik (marinated sliced beef cooked, for two or more, right at the table).

The family-style dinners are a good way to sample a variety of dishes if you're unfamiliar with Korean cuisine. Kim's, a Korean grocery store formerly on Payne, is now located behind the restaurant. (For more information about the store, see listing further on in this chapter).

book by its cover, but most of us do anyway, and we go for the attractive ones with real eye appeal. You shouldn't judge a restaurant by its décor either, but most of us do that, too. So when you walk into this tiny Korean joint you may feel a tremor of disappointment. It's true there's fake wood paneling on the walls (and not much else except for a single decorative black-and-white cloth hanging), but there's real food on the plates.

What's lacking in atmosphere, service, and even English-language skills (I don't recommend attempting telephone conversations more complex than "Are you open?" or "A Number 7 and a Number 12 to go, please") is made up for in the authenticity of the food. Eat here and you eat as Koreans do. Entrées range from whole-meal soups like the beefy yook ge jang and nang myon (buckwheat noodles in cold broth) to broiled beef ribs (kalbi), a spicy rice-and-vegetable dish called dolsotbibimbab (better known as Number 16), and a meat dumpling and rice cake combo (ttok mandukuk). Most dishes come with a variety of side-dish condiments as well as steamed rice. If you like beef or you want a vegetarian dish, you'll have several choices. But there's only one pork dish, one chicken dish, and no fish dishes on the 21-item menu. Dessert comes in liquid form, and there are just two of them: sikye, which is a sweet rice drink, and sujong gwa, the intriguing persimmon punch.

You'll find the restaurant in a tiny little shopping strip with parking in front.

## Seoul Garden
☎ (330) 929-9971

CITY: **Cuyahoga Falls**   AREA: **Farther South**
ATMOSPHERE: **Relaxed**   COST: $$$$

**ADDRESS:** 2559 State Rd.
**HOURS:** Mon–Sat 11:30 a.m.–10 p.m.; closed Sun **RESERVATIONS:** Not taken **PAYMENT:** MC, VS
**BAR:** Beer **TAKEOUT:** Yes **ACCESS:** ✦ Limited

We all know you shouldn't judge a

## Seoul Hot Pot

☎ (216) 881-1221

CITY: **Cleveland** AREA: **Near East Side**
ATMOSPHERE: **Casual** COST: $$$$$

**ADDRESS:** 3709 Payne Ave.
**HOURS:** Mon–Sat 10 a.m.–10 p.m.; closed Sun
**RESERVATIONS:** Taken, recommended for large
groups **PAYMENT:** MC, VS, AX **BAR:** Beer, wine
**TAKEOUT:** Yes **ACCESS:** ♿ None

This small restaurant (it seats about 40) was once the only place around where one person could order a meatball sub and the other jaeyook bokum (marinated pork) and twikim mandu (fried dumpling). When the owners, who came here from Korea, went into business they thought success was to be found in pizzas and subs, so they bought a downtown pizzeria, kept the name, and learned to cook Italian-style. But their Korean friends, including homesick exchange students, kept asking them to use the restaurant kitchen to make traditional Korean dishes. Fearing that Clevelanders would never take to Korean food, they decided the best business would be both businesses and for years served pizzas and naeng myun (noodles).

I'm pleased to report that since the first publication of *Cleveland Ethnic Eats* there's been so much interest in the Korean half of the menu (which does a good job of explaining what goes into all the dishes so unfamiliar to most Americans), that the family has chosen to focus strictly on their native cuisine. So now those with bold palates can sample gejan bekban (raw crab in hot sauce), kimbob (a sort of egg roll made with seaweed), or rice cakes and seafood cakes. Some tables have built-in grills for cooking your own meat, Korean-style. The beef is top quality, marinated, and cooks up so tender you can cut it with a fork. But you're not

supposed to. The protocol, if you want to do as the Koreans do, is to wrap a bite-size piece in a lettuce leaf, pick it up with your hands, and pop the whole thing in your mouth. Like all the entrées, it is accompanied by a variety of side dishes and condiments, including pickled vegetables, rice, and hot sauce. Don't be put off by the uninviting exterior; the inside is simple but pleasant. Parking lot for 10 cars; also on-street parking.

# Thai

## Bangkok Thai Cuisine

☎ (440) 684-1982

CITY: **Lyndhurst** AREA: **East Side**
ATMOSPHERE: **Relaxed** COST: $$$$$

**ADDRESS:** 5359 Mayfield Rd.
**HOURS:** Lunch Tue–Fri 11:30 a.m.–3 p.m.;
Dinner Mon–Thu 5–10 p.m., Fri 5–10:30
p.m., Sat 4–10:30 p.m., Sun 4–9:30 p.m.
**RESERVATIONS:** Taken **PAYMENT:** MC, VS, DIS **BAR:**
None **TAKEOUT:** Yes **ACCESS:** ♿ Full access

Originally on Warrensville Center Road, this modest mom-and-pop business relocated here in 2007. Formerly a carry-out operation, it's now a modest but full-service restaurant where you can enjoy orders of super spicy seafood basil rice or string bean curry. The dining room is nothing fancy but pleasant enough: a mix of booths and tables, with traditional Thai arts and crafts decorating the walls. The food is top notch. Chef and owner Preecha Promploy was formerly with Lemon Grass, and his skill in the kitchen is well known. The menu he's put together for his own place has Thai touchstones such as coconut soup, chili duck, and emerald noodles. But it shows some personal perspective, too. The crispy vegetarian gyoza are filled with a mix of potatoes, sweet potatoes, carrots, celery, and peanuts. And in mee yok mu, pork, beef, or chicken is sautéed in orange juice with vegetables and soy sauce. Build your own entrées by choosing a protein—chicken, beef, pork, duck, squid, shrimp, scallops, or tofu—then choose from a list of sauce and vegetable stylings: cashew nut, garlic and snow pea, ginger and mushroom, or red curry with eggplant and bamboo shoots. Other intriguing options include chicken or fish in tamarind sauce and bang bang, an appetizer made from ground chicken and shrimp. There are six different kinds of soup, four salads, and a sizable number of options for vegetarians. By request, diners can dial the heat level up and down in most dishes. Sweet rice desserts make a fine finish. The storefront spot, located in a shopping strip with parking, is a block from the Lyndhurst City Hall.

## Charm Thai Restaurant
☎ (216) 642-0301
CITY: **Parma**    AREA: **Southwest**
ATMOSPHERE: **Casual**    COST: $$$$$

**ADDRESS:** 7426 Broadview Rd.
**HOURS:** Lunch Mon–Fri 11 a.m.–3 p.m., Sat–Sun noon–4 p.m.; Dinner Mon–Thu 4–9:30 p.m., Fri–Sat 4–10 p.m., Sun 4–9 p.m.; closed between lunch and dinner **RESERVATIONS:** Taken **PAYMENT:** MC, VS, DIS **BAR:** Beer, wine, liquor **TAKEOUT:** Yes **ACCESS:** ♿ Full access **OTHER ETHNIC:** Japanese

Exceptionally fresh ingredients prepared with a deft and delicate touch characterize the food. The selection focuses on Thai favorites—duck choo chee, beef macadamia, lemongrass chicken, curries, and noodle dishes. But there are a few surprises, too, among them a crunchy chive pancake appetizer that is delightfully different from the Chinese version, steamed chicken

dumplings in a ginger soy sauce, a spicy country-style version of pad Thai, and wild boar basil. An unusual sweet and zippy honey lemon sauce flavors the shellfish, cashews, fruit, and vegetables in a preparation called shrimp himaparn. Those who have a taste for uncooked clams, fluke, mackerel, and freshwater eel can dine on sushi and sashimi. Sit at the bar to see your order assembled. A house creation celebrates the restaurant's address: The Broadview Maki roll is filled with shrimp tempura, cream cheese, tobiko (flying fish roe), tuna, and salmon. There are a few other choices that lean Japanese, including soft, fried agedashi tofu, lightly salted edamame (soybeans), miso soup, and seaweed salad. The spiral-bound menu is easy to navigate, with descriptive explanations for each listing. Enjoy a cup of toasted barley tea while you ponder what to eat.

The restaurant opened in June 2008. The dining room has an appealing contemporary look, done up in earthy food tones of tangerine, mustard, sage, celery, and aubergine, lots of natural wood, and stylish lighting. The furnishings, colors, and layout of the tables lend personality to what might otherwise be a bland, square space in boxy strip of new storefronts.

## Koko Bakery
☎ (216) 881-7600
CITY: **Cleveland**    AREA: **Near East Side**
ATMOSPHERE: **Relaxed**    COST: $$$$$

**ADDRESS:** 3710 Payne Ave.
**HOURS:** Mon–Sun 8:30 a.m.–7 p.m.
**RESERVATIONS:** Not taken **PAYMENT:** MC, VS **BAR:** None **TAKEOUT:** Yes **ACCESS:** ♿ Full access **OTHER ETHNIC:** Chinese, Japanese

There are a handful of tables but no table service at this small café and bakery. Most of the culinary action is focused on sweet and savory buns, pastries, and cakes for eating in or taking home. But there is a small menu of rice bowls, Asian-inspired salads and sandwiches, and daily specials such as scallion pancakes, curry chicken, and teriyaki tilapia. When it comes to liquid refreshment beyond the ordinary, consider bubble tea, a kumquat fruit smoothie, a Vietnamese coffee, or a cup of hot longan date tea. For dessert the list of choices is long, and options include a variety of Taiwanese and Hong Kong–style sweets such as lotus and duck egg pastries, buns filled with lemon jam, moon cakes, and shaved ice with more than a dozen flavored toppings. (For more information about the bakery, see listing in the market section of this chapter.) Free head-in parking is available in a lot that fronts this small plaza.

## Lemon Grass Thai Cuisine

☎ (216) 321-0210

CITY: **Cleveland Heights**   AREA: **East Side**
ATMOSPHERE: **Casual**   COST: **$$$**$$

**ADDRESS:** 2179 Lee Rd.
**HOURS:** Lunch Mon–Fri, 11:30 a.m.–2:30 p.m.; Dinner Mon–Thu 5–10 p.m., Fri–Sat 5–11 p.m., Sun 4–9 p.m. **RESERVATIONS:** Taken, for groups of 6+ **PAYMENT:** MC, VS, AX, DIS **BAR:** Beer, wine, liquor **TAKEOUT:** Yes **ACCESS:** ⅃ Full access

Eat here if you're a vegetarian or a die-hard carnivore; an enthusiast of the hot and spicy, in need of mild and light, or a devotee of fresh and healthy; a seeker of classic Thai cuisine or unusual Thai-inspired creations, some of which you can combine to your own taste. Lemon Grass has it all and offers diners a range of choices in environment and food.

The 94-seat sunroom, so called because of all the windows that face onto a pocket park, has a laid-back feel with stone tile floors, a view of the bar, and big-screen televisions tuned to whatever game is the current hot topic of conversation. The other room has a softer, more refined look and a quieter atmosphere. The warm-toned beige walls are decorated with works by Thai artists, the floor is covered in richly colored carpeting with a design inspired by Oriental rugs.

Both rooms offer the same authentic dishes made by chef and owner Eddie Premwattana. He bought the restaurant in 2007 and has added his own signature dishes to the established lineup of pad Thai noodles; lemon grass soup; coconut shrimp; chicken prepared with pine nuts or cashews; a spicy cold beef salad; a variety of seafood dishes; and homemade coconut ice cream. He does duck nine different ways, bakes shrimp in a traditional clay pot, and prepares an interesting pork dish by marinating medallions of meat in garlic oil and coriander root. The regular menu also has a varied selection of meatless dishes including spring rolls made with bean curd, cucumber, lettuce, and carrots; rice noodle and fried rice dishes; and "Green Garden," steamed vegetables in peanut sauce. There's always a choice of yellow, red, masaman, and green curries prepared with your choice of shrimp, tofu, duck, chicken, or beef: yellow is the mildest, red the hottest. All dishes are well described on the menu so you know just what you're getting into when you order, and the spicing can be adjusted at your request.

Readers of *Cleveland* magazine and *Northern Ohio Live* regularly vote this the best Thai in town. In good weather, there's an outdoor patio where this same food is also served. Plenty of parking in a city lot at the rear of the restaurant, and because it's just a few doors away from the Cedar Lee Theatre, a great choice for pre- or post-movie dining.

## Mekong River

☎ (216) 371-9575

CITY: **Cleveland Heights**   AREA: **East Side**
ATMOSPHERE: **Casual**   COST: **$$$**$$

ADDRESS: 1918 Lee Rd.
HOURS: Mon–Sat 4–10 p.m., Sun 4–9 p.m.
RESERVATIONS: Taken, recommended on
weekends PAYMENT: MC, VS, DIS BAR: Beer,
wine, liquor TAKEOUT: Yes ACCESS: ⅃ Full access
*Not recommended for children OTHER ETHNIC:
Cambodian

A board listing specials greets diners at the door. You might see crispy tangerine duck and wild rice, simmered lamb shanks; or a variation on one of the many Thai-style curries that are a part of the regular menu. And if that's not enough to get your juices flowing and your taste buds tingling, wait until you get beyond anticipation and start eating the highly spiced dishes that characterize Thai and Cambodian cooking. Expect an out-of-the-ordinary mix of tastes, textures, and colors, with crisp vegetables, chopped peanuts, overtones and undertones of coconut, lime, and cilantro, and, more often than not, the smack of hot chilies.

If you're not sure what to order, owners Sosophy and Sarin Chham, who are from Cambodia, will be glad to make a recommendation. Depending on your preferences, Sarin can steer you toward some serious heat or help you identify the mild-to-your-mouth dishes that are also part of his wife Sosophy's culinary repertoire. There's a good selection of the standard Thai foods found in restaurants here, plus a number of more unusual Thai and Cambodian specialties: lop (a Thai dish made with ground chicken or pork and roasted ground rice); Cambodian gumbo with papaya and pumpkin; trey chean (fish with ginger gravy); and for dessert, sweet sticky rice with mango.

The menu is also coded for heat: "no stars" means you're safe; one star has a bite; three stars are only for the very bold or the experienced. Appetizers like fish cakes, Mekong chicken wings, and Thai curry puffs plus a papaya salad make a meal. Vegetarian options get a page of their own on the menu. Chham started this restaurant in the space formerly occupied by Siam Cuisine. His former career involved neon, which accounts for the distinctive purple neon signage in the restaurant's front window.

It's diagonally across the street from Cain Park, making it an excellent pit stop in the warm-weather months on your way to or from a play or a concert at the outdoor theaters there. But any time of year is a good time to take this taste trip to Southeast Asia. Expect a comfortable, casual atmosphere where jeans or jackets are acceptable, and you'll find people of all ages, from the high-chair set to card-carrying members of the Golden Buckeye club. Equally good for a date, a girls' night out, or a cross-generational gathering. A small five-seat bar area with chilled Thai beer at the ready. Parking on the street and at the rear of the building.

## Mint Café

☎ (216) 320-9915

CITY: **Cleveland Heights**   AREA: **East Side**
ATMOSPHERE: **Relaxed**   COST: **$$$**$$

ADDRESS: 1791 Coventry Rd.
HOURS: Lunch Mon–Sat 11:30 a.m.–3 p.m.;
Dinner Mon–Thu 5–10 p.m., Fri–Sat 5–10:30
p.m., Sun 4–9:30 p.m.; closed between lunch
and dinner RESERVATIONS: Taken, for groups of
3+; recommended for Fri, Sat nights PAYMENT:
MC, VS, AX, DIS BAR: Beer, wine, liquor
TAKEOUT: Yes ACCESS: ⅃ Full access

I have a definite thing for Tom Khar Gai. That's not a man's name; it's soup. The combination of coconut milk, galanga, lime juice, mushrooms, and velvety slices of chicken is prepared to perfection here. Luckily the restaurant is not far from where I live so I can feed my craving often without much effort. A takeout order combined with a few appetizers constitutes a feast: golden bags (steamed and fried sacks of ground shrimp and mushroom deliciousness); beef satay, Siam rolls, shumai (dumplings), spicy Devil wings, and tofu triangles.

The restaurant opened in early 2006. Over the years I've eaten my way through most of the menu and have yet to find anything that failed to deliver a satisfying experience. They do a nice job saucing and seasoning grilled fish and meat, curries, fried rice, and noodles. Among the most intriguing signature dishes are scallop eggplant, tamarind duck, Lady in Green (salmon steamed in napa cabbage leaves), and something dubbed Coventry Road Madness, a seafood combination spiked with a kicky Thai basil sauce.

Those who eschew meat will be happy to see a section of the menu marked Vegetarian's Corner. Pretty plate presentations add eye appeal to all the kitchen's preparations. Don't quit until you've had dessert. My recommendations are a bowl of coconut, ginger, or green tea ice cream, an ice cream spring roll, or lychees on ice. In addition to wine, beer, and spirits, you can quench a thirst with bubble tea, fruit smoothies, house-made limeade, and Thai iced coffee or tea.

The double storefront is divided into two rooms: One is bigger than the other, but neither is large, and both are decorated with pieces of traditional and Buddhist artwork. During the day, light streams in from the big windows at one end. Tables are covered in white cloths under glass and illuminated by modern blue, red, and orange pendant lamps. Servers are dependably efficient, helpful, and full of smiles. Have change for meters out front and in a parking garage on the next block.

## Pad Thai Restaurant

☎ (330) 650-9998

CITY: **Hudson**  AREA: **Farther South**
ATMOSPHERE: **Casual**  COST: **$$$**$$

ADDRESS: 5657 Darrow Rd.
HOURS: Mon–Thu 11 a.m.–10 p.m., Fri–Sat 11 a.m.–10:30 p.m., Sun 11 a.m.–10 p.m.
RESERVATIONS: Taken, recommended on weekends PAYMENT: MC, VS, AX, DIS BAR: Beer, wine, liquor TAKEOUT: Yes ACCESS: ♿ Full access OTHER ETHNIC: Chinese

You can't miss this stop on Hudson's dining circuit. I mean that both in terms of it being easy to spot—a large, arresting stand-alone building with a beautiful Asian-inspired wooden entrance facade, with the restaurant's name lettered in both English and distinctive Thai script, a copper roof, and red awnings—and the fact that it's a must-visit place for fans of Thai food. It's owned and operated by Joanne and Timothy Ly, the same couple who do such a great job at Thai Gourmet, in Stow.

The menu features an abundant and distinctive array of appetizers; soups; salads; and chicken, beef, pork, seafood, and vegetarian entrées. Their green curry duck is an acknowledged standout. Two eggplant dishes, along with two others that feature hot curry paste and tomato chili paste sauce, respectively, fresh basil rolls, marinated Rock Cornish hen, and avocado ice cream are not often found in these parts. The spice "spigot" on everything can be adjusted to taste with merely a word to your server.

The restaurant has banquet facilities and does catering for events on and off the premises. There are four dining areas, all tastefully appointed with colonial-style rattan-look chairs and traditional arts, crafts, and sculptures. The lounge area is inviting for drinking and eating. Plenty of parking in a lot that separates the restaurant from the traffic whizzing by.

## Pad Thai Restaurant

☎ (330) 668-9981

CITY: **Akron** AREA: **Farther South**
ATMOSPHERE: **Casual** COST: **$$$$$**

**ADDRESS:** 3545 Brookwall Dr.
**HOURS:** Mon–Sat 11 a.m.–10 p.m., Sun 11 a.m.–9 p.m. **RESERVATIONS:** Taken, recommended on weekends **PAYMENT:** MC, VS, AX, DIS **BAR:** Beer, wine, liquor **TAKEOUT:** Yes **ACCESS:** ♿ Full access **OTHER ETHNIC:** Chinese

See Hudson listing for more information.

## Peppermint Thai Cuisine

☎ (216) 464-5432

CITY: **Pepper Pike** AREA: **Southeast**
ATMOSPHERE: **Casual** COST: **$$$$$**

**ADDRESS:** 30769 Pinetree Rd.
**HOURS:** Lunch Mon–Sat 11:30 a.m.–3 p.m.; Dinner Mon–Thu 5–10 p.m., Sat 5–10:30 p.m., Sun 4–9:30 p.m.; closed between lunch and dinner **RESERVATIONS:** Taken, recommended on weekends **PAYMENT:** MC, VS, AX, DIS **BAR:** Beer, wine, liquor **TAKEOUT:** Yes **ACCESS:** ♿ Full access

The restaurant's name is a clever combination of its Pepper Pike location and owner Matt Kanegkasikorn's first Cleveland restaurant on Coventry Road, Mint Café. This spot in Landerwood Plaza gives him a spacious 90-seat dining room, allowing more people to enjoy his expertly prepared Thai dishes. The décor and atmosphere here are slightly more upscale and contemporary, and the venue is ideal for large groups. For information about the menu, a duplicate of the one at his original place, see listing for Mint Café.

## Sweet Mango

☎ (440) 238-9921

CITY: **Strongsville** AREA: **Southwest**
ATMOSPHERE: **Casual** COST: **$$$$$**

**ADDRESS:** 14610 Pearl Rd.
**HOURS:** Lunch Mon–Sat 11:30 a.m.–3 p.m., Sun 12:30–3 p.m.; Dinner Mon–Thu 4–9:30 p.m., Fri–Sat, 4–10:30 p.m., Sun 3–9 p.m.
**RESERVATIONS:** Taken, recommended for dinner
**PAYMENT:** MC, VS, AX, DIS **BAR:** Beer, wine, liquor **TAKEOUT:** Yes **ACCESS:** ♿ Full access

Strongsville, a community with few options for adventurous diners, got an infusion of Southeast Asian excitement when this restaurant opened in August 2007. The chef and owners are from Thailand, and they're serving traditional fare made to the highest standards.

Dishes feature the flavors of coconut milk, lemongrass, chilies, kaffir lime leaves, fresh mangoes, and spicy basil. Among the house's signature dishes are steamed salmon in a choo chee curry sauce; shrimp himaparn prepared with pineapple and cashews in a honey lemon sauce; and beef macadamia. Vegetarians will happily find much to entice them. Anyone who wants to eat on the edge can try Wild Boar Basil. There are many ways to have it your way here. Six kinds of curry can be customized with the addition of chicken, beef, pork, shrimp, duck, tofu, or vegetables. Spiciness of individual dishes can be adjusted. Both jasmine and brown rice are available.

Part of a four-store strip with a parking lot in front, it doesn't look like much from the outside. But the interior is a handsome, modern-looking space. Wood tables are finished to a high satiny gloss and illuminated by trendy little overhead spotlights. If you live nearby, this could easily become a favorite destination. If you don't, the quality of the food and attractive setting make it worth a trip.

## Thai Gourmet
☎ (330) 688-0880

CITY: **Stow**   AREA: **Farther South**
ATMOSPHERE: **Casual**   COST: **$$$**$$

ADDRESS: 3732 Darrow Rd.
HOURS: Mon–Fri 11 a.m.–9:30 p.m., Sat–Sun 11 a.m.–10:30 p.m. RESERVATIONS: Taken, recommended for large groups PAYMENT: MC, VS, AX BAR: Beer, wine TAKEOUT: Yes ACCESS: ♿ Full access OTHER ETHNIC: Chinese

Tucked between megamarts and chain stores at a busy intersection between Cleveland and Akron, this is an unlikely location for a top-quality one-of-a-kind place, a bright spot of uniqueness in a zone of mediocre commercial sameness. The strip-mall exterior is generic, but there are surprises and rewards inside for those who crave an extraordinary meal in pleasant and comfortable surroundings.

It was risky, admits Joanne Ly, who runs the restaurant with her chef-husband, to open a Thai restaurant here. "We weren't sure if people in this area would be interested, and in the beginning many of our customers did choose familiar dishes from the Chinese section of our menu. They were afraid of the spiciness that is part of Thai cooking and very hesitant to try new things." So Joanne, who is beautiful, articulate, and personable, with a smile that makes you feel special, took it upon herself to coax, charm, and convince people to get acquainted with the food of her homeland—and she's succeeded. "In five years' time, we've developed a large group of enthusiastic regulars, many of whom had never tasted Thai food before coming here, and now they've graduated from wanting only mild spicing to asking for it very hot!"

Fans come from as far away as Twinsburg and Hudson, some willing to drive 45 minutes to get a bowl of the savory coconut soup that is surely as much tonic as food, a platter of fish in chili pepper sauce, or an order of basil mussels. Once you've tried their Thai coconut spaghetti, your ideas of what's possible with pasta will be forever changed.

The menu is divided into separate Chinese and Thai sections. Entrées combine frequently seen, popular items like pad Thai, red, green, and yellow curries, lo mein, governor's chicken, and orange beef with other, less common options including hot pepper duck, Bangkok fish, Siam eggplant, lobster with ginger sauce, crystal shrimp, and Szechuan bean curd. Dishes that pack heat are clearly marked. A large list of meatless dishes makes this a destination for vegetarians.

Most vegetables are steamed, and coconut milk is used with a light hand. Dessert choices range from non-Asian chocolate or vanilla ice cream, tiramisu, or walnut cake to homemade Thai coconut ice cream, banana dumplings, fried bananas with peanut or sesame topping, and shankaya (sweet brown coconut rice).

This is a good place for celebrations; tables down the center can easily be pushed together for large groups, and there's a birthday cake on the menu that serves four to 10 (let them know in advance that you'll be coming and tell them the number of people in your party). Beers from Thailand, Vietnam, India, Japan, and China are available along with brews from England, Ireland, Holland, Germany, and the U.S. of A. California reds and whites are available by the glass, as well as a small but interesting mix of domestic and imported wines by the bottle, plus plum wine and hot or cold sake.

Though far from formal, the small restaurant aims for a certain polish. Cloth napkins are folded like fans and stand upright on each plate. The decorations and furnishings are tasteful, with seats that make it inviting to take your time. High chairs are available, and there's a small waiting area at the front. You'll never have to search for a parking spot in the massive lot out front, where Graham Road meets Route 91 (Darrow Road).

## Thai Hut
☎ (216) 228-0110
CITY: **Lakewood**    AREA: **Near West Side**
ATMOSPHERE: **Relaxed**    COST: **$$**$$$

**ADDRESS:** 13359 Madison Ave.
**HOURS:** Mon–Sat 11 a.m.–10 p.m., Sun 4–10 p.m. **RESERVATIONS:** Not taken **PAYMENT:** MC, VS, AX **BAR:** None **TAKEOUT:** Yes **ACCESS:** ♿ Full access

Dial your expectations to unimposing, authentic, and friendly, and this small spot, open since the autumn of 2005, will be a good choice. Everybody who fills one of the 30 seats gets a warm greeting, attentive service, and the chance to enjoy home-style Thai food. The names of some dishes make you smile even before you've tasted them: Cozy Shrimp (a version of spring rolls); Crazy Noodles (pan-fried rice noodles with chicken, green beans, and spicy seasonings); Fisherman's Fury (a fiery mix of scallops, shrimp, and squid); Friendship (sautéed shrimp and chicken with fresh vegetables); and Excited Tofu (a combination of soybean curd, vegetables, and a hot sauce). Be sure to try chive dumplings, spicy beef salad, and beef or tofu prepared pit-king, style with green and red peppers, pine nuts, and chili ginger sauce. Build a curry, much as you do a pizza, selecting from a list

of ingredients. Portions for everything on the menu are generous.

## Thai Kitchen
☎ (216) 226-4450
CITY: **Lakewood**    AREA: **West Side**
ATMOSPHERE: **Casual**    COST: **$$**$$$

**ADDRESS:** 12210 Madison Ave.
**HOURS:** Mon & Thu 11:30 a.m.–9 p.m., Fri–Sat 11:30 a.m.–10 p.m., Sun 1–9 p.m.; closed Tue–Wed **RESERVATIONS:** Not taken **PAYMENT:** Cash only **BAR:** None **TAKEOUT:** Yes **ACCESS:** ♿ None

If there's such a thing as Thai kitsch, this is it. Every available surface, including the ceiling, is festooned with the Asian version of bric-a-brac, travel posters, and paper mobiles. But the result is a charmingly tacky backdrop for very interesting and extremely healthy food. There's a good selection of rice and rice noodle dishes, soups, curries, salads, and meat, vegetable, and seafood entrées flavored with the traditional aromatic Thai seasonings of lime, curry, basil, lemongrass, ginger, and coriander. Many dishes have a spicy bite that's balanced by the use of coconut milk, honey, or crisp vegetables. Peanut and fish sauces are common.

The Thai Kitchen is frequented by many of Cleveland's Thai residents when they want "a taste of home." The chef prepares each dish using authentic Thai methods with traditional seasonings. She makes each item to order with only the freshest ingredients, honoring individual preferences for vegetarian, spicy, or mild dishes and never uses MSG. Although the names are often long and unfamiliar—khao bai-gra-pao khai-down (stir-fried chicken with sweet basil and hot chilies) and kaeng choed phug-gard-dong (pickled mustard vegetable soup with pork and sautéed garlic)—each dish is well described on the menu, and staff will happily answer all your questions.

The restaurant is small, only seven tables and 16 chairs grouped around the L-shaped kitchen. Recorded popular Thai music plays in the background. In terms of the setting, eating out doesn't get much homier than this. But the food will transport you to another world. Owners Suriya and Numtip Chuaypradit always welcome visitors warmly and treat every diner as if they were family.

## V-Li's Thai Cuisine
### ☎ (330) 854-5344
CITY: **Canal Fulton**  AREA: **Farther South**
ATMOSPHERE: **Casual**  COST: **$$$**$$

**ADDRESS:** 129 N. Canal St.
**HOURS:** Tue–Fri 11:30 a.m.–2:30 p.m. & 5–9 p.m., Sat 4–9:30 p.m.; closed Sun–Mon
**RESERVATIONS:** Not taken **PAYMENT:** MC, VS, AX
**BAR:** Beer, wine, liquor **TAKEOUT:** Yes **ACCESS:** ♿ Limited

This is an unlikely location for a restaurant so good that it received a Readers' Choice Award for "Best Thai" from *Northern Ohio Live* magazine. Canal Fulton, after all, would never be considered a hub of fine dining or an ethnic enclave. But V-Li Van Sickel lives nearby with her husband and family, and when she decided to open her own place, she chose a place close to home. She was also attracted to the building itself, a 100-year-old Federal-style brick structure on the town's picturesque Main Street (also the main street), which once served as the Odd Fellows lodge. (Note to self—look up Odd Fellows on the Internet and find out, once and for all, who and what they are.)

The restaurant has proved to be an important addition to local commerce as it draws a steady stream of customers, many willing to travel the distance from Akron, Cleveland, Wooster, and even a couple from Parkersburg, West Virginia (who usually leave with a big box of carryout to eat later). Highways make the trip easy and relatively fast, and V-Li's cooking makes it worth the effort. She has a sizable number of weekly "regulars," and even her employees come to the restaurant in their off-hours to eat her food. She learned to cook growing up in Thailand. After her marriage to Ohio native Roger Van Sickel in 1973, she came to America and perfected her skills working in restaurant kitchens. She loves to cook and passed that enthusiasm on to her son Phillip, who trained to be a chef and now works with her.

Together they prepare a variety of Thai dishes, some familiar like satay, pad Thai, and red, yellow, or emerald curry, others less well known in these parts—cinnamon soup, honey pork, triple-flavored fish, and grilled giant prawns (a weekend special). All the food is light and healthy. Hot dishes get a one- or two-chili rating on the menu. Some of her customers are not the type to try new things, and members of this group tend to order the same one or two dishes they know and love. She brings them what they want, of course, but encourages them in her gentle, charming way to try new things.

Desserts offer a lovely choice: there's sweet rice with custard, fried bananas, coconut ice cream, her own Siam Sundae, and tapioca with young coconut meat. The wine list is good: there's a reserve list of expensive bottles, a choice of quality reds and whites, both with good descriptions of each vintage, and several other house wines offered by the glass.

The setting is pleasant and easy on the eyes: natural wood, a palette of natural colors, and lovely Thai artwork.

# Vietnamese

## #1 Pho
☎ (216) 781-1176

CITY: **Cleveland**   AREA: **Near East Side**
ATMOSPHERE: **Casual**   COST: **$$$**$$

ADDRESS: 3120 Superior Ave.
HOURS: Sun–Thu 11 a.m.–9:30 p.m., Fri–Sat 11 a.m.–10:30 p.m. RESERVATIONS: Taken PAYMENT: MC, VS, AX, DIS BAR: Beer, wine, liquor
TAKEOUT: Yes ACCESS: ♿ Limited

Soon after this place opened in September 2002, I began receiving e-mail messages from friends and readers who wanted to clue me in to what they variously described as their exciting, great, amazing new "find." And I'm so glad they did. It's a wonderful addition to the downtown dining scene, a lovely plus for the street, and a terrific, and popular, place to eat. The refurbished and remodeled double storefront building is attractive inside and out. The two dining rooms are spacious and nicely appointed with oak floors stripped, buffed, and varnished to a high shine; modern lighting, polished wooden tables; and a fashionable red and buttery cream color scheme.

The menu qualifies as a tome, and you'll have to eat here many times in order to thoroughly sample all it has to offer. Soups, the mainstay of Vietnamese cuisine, dominate, of course, but they go way beyond the pho you know, or have yet to discover: soups include spicy lemongrass, tomato crab, and sweet and sour fish. There are 17 different appetizers that run the gamut from crispy spring rolls and shrimp on a sugarcane to the more esoteric lotus root salad and salt-baked squid; a variety of bún (rice noodle) and còm tâm (broken rice) dishes; half a page of options for vegetarians; and 14 entrées made with shrimp, squid, or other fish. The beverages, which comprise a full page, are in a class by themselves and a liquid experience that will surely take most people's taste buds to new places. Consider some of the possibilities: drinks made with durian (not for the timid), soursop, mung beans, logan, and jackfruit.

Service in this 80-seat eatery is consistently attentive, and there is a small but comfortable waiting area. Parking is free on the street, and spaces are generally plentiful.

## Asia Tea House
☎ (216) 621-1681

CITY: **Cleveland**   AREA: **Downtown**
ATMOSPHERE: **Relaxed**   COST: **$**$$$$

ADDRESS: 3126 St. Clair Ave.
HOURS: Tue–Thu 9 a.m.–7 p.m., Fri–Sat 9 a.m.–8 p.m., Sun 9 a.m.–7 p.m. RESERVATIONS: Taken PAYMENT: MC, VS, DIS BAR: None
TAKEOUT: Yes ACCESS: ♿ Limited

This small, plain, and thoroughly authentic Vietnamese eatery is hidden inside and at the back of the Asia Food Market. (For more information about the market, see listing later in this chapter.) There are seats for 30, but the restaurant's brisk takeout business accommodates many more who are hungry for goi cuon (chewy rice-paper rolls stuffed with crisp fresh vegetables and herbs, shrimp, and pork) or banh cuon cha lua (steamed rice roll with pork). I like to place my order, do some grocery shopping while it's being prepared and packed up, and then bring dinner home for the family along with supplies for the rest of the week.

They don't cater much to Western tastes here. The menu is only 17 items long, featuring the most popular combination in homestyle Vietnamese cookery—noodles in soup. Pho dac biet, the house special soup, is made with a combination of rare and well-done beef. The kitchen also prepares broken-rice dishes, a specialty of central and southern Vietnam. Grains of jasmine rice that chipped and splintered during harvest and processing, called com tam, are the central ingredient. In Vietnam this rice is less expensive than regular jasmine rice, but in America it's a sort of delicacy and costs more.

In an article in the *L.A. Times*, Jonathan Gold wrote that com tam is "one of the great Vietnamese working-class foods, the basis of a million lunch plates." At this inconspicuous little spot, broken rice can be ordered with grilled chicken, grilled pork chops, shredded pork, pork skin (big with Vietnamese, decidedly less so among most Americans), and egg. There are also a few Hong Kong–style dishes—roast pork and roast pig (I'm not sure of the difference—maybe a question of body parts and where on the animal they come from), roast duck, and soy sauce chicken. Park in the lot adjacent to the market.

Note that as of this writing, the market and the kitchen share a phone number, so when phoning be sure to say you want the Asia Tea House.

## Khiem's Vietnamese Cuisine
☎ (216) 228-4414
CITY: **Lakewood**   AREA: **West Side**
ATMOSPHERE: **Relaxed**   COST: **$$**$$

**ADDRESS:** 13735 Madison Ave.
**HOURS:** Daily 11 a.m.–9 p.m. **RESERVATIONS:** Not taken **PAYMENT:** Cash only **BAR:** None
**TAKEOUT:** Yes **ACCESS:** ⟁ Limited

An odd little spot, this is a combination Vietnamese restaurant, coffee shop, and ice-cream parlor. It's set in a storefront with a décor that seems left over from something else: striped wallpaper

with flowered borders, mix-and-match tables and chairs, a couple of very faux Tiffany lamp shades, with most everything a little worse for wear. It's small: only 15 seats plus a couple of stools at the counter, and much of the business is carryout.

The menu is small, too, but the food selection is interesting, the prices very reasonable, and it's a favorite with many who enjoy Vietnamese food. There's a dish made with marinated beef in garlic sauce, a chicken stew, and a "salad" made with rice noodles, pieces of egg roll, bean sprouts, vegetables, and a spicy vinegar dressing. Some dishes can be ordered in three sizes—small, medium, or large. Metered parking on the street.

## Minh-Anh Vietnamese Restaurant & Market
☎ (216) 961-9671
CITY: **Cleveland**   AREA: **Near West Side**
ATMOSPHERE: **Casual**   COST: **$$**$$

**ADDRESS:** 5428 Detroit Ave.
**HOURS:** Mon–Thu 11 a.m.–9:45 p.m., Fri 11 a.m.–10:45 p.m., Sat noon–10:45 p.m., Sun noon–8:45 p.m. **RESERVATIONS:** Taken, recommended for large groups **PAYMENT:** MC, VS, DIS **BAR:** Beer, wine **TAKEOUT:** Yes **ACCESS:** ⟁ None

This is a small family-style restaurant where children can feel free to get up and watch the fish in the aquarium. The walls are wood paneled, and the tables are covered in white oilcloth; there are a few green plants, and soft rock plays quietly on the radio. One waitress describes it as "a mellow little place."

Vietnamese food makes use of many of the same ingredients as the cuisines of neighboring Thailand and Cambodia, so you'll find many dishes that use coconut milk, lemongrass, and peanuts. Owner Camla Wadsworth and her brother, the cook, are from Vietnam, but they use more familiar Chinese terms to help diners understand what they're ordering; so although the menu lists egg rolls, spring rolls, chow mein, and lo mein, you'll get the Vietnamese version. One of the most popular menu selections is a crepe, banh xeo, filled with bean sprouts, mushrooms, and chicken, pork, or shrimp. And there are some less common items as well: heo xao tuong (made with pork and spinach in a hot and sweet bean paste), tom rim (a dish of caramelized shrimp), and pho Saigon (beef and rice-noodle soup flavored with cinnamon). There is a decent selection of vegetarian dishes, and some surprises among the beverages: ginseng, jasmine, or sweet chrysanthemum tea, served hot or cold; mango or guava juice, soybean milk, and coconut or ginseng soda.

Parking in the rear, enter from the front. A Vietnamese grocery store is in the space adjacent to the restaurant. (See listing under markets in this chapter for more information.)

## Nam Wah
☎ (440) 243-8181
CITY: **Berea**   AREA: **Southwest**
ATMOSPHERE: **Casual**   COST: **$$**$$

**ADDRESS:** 392 W. Bagley Rd.
**HOURS:** Mon–Thu 11:30 a.m.–10 p.m., Fri 11:30 a.m.–11 p.m., Sat noon–11 p.m., Sun noon–10 p.m. **RESERVATIONS:** Taken **PAYMENT:** MC, VS, AX, DIS, checks **BAR:** Beer, wine, liquor **TAKEOUT:** Yes **ACCESS:** ♿ Full access **OTHER ETHNIC:** Chinese

This family-owned and -operated restaurant has been around since 1989 but moved to its present location when a fire damaged the old place. A first-time visitor may have difficulty finding this incarnation of Nam Wah; it's in a nondescript building in a small strip mall,

behind McDonald's, near the Baldwin-Wallace campus. It's a real neighborhood place, nothing fancy, with seating for about 150 people. It seems to attract working couples who want to relax over an inexpensive meal and would be a nice place for a group of friends to meet and eat. The employees are all Chinese and Vietnamese, some newly arrived in the U.S., and though their English may not always be perfect, the service they provide is friendly without being, as one visitor put it, suffocating.

The midsized menu features both Chinese and Vietnamese dishes. Some unusual dishes from the Chinese portion are bean cake with roast pork soup, Singapore-style rice noodles, and wild pepper chicken. The Vietnamese food is light yet surprisingly filling. Appetizers like grilled meatballs and shrimp on sugarcane are served with rice noodles and vegetables rolled up in rice paper with a sweet vinegar dipping sauce. Two diners told me they'd never tasted Vietnamese food before eating here. One ordered bun thit nuong (pork bowl), and the other scallops in lemongrass. "We have three words to describe the food," she told me, "yum, yum, yum."

## Saigon Restaurant and Bar
☎ (216) 344-2020
CITY: **Cleveland**   AREA: **Downtown**
ATMOSPHERE: **Casual**   COST: **$$$**$$

**ADDRESS:** 2061 E. 4th St.
**HOURS:** Mon–Thu 11 a.m.–10 p.m., Fri 11 a.m.–11 p.m., Sat 5–11 p.m., Sun 5–10 p.m. **RESERVATIONS:** Taken, recommended for groups of 7+ on Fri, Sat nights **PAYMENT:** MC, VS, DIS **BAR:** Beer, wine, liquor **TAKEOUT:** Yes **ACCESS:** ♿ Full access

This 2008 addition to the lively multicultural dining community that has sprung up downtown on East 4th Street is the glam younger sibling of #1 Pho at 30th and Superior. It opened at the end of February. The same folks run both places. This location has an almost identical selection of soups, cold rice noodle and broken rice dishes. The menu here also includes easy-to-navigate sections devoted to fish, squid, shrimp and scallops, beef, chicken, and vegetarian options, but many selections are available only for dinner. Appetizers can be treated like small plates for sharing and grazing. A spread might include sugarcane skewers of minced grilled shrimp, a crepe stuffed with pork, bean sprouts and shrimp, fried tofu, salt-baked squid, and crispy spring rolls. Two fine salads—one with lotus root and the other with cabbage—can be a meal unto themselves. Beverages can be an adventure if you order bubble tea, pau má (penny wort), coconut juice, or go with an Asian-inspired cocktail from the bar.

Bamboo accents the stylish, contemporary décor in this eye-appealing dining room. Tables tucked in what were once store display windows provide a great view, and outdoor seating makes this a fine choice in good weather. Be prepared to pay for parking.

For a more detailed description of the menu see listing for #1 Pho.

## Siam Cafe
### ☎ (216) 361-2323
CITY: **Cleveland**   AREA: **Near East Side**
ATMOSPHERE: **Casual**   COST: **$$$**$$

ADDRESS: 3951 St. Clair Ave.
HOURS: Mon–Sat 11 a.m.–11:30 p.m., Sun 11 a.m.–11 p.m. RESERVATIONS: Taken PAYMENT: MC, VS, AX, DIS BAR: Beer, wine, liquor TAKEOUT: Yes ACCESS: ♿ Full access OTHER ETHNIC: Thai

Opened in 1994, this restaurant boasts a genuinely exotic, varied, and unusual menu, and eating here is an adventure.

There are 18 choices of nonalcoholic hot and cold beverages, including da ba mau (made with palm sugar syrup, coconut juice, and tropical fruit), sinh to mang cau sim (a milkshake made with soursop nectar, ginger tea, and soybean milk), and richly flavored coffee made with sweetened condensed milk. The selection of soups, appetizers, noodle dishes, and other entrées that feature roasted duck, sea scallops, grilled pork, and marinated beef is equally varied. Many ingredients are common to Thai and Vietnamese cuisine—both kinds are featured here—though each is distinctive in its preparation. "Vietnamese cooking," explained owner Michael Hong, "has been influenced by the French and Chinese, and tends toward the sweet and salty. Thai food, which has incorporated Malaysian and Indian flavors, is much more spicy, or sour, or a combination of both." The kitchen will adjust the hot-and-spicy level to suit diners' tastes and can prepare most dishes vegetarian-style. The fish you order may be more than fresh—it's likely to be scooped right out of the tank where it's swimming and into the chef's pan. Portions on all dishes are large.

A hostess seats guests at booths or tables, and the ambience is pleasant and relaxed, a setting of light woods and polished brass with deep green accents. The restaurant's seating capacity doubled following renovations in 2002 that relocated the kitchen. Per person prices for preplanned banquet meals are very reasonable, and the selection of foods is stunning, visually and for the taste buds, too. I chose this option for 11 guests to celebrate my oldest son's graduation from high school and the twins' simultaneous completion of elementary school. We were able to sit in a booth, at a large round table, and food was placed on a lazy Susan that was in almost constant rotation, as everyone served themselves some of everything, and then some more.

Because the kitchen stays open late, this is also a great place to get a meal at an unconventional hour—I like stopping here on the way home from the airport after a missed dinner and an evening flight that offered nothing but a handful of peanuts. A meal-in-a-bowl soup or a plate of pad Thai is perfect. And I have found that the later it gets, the more interesting the crowd.

Be forewarned—there's something incongruous about the place from the outside until you realize that Siam Cafe is housed in a converted Country Kitchen restaurant. The resulting exterior is a sort of barn with an Asian motif and neon highlights. Plenty of parking on the east and west sides of the building.

## Superior Pho

☎ (216) 781-7462

CITY: **Cleveland**   AREA: **Near East Side**
ATMOSPHERE: **Relaxed**   COST: **$**$$$$

ADDRESS: 3030 Superior Ave., Golden Plaza
HOURS: Tue–Sat 11 a.m.–8 p.m., Sun 11 a.m.–7 p.m.; closed Mon   RESERVATIONS: Not taken
PAYMENT: MC, VS, DIS   BAR: None   TAKEOUT: Yes
ACCESS: ♿ Full access

To express my enthusiasm about this place and encourage everyone to give it a try, I desperately wanted to write "Go Pho It." Unfortunately, after I developed a literary attachment to this corny yet, to my mind, endearing pun, I learned that the correct pronunciation of the Vietnamese word for soup is "fuh," not "foe." Oh well, Pho-ged-aboud-it. The important thing is that this is a true Vietnamese soup bar, a kind of simple, inexpensive fast-food eatery that's common on the coasts. But there was nothing like it here when Manh Nguyen opened it in 2002. It has proven to be an enduring and very popular addition to our local food community.

Like all pho shops, this place makes one thing very, very well, then tweaks the basic dish to get variations, and serves them in two sizes: small (which was big enough for my lunch) and large. The soup begins with a light, clear, but intensely flavorful beef broth. The intensity is the result of slow cooking and a mix of herbs and spices. Rice noodles are part of every bowlful, which also comes with a side platter of fresh, crisp bean sprouts, hot peppers, Asian basil leaves, recao (a green herb similar in taste to cilantro), and a wedge of lime. Variations are about meat—beef and beef parts cut up and cooked all kinds of ways. Choose from thin slices of brisket, eye of round, flank steak, shank, tripe, and meatballs, alone or in combination with each other. Add all the crunchy stuff to the hot broth, squeeze in the lime juice, and eat. You'll need chopsticks and a deep-bowled Asian soup spoon to get every last drop and sliver of this bargain-priced one-dish meal, and both are found on the table. If you need more zing to the thing, there are also bottled condiments within easy reach of each of the restaurant's 38 seats: red hot sauce; salty fish sauce; and thick soy paste.

You can also order sides of steamed green onions or pickled onions, a dessert called marmalade on the menu that is more like canned fruit cocktail, and traditional drinks—soybean milk and pennywort, coconut juice, and hot or cold Vietnamese drip coffee. A wonderful French bread sandwich made with pate and roast pork debuted in 2003. Also on the menu are: chicken cabbage salad; summer rolls; several vermicelli noodle dishes and others made with rice; and bubble tea, a kind of Asian shake featuring black tapioca pearls.

Don't expect trendy décor. This is a simple place with a relaxed atmosphere that's all about offering delicious, healthy, inexpensive food. Although picky young eaters are unlikely to find anything to their taste here, kids are welcome and booster seats are available. The restaurant is located at the rear of Golden Plaza, an urban mini-mall with an Asian essence. Parking on the street or in a lot behind the building, which has a back entrance.

## Tay Do
☎ (440) 842-0392
CITY: **Parma**   AREA: **Southwest**
ATMOSPHERE: **Relaxed**   COST: **$$**$$

**ADDRESS:** 11725 Snow Rd.
**HOURS:** Mon–Thu 11 a.m.–10:30 p.m., Fri–Sat 11 a.m.–11 p.m., Sun noon–10 p.m.
**RESERVATIONS:** Taken **PAYMENT:** MC, VS, DIS **BAR:** None **TAKEOUT:** Yes **ACCESS:** & Full access **OTHER ETHNIC:** Chinese

Craving a big bowl of steaming pho brimming with thin slices of beef brisket or cold vermicelli noodles flecked with pork and crumbled spring rolls? Here's the place to get what you're hankering for seven days a week. There's real know-how in the kitchen of this little mom-and-pop restaurant. Everything that comes to the table is done well, from the tofu in sweet sesame sauce, crisp cabbage salad, to the slow-cooked clay pot catfish (must be ordered in advance). Cooking provides a soundtrack for every meal. You can hear the sizzle as orders hit the hot wok and the steady clang-and-clatter rhythms of stirring spoons. In addition to the dishes that appear on most Vietnamese menus, look for six tamarind broth soups, stir fries made with caramelized ginger or peppery tomatoes, and a few dishes made with squid.

This is a no-frills operation. Tables are formica, the plants are plastic, and everything looks a bit worse for wear.

You won't find much English spoken either, and the language barrier is easy to misinterpret as a lack of friendliness. Don't be put off, but don't ask too many questions. Just point to the numbered item on the menu that you want to eat, wait patiently while it's being prepared, and then enjoy.

# MARKETS

# Asian mix

## Asia Food Market
☎ (216) 621-1681
CITY: **Cleveland**   AREA: **Near East Side**

**ADDRESS:** 3126 St. Clair Ave.
**FOOD AVAIL.:** Meat (fresh, deli, frozen), fish (fresh, frozen), produce, grains, beans, flour, rice, baked goods, canned & packaged goods, spices, condiments, beverages, tea, coffee, prepared frozen foods, takeout meals **HOURS:** Mon–Thu 9 a.m.–7 p.m., Fri–Sat 9 a.m.–8 p.m. **PAYMENT:** MC, VS, DIS, checks **ACCESS:** & Limited **OTHER ETHNIC:** Chinese, Filipino, Indonesian, Korean, Laotian, Thai, Vietnamese

The Duong family owns and operates this wholesale and retail business. They are from Vietnam and stock food products from their native country as well as from Laos, Thailand, and Korea, but the emphasis is on Chinese imports.

This is a full-service neighborhood grocery, and the manager, Alex Duong, describes it as typical of those you'd find in any large city in Southeast Asia. "We strive," he says, "to be a one-stop market for all your Asian grocery needs." And whether those needs include a freshly roasted duck, a jar of fish sauce, a bag of frozen pot stickers, some star anise, bean threads, or a pound of leafy green Chinese broccoli, you'll likely get what you came for and more. Inside, you'll find a butcher and a fresh-fish market, lots of prepared foods to go, an Asian pharmacy, and a Vietnamese restaurant (see listing earlier this chapter).

## Asian Food Market
☎ (330) 928-1969
CITY: **Cuyahoga Falls**    AREA: **Farther South**

ADDRESS: 2603 State Rd.
FOOD AVAIL.: Fish (frozen), produce, grains, beans, flour, rice, canned & packaged goods, spices, condiments, beverages, tea, prepared frozen foods HOURS: Mon–Sat 10 a.m.–8 p.m.; closed Sun PAYMENT: Checks ACCESS: ⚬ None OTHER ETHNIC: Chinese, Japanese, Korean, Thai

Korean-born Dong Park and his wife have been in the grocery business since the 1980s. Their midsize market serves a clientele that by his estimate is 50% Asian and 50% American. All seem to know what to do with the Korean, Japanese, Chinese, and Thai ingredients he stocks. For those who don't want to start from scratch, the freezer case has prepared foods like dumplings and egg rolls. Among the produce you'll find gnarly chunks of ginger root, white radishes so big they look as if they were raised with growth hormones (they weren't), a variety of hot and even hotter peppers, and purple Asian eggplants. If you want your table to be as authentic as your food, you can also purchase rice bowls and sushi plates here. In a small

strip of stores with parking in front and in back.

## Dong Duong Indochina Grocery
☎ (216) 651-8796
CITY: **Cleveland**    AREA: **Near West Side**

ADDRESS: 6406 Lorain Ave.
FOOD AVAIL.: Fish (frozen, dried), produce, grains, beans, flour, canned & packaged goods, spices, condiments, tea HOURS: Daily 10 a.m.–7 p.m. PAYMENT: Checks ACCESS: ⚬ None OTHER ETHNIC: Cambodian, Chinese, Laotian, Thai, Vietnamese

Open since 1987, this is another small family-owned store that carries a variety of food products imported from Thailand, Vietnam, China, Singapore, and Cambodia. They also sell electric rice cookers and woks. Store owners Srey Trinh and her husband, Phung, are from Cambodia but are well versed in all the products they sell and how to use them. They're happy to answer questions.

## Kobawoo Oriental Food Market
☎ (216) 741-0688
CITY: **Cleveland**    AREA: **Near West Side**

ADDRESS: 4709 Pearl Rd.
FOOD AVAIL.: Meat (frozen), fish (frozen, dried), produce, grains, beans, flour, rice, canned & packaged goods, spices, condiments, tea, prepared frozen foods HOURS: Mon–Sat 10 a.m.–9 p.m., Sun noon–7 p.m. PAYMENT: MC, VS, DIS, checks ACCESS: ⚬ None OTHER ETHNIC: Chinese, Japanese, Korean

Well stocked with products from Korea, plus a small selection of ingredients for Chinese and Japanese cookery, this store replaces Kim's Oriental Food Company, formerly at this location. Though most of their clientele is Korean, the current owners, like their predecessors, also cater to the growing number of Americans interested in preparing Korean dishes in their own kitchens, and in using Asian flavorings to spice up American foods. You can find seasonings in both powder and liquid form here, as well as many varieties of canned and jarred pickled vegetables and kimchee. Though small, Kobawoo prides itself on its selection of fresh produce. The store has its own parking lot.

## Oriental Food & Gifts

☎ (216) 291-1241

CITY: **South Euclid**   AREA: **East Side**

**ADDRESS:** 4271 Mayfield Rd.
**FOOD AVAIL.:** Meat (fresh, frozen), fish (fresh, frozen), produce, grains, beans, flour, rice, canned & packaged goods, spices, condiments, beverages, tea, wine, prepared frozen foods, takeout meals **HOURS:** Mon–Sat 10 a.m.–8 p.m., Sun noon–7 p.m. **PAYMENT:** MC, VS, AX, DIS **ACCESS:** ♿ Full access

. . . . . . . . . . . . . . . . . . . . . . . . . . . .

Located at the corner of Belvoir and Mayfield in a strip mall that offers ample parking, this is a large, well-stocked supermarket with products from almost all the Pacific Rim nations. You can find tubes of Japanese wasabi (horseradish), Vietnamese hot sauce, cans of pennywort and sugarcane juice for Thai recipes, five-gallon jars of Korean bean paste, and dried Chinese mushrooms. Rice can be purchased in amounts ranging from 2- to 50-pound bags, soy sauce and sesame oil by the gallon, and exotic spices in 5-pound sacks. The selection is staggering: there are shelves and shelves of different sorts of cookies and crackers, noodles, flours, and teas of every type. In one visit I found yam noodles, acorn starch, and roasted barley tea. Freezer cases and refrigerators hold such specialties as duck and quail eggs, baby octopus and seasoned cuttlefish, fermented turnip greens and cabbage kimchee.

Aisles are wide, lighting is bright, and staff are helpful. A deli-type display case features a variety of ready-to-eat noodle, fish, and vegetable dishes, and the produce section has most of the Asian vegetables you'd ever need, and some I've never seen before. They also carry all the ingredients needed to prepare Japanese sushi at home. You'll also find Asian-brand cosmetics, kitchen utensils, housewares, and even furniture. They even have Asian-language videos for rent. This place qualifies as an American-style superstore with a purely Asian flavor. They also do catering and restaurant supply services.

## Sugarland Food Mart

☎ (440) 843-8646

CITY: **Parma**   AREA: **Southwest**

**ADDRESS:** 5790 Ridge Rd.
**FOOD AVAIL.:** Meat (frozen), fish (fresh, frozen, dried), beans, rice, baked goods, canned & packaged goods, spices, condiments, tea, prepared frozen foods **HOURS:** Mon–Sat 9 a.m.–6:30 p.m., Sun 11 a.m.–5:30 p.m. **PAYMENT:** MC, VS, checks **ACCESS:** ♿ Limited

. . . . . . . . . . . . . . . . . . . . . . . . . . . .

The emphasis at this small neighborhood store is on products from the Philippines, but this family operation, in business since 1987, also carries imported foods for all types of Asian cooking. There are many varieties of noodles, rice, and soy sauce. This is a good source for the kinds of specialized ingredients necessary for many Southeast Asian dishes: palm sugar, canned coconut, coconut and mango jellies, canned tropical fruits, and chili sauces. They even stock quail eggs.

## Tink Holl Food Market
☎ (216) 881-6996
CITY: **Cleveland**   AREA: **Near East Side**

**ADDRESS:** 1735 E. 36th St.
**FOOD AVAIL.:** Meat (fresh, frozen), fish (fresh, frozen, dried), produce, grains, beans, flour, rice, baked goods, canned & packaged goods, spices, condiments, beverages, tea, prepared frozen foods **HOURS:** Mon–Sat 9 a.m.–8 p.m., Sun 9 a.m.–7 p.m. **PAYMENT:** MC, VS, DIS, checks **ACCESS:** ♿ Full access

Formerly located in Asia Plaza, the Tink got even bigger in 2005 when it moved to its current address a few blocks away. It's now among the largest grocery stores of its kind in Ohio. Dragons guard the brightly colored red and yellow entryway, heralding the fact that this is no ordinary supermarket. Like most big grocery stores, this sprawling 13,000 square feet of space is demarcated by rows of shelves, bright lights, and wheeled metal carts, but don't expect to find peanut butter and jelly here. The market stocks strictly Asian products, and the variety spans the entire Pacific Rim from China to Vietnam, Japan to the Philippines. So instead of directing shoppers to the cereal and soda, signs point the way to duck eggs, shrimp chips, rice sticks, and salted radishes. This is the place to find bean paste, pickled garlic, cans of lotus root, agar-agar, dried cloud ears, five spice powder (a blend of anise, fennel, cinnamon, Szechuan pepper, and cloves), and kombu, a sea vegetable used by Japanese cooks to make stock.

It's easy to make your way down the wide aisles, but hard to choose from among the many different types of noodles, sauces, and oils. In the seafood department, some potential meals are still swimming while others cool their fins and shells on beds of ice. The produce section is awesome—and mysterious to the uninformed. Only a few items have English language labels. Refrigerated cases hold a mind-boggling array of dumplings and buns, and more esoteric ingredients such as beef tendon, edamame (a kind of soy bean), and mochi ice cream.

If all this is not just groceries to you, as it is to the many Asians who shop here, it's fun to just wander around like a tourist, eyeballing crackers, candies, and snacks that will surely open up new vistas of what eating is all about. There's also a large selection of traditional cooking and serving utensils. Entrances on both Payne Avenue and East 36th Street. Ample parking in private lot.

# Chinese

## Good Harvest Foods
☎ (216) 861-8018
CITY: **Cleveland**   AREA: **Near East Side**

**ADDRESS:** 3038 Payne Ave.
**FOOD AVAIL.:** Meat (fresh, frozen, dried), fish (fresh, frozen, dried), produce, rice, canned & packaged goods, spices, condiments, beverages, tea, coffee, prepared frozen foods **HOURS:** Daily 9 a.m.–8 p.m. **PAYMENT:** MC, VS, AX, DIS **ACCESS:** ♿ Full access **OTHER ETHNIC:** Japanese, Korean, Thai, Vietnamese

Just a short block from Asia Plaza, in Cleveland's small but lively and growing Asia Town, is a large white building with dragon heads flanking the front door. A sign identifies this as the Hong Kong Supermarket, and the inside does look and sound like a supermarket. The aisles are wide and brightly lit. Shelves, refrigerated coolers, and glass-doored freezers are well stocked, there's a produce section and a counter with fish kept cool on chopped ice, and the choices in every department are abundant. There are carts and baskets for your selections, and multiple cashiers at checkout lines are ready to take your money. But here the resemblance between this place and where I generally go for my quart of milk and can of tuna ends. At 5' 7" I feel like a giant next to the elderly Chinese ladies who are shopping here. Signs are written in both English and Chinese, and most of the employees are more fluent in the latter than the former. There are pungent smells I can't identify, vegetables I don't recognize, cuts of meat I've never seen (and suspect come from parts of the animal I've never considered consuming).

Among the teas are ginseng, roasted barley, jasmine, chrysanthemum, ginger, lichee black, and China green. There are medicinal teas and diet teas, teas in bags and loose leaves in lovely tins. For munching, perhaps carrot crackers, burdock, chili salt, or bamboo shoot biscuits, sweet potato cookies, and prawn-flavored or cuttlefish chips. Making a fruit salad? Forget about the canned peaches—choose lychees, loquats, longan, sapota, or rambutan in heavy syrup. Add some spark to your meals with wasabi or curry paste. Dried shiitake mushrooms come in 5-pound bags as big as a couch pillow, and the cost is astonishingly reasonable. Jasmine rice from Thailand can be bought in a 1-pound or a 50-pound sack. Sauces, spices, herbs, condiments, oils, vinegars, noodles, and beans abound. Esoteric ingredients are available—almond powder, lotus seed meal, red yeast, condensed plum syrup, grass jelly drink. So is everything and anything fresh, dried, pickled, and preserved, canned, bottled, bagged, and frozen that's likely to be called for in Chinese, Thai, Vietnamese, Korean, and Japanese cooking. Skip the cow juice—there's coconut and soy milk. Instead of cheese, there's a selection of tofu. Oddly, you'll also find anomalies like Ovaltine and

cans of Campbell's pork and beans—who knew? Mundane apples, strawberries, and bananas sit side by side with exotic star squash, lotus root, bitter melon, opo, stalks of lemongrass, and miniature heads of baby choy. There's also a Chinese pharmacy, kitchen and cooking supplies, and housewares. The store's parking lot is on the 31st Street side of the building.

# Filipino

## Nipa Hut
☎ (440) 842-7333
CITY: **Parma Heights**   AREA: **Southwest**

**ADDRESS:** 6775 W. 130th St.
**FOOD AVAIL.:** Meat (fresh, frozen), fish (fresh, frozen), produce, grains, beans, flour, rice, baked goods, canned & packaged goods, spices, condiments, beverages, tea, coffee, wine, prepared frozen foods, takeout meals
**HOURS:** Mon–Sat 8:30 a.m.–8 p.m.; closed Sun **PAYMENT:** MC, VS, DIS, checks **ACCESS:** ♿ Full access **OTHER ETHNIC:** Chinese, Indian, Japanese, Korean, Thai

The market has the look and feel of a large convenience store. And it certainly is convenient if you're looking for a jar of Filipino Mang Tomas All Around Sarsa Sauce, papaya pickles, mango preserves, or tamarind concentrate. The brightly lit place is packed with products from virtually every nation in the Pacific Rim, stacked on industrial shelving, in refrigerator and freezer cases, and in boxes piled one on top of the other. But foodstuffs from the Philippines dominate, and you'll find things here that you are unlikely to find anywhere else. There are dried and frozen taro and hot pepper leaves; whole beef tongues; packaged hopia cakes laced with pineapple, red beans, or winter melon, and ginataan by the pint (a dessert made with sweet rice, coconut milk, sweet potatoes, taro root, and jackfruit). The fresh produce section offers upo (a green vegetable shaped like an eggplant), sitaw (long green beans), gabe (a leafy green), mangoes, and cassava and taro root. Milkfish, a favorite in the Philippines, is available fresh, frozen, dried, and fried, along with a nice selection of other types of fresh fish. If you want anchovy sauce, shrimp paste, pickled ginger, dried lily flowers, banana sauce, fried garlic crumbs, and agar-agar this is the place. There is also a large selection of prepared foods that can be packaged for carryout or eaten in the store. (For information about the Nipa Hut as a restaurant, see listing earlier in this chapter).

# Japanese

## Columbia Asian Food & Gift
☎ (440) 716-0808
CITY: **North Olmsted**   AREA: **West Side**

ADDRESS: 24529 Lorain Rd.
FOOD AVAIL.: Meat (frozen), fish (frozen, dried), produce, grains, beans, baked goods, canned & packaged goods, spices, condiments, beverages, tea, coffee, prepared frozen foods HOURS: Mon–Sat 10 a.m.–8 p.m., Sun 1:30–7 p.m. PAYMENT: MC, VS, checks ACCESS: & Full access OTHER ETHNIC: Chinese, Filipino, Korean, Vietnamese

Thanks to a *Cleveland Ethnic Eats* reader for telling me about this market, which features a very good selection of Pacific Rim products that goes beyond the ordinary. This is the place if you're looking for a whole, frozen squid, a gallon jar of kimchee, dried sardines, roasted soybean powder, black vinegar, green-tea ice cream, or seaweed

in three-foot strips. Freezer cases hold fish cakes and a selection of pot stickers and dumplings. There's a large variety of noodles, fresh and canned vegetables, and sauces. I was happy to find ponzu, a citrus marinade that I like to keep on hand, and Hanayuki flakes, honey-sweetened bread crumbs that make a great coating for frying and baking. Lovely imported dishes and tableware, rice cookers, and specialized utensils fill an entire aisle. This market is in a brace of stores set back from the road by a huge parking lot. Aoeshi, a Japanese restaurant, is next door (see listing in this chapter).

## Hana Asian Food
☎ (440) 461-2800
CITY: **Lyndhurst**   AREA: **East Side**

ADDRESS: 5121 Mayfield Rd.
FOOD AVAIL.: Fish (frozen), produce, grains, beans, spices, beverages, tea HOURS: Mon–Sat 10 a.m.–8:30 p.m., Sun 12:30–7 p.m. PAYMENT: MC, VS, AX ACCESS: & Full access OTHER ETHNIC: Korean, Thai

This strip mall store has a limited selection of fresh produce but lots of frozen products, from pot stickers and spring rolls to containers of mochi ice cream. The refrigerator case offers jars of kimchee and salted shrimp, sweet rice powder, and soybean paste. Shoppers who can't read the Asian-language labels on many of the products are at somewhat of a disadvantage. Either you know exactly what you want or you're willing to take a flyer. I was amused to see a few Western items, like Worcestershire sauce and Spam, packaged for a Korean-speaking audience. The three-aisle market offers some cookware and health and personal care items, 50-pound bags of rice, a variety of dried noodles and beans, snack foods, and candy. Parking lot.

# Korean

## Kim's Oriental Food

☎ (216) 391-5485

CITY: **Cleveland**   AREA: **Near East Side**

ADDRESS: 3700 Superior Ave.
FOOD AVAIL.: Meat (frozen), fish (fresh, frozen), produce, grains, beans, flour, canned & packaged goods, spices, condiments, tea, prepared frozen foods HOURS: Tue–Sat 10 a.m.–9 p.m., Sun 10 a.m.–8 p.m.; closed Mon PAYMENT: MC, VS, AX, checks ACCESS: ⅃ Full access OTHER ETHNIC: Japanese

This is one of the best sources for Korean foods in the area. It's located behind the Korea House restaurant, both in a remodeled commercial building, and the two establishments share a large, fenced-in parking lot. The store has a bright, clean, roomy look. Many varieties of rice are available in quantities ranging from 1 pound to 100 pounds, and there's also an extensive selection of noodles, different kinds of kimchee, and frozen dumplings. This is a place where the experienced cook can find obscure and unusual ingredients and a beginner can stock up on everything needed to get started in Korean cooking.

## Seoul Asian Food

☎ (216) 741-0688

CITY: **Cleveland**   AREA: **Near West Side**

ADDRESS: 4847 Pearl Rd.
FOOD AVAIL.: Meat (frozen), fish (frozen, dried), produce, grains, beans, canned & packaged goods, spices, condiments, beverages, tea, coffee, prepared frozen foods HOURS: Mon–Sat 10 a.m.–9 p.m., Sun noon–7 p.m. PAYMENT: MC, VS ACCESS: ⅃ Limited OTHER ETHNIC: Chinese, Japanese, Thai, Vietnamese

The market is smaller than the average convenience store, but shelves, coolers, and freezer cases are crammed with a wide selection of ingredients used in a variety of Pacific Rim cuisines. On a quick walk through I spotted sacks of barley tea, packages of spicy squid, big bags of frozen anchovies, fish cakes, quail eggs, cans of lotus root, sweet rice flour, seasoned soybean curd, and roasted seaweed. But Korean products predominate as evidenced by the many jars of kimchee. The selection of fresh items is limited. The store is located next to the Korean Presbyterian Church and the two venues share a parking lot.

# Thai

## Koko Bakery

☎ (216) 881-7600

CITY: **Cleveland**   AREA: **Near East Side**

ADDRESS: 3710 Payne Ave.
FOOD AVAIL.: Baked goods, takeout meals HOURS: Mon–Sun 8:30 a.m.–7 p.m. PAYMENT: MC, VS ACCESS: ⅃ Full access OTHER ETHNIC: Chinese, Japanese, Korean

Sample dessert Taiwanese style. A display of beautifully decorated cakes is the first thing you notice on walking into the small, tidy, and well-lit space. But there are a variety of tempting options here, including fruit tarts, egg custard, Chinese donuts, green tea cookies, almond shortbread, and winter melon and lotus pastries. Steamed, baked, and fried buns line the shelves of a see-through cupboard, and the protocol is self serve—grab a paper-lined tray and a pair of tongs from underneath the cabinet and take what you want. Every item is clearly labeled. Some are stuffed with taro or red bean paste, cream, or lemon jam. Others, featuring fillings of curry beef, chicken and mushrooms, barbecued pork, or sour vegetables and meat, are more main course than the finish to a meal. Equal parts store, coffee shop, and café, you can take the sweet and savory swag home or enjoy it on the spot. To wash it down there's bubble tea in a dozen flavors, Hong Kong milk tea, and smoothies plus espresso, coffee, and unusual teas such as longan, rose, and jujube date. Try pairing up a slice of moon cake or a few white sesame cookies with a bowl of flavored Taiwanese or Korean shaved ice. There's also a small menu of entrées, rice bowls, and sandwiches. (See listing in the restaurant section of this chapter.)

The bakery is part of a three-store strip fronted by a parking lot.

# Vietnamese

## Saigon Trading USA
☎ (216) 252-3979
CITY: **Cleveland**　AREA: **West Side**

ADDRESS: 10246 Lorain Ave.
FOOD AVAIL.: Fish (frozen, dried), produce, rice, canned & packaged goods, spices, condiments, beverages, tea, prepared frozen foods HOURS: Vary; call first PAYMENT: Checks ACCESS: & Limited OTHER ETHNIC: Chinese, Japanese

Situated in a short strip of attached brick-fronted shops with apartments above, this is a very small store. Considering the size of the space, the selection of food products from Thailand, Vietnam, China, and Japan is surprising. It includes fresh vegetables, frozen fish and prepared foods, vegetarian dishes, and an assortment of products in cans, bags, and jars. Among all the things you'd expect to see, such as tea, fish sauce and egg roll wrappers, some

less common items can be found, such as pickled mustard, dried turnips, tapioca flakes, and preserved radish. This is a one-person operation, so hours are "flexible." To insure that it's open when you arrive, call first. Parking at the rear of the store.

## Vietnam Market
☎ (216) 281-7724
CITY: **Cleveland**　AREA: **Near West Side**

ADDRESS: 5506 Detroit Ave.
FOOD AVAIL.: Fish (frozen, dried), produce, grains, beans, rice, canned & packaged goods, spices, condiments, beverages, tea, coffee, prepared frozen foods HOURS: Mon–Fri 9 a.m.–10 p.m., Sat 9 a.m.–11 p.m., Sun 9 a.m.–10 p.m. PAYMENT: MC, VS, checks ACCESS: & Limited OTHER ETHNIC: Chinese, Thai

When the fire-eater swallows a burning brand, the ringmaster always reminds the audience that they should not try this at home. But if you eat something you like at the Vietnamese restaurant Minh Anh, you really can try it at home by going next door to the Vietnam Market, buying the necessary ingredients, and preparing it yourself. Everything you'd need for virtually any Vietnamese dish, as well as a selection of essentials for Chinese and Thai cooking, can be found here. The store, which opened shortly after the second edition of this book went to press in 1998, can be accessed both from within the restaurant and through a separate street entrance. In addition to all the canned, bottled, and packaged foods you'd expect to see in a grocery catering to an Asian clientele, there is a small selection of fresh fruits and vegetables. You can shop every day, and much of the night—the store is open seven days a week until late. There's parking in a small lot behind the store and restaurant, or on the street.

# MIDDLE EAST, AFRICA, INDIA, AND TURKEY

This chapter, a sort of patchwork quilt, pieces together an eclectic assortment of countries from multiple continents that share a kinship in matters of food.

I included India, though it is geographically closer to China, because its cuisine is unlike those of the rest of Asia. The use of lentils, flat breads, butter, and other dairy products relate it more to Middle Eastern cuisine. In addition, a significant portion of India's population is Moslem, which links them spiritually as well to that part of the globe. And though Ethiopia, situated on the east coast of Africa, is literally and figuratively worlds apart from India, its traditional wats, fiery hot stews served with injera, a pancake-like bread, bear a close resemblance to spicy Indian curries eaten with roti, an unleavened round bread. As in the Middle East, the Ethiopian tradition is to eat at low tables without utensils, scooping up food with prewashed hands and pieces of bread. And in all these countries, meatless dishes are a major part of the daily diet.

What they also have in common: people from each of these countries have opened restaurants or markets in Greater Cleveland, which gives the rest of us a chance to be "table travelers" through these parts of the world.

There is no Ethiopian community to speak of in Cleveland. The story of Ethiopian cuisine is probably best told by the one restaurant in town that serves it, for in the modern Western mind this country is profoundly linked only to images of famine and scarcity. It's difficult to imagine Ethiopia having a tasty and inviting food culture. But it does. Ethiopian food, reflecting a heritage that dates back thousands of years to the ancient Abyssinians, is especially interesting in that it has remained relatively free of European influences. It features a bread made with a form of millet called teff that grows only in Ethiopia. Berbere, a blend of ground chilies and other herbs and spices such as rue seed, ginger, cloves, bishop's weed, and cinnamon, is an often-used seasoning. Hot and hotter is to be expected. A typical main meal consists of some type of stewed legumes, vegetables, and sometimes meat or poultry. Dorowot is made with chicken and is considered a national dish.

Until very recently, Cleveland did not have any Turkish restaurants. But now there are two, offering venues for "food journeying" to what has long been considered the crossroads of European, Asian, and Middle Eastern cultures. Turkey's culinary traditions reflect this mix in dishes that combine a Mediterranean, Armenian, and Persian sensibility with ingredients and cooking styles common to Arabic, Indian, and North African kitchens. Garlic and dill are favored flavorings. Tomatoes, lentils, chickpeas, eggplant, yogurt, and rice play a role in many dishes. Lamb and chicken are the most commonly used meats.

Currently there are approximately 100,000 Arab Americans in Northeast Ohio (half that number arrived in the 1990s) representing Christians and Moslems from 23 different homelands. Historically the Arab world has not been a cohesive one, but in Cleveland all the different nationality groups and religious sects have formed an unprecedented working relationship. "We've been able to unite as Arab Americans," said Ed Farage, founder of CAMEO (Cleveland American Middle East Organization), an association dedicated to helping this constituency into the political mainstream. "We concentrate on what brings us together," Farage says, "and CAMEO, for example, is the only local group of its kind in the country. We don't define ourselves by religion or where we come from, but rather by our mutual concerns as American Arabs. Our membership is very diversified, from laborers to lawyers. Language is one thing we have in common, and another is food. We all eat the same things. The ingredients may be slightly different, but no matter where you go in the Arab world, you can get kibbee."

Lamb is the most popular meat throughout the Middle East and when mixed with bulgur, a nutty-flavored cracked wheat, it becomes kibbee. It may be prepared in countless ways: eaten raw, shaped into patties and baked, or stuffed and fried. Kibbee is the national dish of Lebanon, and it is Lebanese cooking that dominates our local Middle Eastern food scene. Like much of Arab cuisine, it is characterized by subtle, rich spicing using fennel, mint, parsley, cardamom, ginger, nutmeg, saffron, and turmeric. This is as much about history as taste and tradition: Arabs controlled the spice trade between East and West throughout the Middle Ages. Lemons, onions, and garlic also play a significant role. Beans, fruit, vegetables (especially eggplant), and cereal grains are staples. Bulgur may be steamed and eaten on its own like rice or combined with tomatoes and chickpeas for tabouleh, a highly seasoned salad. Almonds and pine nuts are basic to the cuisine, and yogurt, as in Indian cuisine, is much more than the snack and breakfast food it is in this country, used as a marinade, in sauces and dressings, and as a side dish.

Many members of Cleveland's Indian community arrived in the 1960s. A second wave, often their relatives, followed over the next two decades. Many are highly educated, taking their place in this country as doctors, professors, engineers, and research scholars. Approximately 3,000 Indian families live in Greater Cleveland, and most try to maintain their Indian way of living, according to Mukund Mehta, former editor of *The Lotus*, an Indian community newspaper. "We want very much to keep our culture intact," explained Mehta, "and contribute its richness to American life. I am delighted when I see Americans enjoying the food in Indian restaurants."

Mehta and other members of the Indian community are justifiably proud of their cuisine. An ancient wisdom informs their cooking, and it is as much about a way of life as a way of eating. Rooted in a knowledge of how the body works, Indian cuisine is traditionally healthy, nutritious, and well balanced. Many of the spices were first used as medicines.

Ingredients such as onions, tomatoes, lentils, yogurt, rice, cauliflower, peas, and potatoes are typical. Many vegetables are pickled. Meat plays a minor role, though the food found in restaurants gives it a more prominent place to accommodate American tastes. The characteristic heat and complex flavor of Indian cuisine—and there are distinctive regional differences—is achieved by the use of masalas, which are aromatic blends of spices such as cardamom, mace, nutmeg, cumin, and coriander, mustard seed, chilies, pepper, and cloves. Curry powder is actually only one type of masala. Cooling fruit relishes called chutney, and yogurt side dishes, are served as a counterbalance.

"We are taught from the earliest age," said Sheela Sogal, former owner of the Saffron Patch restaurant, "that a cook should take no shortcuts. Care and love is the best spice of all. Everything in the kitchen should be done with heart and soul."

# RESTAURANTS

## Ethiopian

### Empress Taytu Ethiopian Restaurant
☎ (216) 391-9400
CITY: **Cleveland**   AREA: **Near East Side**
ATMOSPHERE: **Casual**   COST: $$$$$

**ADDRESS:** 6125 St. Clair Ave.
**HOURS:** Tue–Thu 5–9 p.m., Fri–Sat 5–10:30 p.m.; closed Sun–Mon **RESERVATIONS:** Taken, recommended on weekends **PAYMENT:** MC, VS, AX **BAR:** Beer, wine, liquor **TAKEOUT:** Yes **ACCESS:** ᕪ Full access

Cleveland's only Ethiopian restaurant serves the traditional spicy cuisine of ancient Abyssinia, most of which is eaten sans silverware by scooping up stews and purees with pieces of injera, a soft flat bread that is made on the premises. Food arrives on large platters for sharing, and there are numerous combination plates on the menu that give newcomers to this cuisine a chance to sample a variety of dishes, which are primarily stews of meats, vegetables, or legumes. Chicken in a sauce that resembles our barbecue, but does contain tomatoes, is called dorowat and is made with onions, ginger, hot red peppers, rue, basil, cinnamon, cloves, and a flavoring called bishop's weed. T'ibs features small chunks of beef or lamb sautéed in spiced butter with herbs and onions. There are many completely vegetarian dishes.

The décor is exotic, designed to duplicate native thatched-roof huts, and you can choose to eat at a regular table or from traditional low tables and stools—made comfortable by the addition of cushions and back rests. (If you want to sit at one of these traditional basket tables be sure to let them know when you make your reservation—they are very popular.) Warm, moist cloths for cleaning your hands are served before and after the meal by women in long white dresses. Enter through the back door from the restaurant's own parking lot. You pass by the kitchen and can look inside. Large photographs from Ethiopia are on the walls.

For a very special experience, request the Ethiopian coffee ceremony. The green beans are roasted to order on the stove and brought to your table still hot; incense is lit, and the brew is made in a clay pot.

## Indian

### Bombay Sitar
☎ (330) 493-0671
CITY: **Canton**   AREA: **Farther South**
ATMOSPHERE: **Relaxed**   COST: $$$$$

**ADDRESS:** 4633 Belden Village St. NW
**HOURS:** Lunch Mon–Fri 11 a.m.–2:30 p.m., Sat 11:30 a.m.–3 p.m., Sun noon–3 p.m.; Dinner daily 5–10 p.m. **RESERVATIONS:** Taken, recommended on weekends **PAYMENT:** MC, VS **BAR:** Beer, wine, liquor **TAKEOUT:** Yes **ACCESS:** ᕪ Full access

I'm not a fan of sitar music—just ask my husband, who took up the instrument along with George Harrison back in the day—but I'm a big fan of the food served at Bombay Sitar, Canton's first and only Indian eatery. It's a real find out there in mall-world, where franchise food rules. The kitchen stakes out a unique culinary territory, producing an array of dishes seldom seen in these parts: a Bombay-style chicken and spinach soup; achar, spicy pickled vegetables; a pullao mix of rice, peas, and fruits; kofta lajawab, vegetable balls stuffed with cheese in a mild creamy sauce; black lentil dal; tandoori eggplant; chicken patta made with sweet and sour mangoes; Karachi lamb made in an iron skillet; and a sweet milk drink called falooda. Among the more commonly found items, the mulligatawny soup, vegetable korma, and lamb rogan josh are memorable. Two combination dinners provide a chance to sample many different things at a great price.

Unlike any other Indian restaurant I've ever been to, servers brought complimentary munchies immediately after we were seated—a plate of crispy rice crackers, refilled after we quickly gobbled them all down, and two tasty dipping sauces. Basmati rice and mint chutney, which often must be ordered à la carte at other places, come with most entrées. Spicing is to order from mild to Indian hot (don't go there unless you're a pro).

There are two dining areas, with the daily luncheon buffet set up in between. The location was once an Aladdin's, and their signature décor is still visible—in fact, the former tenants like to come back here to eat. The atmosphere is jeans casual. Located in a short brace of stores with a big red sign that makes it easy to spot from the road. They will cater parties of any size.

## Cafe Tandoor
☎ (216) 371-8500
CITY: **Cleveland Heights**  AREA: **East Side**
ATMOSPHERE: **Casual**  COST: **$$$**$$

**ADDRESS:** 2096 S. Taylor Rd.
**HOURS:** Lunch Mon–Sat 11:30 a.m.–2 p.m.; Dinner Mon–Sat 5:30–10 p.m., Sun 3–9 p.m.
**RESERVATIONS:** Recommended **PAYMENT:** MC, VS, AX, DIS **BAR:** Beer, wine, liquor **TAKEOUT:** Yes
**ACCESS:** ♿ Full access

The smells that greet you at the door of this attractive, well-lit restaurant are exotic. You can pick up whiffs of cinnamon, cumin, ginger, and garlic. The second thing you notice on entering is that many Indian families are eating here, a sure sign that the food is authentically prepared. Divided into two rooms, the place seats about 100 at cloth-covered tables. Storefront windows are filled with plants.

The menu is all Indian, but that doesn't mean you'll only find curries or other dishes with over-the-top heat. Owner Raj Singh, who runs the restaurant along with his wife, Beverly, is from the region of northern India near Nepal, and he did not grow up eating hot food. "Our food is intensely flavorful because of the spices and spice combinations we use," explains Raj. "People think all Indian food is spicy. It's not— but it is spiced." If you're not familiar with any of the dishes on the menu, the staff is knowledgeable and will graciously assist. Anything that does pack heat can be ordered mild, medium, or four-alarm. Typical of Indian cuisine, there are many vegetarian selections, but the menu includes a large choice of chicken, lamb, and shrimp entrées, too. When prepared in a clay tandoori oven, these are great choices for the fat- and weight-conscious, as the cooking method requires no oil. Traditional fried foods like pakora (batter-dipped meat or vegetables) are not at all greasy, and flavorful tandoori breads are made on the premises. Empty plates are brought warm from the kitchen, and food arrives beautifully arranged on large platters set in the middle of the table.

Portions are generous, but desserts are worth saving room for. Cafe Tandoor has been ranked among the best Indian restaurants in the country by the *Zagat* guide, and *Northern Ohio Live* magazine readers have voted it the Best Indian Restaurant eight years running. Ample parking on the street and in back. The Singhs have opened additional locations; see following listings.

## Cafe Tandoor
☎ (330) 562-5334
CITY: **Aurora**   AREA: **Farther East**
ATMOSPHERE: **Casual**   COST: $$$$$

ADDRESS: 96 Barrington Town Center
HOURS: Tue–Sat 11:30 a.m.–2 p.m. & 5:30–10 p.m., Sun 3–9 p.m.; closed Mon RESERVATIONS: Recommended PAYMENT: MC, VS, AX, DIS BAR: Beer, wine, liquor TAKEOUT: Yes ACCESS: & Full access

The 70-seat Cafe Tandoor in Aurora is a twin of the restaurant in Cleveland Heights, and the place to go for Indian food in the area, which heretofore has been starved for vegetable samosas, marinated and charcoal-baked lamb chops, and pishori naan, a baked-to-order bread topped with ground pistachios and almonds. Plenty of free parking. For more information, see previous listing for the original restaurant.

## Cafe Tandoor
☎ (440) 835-7999
CITY: **Westlake**   AREA: **West Side**
ATMOSPHERE: **Casual**   COST: $$$$$

ADDRESS: 30030 Detroit Rd.
HOURS: Mon–Sat 11:30 a.m.–2 p.m. & 5:30–10 p.m., Sun 3–9 p.m. RESERVATIONS: Recommended PAYMENT: MC, VS, AX, DIS BAR: Beer, wine, liquor TAKEOUT: Yes ACCESS: & Full access

The famous East Side location has expanded to the west at last, and taken up residence in Westbay Plaza. For more information, see listing for Cafe Tandoor in Cleveland Heights.

## Cuisine of India
☎ (440) 842-5907
CITY: **Parma Heights**   AREA: **Southwest**
ATMOSPHERE: **Casual**   COST: $$$$$

ADDRESS: 6857 W. 130th St.
HOURS: Lunch Mon–Fri 11:30 a.m.–2:30 p.m., Sat–Sun noon–3 p.m.; Dinner Mon–Sun 5–10 p.m.; closed between lunch and dinner RESERVATIONS: Taken PAYMENT: MC, VS, AX, DIS BAR: Beer, wine, liquor TAKEOUT: Yes ACCESS: & Full access

With its tangerine- and red-colored walls, this is a pleasant spot to enjoy kabobs cooked in a clay tandoori oven, spicy curries, and freshly baked rounds of Indian bread. If that's not enough to get you in the door, consider the fact that it's among the few places in the area to taste Indo-Chinese cuisine. This blending of cooking cultures— the result of immigration and a shared border—doesn't get a special section on the menu other than the listing for hot and sour soup, but those who request it will be rewarded with a small selection of uncommon and tasty meat, rice, and vegetables. Don't miss the Manchurian chicken. For fans of more traditional Indian food, the selection is varied, interesting, and prepared with skill. Of special note are potato cutlets (aoloo tikki), onions coated in chickpea flour batter and deep-fried (onions bhajia), a Punjabi-style puloo made with rice and peas, and a lamb biryani garnished with eggs. The Peshwari naan is memorable—a warm, doughy pocket filled with spiced cheese, nuts, and raisins. A few preparations are made with goat meat, and others feature lobster or salmon. The kitchen is willing to make vegan versions of most vegetarian dishes.

A flat-screen TV in one corner shows Bollywood extravaganzas—a great distraction if conversation at your table flags. The main dining room offers cozy booths, and a second space is ideal for large gatherings and private parties. The restaurant is located in a strip mall with many empty storefronts that make a bleak first impression. But inside all is warm, welcoming, stylish, and lively.

## Flavors of India
☎ (440) 779-5774
CITY: **North Olmsted**    AREA: **West Side**
ATMOSPHERE: **Casual**    COST: **$$$**$$

**ADDRESS:** 26703 Brookpark Rd. Ext.
**HOURS:** Tue–Fri lunch 11:30 a.m.–3 p.m., Dinner 5–10 p.m., Sat lunch noon–3 p.m.; closed Mondays and between lunch and dinner. **RESERVATIONS:** Taken, recommended on weekends and for groups of 5+ **PAYMENT:** MC, VS, AX, DIS, checks **BAR:** Beer **TAKEOUT:** Yes **ACCESS:** ♿ Full access

An Indian restaurant of another name was previously at this location. Jay Patel took it over in January 2008 and has done a great job of spicing up the menu. You'll find some dishes not often found elsewhere: tandoori baingan (a baked eggplant appetizer); batatavada (pea and potato balls coated in chickpea flour and deep fried); neelgiri korma, featuring chicken in a cilantro cream sauce; ginger-flavored lamb karahi; and yellow lentils cooked with cumin. There are also nine Bombay specials, including a popular regional preparation called bhel puri made with puffed rice and sweet and sour chutney. More familiar selections including samosas (appetizer pastries stuffed with potatoes and peas); pakoras (chickpea flour fritters); a variety of breads; tandoori dishes; and biryanis (basmati rice cooked with meat, fish, or vegetables, striped with saffron, the world's most costly spice, and topped with raisins and nuts)—all evidence of the great amount of time and labor that characterize this cuisine. Thanks to the talented chef on staff, those of us who have neither the hours nor the expertise to invest in such a task need not miss out on the pleasures of eating Indian food.

Desserts and drinks are worth a mention: There's a luscious fruit-flavored lassi (like a milkshake made with yogurt) and masala chai (spiced, milky tea); a small selection of beers that includes two Indian imports, King Fisher and the 22-ounce Taj Mahal; and kulfi, a traditional ice cream laced with pistachios, cardamom, and saffron, so thick it almost requires chewing.

The main dining area seats about 45 at tables draped in teal cloths topped with lovely paisley "scarves" under glass. A second room seats 25 and can be reserved for private parties or meetings. A small serving area at the back is used for the lunchtime buffet. There are high chairs and booster seats available as well as a roomy waiting area. On- and off-site catering services are available. Note: If you don't know the area, Brookpark Road Extension can be hard to find. It's not even listed on some local maps. Brookpark and Lorain merge, and the Extension is a small side street near the merge, also marked as "Sparky." Make your way past parking lots and chain stores lined up one after another, into a strip mall. Behind the restaurant's bland facade is an attractive and inviting dining room that feels—and smells—a million miles away from the overdeveloped suburban landscape outside.

## India Garden
☎ (216) 221-0676
CITY: **Lakewood**   AREA: **West Side**
ATMOSPHERE: **Relaxed**   COST: $$$$$

**ADDRESS:** 18405 Detroit Ave.
**HOURS:** Lunch Mon–Fri 11 a.m.–2:30 p.m., Sat–Sun, noon–3 p.m.; Dinner Mon–Sun 5–10 p.m.; closed between lunch and dinner
**RESERVATIONS:** Recommended **PAYMENT:** MC, VS **BAR:** Beer, wine, liquor **TAKEOUT:** Yes **ACCESS:** ♿ Limited

The 50-seat restaurant is set back from the road at the far end of a parking lot. It doesn't look like much from the outside and the interior is nothing fancy—a small, pleasant room with golden yellow walls. It's the food that makes this spot a standout. With each visit I discover a new favorite. Eat your way through the usual and excellently prepared suspects—meats, chicken, and seafood roasted in a tandoori oven, marinated in yogurt, and simmered with tomatoes—and you won't be disappointed. Indulge in masalas, creamy coconut-based kormas, curries, and fiery vindaloos. But give yourself a treat and break out into what may be less familiar territory: banana peppers stuffed with spiced potatoes and cheese; minced lamb and green peas; a seasonal dish made with okra and cumin seeds; and preparations featuring mutton and goat. The vegetarian fare and the fresh breads are exceptional. Don't miss the Indo-Chinese specialties like zesty deep-fried "chilly" chicken, a noodle dish called haka chow mein, and gobi Manchurian—cauliflower cooked in a spicy sweet and sour sauce. The cross-cultural cuisine reinvents Chinese dishes to suit the Indian palate, and it is quite popular in cities there today. When it comes to beverages, there's a small but interesting selection of wines and beers, plus sweet, salty, or fruity lassi (yogurt drinks), chai, and Indian coffee. There's a lunch buffet every day of the week.

## India's Cafe & Kitchen
☎ (440) 842-7724
CITY: **Parma**   AREA: **Southwest**
ATMOSPHERE: **Relaxed**   COST: $$$$$

**ADDRESS:** 5549 Ridge Rd.
**HOURS:** Tue–Thu 11:30 a.m.–2 p.m. & 4:30 p.m.–9 p.m.; Fri 11:30 a.m.–2 p.m. & 4:30 p.m.–9:30 p.m., Sat 11:30 a.m.–9:30 p.m., Sun noon–8 p.m. **RESERVATIONS:** Not taken **PAYMENT:** MC, VS, checks **BAR:** None **TAKEOUT:** Yes **ACCESS:** ♿ Full Access

Owner Gajendra Shrivastav promotes her little Parma place as a source of homestyle food. So in addition to offering the lamb and chicken dishes favored by Americans that show up on most Indian restaurant menus, her menu is heavy on vegetarian dishes and simple things like rice cooked with cumin seeds (jeera), daal makhani (beans and onions in garlic ginger cream sauce), and Punjabi cholle (chickpeas in tomato gravy) that seem more suited to family meals than company dinners. She also makes traditional snacks often sold by street vendors, fried lentil donuts, and a rice and milk dessert called khir. Compared to other places, the breads are a real bargain, and freshly made chapatis and paratha can be purchased in quantity.

Although there are four two-top tables this is really about curry to go. Eating in means eating out of Styrofoam containers amid people waiting to pick up their orders, and I don't recommend it. The big kitchen is just on the other side of the order counter, and there are no walls or doors to hide the cooking mess. So be forewarned, what you see is a work space, not a showplace or a set on the Food Channel, and it's neither pretty nor pristine. But what comes out of that kitchen is top-notch, authentic, and delicious. And you can have platters of their best at your next event because Shrivastav caters. The corner building is nondescript. Park on the street.

## Jaipur Junction

☎ (440) 842-3555

CITY: **North Royalton**   AREA: **Southwest**
ATMOSPHERE: **Relaxed**   COST: **$$$**$$

**ADDRESS:** 9377 Sprague Rd.
**HOURS:** Mon noon–3 p.m. & 5–9 p.m., Tue–Sat noon–3 p.m. & 5–10 p.m., Sun noon–3 p.m. & 5–9 p.m. **RESERVATIONS:** Not taken
**PAYMENT:** MC, VS, AX, DIS, checks **BAR:** None
**TAKEOUT:** Yes **ACCESS:** ♿ Full access

Responding to the many requests she received to bring Indian food to the West Side (and make it fast, too, her customers told her), Sheela Sogal, former owner of the Saffron Patch (see listing further on in this chapter), opened what she calls a "gourmet-on-the-go" restaurant in the spring of 1997. Its listing in the Yellow Pages refers to it as an oasis of vegetarian cuisine, which it is, and a "bhel-poori chat bar." What, I asked Ms. Sogal, does that mean? Bhel-poori is a crunchy mix of assorted fried foods, and chat are snacks and cold appetizers. The restaurant offers many of these foods, typically sold by the street

vendors of Jaipur, India: lamb or fish kabobs; charbroiled chicken wrapped in fresh-baked naan (bread); masala dosa, rice crepes filled with potatoes and onions; tava-tikki, a potato patty topped with vegetable chili; and kheema paratha, a grilled sandwich stuffed with seasoned ground lamb.

There is also a selection of larger, heartier entrées similar to those on the menu at the Saffron Patch, including shrimp tandoor (baked in a special oven), nine different versions of curry, and three types of biryani (stew) made with either vegetables, chicken, or shrimp. If you're eating on the premises, you can try a sampler approach, selecting one dish at a time. There are also sides of relish, pickles, bread, and sauces, and a wonderful selection of hot and cold drinks (not available for carryout), including tea with cardamom; a minty milk tea; thandai, a mix of milk, fruit juice, and almond paste; lassi, made with yogurt and ginger; and a mango milkshake. You place your order at the counter; a server brings it to your table, one of about 10 four-tops. The food can be prepared mild, hot, or, in the words of one employee, "Indian hot, which makes most Americans wish they were somewhere else."

The restaurant is usually crowded with Indian customers who tend to beam on non-Indians eating there, as if to say, "Oh, how nice you like our food." The staff, who are all Indian, are also particularly warm and helpful. From the outside, this storefront restaurant, in the Timber Ridge Plaza behind a Blockbuster Video, appears rather ordinary. But inside there's a most unusual ambience created by original and large-scale artwork. There's a stunning full-wall mural, a detailed rendering of an early-20th-century Indian kitchen, complete with mud ovens, stacked baskets and pots, suitcase, a dresser, plates on shelves, and linens. A smiling woman in a sari can be seen in a doorway. A large window in the center of the scene looks down into a courtyard and out onto a desert village. In the distance, a train chugs along the tracks. Jaipur is a desert city on a heavily traveled route, and the painting, done by Ann Marie Place, an Australian woman living in Twinsburg, depicts a scene that one would see there. It's meant to make people feel as though they were in a country home in that part of India, and the response of first-time visitors is usually an emphatic "Wow." Elsewhere, shelves display Indian dolls, colored bottles, and decorative clay pots. The wall to the right of the entrance is reserved for comments; patrons are encouraged to get a Magic Marker from the counter and leave messages either in words or pictures.

Easily accessed from I-77 or I-71, with detailed directions from downtown, south, east, and west printed on the back of the takeout menu.

## Raj Mahal Indian Cuisine
☎ (330) 926-0795
CITY: **Cuyahoga Falls**   AREA: **Farther South**
ATMOSPHERE: **Casual**   COST: **$$$**$$

ADDRESS: 2033 State Rd.
HOURS: Daily 11:30 a.m.–2:30 p.m. (lunch buffet) & 4:30–10 p.m. RESERVATIONS: Taken, recommended for large groups PAYMENT: MC, VS, DIS BAR: None TAKEOUT: Yes ACCESS: ♿ Full access

My father, who has a certain meat-and-potatoes bent to his preferences, a lack of interest in all things legume, and little affection for spice-generated heat, ate his very first Indian meal here and came away with a newfound appreciation for this cuisine, saying he found the food "very tasty." He was especially enthusiastic about kulfee, a homemade ice cream flavored with almonds and rose-

water (also with mango or pistachio), describing it as "absolutely delicious." When he and my mother visited the restaurant, they spoke with a couple who said they come almost every day for the luncheon buffet, a self-serve spread that features a changing assortment of dishes from the regular menu, and sometimes come back for dinner. These people seemed to be knowledgeable about Indian food and gave this restaurant high marks compared to other places they've eaten. All this should equal enough endorsement for connoisseurs of Indian food, hesitant novices, and everyone in between.

The choice of entrées featuring chicken, beef, lamb, seafood, vegetables, and rice specialties is extensive, and the possibilities become almost dizzying when you mix and match appetizers (including soups, samosa, vegetable fritters, and potato pancakes), accompaniments like dal (spicy pureed lentils), homemade yogurt, mango chutney, spicy mixed pickles, and raita (yogurt with cucumbers and tomatoes), and freshly baked or fired Indian breads. The menu, which you can study online, offers a crash course in Indian cookery. From it you learn that makhani dishes are prepared in a butter and cream sauce with cashews and raisins; josh dishes include a yogurt-based sauce; masala-style dishes are made with tomatoes, ginger, onions, and bell peppers; anything done à la palak has curried spinach in it; rice is the central ingredient in a biryani; and if it's vindaloo, it's got to be floating in a tomato-based sauce.

Indian drinks and desserts are a world unto themselves (a world, I might add, where dairy reigns supreme), and one I recommend you visit unless you are lactose intolerant. In addition to the kulfee my father liked so much, there's rice pudding (kheer), cheese in a sweet milk sauce (rasmalai), deep-fried milk balls in a sweetish syrup, and a yogurt drink called lassi.

As with so many locations featured in this book, these interesting and decidedly non-Ohio flavors are to be found in an uninteresting shopping plaza, behind an inconspicuous facade, in a place that puts more emphasis on food than décor. However, summer 2003 saw the restaurant close briefly while the interior got a complete face-lift. The result is fresh and attractive, and more seating has been added. Tables are in two rooms, one with big storefront windows, the other with no windows at all. Some Indian artwork is on the walls. But great care is paid to the details: napkins may be paper, but they're carefully folded and placed in tall water glasses; place mats are paper, but underneath there's a real tablecloth. Servers are attentive and well dressed in white shirts, black pants, bow ties, and vests. A big eyesore of a sign makes the place easy to find, and a map on their Web site (www.rajmahal.us) also helps first-timers. The kitchen provides a full range of catering services.

## Saffron Patch
☎ (216) 295-0400
CITY: **Shaker Heights**   AREA: **East Side**
ATMOSPHERE: **Dressy**   COST: **$$$**$$

**ADDRESS:** 20600 Chagrin Blvd. (Tower East Building)
**HOURS:** Lunch Mon–Fri 11:30 a.m.–3 p.m., Sat–Sun noon–3 p.m.; Dinner Mon 5–8:30 p.m., Tue–Sat 5–9:30 p.m., Sun 5–9 p.m.
**RESERVATIONS:** Recommended **PAYMENT:** MC, VS, AX, DIS **BAR:** Beer, wine, liquor **TAKEOUT:** Yes
**ACCESS:** ♿ Full access

Here at Cleveland's first Indian restaurant you'll find exotic fare, and the aroma alone is an adventure. The luncheon buffet provides a great opportunity to sample a wide variety of foods: an okra curry, saffron rice, raita (a salad of cucumbers in yogurt sauce), chicken cooked in a stovetop tandoor oven, rice and lentil crepes filled with onions and potatoes, and naan (a flat bread).

Each region of India has its own style of food preparation. The chefs here prepare some dishes from southern India but focus primarily on the cuisine of the north—spicy, pungent dishes, many vegetarian—and make it the traditional way, from scratch. Lamb chops marinate for three days. Cheese, similar to our farmer cheese (a drier version of cottage cheese), is made in-house. They use authentic ingredients, even when they are costly or hard to obtain. A portion of lobster curry features a pound of fish flesh. Some menu highlights: the Maharaja mixed grill, made with tandoori-cooked chicken, lamb, and shrimp; Pakistani murgh methiwala, a combination of chicken and fenugreek; fish curry; Punjab-style eggplant; hot and spicy lamb vindaloo; alu gobi, a ragout of potatoes, cauliflower, tomatoes, and ginger; and vegetables jal farezi.

Located in the basement of an office building, this is a large (capacity of about 110) and surprisingly lovely place to eat, with white-walled rooms adorned with fabric borders of blue elephants. Partitions divide the space into three sections, lighting is subdued, recorded sitar music plays softly in the background, and the overall effect is one of calm, comfort, and casual sophistication. They sometimes organize special eating events around American holidays, such as Mother's Day, Father's Day, Valentine's Day, and the Hindu festival of Diwali, celebrated in late autumn. Takeout orders can be phoned or faxed in (fax number: 216-295-1320, and a special ready-to-fax version of the menu is available). Ample parking.

## Saffron Patch
☎ (330) 836-7777
CITY: **Akron** AREA: **Farther South**
ATMOSPHERE: **Dressy** COST: $$$$$

**ADDRESS:** 1244 Weathervane Lane
**HOURS:** Mon 5–9 p.m., Tue–Thu Lunch 11:30
a.m.–2:30 p.m.; Dinner 5–9:30 p.m., Fri–Sun
Lunch 11 a.m.–2:30 p.m.; Dinner 5–10
p.m.; closed between lunch and dinner
**RESERVATIONS:** Taken **PAYMENT:** MC, VS, AX, DIS
**BAR:** Beer, wine, liquor **TAKEOUT:** Yes **ACCESS:** &
Full access

The original Cleveland Saffron Patch opened in 1991, and this second location offers the same menu of mostly northern Indian dishes. See previous listing for details. Food is served in two small dining areas that feature attractive and contemporary décor.

Hidden away in what looks like a home from the front, in Liberty Commons, a retail plaza in northwest Akron's Merriman Valley neighborhood.

## Taj India Palace
☎ (440) 461-3737
CITY: **Richmond Heights** AREA: **East Side**
ATMOSPHERE: **Casual** COST: $$$$$

**ADDRESS:** 5156 Wilson Mills Rd.
**HOURS:** Lunch daily 11:30 a.m.–2:30 p.m.;
Dinner daily 5 p.m.–10 p.m. (closed between
lunch and dinner) **RESERVATIONS:** Taken
**PAYMENT:** MC, VS, AX, DIS **BAR:** Beer, wine,
liquor **TAKEOUT:** Yes **ACCESS:** & Full access

This Indian restaurant, located in the shopping plaza opposite Richmond Town Center since 1998, has had multiple names and owners. Its current incarnation began in 2007 when Mohammad Miah took over. The Bengali native has done exciting things with the menu. You can taste the results in dishes like chaat (spiced potatoes in

yogurt); iddly (steamed rice and lentil patties); rice crepes called dosai; bhindi massalla (spice-filled okra cooked with onions and green peppers); sweet and sour shrimp dansak; fiery lemon-spiked lamb madras; and mild, creamy coconut-infused vegetable makonwalla. Don't miss the house special: biryani made with rice, lamb, chicken, shrimp, and nuts; channa masala (a dish of garbanzo beans and onions seasoned with a blend of roasted spices); and the fresh, warm naan and roti specialty breads. Combination dinners and thali platters let you sample multiple preparations in a single entrée. The lunch buffet provides an ever-changing array of dishes. A typical assortment might include lamb curry; tandoori chicken; butter chicken; palak paneer (cheese cubes in a spinach sauce); and aloo gobi (cauliflower and potatoes cooked with ginger and tomatoes). For dessert choose from rice pudding with almonds and pistachios, gulab jaman (tiny fried cake "balls" infused with rosewater, a flavor both sweet and flowery); and Indian ice cream. The front of the restaurant features a nine-stool bar. The spacious dining room seats about 100, with booths along each wall and tables down the center that can be pushed together for large groups. White cloths are spread out under glass, and green cloth napkins fan out from water glasses in a décor that is otherwise nondescript but pleasant enough. The emphasis is clearly on what happens in the kitchen. Enough parking for a full battalion.

## Udupi Cafe
☎ (440) 743-7154
CITY: **Parma Heights** AREA: **Southwest**
ATMOSPHERE: **Casual** COST: $$$$$

**ADDRESS:** 6339 Olde York Rd.
**HOURS:** Mon, Wed–Sun 11:30 a.m.–10 p.m.;
closed Tue; Lunch buffet Mon, Wed–Fri

11:30 a.m.–3 p.m., Sat–Sun 11:30–2:30 p.m.
**RESERVATIONS:** Taken **PAYMENT:** MC, VS, DIS **BAR:** None **TAKEOUT:** Yes **ACCESS:** & Full access

This may well be the most exotic spot to eat in Cleveland, if you define exotic as "having the charm of the unfamiliar, strikingly and intriguingly different." And imagine finding such singularity in a strip mall, in a town not known for the unusual. But the fact is, there's nothing else like this place in Northeast Ohio. That's because the all-vegetarian dishes served represent the cuisine of Udupi, a coastal town in southern India in the state of Karnataka. It's said that food there is a religion, and their style of preparation is renowned throughout the country. In contrast, most Indian restaurants in America offer a northern approach.

Although the two have a palette of ingredients and a few dishes in common, the food at Udupi is a revelation to the uninitiated. I can offer only a sampler here. Iddly are rice and lentil patties; vada are fried lentil donuts; bonda are potato dumplings; and sambhar is a side dish and condiment made with spiced lentils and vegetables. The menu features 13 different dosai. These are among the most famous regional creations—very large, thin, crisp rice flour crepes filled or topped with various combinations of potatoes, onions, or creamed wheat accompanied by chutney and sambar. Another is uthappam—griddle-cooked pancakes topped with tomatoes, onions, peas, chilies, or coconut. Bagala bhath features rice with yogurt, mustard seeds, and cucumber. Avial is a curry made with coconut sauce. In addition to the freshly baked tandoori breads that are typical of Indian restaurants, Udupi's pièce de résistance is the colossal batura, an extraordinary, delicious puff of bread the size of your head that implodes, soufflé-like, as it cools.

The variety and flavor of the food here are so enticing that I'll wager only hard-core carnivores will miss the meat. There are many ways to try many things, from the weekday lunch buffet to the assorted appetizer platter and the thali dinner—or come with a group and promise to share. Some items are quite spicy but the heat in many can be adjusted, so speak up and ask for what you want. Cold milk or fruit drinks and desserts are must-haves—I simply am never too full, no matter how I've stuffed myself, for the homemade ice cream or the badam halwa, a sweet confection made with ground almonds and honey.

The dining room is a sprawling space with seating for about 150, and it is usually populated with Indian families and large groups of young Indian men, students perhaps, who appear delighted to be eating these wonderful things from home. The décor is strictly utilitarian, but that in no way detracts from the reality that this is a meat-free paradise.

# Lebanese

## Cedarland at the Clinic
☎ (216) 791-6606
CITY: **Cleveland**   AREA: **Near East Side**
ATMOSPHERE: **Casual**   COST: **$$**$$

**ADDRESS:** 9491 Euclid Ave.
**HOURS:** Mon–Fri 7 a.m.–10 p.m., Sat 10 a.m.–9 p.m.; closed Sun **RESERVATIONS:** Taken **PAYMENT:** MC, VS, DIS **BAR:** None **TAKEOUT:** Yes **ACCESS:** & Full access

If you have a taste for kabab halabi (spiced ground beef with pine nuts) or mutabal (baked eggplant prepared with garlic, lemon, and olive oil), you're in luck. Serge Elias is cooking in Cleveland. His restaurant is an answer to the prayers of the many people from the

Middle East who are at the Cleveland Clinic as staff or as patients and their families and entourages. All are happy to be able to get familiar foods. And they don't even have to walk across the street to the small mall where the 75-seat restaurant is located. Serge delivers—to the Clinic and to all the institutions in University Circle. In a further attempt to be accommodating, Serge and his staff will make every effort to meet the needs of those with dietary restrictions (such as no-salt or low-spice diets) with one day's advance notice (some minimum charges apply).

The food is already ideally suited to a healthy diet: low fat, fresh, high fiber, and prepared from scratch without additives, preservatives, or chemical flavor enhancers. The chicken noodle soup starts with a stock made on the premises. The menu includes Lebanese versions of vegetarian dishes such as hommus (chickpea dip), baba gannoj (baked eggplant dip), felafel (a batter of ground chickpeas and fava beans made into patties and fried), taboolee (salad made with bulghur wheat and parsley), meatless stuffed grape leaves, and fatoosh (salad topped with crunchy pieces of toasted pita bread). Among the entrées are lamb shish kabob, shish tawook (skewered grilled chicken in garlic sauce), kafta (a combination of freshly gound beef, onions, parsley, and spices), and the uncommon hommus barmaki (hommus topped with ground meat, pine nuts, onions, and the Lebanese equivalent of secret sauce). Elias also offers something he says is not found anywhere else around town, called arayiss—a pita stuffed with a choice of meat or vegetarian fillings and baked. There is also a selection of sandwiches, salads, and sides (Middle Eastern and the more familiar turkey, grilled cheese, coleslaw, french fries, and the like). For breakfast, you can go for a standard scrambled with home fries or branch out and get right with the big health nut in the sky by choosing kamah (a Lebanese improvement on a boring bowl of oatmeal, made with boiled wheat, raisins, and walnuts).

Serge is a philosopher as well as a chef and a businessman, so on each menu he's printed a passage from Kahlil Gibran's book *The Prophet*. The restaurant is often crowded with men in kaftans and women in burkhas. For all you know, you may be sitting beside a foreign queen or prince or a member of their retinues. You may not understand what they are talking about, but you can be sure you have something in common: the pleasure of eating the wonderful food that comes out of Serge Elias's kitchen. There are also some Middle Eastern grocery items available.

## Continental Cuisine
☎ (330) 864-1777
CITY: **Fairlawn**   AREA: **Farther South**
ATMOSPHERE: **Casual**   COST: $$$$$

**ADDRESS:** 55 Ghent Rd.
**HOURS:** Mon–Sat 11 a.m.–9 p.m.; closed Sun
**RESERVATIONS:** Taken, recommended for large groups **PAYMENT:** MC, VS, AX, DIS **BAR:** Beer, wine **TAKEOUT:** Yes **ACCESS:** & Full access

Summit Mall in Fairlawn is the quintessential all-American space, but the neighborhood's not quite as homogenized as it appears. Located just across the road is a small eatery that has some surprises in store for diners in search of an alternative to burgers and fries. In a bright, modern setting, Beshara Sabbagh and his family prepare and serve the classic dishes of Lebanon. You'll find falafel, shawarma, chicken and beef kabobs, and stuffed grape leaves. You can have them for lunch or dinner, eat-in or carryout.

"All our food is fresh and very, very good," insists Sabbagh, "and I'm not just saying that because it's my restaurant. I know it's true because we go to a lot of trouble to do everything right, the traditional way and with only the best ingredients. We use only lemon juice that we squeeze ourselves and extra virgin olive oil. We marinate our chicken and beef for hours. And we make each salad to order—we don't even slice tomatoes or chop lettuce in advance." The menu has grown beyond its Middle Eastern orientation to include hand-tossed pizzas, more salads, beef and chicken gyros, fish, pasta, and filet mignon. There are places for 72 diners with full table service. Catering is also available.

## Sahara

☎ (216) 671-9300

CITY: **Cleveland** AREA: **West Side**

ATMOSPHERE: **Relaxed** COST: **$$**$$$

**ADDRESS:** 12501 Lorain Rd.

**HOURS:** Daily noon–10 p.m. **RESERVATIONS:** Not taken **PAYMENT:** MC, VS **BAR:** None **TAKEOUT:** Yes

**ACCESS:** ♿ Limited

You have a taste for felafel, hummus, and a spinach pie. Your partner craves shish kabob or maybe a beef shawarma sandwich dripping with tahini sauce and tomatoes. And what about the kids, or those in your group with a childlike preference for nothing more challenging than chicken fingers, french fries, and hamburgers? Is there a dining destination that can satisfy everybody? Yes, and this place is it. Reading the menu is like finding an oasis in the desert—at last you have stumbled upon what you need, and the discovery is sure to make you happy. And you'll be even happier when you get the bill because the prices are more than reasonable for the amount and quality of the food.

In addition to Middle Eastern standards, the kitchen prepares some more unusual fare: vegetarian kibbee made with cracked wheat, steamed potatoes, and chickpeas; rotisserie-roasted chicken farroos with garlic sauce; spiced, grilled lamb chops; and kaliyah skillets, spiced and sautéed onions, peppers, and tomatoes available with or without meat. Fire up your burners with a side of homemade hot paste. The many combination plates for those who can't or won't make choices are a nice touch. The qudsia appetizer has both hummus and foul madammas (fava beans with lemon juice, garlic, and olive oil). The Sahara is an entrée in six parts, and the vegetarian version has the same number of meat-free selections. The Family Plate, which promises to feed up to six, packs almost the entire menu into a single order, including but not limited to shish kafta, tawook, kafta, shawarma, kibbee, kabob, grape leaves, baba ganouj, and tabouli. A Friday special is kibbee nayee, a mixture of raw ground meat, cracked wheat, and onions, and Saturday is the only day to get mansaf, a dish made with rice, lamb, yogurt, and almonds.

The two dining rooms are pleasant. Arched doorways, pinkish stucco walls, a mural of a mosque, and Middle Eastern music in the background lend an out-of-Cleveland feel to the storefront space. The kitchen caters special events on- and off-site, and whole rotisserie chickens are available for carryout.

## Taza Lebanese Grill

☎ (216) 464-4000

CITY: **Woodmere** AREA: **Southeast**

ATMOSPHERE: **Casual** COST: **$$$**$$

**ADDRESS:** 28601 Chagrin Blvd.

**HOURS:** Mon–Thu 11 a.m.–10:30 p.m., Fri–Sat 11 a.m.–11 p.m., Sun noon–10 p.m.

**RESERVATIONS:** Not taken **PAYMENT:** MC, VS, AX, DIS **BAR:** Beer, wine, liquor **TAKEOUT:** Yes

**ACCESS:** ♿ Full access

Fans of hummos, falafel, and fattoush who want to dine in classy contemporary surroundings should pull up a chair here. The distinctive fresh and healthy fare that defines this cuisine is the centerpiece of the menu, and it's served in a spacious and handsomely appointed dining room outfitted with dark and gleaming woodwork, shimmering tiles, and earthy colors. It opened for business at the Eton Collection in 2005. Much of the food is the same as what's served at the various Aladdin's Eateries around town. That's no surprise as all are owned and operated by the Chamoun family. The bulk of the menu focuses on soups, salads, dips, wraps, and the usual lineup of shawarma (strips of grilled meat or poultry) and shish kebabs. But they wanted this location to offer a different dining experience than their casual quick-bite outposts, so there are some items only served here. The selection of mezza, small appetizer-sized portions best ordered in multiples and shared, is more extensive and includes soujouk (sausages), bamieh (okra simmered with a pomegranate sauce), jibneh (grilled cheese with olives, pistachios, and tomatoes), and manakish (sort of like pizza). Entrées that are not widely prepared in area restaurants really shine and have won praise from friends who were raised on this food, such as fish (samakeh) done three ways with roasted tomatoes and cardamom; tahini walnut cilantro sauce; or parsley zaatar pesto. A very traditional and very tasty dish is fatteh lamb. The meat is layered with chick peas and toasted pita and doused with a sesame garlic yogurt sauce. A brick baking oven and wood-burning grill, visible behind a glass partition, lend authentic flavor to kabobs and breads. Warm pita with spiced oil for dipping are on the house.

An attractive granite bar area and piped-in Middle Eastern music add a bit of club vibe to the often-packed space that buzzes with conversation. Though lacking a view and much in the way of greenery, there is an outdoor patio where you can enjoy good weather along with a plate of grape leaves and a glass of wine. A full catering menu is on the restaurant Web site, www.mytaza.com.

# Middle Eastern

## Aladdin's Eatery
☎ (216) 521-4005

CITY: **Lakewood**   AREA: **West Side**
ATMOSPHERE: **Casual**   COST: $$$$$

**ADDRESS:** 14536 Detroit Ave.
**HOURS:** Daily 11 a.m.–10:30 p.m. **RESERVATIONS:** Not taken **PAYMENT:** MC, VS **BAR:** Beer, wine
**TAKEOUT:** Yes **ACCESS:** ♿ Full access

Aladdin's is bright, airy, and contemporary. It's located in a corner storefront in Lakewood, part of that city's restaurant renaissance. The décor is casual yet attractive—pale woods with pale green, yellow, and beige accents. The menu, featuring the healthy cuisine of Lebanon and the other countries of the Middle East, includes many vegetarian dishes. The kitchen prides itself on producing authentic dishes using only the freshest natural and preservative-free ingredients. There are a variety of soups, salads, and pita bread sandwiches that come stuffed or rolled. Traditional entrées include mujadara (steamed lentils and rice), sfiha (a meat pie), and shawarma (charbroiled beef and lamb). Some more contemporary variations on Middle Eastern themes can be sampled in the pita "pitzas" that make good use of tahini (sesame) sauce, feta cheese, eggplant puree, and falafel (mildly spiced chickpea-and-fava-bean patties). The menu does a good job of explaining what goes into every dish. A small but interesting wine and beer list. A parking lot in the rear.

Other Aladdin's locations include:

## Aladdin's Eatery
☎ (216) 932-4333

CITY: **Cleveland Heights**   AREA: **East Side**
ATMOSPHERE: **Casual**   COST: $$$$$

ADDRESS: 12447 Cedar Rd. at Fairmount Blvd.
HOURS: Mon–Thu 11 a.m.–10:30 p.m., Fri–Sat 11 a.m.–11:30 p.m., Sunday 11 a.m.–10 p.m.
RESERVATIONS: Not taken  PAYMENT: MC, VS  BAR: Beer, wine  TAKEOUT: Yes  ACCESS: よ Full access

## Aladdin's Eatery
☎ (330) 535-0110

CITY: **Akron**  AREA: **Farther South**
ATMOSPHERE: **Casual**   COST: $$$$$

ADDRESS: 782 W. Market St.
HOURS: Daily 11 a.m.–10:30 p.m.  RESERVATIONS: Not taken  PAYMENT: MC, VS  BAR: Beer, wine
TAKEOUT: Yes  ACCESS: よ Full access

## Aladdin's Eatery
☎ (330) 629-6450

CITY: **Boardman**  AREA: **Farther East**
ATMOSPHERE: **Casual**   COST: $$$$$

ADDRESS: 7325 South Ave.
HOURS: Daily 11 a.m.–10:30 p.m.  RESERVATIONS: Not taken  PAYMENT: MC, VS  BAR: Beer, wine
TAKEOUT: Yes  ACCESS: よ Full access

## Aladdin's Eatery
☎ (330) 656-0560

CITY: **Hudson**  AREA: **Farther South**
ATMOSPHERE: **Casual**   COST: $$$$$

ADDRESS: 44 Park Ln.
HOURS: Mon–Thu 11 a.m.–10:30 p.m., Fri–Sat 11 a.m.–11:30 p.m., Sun 11 a.m.–10:30 p.m.

RESERVATIONS: Not taken  PAYMENT: MC, VS  BAR: Beer, wine  TAKEOUT: Yes  ACCESS: よ Full access

## Aladdin's Eatery
☎ (440) 684-1168

CITY: **Mayfield Village**   AREA: **East Side**
ATMOSPHERE: **Casual**   COST: $$$$$

ADDRESS: 775 SOM Center Rd.
HOURS: Daily 11 a.m.–10:00 p.m.  RESERVATIONS: Not taken  PAYMENT: MC, VS  BAR: Beer, wine
TAKEOUT: Yes  ACCESS: よ Full access

## Aladdin's Eatery
☎ (440) 243-0800

CITY: **Middleburg Hts.**  AREA: **Southwest**
ATMOSPHERE: **Casual**   COST: $$$$$

ADDRESS: 18334 E. Bagley Rd.
HOURS: Mon–Thu 11 a.m.–10:30 p.m., Fri–Sat 11 a.m.–11, Sun 11 a.m.–10:30 p.m.
RESERVATIONS: Not taken  PAYMENT: MC, VS  BAR: Beer, wine  TAKEOUT: Yes  ACCESS: よ Full access

## Aladdin's Eatery
☎ (440) 617-9005

CITY: **Westlake**  AREA: **West Side**
ATMOSPHERE: **Casual**   COST: $$$$$

ADDRESS: 151 Crocker Park Blvd.
HOURS: Mon–Thu 11 a.m.–10:30 p.m., Fri–Sat 11 a.m.–11:30 p.m., Sun 11 a.m.–10 p.m.
RESERVATIONS: Not taken  PAYMENT: MC, VS  BAR: Beer, wine  TAKEOUT: Yes  ACCESS: よ Full access

## Aladdin's Eatery
☎ (216) 642-7550

CITY: **Independence**   AREA: **Southeast**
ATMOSPHERE: **Casual**   COST: $$$$$

ADDRESS: 6901 Rockside Rd.
HOURS: Sat–Thu 11 a.m.–10:30 p.m., Fri 11 a.m.–11 p.m.  RESERVATIONS: Not taken
PAYMENT: MC, VS  BAR: Beer, wine  TAKEOUT: Yes
ACCESS: よ Full access

## Ali Baba Restaurant
☎ (216) 251-2040
CITY: **Cleveland**   AREA: **Near West Side**
ATMOSPHERE: **Casual**   COST: **$$$**$$

ADDRESS: 12021 Lorain Ave.
HOURS: Wed–Sat 5–9:30 p.m. (will stay open later Fri–Sat if there are customers); closed Sun–Tue RESERVATIONS: Taken PAYMENT: Cash only BAR: BYOB TAKEOUT: Yes ACCESS: ⅙ Limited

● ● ● ● ● ● ● ● ● ● ● ● ● ● ● ● ● ● ● ● ● ● ●

This is a tiny storefront restaurant with three booths and four tables. The menu is modestly small. But even so, people are willing to travel here from across town—especially those from the Middle East who are temporarily living and working in Cleveland—for a real taste of home. This casual, low-key restaurant has been around for more than two decades. The owner's husband is from Lebanon, and many of the recipes come from his grandmother. In addition to the dishes we Americans have come to know well, like hummus and spinach pie, there are some other more unusual options here: labnee (a sort of cream cheese made from yogurt), moujaddara (a lentil stew), and loobi bzait (green beans simmered in a vegetable sauce and served over rice). They serve lamb and chicken shish kebabs and an interesting meat dish called soujook made from marinated ground beef.

Everything is prepared without any artificial flavorings or colorings, and MSG is never used. They also offer some creative takeout options: 12- and 16-ounce containers of a variety of salads and dips and little meat and vegetable pies and patties by the dozen.

## Desert Inn
☎ (330) 456-1766
CITY: **Canton**   AREA: **Farther South**
ATMOSPHERE: **Dressy**   COST: **$$$**$$

ADDRESS: 204 12th St. NW
HOURS: Mon–Thu 11 a.m.–2 p.m. & 5–9:30 p.m., Fri 11 a.m.–2 p.m. & 5–10:30 p.m., Sat 5:30–11 p.m.; open Sundays Thanksgiving through Mother's Day noon–8 p.m.
RESERVATIONS: Taken, recommended for dinner PAYMENT: MC, VS, AX, DIS BAR: Beer, wine, liquor TAKEOUT: Yes ACCESS: ⅙ Full access

● ● ● ● ● ● ● ● ● ● ● ● ● ● ● ● ● ● ● ● ● ● ●

The Desert Inn is one of those restaurants so closely identified with the town where it's located that the two are almost inseparable. Everybody knows about the Desert Inn. Locals rave about it. Regulars love the know-your-name atmosphere as much as the food. It's a family-friendly, hanging-out kind of place that attracts politicos, celebrities, and ordinary Joes . . . and Joans, and it's been a part of the Canton scene (Is there a Canton scene?) since 1970. Mark Shaheen, whose father started the business, now runs it with the help of his wife, Tina, and their sons Markos and Joseph.

Hospitality has always been the family's specialty, along with Middle Eastern–style food. They serve Syrian-style baba g'noush, tabooli, hummus, and baked or raw kibee. Shish kabobs are presented on a large platter atop mounds of rice, roasted potatoes, and salad. A self-invented house special is a "Middle Eastern egg roll," consisting of spiced ground lamb, pine nuts, and vegetables wrapped in an egg roll skin and fried. The kitchen also does standard sandwiches and steaks.

The original funky converted house was replaced in 2006 with a brand new building that offers attractive and spacious dining rooms and a lounge. But much of the staff remains the same, the chairs are still comfortable, the atmosphere easygoing, sociable, and welcoming. A belly dancer entertains most Friday nights.

## Falafel Café

☎ (216) 229-9540

CITY: **Cleveland**    AREA: **Near East Side**
ATMOSPHERE: **Relaxed**    COST: **$$**$$$

ADDRESS: 11365 Euclid Ave.
HOURS: Mon–Sat 10:30 a.m.–11 p.m., Sun noon–7 p.m. (Sep–Jun) RESERVATIONS: Taken PAYMENT: MC, VS, AX, DIS BAR: None TAKEOUT: Yes ACCESS: ♿ Full access

. . . . . . . . . . . . . . . . . . . . . . . .

Walk up to counter, place your order, and walk out with very well-made Middle Eastern food, either in a bag or in your belly. The kitchen has a real knack when it comes to hummus, stuffed grape leaves, and baba. Their falafel sandwich gets my personal two thumbs up. The fried chickpea balls are moist and flavorful and come wrapped in a large pita round, with pickled turnips, lettuce, tomatoes, pickles, and sesame sauce. Two made-from-scratch soups—creamy lentil and vegetable—are served daily. In addition to the more familiar Middle Eastern fare, there are some unusual options, especially for those looking for meatless meals, including a red lentil and fava bean stew, another made with okra, and an eggplant casserole called "mousakaa" that bears little resemblance to its Greek namesake. A glass case near the entrance is filled with fatayar made in-house and ready to go, and the variety of these handheld pies is noteworthy: spinach, feta, spicy beef, chicken, vegetables with cheese, and potato with carrots and peas. The dough on these is particularly light. They also make their own baklava, rice pudding, and date cookies, and all go well with a demitasse of their Turkish coffee.

The setting is minimalist—13 wooden tables in a small, spare white-walled space. Late evening hours accommodate the neighborhood's student crowd and anyone else who gets hungry long after dinnertime has come and gone. High chairs on hand for those who tend to eat earlier. Metered on-street parking, if you can find a spot, and a metered lot across the street. The 15-minute stopping right out front is good if you're just running in to pick up your takeout order.

## Kan Zaman

☎ (216) 685-1500

CITY: **Cleveland**    AREA: **Near West Side**
ATMOSPHERE: **Relaxed**    COST: **$$**$$$

ADDRESS: 1917 W. 25th St.
HOURS: Mon–Thu 10 a.m.–9 p.m., Fri 10 a.m.–2 a.m., Sat 10 a.m.–3 a.m., Sun 10 a.m.–midnight RESERVATIONS: Taken PAYMENT: MC, VS, checks BAR: None TAKEOUT: Yes ACCESS: ♿ Full access

. . . . . . . . . . . . . . . . . . . . . . . .

It's midnight, and you've got a craving for shish kabob. . . . The kitchen here is open late and will be happy to get you what you need. But you'll likely find more people smoking than eating in the wee hours. Although this is a full-service restaurant, with a menu that features the predictable Middle Eastern standards from hummus and baba to kibbee and felafel, the real draw is the "hubble bubble" bar. Guests "rent" Arabic water pipes, also known as hookahs. They arrive tableside with a disposable, sealed-in-plastic mouthpiece and your choice of flavored tobacco. The server keeps you stoked with a glowing coal. Fueled with a demitasse of thick, dark coffee or cups of mint tea and the sweet, smooth smoke, you're positioned for some serious leisure.

There is a definite sense of otherness to this place. The TV is perennially tuned to Arabic-language stations.

There is a low and constant thrum of recorded Middle Eastern music just below the surface of conversation, which is as likely to be taking place in Arabic as English. The recorded music is tuned to loud, and the crowd tends to be on the young side. There's no patio or cafe seating, but when the weather's warm, tables are literally dragged out from the darkish interior onto the sidewalk, and the setting takes on urban, jury-rigged kind of immediacy that is more commonly found in other countries. Free parking at the rear of the building, accessed through an alley off West 25th.

## Kan Zaman
☎ (216) 621-2222
CITY: **Cleveland**   AREA: **Near West Side**
ATMOSPHERE: **Casual**   COST: $$$$$

ADDRESS: 1616 W. 25th St.
HOURS: Mon–Thu. 10 a.m.–10 p.m., Fri–Sat 10 p.m.–2:30 a.m.; closed Sunday RESERVATIONS: Taken, recommended on weekends PAYMENT: MC, VS, AX, DIS BAR: Beer, wine, liquor TAKEOUT: Yes ACCESS: ⅋ Full access

The Middle Eastern menu of traditional salads, dips, sandwiches, skewered and broiled meats mirrors the one at the original location down the street (see previous listing). But the dining room is larger and nicer with a mixture of big booths and cloth-covered tables. There's a lunch buffet Mon–Fri from 11 a.m. to 3 in the afternoon. The atmosphere is more family oriented during the day and early evening. On Friday and Saturday nights it morphs into a nightclub after dinner, complete with live performers, a dance floor, and a high-energy party crowd. The kitchen stays open late to accommodate them.

## Main Street Continental Grill
☎ (330) 678-0800
CITY: **Kent**   AREA: **Farther South**
ATMOSPHERE: **Relaxed**   COST: $$$$$

ADDRESS: 911 E. Main St.
HOURS: Sun–Wed 10 a.m.–10 p.m., Thu–Sat 10 a.m.–11 p.m. RESERVATIONS: Not taken PAYMENT: MC, VS, DIS BAR: None TAKEOUT: Yes ACCESS: ⅋ Full access

There aren't many options for eating ethnic in this college town, so I was happy to hear about Continental Grill. Since December 2007 it's been offering a nice line-up of Middle Eastern dishes—along with the hot dogs that made this an iconic Main Street destination for years. It also features a sizable selection of vegetarian options, something else that's in short supply in the area's restaurants. Expect the usual: hummus, baba ghanouj, falafel, tabouli, and stuffed grape leaves. Plenty for carnivores in the form of kabobs, meat pies, and beef and chicken shawarma sandwiches. Students like the prices, and parents feel comfortable bringing children. The restaurant caters parties and prepares box lunches for groups and gatherings.

## Middle East Restaurant
☎ (216) 771-2647
CITY: **Cleveland**   AREA: **Downtown**
ATMOSPHERE: **Casual**   COST: $$$$$

ADDRESS: 1012 Prospect Ave.
HOURS: Mon–Thu 11 a.m.–5 p.m., Fri 11 a.m.–10 p.m., Sat 4 p.m.–1 a.m.; closed Sun RESERVATIONS: Taken, recommended Fri, Sat nights PAYMENT: MC, VS BAR: Beer, wine, liquor TAKEOUT: Yes ACCESS: ⅋ Limited

I first began eating Josephine Abraham's fatiyar (meat- or spinach-filled turnovers), kibbee (lamb with cracked wheat and pine nuts), babaganoj (a dip of grilled eggplant and sesame sauce), and rice pudding in the early 1970s, when the restaurant was located on Bolivar. My husband's mother treated us to a memorable meal there when he graduated from college. In 1974 the restaurant moved to a space in what's now called the Carter Manor and has been winning awards ever since. Josephine finally handed down the spoon to her sister, Margaret, shifting her own role to kitchen consultant and her tempo to semiretirement until her death in 2001. There were more changes in 2004 when Margaret left and ownership of the restaurant passed from the retiring Edward Khouri to his nephew Lee George. But the recipes perfected over time by the Abraham sisters are still being made and served, and the restaurant is better than ever.

Whenever members of the Saudi royal family visit the Cleveland Clinic, they still get their favorite dishes made here and delivered. Menu selections include lamb and chicken kebabs, stuffed eggplant or cabbage, and lima beans or string beans simmered with ground meat in a tomato sauce, plus daily specials. The traditional coffee is always thick and sweet, just as it should be. A blue-and-white Arabic motif decorates the walls, and music from the jukebox, which has only Middle Eastern selections, plays softly in the background. It's easy to get comfortable, make yourself at home, and take your time here, though they are used to accommodating the more hurried pace of lunchtime diners from area office buildings. Parking is not always easy, but there are a number of nearby lots and garages.

## Nate's Deli & Restaurant

☎ (216) 696-7529

CITY: **Cleveland**   AREA: **Near West Side**
ATMOSPHERE: **Casual**   COST: $$$$$

**ADDRESS:** 1923 W. 25th St.
**HOURS:** Mon–Fri 10 a.m.–5 p.m., Sat 10 a.m.–4 p.m.; closed Sun **RESERVATIONS:** Taken, recommended for groups of 4+ **PAYMENT:** Cash only **BAR:** None **TAKEOUT:** Yes **ACCESS:** & Full access

Primarily a lunch place, Nate's is a casual, comfortable storefront restaurant near the West Side Market. Don't let the simple, unadorned look of the place lead you to believe the food is standard luncheonette fare. The menu is a most unusual combination: lunch and dinner entrées include both deli favorites and Middle Eastern specialties. You can get a kosher hot dog, a good corned beef sandwich, or a hot pastrami on rye. But you'll also find authentic, subtly seasoned hummus (a dip made with chickpeas, olive oil, sesame paste, and lemons), or a tabouleh salad (parsley, tomatoes, onions, wheat, and mint). Vegetarian and Middle Eastern entrées include falafel, foul medamas (fava beans with garlic, lemon, and olive oil), shish tawook (marinated, skewered cubes of chicken), and shawarma (strips of lean beef sautéed with onions and tomatoes and served with sesame sauce).

Portions are generous, and a relish plate with tomatoes, hot peppers, and turnips pickled in beet juice arrives at every table, compliments of the house. The 50-seat restaurant is often crowded at midday with business people from downtown. Breakfast offerings are strictly American. There's some metered parking on the street, or use the municipal lot behind the restaurant.

# Turkish

## Anatolia Cafe

☎ (216) 321-4400

CITY: **Cleveland Heights**   AREA: **East Side**
ATMOSPHERE: **Relaxed**   COST: **$$$**$$

ADDRESS: 2270 Lee Rd.
HOURS: Mon–Thu 11 a.m.–midnight, Fri
11 a.m.–11 p.m., Sat noon–11 p.m., Sun
noon–10 p.m. RESERVATIONS: Taken, only for
groups of 7+ PAYMENT: MC, VS, DIS BAR: Beer,
wine, liquor TAKEOUT: Yes ACCESS: ♿ Full access

Anatolia Cafe serves as Cleveland's gateway to Turkey's unique, healthy, and delicious cuisine. Owner Yashar Yildirim learned how to run a restaurant working in the family's Columbus place of the same name. He also learned that Turkish people would drive a long distance for a bowl of good red lentil soup (mercimek) or a plate of stuffed eggplant (karni yarik). Customers from Northeast Ohio convinced him there was a hunger for haydari (yogurt and walnut dip) and kisir (cracked wheat salad) here, so Yildirim set up shop and has been busy ever since. Turns out Russians, equally enthusiastic about this food, are also among his regulars.

Lamb and chicken hold pride of place on the menu, served in a multitude of ways—ground, grilled, marinated, skewered, and topped with yogurt and a light tomato sauce. There are usually two fish entrées and three vegetarian options, but the hot and cold appetizers tend to be meatless, too, and, along with salads, offer plenty of choices for those not inclined to carnivorous pursuits. Many dishes offer the Turkish take on things we know from other countries—hummus, babagannush, felafel, and döner, the Anatolian version of Greek gyros. The stuffed grape leaves are slightly sweet, with a filling of rice, currants, pine nuts, dill, and mint; the spicing of the kofte (grilled ground lamb) sets it apart from its Lebanese counterpart.

Turkish beers and wines are available, as well as raki, a brandy made from raisins and distilled with aniseed that's served watered down and over ice; a yogurt drink; mint tea; sour cherry juice, which also shows up in a delicious cocktail; and demitasse cups of thick, dark coffee.

The restaurant relocated to Lee Road in 2008. It's a gorgeous place, with multiple rooms painted in lip-licking shades of lemon, tangerine, and pomegranate. One dining area has a working fireplace, and the lounge features a copper-topped bar. Rugs, weavings, traditional cooking pots, and clay urns decorate the walls. The kitchen does catering on and off site. A private party room can handle 100 people. Patio seating out front in good weather. Free valet parking on weekends.

## Antalya Red Square

☎ (440) 461-0818

CITY: **Mayfield Heights**   AREA: **East Side**
ATMOSPHERE: **Casual**   COST: **$$$**$$

ADDRESS: 5131 Mayfield Rd.
HOURS: Tue–Thu 11 a.m.–10 p.m., Fri 11
a.m.–11 p.m., Sat–Sun noon–11 p.m.; closed
Mondays RESERVATIONS: Taken PAYMENT: MC,
VS, AX, DIS BAR: None TAKEOUT: Yes ACCESS:
♿ Full access OTHER ETHNIC: Mediterranean,
Russian

Chef Sonmez Bozkurt has a long, professional résumé that starts in Turkey. He came to the U.S. in 1997 and worked in New York, Cincinnati, and at Cleveland's Anatolia Cafe (see previous listing in this chapter) before opening his own restaurant with Emil Markakhayev, who hails from Azerbejian, in September 2007. The menu is packed with traditional preparations that give lamb, rice, and yogurt starring roles. Meats of all kinds are mostly marinated, grilled, and skewered. Legumes show up in such tasty ways as red lentil soup, piyaz—a white bean salad, and barbunya pilaki—kidney beans and vegetables in an olive oil and lemon dressing. Mixed appetizer platters and dinner specials for two or three are a great way to try a variety of dishes at a single sitting.

The place, in a space that has seen numerous eating establishments come and go, has a quirky and split personality. The dining room décor seems slightly outdated and kitschy. The room can feel cavernous with a ghost-town ambience when not crowded. There's a bandstand and a dance floor because the venue does double duty as a club on Saturday nights, catering to a predominantly Russian clientele. Private banquets are hosted in a separate party room.

# MARKETS

# African

## Barwulu/Hookes African Food Market
☎ (216) 261-0553
CITY: **Euclid**   AREA: **East Side**

**ADDRESS:** 917 E. 222 St.
**FOOD AVAIL.:** Meat (frozen), fish (frozen, dried), produce, grains, beans, spices, condiments, beverages, tea, coffee **HOURS:** Mon–Sat 10 a.m.–8 p.m.; closed Sun **PAYMENT:** MC, VS
**ACCESS:** ♿ Limited **OTHER ETHNIC:** Caribbean

William Barwulu Hookes is from Liberia and his wife, Ramona Hookes, is American born. He's been in this country since the 1980s but never lost his taste for the foods of home, and he's banking on the fact that other people from Africa feel the same. That's why the couple decided to buy the business from its former owner in 2001, and are keeping the shelves stocked with African staples and delicacies: stockfish, cassava leaf, potato greens, palm oil, palava sauce, fufu (plantain flour), fermented banku (flour of ground cassava and maize), and kenkey, a cereal from Ghana that's much like farina.

But Barwulu is convinced that Americans will also like some of his products.

"I get frozen free-range chickens flown in from Africa. And I tell you this— once a person has tasted this they will be running here to get some more. It is very special." In addition to all sorts of spices and condiments, as well as the beans, grains, and frozen goat meat that are used in African cooking, shoppers will also find ingredients more familiar to those who prepare Jamaican food. This should come as no surprise if you know anything about the history of the Caribbean—the interplay of indigenous, European, Indian, and African cultures, the result of slavery, colonialism, and immigration, is vividly displayed in the region's cuisine.

There are only two narrow aisles in this tiny store, but the floor-to-ceiling shelves and the boxes on the floor hold a whole world of food. Space for three cars to park head-in directly in front of the store, with additional parking on side streets.

# Indian

## Asian Imports
☎ (440) 777-8101
CITY: **North Olmsted**   AREA: **West Side**

ADDRESS: 26885 Brookpark Ext.
FOOD AVAIL.: Produce, baked goods, canned & packaged goods, spices, condiments, beverages, tea, coffee, prepared frozen foods, takeout meals HOURS: Tue–Sun 11:30 a.m.–7 p.m.; closed Mon PAYMENT: MC, VS, DIS ACCESS: ⅙ Limited

This small market is packed from floor to ceiling. Rice comes in many varieties and quantities. Freezer cases are filled with convenience foods, Indian-style prepared entrées and side dishes, and ready-to-cook naan, roti, and parantha (breads), plus samosa

wrappers for do-it-yourselfers. You can also buy hot homemade samosas and pakoras to go. Also available are spices in abundance, nuts, dried fruit, esoteric ingredients like mango pulp and ginger paste, and fresh produce, including some vegetables with names that sent me to a culinary dictionary— karela (bitter gourd), gawar (a long green bean), and dudhi (white fleshed and pumpkinlike). Specialized cooking utensils, Indian-language videos, and personal care products complete the selection. Located in the same strip as Flavors of India (see listing in this chapter), with ample parking.

## India Food & Spices
☎ (440) 845-0000
CITY: **Parma**   AREA: **Southwest**

ADDRESS: 5543 Ridge Rd.
FOOD AVAIL.: Meat (frozen), produce, grains, beans, flour, baked goods, canned & packaged goods, spices, condiments, beverages, tea, prepared frozen foods HOURS: Tue–Fri 1–7:30 p.m., Sat noon–7 p.m., Sun 1–6 p.m.; closed Mon PAYMENT: Checks ACCESS: ⅙ None

Owner Bhavna Patel has moved her market across the street from its previous location. She takes pride in the fact that although this store is small it can supply customers with virtually any spice they ask for. She carries fruits and vegetables basic to Indian-style dishes, including bitter melon, okra, eggplant, long beans, mangoes, and guavas. A good selection of chutneys, Indian pickles (mango, gooseberry, ginger, lime), and flours made from ground beans— adoo besan, moong, dhokla, urad, and bajari. For an inexpensive weekend of armchair travel, you can stop in, buy some Indian ice cream and pastries, and rent an Indian video. There are a few basic, non-Indian grocery and household items available. Parking available in rear.

## Indo-American Foods

☎ (216) 662-0072

CITY: **North Randall** AREA: **Southeast**

**ADDRESS:** 4614 Warrensville Ctr. Rd.
**FOOD AVAIL.:** Produce, canned & packaged goods, spices, condiments, beverages, tea, prepared frozen foods **HOURS:** Mon–Sat 11 a.m.–8 p.m., Sun noon–8 p.m. **PAYMENT:** MC, VS, AX, DIS, checks **ACCESS:** ♿ None

A small convenience store that's best described as the Indian version of a 7-Eleven. Dried, canned, and packaged staples include rice and spices, mango juice, and movies to rent (Indian and Pakistani with subtitles). Some seasonal produce. This is where local Indian families run when they need a jar of ghee (clarified butter), a can of ginger pickles, or a bottle of coconut oil.

## Lakshmi Plaza

☎ (440) 460-4601

CITY: **Mayfield Heights** AREA: **East Side**

**ADDRESS:** 5880 Mayfield Rd.
**FOOD AVAIL.:** Produce, grains, beans, baked goods, spices, condiments, beverages, tea, coffee **HOURS:** Daily 11 a.m.–8 p.m. **PAYMENT:** MC, VS, DIS, checks **ACCESS:** ♿ Full access

Mayfield Road is becoming a veritable global marketplace, and this is the most recent addition. A full-service Indian grocery store in a small two-aisle space. Opened in April 2002, the market carries fresh vegetables and every sort of spice, condiment, sauce, grain, bean, and flour used in Indian cooking. There are many short-cut mixes for curry, dal, kurma, and biryani; chapati and pappadums (breads) ready to fry; prepared ghee (clarified butter) and paneer (a farmer-type cheese); and some masalas (spice blends). Some of the more esoteric ingredients that caught my eye were green cardamom, mustard oil (a pungent fat from black mustard seeds), and ajwan seed (an herb with a strong thyme-like flavor). The store offers delivery service, a large selection of Indian-language movies, and some specialized cooking utensils. Located in a strip mall with ample parking both in front of and behind the store.

## Patel Brothers

☎ (440) 885-4440

CITY: **Middleburg Heights** AREA: **Southwest**

**ADDRESS:** 6876 Pearl Rd.
**FOOD AVAIL.:** Produce, grains, beans, flour, baked goods, canned & packaged goods, spices, condiments, tea, coffee, prepared frozen foods **HOURS:** Tue–Sat 11 a.m.–8 p.m., Sun 11 a.m.–6 p.m.; closed Mon **PAYMENT:** MC, VS, checks **ACCESS:** ♿ Full access

Tucked among the larger stores that are part of Southland Shopping Center is this small, family-owned shop offering Indian and Pakistani foods. Some basic household staples are shelved with the pickled mangoes, chutney, and chili paste. You'll find fresh items like bitter melon, squash, long beans, Chinese okra, eggplant, guava, mango, rotis (bread), and Indian pastries. A wide selection of masala (spice mixtures) and sambal (spicy condiments).

## Raj Mahal Indian Foods

☎ (330) 926-0369

CITY: **Cuyahoga Falls** AREA: **Farther South**

**ADDRESS:** 2037 State Rd.
**FOOD AVAIL.:** Produce, grains, beans, baked goods, canned & packaged goods, spices, condiments, beverages, tea, prepared frozen

foods **HOURS:** Mon–Sun 11:30 a.m.–10 p.m.
**PAYMENT:** MC, VS, AX, DIS **ACCESS:** & Limited

Owner Kala Chima, who also is the proprietor of the Raj Mahal Restaurant next door (see listing in Restaurants section), has filled this three-aisle shop with a great mix of foods. In addition to the standard Indian cooking ingredients, there are vegetables I do not recognize by sight with names I must come home and look up (and even then, I still don't know what they are or what to do with them): arbi (colocasia or elephant ears); karela (bitter gourd); dudhi (bottle gourd); and turai (a relative of zucchini). On the shelves you'll find mango pulp, gooseberries in sugar syrup, lime pickles, green and black cardamom, puffed rice, and dried tamarind. A freezer case holds breads—naan, roti, and parantha. I was entranced by 15-pound canvas sacks of basmati rice. The Royal brand graphics on the bag are charming, and the copy reads "from the foothills of the Himalayas to your table." Busy commercial strip with easy head-in parking.

## Spice Corner
☎ (330) 535-1033
CITY: **Akron**     AREA: **Farther South**

**ADDRESS:** 319 E. Market St.
**FOOD AVAIL.:** Produce, grains, beans, flour, canned & packaged goods, spices, condiments, beverages, tea **HOURS:** Tue–Sun 11 a.m.–7 p.m. **PAYMENT:** MC, VS, checks **ACCESS:** & Full access **OTHER ETHNIC:** Malaysian, Pakistani

As its name suggests, this store specializes in spices and is a good source for hard-to-find flavorings essential to many traditional Indian, Pakistani, and Malaysian dishes. Their aromas mingle with the smell of incense, the only nonfood item available here, and the

air is thick with the exotic scents. Produce available in season includes bitter melon, long squash, guavas, and Asian vegetables. There are jars of relishes and pickles from India, a variety of lentils and rice, and flour specially ground for making chapati (Indian flat bread) as well as ready-made frozen chapati. As so much Indian cuisine is meatless, this is a great source of food ideas and products for vegetarians.

# Lebanese

## Jasmine Pita Bakery
☎ (216) 251-3838
CITY: **Cleveland**     AREA: **West Side**

**ADDRESS:** 16700 Lorain Rd.
**FOOD AVAIL.:** Produce, grains, beans, flour, rice, baked goods, canned & packaged goods, spices, condiments, beverages, tea, coffee, prepared frozen foods, takeout meals **HOURS:** Mon–Sat 9 a.m.–9 p.m., Sun 10 a.m.–4 p.m. **PAYMENT:** MC, VS, DIS, checks **ACCESS:** & Full access **OTHER ETHNIC:** Middle Eastern

Take advantage of the head-in parking in front of the renovated business strip when you shop here. Large windows offer a sneak preview of the pleasant shopping and eating environment inside. You'll see a bright, spacious, uncluttered room, gleaming industrial shelving, large refrigerators, and sparkling glass cases, all filled with Middle Eastern delicacies. There's a good selection of prepared foods including hummus, baba ghannouj, kibbee, stuffed grape leaves, meat and spinach pies, felafel, and tabouli; a self-serve olive bar with at least six different varieties, plus turnip and cauliflower pickles; a bakery counter; cheeses and yogurt products; and a cooler stocked with drinks like guava and mango nectar. They carry pita, lavash (a thin, crepe-like bread), and seasoned breads. In addition to the ingredients you'd expect to find, such as tahini and olive oil, you'll also encounter some delightful specialties—fig marmalade, date honey, and large hunks of halvah (a candy made from crushed sesame seeds and honey). Two tables at the front of the store provide a place to dine on your counter purchases or to simply pause and enjoy the aroma.

# Middle Eastern

## Aladdin's Baking Company
☎ (216) 861-0317
CITY: **Cleveland**   AREA: **Downtown**

**ADDRESS:** 1301 Carnegie Ave.
**FOOD AVAIL.:** Produce, grains, beans, flour, rice, baked goods, canned & packaged goods, spices, condiments, beverages, tea, coffee, prepared frozen foods, takeout meals **HOURS:** Mon–Sat 7:30 a.m.–6 p.m., Sun 9:30 a.m.–1:30 p.m. (open Mon–Sat until 7 p.m. during baseball season) **PAYMENT:** MC, VS, AX, DIS, checks **ACCESS:** ♿ Limited

Freshly baked pita, a traditional flat pocket bread made without sugar, oil, or fat, is the specialty here. A selection of Middle Eastern dishes is available daily, and you can purchase a full meal, already prepared. There's fatiyar (spinach or meat pies), beef or chicken shawarma (cooked by rotisserie), kafta (meatballs), kibbee (ground lamb and pine nuts), and shish kabob. You can get containers of tabouli (a salad made with bulgur wheat, onions, mint, tomatoes, olive oil, and lemon juice), hummus (chickpea spread), and baba ghannouj (eggplant spread). For dessert, choose from Middle Eastern and Mediterranean-style pastries, including Beirut-style baklava, and pick up Turk-

ish or Lebanese coffee. For use in your own recipes, they stock feta cheese, a wide variety of olives, olive oils, nuts, spices, and condiments. Call ahead to order prepared meals for one or one hundred.

## Almadina Imports
☎ (216) 671-4661
CITY: **Cleveland**   AREA: **Near West Side**

**ADDRESS:** 11550 Lorain Ave.
**FOOD AVAIL.:** Meat (fresh, deli, frozen), fish (fresh, frozen), produce, grains, beans, baked goods, spices, condiments, beverages, tea, coffee, takeout meals **HOURS:** Mon–Sat 8 a.m.–10 p.m., Sun 8 a.m.–9 p.m. **PAYMENT:** MC, VS, DIS, checks **ACCESS:** ♿ Limited

This spacious, full-service market, easily found by virtue of the big burgundy-colored awning over the front door, offers all things Middle Eastern, from pomegranate juice to sesame paste, as well as a large variety of nonethnic produce and household products. Halal meats, from animals slaughtered according to Islamic guidelines, are available fresh and frozen.

In addition to an olive bar, there's a nut bar—something I've never seen in any other Middle Eastern store in the region—with a large selection that includes spiced and flavored nuts and nut mixtures. They also carry the biggest rounds of fresh pita bread I've ever encountered—about 12 inches across. You could use one for a pizza or an edible platter. But the prepared foods really make this place stand out from the many other similar markets in town— definitely not your garden-variety takeout.

Breakfast offerings include eggs with Halal beef bacon; eggs ageh made with parsley, mint, and spices; egg pies; and zatar (bread spread with sesame seeds, olive oil, herbs, and spices) with cheese.

For later in the day and into the wee hours, in addition to typical entrées such as shish kabob, shish tawook (chicken) and shawarma (ground beef), hummus, salads, and rice pilaf, there are sandwiches made with lamb liver, lamb brains, lamb spleen, and lamb hearts.

## Assad Bakery
☎ (216) 251-5777
CITY: Cleveland   AREA: West Side

ADDRESS: 12719 Lorain Ave.
FOOD AVAIL.: Meat (fresh, deli), fish (dried), produce, grains, beans, flour, rice, baked goods, canned & packaged goods, spices, beverages, tea, coffee, prepared frozen foods, takeout meals HOURS: Mon–Sat 9 a.m.–9 p.m., Sun 9 a.m.–8 p.m. PAYMENT: MC, VS, AX, checks ACCESS: ₺ Full access

Don't be misled by the name—this is much more than a bakery. Brothers Mike and Fred Assad founded the business in 1990 and employ almost all their extended family. They bake fresh pita on the premises and prepare meat and spinach pies as well as Middle Eastern pastries. Exotic fruits and vegetables such as raw dates, fresh figs, loquats, and cactus pears are available seasonally. There's an interesting selection of cheeses, olives, nuts, spices, and olive oils. They also stock some unusual cookware, Middle Eastern drums, and Arab clothing. Mike describes his clientele, many regulars who enjoy the friendly, personal service, as "like a United Nations."

## Halal Meats
☎ (216) 281-1900
CITY: Cleveland   AREA: Near West Side

ADDRESS: 9418 Detroit Ave.
FOOD AVAIL.: Meat (fresh, deli, frozen), produce, grains, beans, baked goods, spices,

condiments, beverages, tea, coffee HOURS: Mon–Sat 9 a.m.–9 p.m., Sun 10 a.m.–7 p.m. PAYMENT: MC, VS, AX, DIS, checks ACCESS: ₺ Limited

Whether you're in search of dried Egyptian okra, tamarind syrup, a can of Moroccan sardines, labneh (a cream cheese made from yogurt-like cultured milk), or a foot-long kebab skewer, this is the place. The selection of products used in Middle Eastern cookery is extensive and includes many esoteric ingredients and Halal meats (prepared according to Muslim law). Indian foods are also well represented: sauce mixes, chutney, tandoori paste, chili pickles, basmati rice, and mango jam. Rice, sugar, olive oil, and even pickled cucumbers are sold in large, cost-saving sizes. Some shelf space is devoted to Goya products, used in Latin American cooking, and the freezer case contains Goya frozen banana leaves alongside the filo dough and felafel. The only category of food not well represented is fresh produce—the variety and quantity are limited. Although I just discovered this market, it's been in operation since 1985, one of the first places in the state to sell Halal meats. The store, renovated in 2001, is brightly lit, and maneuvering around the aisles is easy.

## Holyland Imports
☎ (216) 671-7736
CITY: Cleveland   AREA: West Side

ADDRESS: 11717 Lorain Ave.
FOOD AVAIL.: Meat (fresh), produce, grains, beans, flour, rice, baked goods, canned & packaged goods, spices, condiments, beverages, tea, coffee, prepared frozen foods HOURS: Mon–Sat 9 a.m.–9 p.m., Sun 9 a.m.–7 p.m. PAYMENT: MC, VS, AX, DIS, checks ACCESS: ₺ Full access OTHER ETHNIC: Greek, Indian

Arabic-language videos play on a

television perched above the refrigerator case, and the sound adds to the sensation of having journeyed to another country. A move in January 2008 added more square footage and a space that provides a pleasant shopping environment. The array of Middle Eastern food products and cookware is impressive, and you can find ingredients typically featured in Greek and Indian recipes as well. Large bins hold almonds, pistachios, walnuts, and pine nuts, and the prices for these, which you scoop up yourself, are noticeably lower per pound than the packaged counterparts available at regular grocery or gourmet stores. Other containers are filled with olives and delicacies such as pickled turnips and pickled peppers. The place is run by the five Mohammad brothers. They all take turns behind the counter, keeping the store open seven days a week.

## The Near East Market

☎ (330) 475-0538
CITY: **Cuyahoga Falls**   AREA: **Farther South**

ADDRESS: 3461 Hudson Dr.
FOOD AVAIL.: Meat (fresh), produce, grains, beans, baked goods, canned & packaged goods, beverages, tea, coffee, prepared frozen foods, takeout meals HOURS: Daily 10 a.m.–8 p.m. PAYMENT: MC, VS, AX, DIS, checks ACCESS: ⚬ Full access OTHER ETHNIC: African, Indian, Pakistani, Turkish

Fan, ace librarian (Cleveland Heights-University Heights), and true food enthusiast Helene Stern tipped me off to this place. She and her husband, Bud, found it, shortly after it opened in June 2003, on their way home from the Akron Art Museum. Lucky thing, because they were hungry and looking for a place to get a late lunch. Unfortunately there were no tables, though plans are in the works to remedy that. But there was a great deal of great food to carry out, much of it prepared on the premises. Among their choices were meat, cheese, and spinach pies; kibbeh balls (in meat and vegetarian versions); hummus; eggplant dip; stuffed grape leaves; lentils and rice; shawarma and felafel sandwiches; and fattoosh and tabouleh salads. Pastries are shipped in from bakeries in Detroit and Toronto, including a few different versions of baklava.

The spacious modern market, situated at the corner of Graham Road and Hudson Drive, offers a mix of ready-to-eat and groceries. Big self-serve buckets of olives sit on the floor, and store owner Moamar Mustafa cures some varieties himself. A refrigerator case features a large selection of Middle Eastern and European cheeses. Special finds in the produce section—fresh fava beans, green chickpeas, green almonds, and fresh figs Helene says are the best she's ever had. An aisle is devoted to spices and sauces. You can find all the canned, boxed, and jarred things you'd expect, plus some you wouldn't, like pickled wild cucumbers, Syrian sweets, pieces of nougat, and Turkish Delight candies. Supplies of fresh Halal lamb, beef, and chicken arrive every week.

The big sign out front makes it easy to spot, and ample parking makes it hassle free.

## Petra Food

☎ (330) 633-3830
CITY: **Tallmadge**   AREA: **Farther South**

ADDRESS: 57 Midway Plaza
FOOD AVAIL.: Meat (fresh), produce, grains, beans, flour, rice, baked goods, canned & packaged goods, spices, condiments, beverages, tea, coffee, prepared frozen foods, takeout meals HOURS: Mon–Sat 10 a.m.–8 p.m., Sun 11 a.m.–5 p.m. PAYMENT: MC, VS ACCESS: ⚬ Full access OTHER ETHNIC: Bosnian, Greek, Indian, Italian, Pakistani

The store opened in 1994 because a man and his wife got tired of driving to Cleveland to purchase the Middle Eastern and North African groceries they needed. They realized that if they wanted a store that sold these things a little closer to where they lived, others probably did as well. They don't own the business anymore, but the current proprietor continues to serve shoppers from Akron, Kent, and Canton who need Halal lamb and goat meat; semolina, farina, and chickpea flour; basmati rice and bulgur wheat; and tahini (sesame paste). A good source of unusual fresh and frozen fruits and vegetables like baby eggplants, mikete (a sort of cucumber), and kseu (a type of zucchini). And some hard-to-find ingredients such as dried fava beans and jamid, dried yogurt used in the preparation of meats. Prepared felafel, kibbee (baked ground meat), and fresh pita bread are for sale along with dairy products and specialized kitchen utensils. They also stock more than 60 different spices and spice blends, all in bulk, so you can purchase just the amount you need. Parking is plentiful in the plaza lot.

## Sanabel Middle East Bakery
☎ (330) 253-4505
CITY: **Akron**   AREA: **Farther South**

ADDRESS: 308 E. South St.
FOOD AVAIL.: Grains, beans, baked goods, canned & packaged goods, spices, condiments, beverages, tea, coffee, takeout meals **HOURS:** Mon–Fri 9 a.m.–5:30 p.m., Sat 9 a.m.–3:00 p.m.; Sun closed **PAYMENT:** MC, VS, checks **ACCESS:** & Full access

The neighborhood's a little run down, with cracks in the sidewalk and weeds in the cracks, but the bakery space, in a World War II–era building, is nicely spiffed up. Since 1998, the shop's been a source of Middle Eastern favorites including stuffed grape leaves; hummus, felafel; kibbeh; and meat, spinach, cheese, and chicken pies. Sandwiches are served on Norma Touma's fresh pita. For those who'd rather dine in than take out, there are a few tables set amid shelves and cases of canned and jarred foods, dairy products, and spices. If you're in search of Egyptian tobacco for your hookah, you'll find it here, too.

## Vine Valley Mediterranean Market
☎ (330) 865-6777
CITY: **Akron**   AREA: **Farther South**

ADDRESS: 1450 Portage Path
FOOD AVAIL.: Grains, beans, baked goods, canned & packaged goods, spices, condiments, beverages, tea, coffee, takeout meals **HOURS:** Mon–Fri 10 a.m.–6 p.m., Sat 10 a.m.–5 p.m., Sun closed **PAYMENT:** MC, VS
ACCESS: & Full access

The Merriman Valley is becoming a bit of an ethnic eats hub, and this little market is a standout for its freezer case stocked during the summer with quarts of Lebanese-style ice cream, made in Detroit. The most unusual is flavored with rosewater, but there's also mango, pistachio, and apricot. They prepare their own traditional Middle Eastern fare—meat and spinach pies, kibbeh, rolled grape leaves, zatar, and shawarma sandwiches. Shoppers will find an array of ingredients, from oils and spices to cheeses and fresh vegetables, in these two aisles and can even go home with their very own hookah. Located at one end of the strip in Parkway Plaza.

# MEDITERRANEAN

The term "Mediterranean" generally refers to the coastal regions of the countries surrounding the sea of that name. I've used it here rather cavalierly to provide a collective heading for a diverse group of countries and areas in Southern Europe. What ties them together in my mind is the robust, earthy flavor of their foods. Mediterranean cooking is characterized by its reliance on olives and olive oil, garlic, onions, lemons, grapes and the wines that can be made from them, capers (the pickled flower bud of a shrub that grows in the region), tomatoes, and green herbs like thyme, parsley, rosemary, basil, fennel, and bay leaves. Good bread and fresh fruit are seen as essential parts of every meal. With its emphasis on seafood and fresh garden vegetables, Mediterranean cuisine is considered to be one of the healthiest diets in the world. Both the tastes and simple techniques are well suited to the contemporary American lifestyle, and this approach to food has grown increasingly popular in recent years. In Cleveland, restaurants provide diners with a chance to explore Mediterranean cuisine as it is prepared in Greece, Italy, and southern France.

Between 1890 and 1920, 5,000 Greeks settled in Cleveland. They were mostly males intending to stay only long enough to make their fortunes and then return home. These *protporoi* (pioneers) took low-paying, menial jobs at first, but once they decided to remain and establish roots in the community many started their own small businesses. They sent for their wives or returned home to find a bride to bring back to Cleveland. By 1922 there were at least 137 Greek-owned businesses in town, among them coffeehouses, candy stores, and restaurants.

Much of Greek cultural and social life, even for second-, third-, and fourth-generation Greek Americans, centers around the city's four Greek Orthodox churches. "I have to travel far to get to church," said Debbie Alexandrou, who was born on the island of Samos. "But I love it there, because it's just like being in Greece. I can pretend that I am back home."

Small in number and close-knit, the Greek community of Cleveland is very dedicated not only to preserving their cultural heritage, but to sharing it, and they sponsor many festivals around town. Food is always an important element. "All our events include food," said Penny Sikoutris, born here to Greek immigrant parents. "When Greeks get together, they eat. Years ago, the general public was not so familiar with our cuisine. Now that they've grown accustomed to it, they seem to like it as much as we do!"

Beyond its commonalities with all Mediterranean cooking, some ingredients are particular to Greek cuisine. Dill, sage (which seems to flourish in the sea air), oregano, and mint are used often. Lamb is the favored meat, and cheeses are made from goat's milk. Phyllo, thin sheets of pastry dough, goes into a variety of dishes. Honey is used with abandon in pastries.

I once attended a festival held at the Church of the Annunciation, the oldest Greek Orthodox church in the city. It was built on a parcel of land on West 14th, just across the river from "Greek Town," that was purchased in 1912. The array of food was staggering, as it always is at this annual celebration: there was pastitsio, moussaka, dolmathes, tiropeta, and spanakopeta, lamb shanks, baked fish, and souvlakia. And tray after tray of desserts, almost floating in a sea of golden sweetness: baklava, galaktoboureko, and kataife. To no one in particular I said, "What would Greeks do without honey?" The man behind me replied, "Not have a reason to live."

Italians have long been one of the largest ethnic groups in Cleveland. The earliest immigrants came from northern Italy after the Civil War, followed in the years just preceding World War I by people from the central and southern regions. Between 1889 and 1924, 25,000 Italians came to settle here. They were stonemasons, bootmakers, quarrymen, and produce sellers. They tended to live in close proximity to one another, build their own churches, and attend to all their needs through hometown societies. Big Italy, which no longer exists, was a downtown area that stretched from Ontario to East 40th Street. Little Italy was, and is, perched on Murray Hill along Mayfield Road, much like a little hill town in the old country. By 1911, 96 percent of the people who lived there were Italian born and most were from the Abruzzi region.

Americans of Italian descent are for the most part fully assimilated into the mainstream of American life. Though Little Italy continues to be a densely populated Italian enclave and home to some of the city's best-known Italian restaurants and stores, Italian Americans are spread throughout Greater Cleveland now. But for many, no matter where they live, Italian-American clubs that promote cultural awareness and pride provide a link with their heritage. Local cookbook author Maria Volpe Paganini says much of this cultural legacy is expressed through food and family, the two basic and essential elements of the Italian soul.

"To Italians, family is what matters most and food is at the center of day-to-day family life. Food is more important to us than politics or money and we think about it a great deal. We gather around the table, and while we eat good food, we talk."

Italian cuisine has profoundly influenced how Americans eat, though the Italian dishes we're most accustomed to bear little resemblance to the real thing. Even the term "Italian food" is misleading. There are approximately 20 regions in that country, and every one has its own culinary heritage. In each, the unique foods produced there represent the area's distinctive style: Modena is the one true source for balsamic vinegar, Parma for prosciutto ham, and Emilia-Romagna for genuine Parmigiano-Reggiano cheese.

Pasta, however (and there are over 200 different types and shapes), is common to all. Cooks throughout the country also appreciate the qualities of Italian varieties of rice (arborio, vialone nano, carnaroli); polenta (a cornmeal mush); cannellini and other beans; and anchovies. And they do wondrous things with veal.

Though the cooks of southern France are a breed unto themselves, their culinary traditions are inextricably linked to their Italian neighbors. But as a group they have no real Cleveland history to speak of, for, as someone from Provence once said to me, "Why would they leave?" Which leaves me with only their cuisine to write about.

It's been described as full of gusto, passion, and vitality, imbued with the warm sunshine of their climate and the peasant's appreciation for nature's bounty. Their soups are said to have distinctive personality, and their lamb, which grazes on wild herbs, is like no other. In addition to the ingredients favored by all Mediterranean cooks, the kitchens of southern France are stocked with mushrooms, potatoes, shallots, and leeks. But it is not the type of ingredients so much as their freshness and the way in which they are combined to let the flavor of each shine through that characterizes this style of cooking. Ultimately it is the art of beautiful and savory simplicity.

# RESTAURANTS

# Greek

## Athens Restaurant
☎ (330) 453-6800
CITY: **Canton**    AREA: **Farther South**
ATMOSPHERE: **Relaxed**    COST: **$$**$$

ADDRESS: 816 Harrison Ave. SW
HOURS: Mon–Sat 6 a.m.–3 p.m. **RESERVATIONS:**
Taken **PAYMENT:** MC, VS, AX, DIS **BAR:** None
**TAKEOUT:** Yes **ACCESS:** ♿ Full access

Ted Karasarides opened this restaurant in 1976, and now his glamorous-looking daughter Dimitria (known to all as Dee), who has been helping out since she was 14, runs the place, and her mom, Maria, still prepares the daily Greek specials. Most of the staff have been working here almost as long as Dee and Maria, some for 20 years, and they are all part of the family. Regular customers are part of the family, too, and everybody calls each other by name. The early-morning hours bring retirees, folks getting off the night shift, police officers, and bus drivers. At lunchtime you see company people, both suits and non-suits, from nearby corporations like Timken and Diebold, and hospital workers, plus others of unidentified occupation and age enjoying the increasingly rare opportunity to sit wherever they want and smoke as much as they want.

There's a long lunch counter that stretches all the way from the front of the restaurant to the kitchen, and the low stools have real wooden tops, burnished silky and golden by all the seats that have sat on them. In 2004 the dining room got a fresh coat of bright, sunny Mediterranean color. Tables are covered in green vinyl, and Greek scenes painted on the walls complete the decorative flourishes. Carryout business is always brisk. Breakfast is served until 11:30 on weekdays and all day Saturday.

Saganaki (flaming cheese), Greek salads, mbefteki (chopped, spiced steak), gyros, soutsoukakia (sausages of northern Greece), rice pudding, Greek pastries, and Greek coffee are on the regular menu, along with standard American diner fare. Specials include roasted lamb shanks, sarmathes (stuffed cabbage leaves in egg-lemon sauce), yovecci (beef tips with rosemary and kasseri cheese), stifado (stew), pastitsio, mousaka, baked pork chops Thessalonika-style, and keftedes (meatballs with rice). A small bakery counter at the front offers baklava, cookies, and other traditional pastries for sale. A separate room called "The Athenian" is available for private gatherings or large groups.

The restaurant is easy to spot as the lone white corner building is done in faux-Parthenon with distinctive white columns in front. Plenty of parking in a lot to the side and another across the street.

## Casablanca
☎ (330) 735-3304
CITY: **Dellroy**   AREA: **Farther South**
ATMOSPHERE: **Relaxed**   COST: $$$$$

**ADDRESS:** 27 N. Smith St.
**HOURS:** Daily, two seating times: 6 p.m. and 8 p.m., by reservation only **RESERVATIONS:** Required **PAYMENT:** Checks **BAR:** BYOB **TAKEOUT:** **ACCESS:** ♿ Full access **OTHER ETHNIC:** Mediterranean

This is a truly unique dining destination, as unlike a restaurant as a restaurant could be. There are only four tables, and you can't get one unless you've got a reservation. The tables are in the dining room of a two-story house where owners Jim and Karen also live. There's a spectacular view of Atwood Lake from the dining room, and if you time your visit properly, you get to watch the sun set. Jim greets, seats, and serves while Karen handles the kitchen. You can see her at work, because only a counter separates the two rooms in this century home that the couple gutted and renovated to function as both home and workplace. They've been in business since 1995 and have never advertised, relying instead on word-of-mouth recommendations. People come from all over the region, and they are usually booked well in advance on the weekends and every night throughout the summer.

Jim generally wears a tuxedo and provides the kind of personal and attentive service found in high-end restaurants. The tables sport white linens and fresh flowers, and fine art decorates the walls. Even so, the atmosphere is informal, the pricing moderate, and the dress code casual—although if you want to put on your prom clothes and compete with Jim you won't feel out of place.

The menu selection is not large, but it is interesting, and the inspiration is Mediterranean with Greek cuisine at the forefront. Among the appetizers are tiropita (cheese-filled triangles of phyllo dough) and keftedes (meatballs), and entrées include plaki (Greek-style fish); chicken rigani made with feta and Kalamata olives; a slow-roasted Cretan pork done with rosemary and lemon; and rack of lamb seasoned with garlic and oregano. Writing for the *Canton Repository*, Saimi Rote Bergmann urged diners not to leave without trying the Greek coffee. They also do prime strip steak, crab cakes that everyone raves about, surf and turf, and some Italianish dishes.

The nearby Whispering Pines Bed and Breakfast (read more about it in *Bed & Breakfast Getaways from Cleveland*) offers a weekend getaway package that includes a voucher for dinner here (330-735-2824, info@atwoodlake.com).

## The Greek Express
☎ (216) 357-2960
CITY: **Cleveland**   AREA: **Downtown**
ATMOSPHERE: **Casual**   COST: $$$$$

**ADDRESS:** 401 Euclid, Suite 55
**HOURS:** Mon–Sat 11 a.m.–4 p.m.; closed Sun
**RESERVATIONS:** Not taken **PAYMENT:** MC, VS, DIS, checks **BAR:** None **TAKEOUT:** Yes **ACCESS:** ♿ Full access

This small eatery in the Food Court of the Old Arcade caters to a busy business crowd in a hurry. At first glance the order-at-the-counter service, plastic tableware, and Styrofoam plates give the impression this is just another fast-food joint. But the quality, freshness, and authentic Greek taste convey a different message. You wouldn't choose this spot for a romantic tête-à-tête (though the charm of the landmark Arcade creates its own special atmosphere) or a leisurely meeting over lunch. But it is a good choice for a quick, interesting, and inexpensive meal. The menu offers a selection of traditional dishes—avgolemono (egg lemon) soup, gyros, spanakopita, moussaka, rice pilaf, and chicken kebobs—plus an eclectic mix of curries, salads, hummus, and baba ghanouj. Nice tables and chairs and even a few couches just outside the door where you can enjoy your meal.

Phone orders are accepted for take-out.

## The Mad Greek
☎ (216) 421-3333
CITY: **Cleveland Heights**   AREA: **East Side**
ATMOSPHERE: **Casual**   COST: $$$$$

**ADDRESS:** 2466 Fairmount Blvd.
**HOURS:** Mon 11:30 a.m.–10 p.m., Tue–Thu 11:30 a.m.–10:30 p.m., Fri–Sat 11:30 a.m.–11 p.m., Sun 4–10 p.m. **RESERVATIONS:** Taken, recommended Fri, Sat **PAYMENT:** MC, VS, AX, DIS **BAR:** Beer, wine, liquor **TAKEOUT:** Yes **ACCESS:** & Limited **OTHER ETHNIC:** Indian

The Mad Greek is well known for serving a unique combination of Greek and Indian foods since 1976 that reflected the heritage—by birth and marriage—of the restaurant's original owners. Moussaka, a special of fisherman's stew or loukaniko sausage, spanakopita, and dolmades peacefully coexist on the menu with Goan coconut curry, shrimp rangoon, samosas, and chicken biryani. You can go Indian on your soup course with a bowl of mulligatawny or dal, then shift international gears and dig into Apollo chicken made with Kalamata olives and feta. Or get cross-cultural with someone else at your table and trade half your gyro platter for half of a Masala-spiced salmon entrée. Current owners Chris Chopra and Bill LaRue have the chef doing a few pasta dishes, too. Think of it as a postmodern expression of ethnic eating—a little of this and some of that make lots of different customers

happy. The main dining room is done with a classic Med décor—white walls accented with colorful ceramic tiles and lots of green plants. The attractive cafe-bar area, which features live jazz on Friday and Saturday nights, is a great spot for happy hour, where you can try Greek or Indian beers and nibble Greek bruschetta, Mediterranean flatbread, or paneer tikka (homemade cheese broiled and presented with a trio of chutneys). The place goes alfresco when the warm weather arrives; huge windows open to create a very appealing inside/outside experience. There's also a secluded patio in back.

## Mardi Gras Lounge & Grill
☎ (216) 566-9094
CITY: **Cleveland**   AREA: **Downtown**
ATMOSPHERE: **Casual**   COST: $$$$$

**ADDRESS:** 1423 E. 21st St.
**HOURS:** Thu 3 p.m.–10 p.m., Fri 3 p.m.–3 a.m., Sat 5 p.m.–3 a.m.; closed Sun–Wed **RESERVATIONS:** Taken **PAYMENT:** MC, VS, AX, DIS, checks **BAR:** Beer, wine, liquor **TAKEOUT:** Yes **ACCESS:** & Full access *Not recommended for children

You might come here for the food alone—the menu is peppered with Greek specialties such as pastitsio and moussaka, plus a few spicy Cajun dishes like shrimp Creole and blackened chicken. It's the only place in town you can get saganaki (flaming Greek kasseri cheese) or a souvlaki (marinated broiled lamb) at 3 a.m. on a Thursday. But this is no typical ethnic restaurant, and people are just as likely to find their way here because the bar is open late and the music is hot. Bands play at the front of the bar area that fills the center space. Tables on the mezzanine level (adjacent to the bar) and a few others parallel to the bar offer a good view of the performers. Another dining area is removed from the scene in a separate room. A favorite lunchtime hangout for *Plain Dealer* employees, with a standard selection of salads and sandwiches, it also attracts audiences for live jazz, blues, and R&B three nights a week. Any time of the day or night, the clientele is a mix of white- and blue-collar folks, and the ambience is dark and funky. An ATM in the bar is handy, though I suppose it could easily lead some down the paths of overconsumption or overspending. There's a parking lot across the street and never a cover charge.

# Italian

## Agostino's Ristorante
☎ (216) 741-6522
CITY: **Brooklyn**   AREA: **Near West Side**
ATMOSPHERE: **Casual**   COST: $$$$$

**ADDRESS:** 4218 Ridge Rd.
**HOURS:** Tue–Fri 11 a.m.–10 p.m., Sat 3–11 p.m., Sun noon–8 p.m. **RESERVATIONS:** Taken, weekdays for groups of 5+ only; required on weekends **PAYMENT:** MC, VS, AX, DIS **BAR:** Beer, wine, liquor **TAKEOUT:** Yes **ACCESS:** ♿ Full access

The sign out front leads you to believe this is a typical Italian-American pizza-and-spaghetti place. It's not. This is the kind of restaurant that attracts hard-core Italian eaters who generally avoid food that's not prepared at home by a family member.

The menu offers simple, well-loved dishes that few area restaurants do well, such as trippa (tripe, which, if you really must know, is made from the stomach lining of cattle or oxen, in a tomato and bell pepper broth), wedding soup, tortellini with ham and peas, and escarola (greens steamed in a garlic and oil broth). The kitchen also does more things with calamari than any other single place I've visited: in addition to the usual frying, it's marinated and served cold in a salad; stuffed; grilled; sautéed; used in a seafood sauce for pasta and to make a zuppa di pesce (fish soup). The bread is fresh and plentiful, the oil for dipping it in is herbed, the house dressing is a balsamic vinaigrette, and there's a nice selection of veal, chicken, and pasta dishes. For dessert expect tiramisu, spumoni, and real Italian lemon ice.

Owner and staff take pride in the restaurant and it shows in the level of hospitality and service. Customers are never rushed. Everyone is welcome to sit, eat, and talk as long as they like, just as if they were in their own home. When a woman asked for "lotsa sauce," I heard the waiter reply, "No problem, I'll bring you a nice big bowlful on the side, you can eat what you want and take the rest with you."

Agostino's has grown from the original 10-table place it was years ago to three rooms that can seat about 175 diners. That first room is a darkish little brick and stucco space with lots of character. Along with the adjacent bar area, equipped with some tables and a television, it formed the original restaurant. The other two dining areas are larger, brighter, newer, and a bit more formal in appearance, comfortably accommodating large groups. There's also a banquet hall that can hold 150. Recorded singers crooning in Italian alternate with Frank Sinatra as soft background music, and on Wednesday, Saturday, and Sunday evenings a mandolin and guitar duo entertain. Periodically, the restaurant becomes a cabaret, and a special seven-course meal is offered along with a floor show.

There's valet parking and a convenient pick-up window for takeout orders around the back. Easy to find, just north of I-480 and the intersection of Ridge and Memphis.

## Alberini's

☎ (330) 652-5895

CITY: **Niles**   AREA: **Farther South**
ATMOSPHERE: **Casual**   COST: $$$$$

ADDRESS: 1201 Youngstown-Warren Rd.
HOURS: Tue–Thu 4 p.m.–10 p.m., Fri–Sat 4 p.m.–11 p.m.; closed Sun, Mon, holidays
RESERVATIONS: Taken, recommended Fri, Sat
PAYMENT: MC, VS, AX, DIS, checks BAR: Beer, wine, liquor TAKEOUT: Yes ACCESS: & Full access

"I'm an American Italian," says Richard Alberini, "and so's my wife, Gilda. We were born knowing about good food. When I got out of the navy, I learned about the restaurant business, and we opened this place together 40 years ago."

Back then it was in a building about a mile away from their present location, and the rent was only $55 a month. The couple did everything from cooking to cleaning. In 1960 they built a place of their own and kept adding to it over the years so it's now a sprawling collection of six distinctive dining rooms—and a local institution. Longtime customers bring their kids, and their kids' kids, and Richard, who continues to come to work every day, even though he's handed over the management of kitchen and business to his two sons, always sees someone he knows.

Although dining habits have changed since the restaurant opened, much about Alberini's hasn't, and that's part of its appeal. The décor is in the time-honored white-tablecloth style, where formality intersects with comfort. The heart of the menu is still classic, hearty Italian dishes like fried calamari, wedding soup, veal Parmigiana, spaghetti and meatballs, gnocchi with a Bolognese meat sauce, ravioli, linguini with clam sauce, and lasagna. And they still offer their own interpretation of dishes long associated with special occasions and deluxe dining: shrimp cocktail, escargots, Caesar salad, roast duck, rack of lamb, bananas Foster, and cherries jubilee.

But the old pairs well with the new in traditional offerings with a contemporary flair: chicken with fresh artichokes and a tomatoes concasse in a balsamic sauce; roasted garlic risotto; baked oysters with spinach and anisette; osso bucco made with a gremolata of parsley, rosemary, lemon zest and garlic; and a filet of beef with portabella mushrooms in red Barolo wine sauce accompanied by Parmigiano potato fritellas.

Wine is important here. The award-winning wine list features over 800 selections, and the cellar racks hold 10,000 bottles. Diners are encouraged to make their selection early on so it can be properly decanted, with time to breathe or chill. Thirty-eight different wines are available by the glass. But the large selection of alcoholic beverages doesn't end with wine: there are over 20 fine ports; 17 aged single-malt Scotches; 13 kinds of cognac and brandy; a rare Armagnac; and 16 cordials, including Strega and Romano Sambuca.

The spacious restaurant offers excellent party and banquet facilities and is a popular choice for large groups. Smaller rooms, such as the wine cellar, offer more intimate settings. Chooks (in honor of chef "Chook" Alberini who runs the restaurant kitchen) is a wine bar and grill offering lighter fare and a casual atmosphere. Cigars are sold and can be smoked in this room. A retail shop called Cork and More Shoppe is also on the premises, selling wine and prepared gourmet foods. (For more information see listing in the market section of this chapter.) There's live piano music in the lounge Friday and Saturday evenings. Plenty of parking in the restaurant lot.

## Aldo's

☎ (216) 749-7060

CITY: **Brooklyn** AREA: **Near West Side**
ATMOSPHERE: **Casual** COST: $$$$$

**ADDRESS:** 8459 Memphis Ave.
**HOURS:** Tue 11:30 a.m.–9 p.m., Wed 11:30
a.m.–10 p.m., Thu 11:30 a.m.–10 p.m., Fri
11:30 a.m.–11 p.m., Sat 4–11 p.m., Sun 4–9
p.m.; closed Mon **RESERVATIONS:** Taken, for
groups of 5+ **PAYMENT:** MC, VS, AX, checks
**BAR:** Beer, wine, liquor **TAKEOUT:** Yes **ACCESS:** &
Full access

The question is, how can Aldo's still be considered one of Cleveland's best-kept secrets when the restaurant has been enthusiastically reviewed by *Northern Ohio Live, Cleveland* magazine, the *Plain Dealer, Currents,* and the *Akron Beacon Journal*? But that's how folks at nearby American Greetings corporate headquarters and food aficionados from all over (some of whom say they come three or four times a month) describe this intimate little place.

Tucked inconspicuously behind a nondescript facade in a six-store strip mall (part of the Memphis-Ridge business district), Aldo's serves traditional, but never standard, Italian fare. Each forkful is to be savored, and every meal is really a celebration of the joys of good food. On any given night, the 13-14 specials could include bruschetta with roasted peppers and bocconcini, pasta fagiole, spezzatino di vitelle (veal stew), crepes stuffed with veal in basil sauce with escarole, and tripe in fresh tomato sauce. Kitchen skills are especially evident when it comes to pasta, seafood, and veal dishes.

The décor is modern, but the Zappa family photos on the wall lend a homey touch. It's painfully small, seating just 35. If you have to wait for a table, your only option is to stand in the narrow entryway, but no one seems to mind, and

newcomers chat with Aldo regulars. Customers, some in sweatshirts, some in suits and silk, call out greetings to Aldo, who often stops and visits, and everyone ends up feeling like a guest in his home rather than a customer. Service is impeccable and at the same time friendly. This is a place you'll want to remember. More than likely, they'll remember you, too.

## Anthony's

☎ (216) 791-0700

CITY: **Cleveland** AREA: **Near East Side**
ATMOSPHERE: **Relaxed** COST: $$$$$

**ADDRESS:** 12018 Mayfield Rd.
**HOURS:** Mon–Thu 11 a.m.–9 p.m., Fri–Sat
11 a.m.–11 p.m., Sun 11 a.m.–9 p.m.
**RESERVATIONS:** Not taken **PAYMENT:** MC, VS, AX,
DIS **BAR:** None **TAKEOUT:** Yes **ACCESS:** & Full
access

Not much décor or service but plenty of good food to enjoy on-site or take home. For dining on the premises, order at the counter, pay, carry your food to the table yourself, and throw away your own plastic place setting when you're done. Take your time or get in and out in a hurry, linger over a hot meal or inhale a slice or three of pizza.

The lunch menu changes daily—there's always a special and a selection of veal, chicken, and sausage dishes, plus pasta, meatballs, subs, sandwiches, stromboli, and salads. Try the grilled pesto chicken panini: warm ciabatta bread stuffed with basil-dressed chicken that qualifies as a complete meal. Turn it into a multicourse event with an Italian pastry or some real gelato (Italian ice cream that packs more creamy flavor in every spoonful than its American cousin) for dessert and a cup of freshly brewed espresso or cappuccino.

The atmosphere is self-serve relaxed, so don't hesitate to bring young lunchers who haven't quite gotten up to speed in the table manners department. Expect to mingle with neighborhood residents, CWRU students, and folks who work in University Circle. Make Sunday morning special with a breakfast panini or a frittata (Italian-style omelet). A few small tables outdoors on the sidewalk, weather permitting, are perfect for enjoying a cannoli and a cup of cappuccino. Meatballs, lasagna, manicotti, and pizza are all available for takeout along with a variety of subs and cold sandwiches.

The catering end of the business offers a special menu of party trays and entrées to choose from, including chicken Marsala, cavatelli, and garlic-roasted potatoes with sausage and peppers. Remember that parking is always tricky in this old and densely populated neighborhood.

## Aroma Ristorante

☎ (440) 933-4360

CITY: **Avon Lake**    AREA: **Farther West**
ATMOSPHERE: **Casual**    COST: **$$$**$$

**ADDRESS:** 33481 Lake Rd.
**HOURS:** Dinner Mon–Sat 5–10 p.m.; Lunch Thu–Fri 11:30 a.m.–2:30 p.m.; closed Sun
**RESERVATIONS:** Recommended **PAYMENT:** MC, VS, DIS **BAR:** Beer, wine, liquor **TAKEOUT:** Yes
**ACCESS:** ♿ Full access *Not recommended for children

Mario Marotta spells the name of his restaurant "Aroma." And it's appropriate because to walk in is to be swept up in a profusion of wonderful smells, a glorious mix of garlic, basil, rosemary, aged cheeses, and slow-simmered sauces and stews. But he could just as well have called it "Ah Roma," because he has managed to create a little bit of Italy in this western suburb. Marotta comes from the southern town of Salerno. He prepares regional dishes from Lazio,

Friuli, Abruzzo, Calabria, Liguria, and the rest of the country. That means diners can enjoy dishes such as calamaretti picanti all Venezia, which translates as sautéed squid with tomatoes, garlic, and herbs; spaghetti San Remo, made with sun-dried tomatoes, zucchini, and roasted pine nuts; saltimbocca alla Romana, a sage- and wine-flavored veal scallopine; and formaggi regionali con miele di Acacia, a dessert of provincial Italian cheeses, honey, and aged balsamic vinegar.

The menu is packed with traditional and creative renditions of pasta, fish, and meat, and choosing what to eat is no easy task. Should it be a homey bowl of escarole and beans in tomato Parmesan broth; fettucine in cream sauce with prosciutto and peas; rigatoni and sausage made with broccoli florets; spinach gnocchi with mascarpone; or something more substantial like osso bucco, pork tenderloin with fresh figs, salmon with pesto? To further complicate matters, there are nightly specials—crabmeat ravioli with basil cream, grouper in a caper lemon sauce, a veal chop done in Barolo, a risotto of the day. Happily, the price of a generously portioned entrée includes a salad and vegetables. This, I think, justifies splurging on appetizers—the stuzzicherie della casa offers a selection of the house's best—a bottle of really good wine from his all-Italian list, or an ever-changing array of desserts.

Little touches add to the overall enjoyment. Bread is always fresh and crusty, and the butter is studded with bits of green herbs. Service is professional: smooth, attentive, and unobtrusive—a level uncommon at such a reasonably priced venue. The pretty space is long and narrow and resembles a wine cellar with windows. A couple of tables in the tiny bar area provide seating for smokers, and there are tables outside in good weather. The quality of the food, atmosphere, and service make me feel as though I've found my way into a little corner of Italian heaven. The strip-mall location, set back and separated from the road by a vast parking lot, and the bait and tackle shop next door are reminders that it's in Avon Lake. The result is an interesting juxtaposition of realities. The name is emblazoned in bright yellow neon out front, making it easy to locate.

## Arrabiata's

☎ (440) 442-2600

CITY: **Mayfield Heights** AREA: **East Side**

ATMOSPHERE: **Casual** COST: **$$$**$$

**ADDRESS:** 6169 Mayfield Rd.
**HOURS:** Mon 11:30 a.m.–2:30 p.m. & 5–9 p.m., Tue–Thu 11:30 a.m.–2:30 p.m. & 4:30–10 p.m., Fri 11:30 a.m.–2:30 p.m. & 4:30–11 p.m., Sat 5–11 p.m., Sun 5–9 p.m. **RESERVATIONS:** Taken, recommended for groups of 5+
**PAYMENT:** MC, VS, AX, DIS **BAR:** Beer, liquor
**TAKEOUT:** Yes **ACCESS:** ♿ Full access

What do you get when two sets of brothers with Italian roots go into the restaurant business together? Sibling rivalry? No. A food fight? Maybe, but if so, it's always after hours and nobody's 'fessing up. Escarola fagioli, fettucine alfredo, and zuppa di pesce? Yes. When the former owners of Arrabiata's put it up for sale in 1998, John and Nick D'Angelo and Joe and Paul Rini decided to buy. These guys have known each other since first grade (currently all are in their 20s); they grew up together, and each has worked here at one time or another. Nick got additional restaurant experience in Florida, while Joe honed his skills in New York, and they run the front of the house. Their younger brothers John and Paul (do they sing as well as cook? I ask myself) studied with Loretta Paganini at her cooking school in Hudson, and they man the kitchen. They repainted and redecorated. The result is a sleek, modern-looking space done up in black, white, and eggplant purple, where people can expect to be comfortable and eat well.

The kitchen has a set of styles, culinary templates if you will, that are applied to a variety of pasta, meats, fish, and vegetables. If the veal or chicken is D'Agnese, it's served in a lemon butter sauce with artichoke hearts, but if it's a cacciatore, it will be in a plum tomato sauce with onions, green peppers, and mushrooms. Linguine, rigatoni, calamari, shrimp, a clam and mussel combination, and orange roughy get the "house special Arrabiata treatment"—a spicy marinara sauce studded with imported olives, cherry and banana peppers, and onions. Eggplant comes a la rollatini (rolled and stuffed), and so does chicken. Eggplant Parmigiana is a dish unto itself, but chicken and veal Sicilian style come with the stuff as a topping. You can get your beef (a filet mignon) done Arrabiata, D'Agnese, Cacciatore, or Pasqualina (with mushrooms, artichokes, roasted red peppers, and a Marsala wine sauce; a boneless breast of chicken is done this way, too).

The guys are enthusiastic hosts. "We want to make sure all our customers leave with full stomachs and smiles on their faces," says Nick D'Angelo. Kids with small appetites or picky tastes can get a side order of pasta as their entrée (with or without meatballs or sausage) or a couple of other child-friendly choices. The bar seats 12, and there's a nice selection of wines, domestic and imported, by the glass and the bottle. Private catering services are offered, and the restaurant is available for private parties when it is not open to the public. It's located in a shopping strip at the corner of Mayfield and Commonwealth, close to I-271, with ample parking.

## Arrabiata's
☎ (440) 835-9100
CITY: **Bay Village**  AREA: **West Side**
ATMOSPHERE: **Casual**  COST: $$$$$

ADDRESS: 600 Dover Center Rd.
HOURS: Lunch Mon–Fri 11:30 a.m.–3 p.m.;
Dinner Mon 3–9 p.m., Tue–Thu 3–10 p.m., Fri
3–11 p.m., Sun 4–8 p.m. RESERVATIONS: Taken,
recommended for groups of 5+ PAYMENT: MC,
VS, DIS BAR: Beer, wine, liquor TAKEOUT: Yes
ACCESS: ♿ Full access

See listing for Arrabiata's on Mayfield
Rd. in Mayfield Heights for more information.

## The Baricelli Inn
☎ (216) 791-6500
CITY: **Cleveland**  AREA: **Near East Side**
ATMOSPHERE: **Casual**  COST: $$$$$

ADDRESS: 2203 Cornell Rd.
HOURS: Mon–Thu 5–10 p.m., Fri–Sat 5–11 p.m.
RESERVATIONS: Recommended PAYMENT: MC, VS,
AX, DIS BAR: Beer, wine, liquor TAKEOUT: No
ACCESS: ♿ Full access *Not recommended for
children

When owner and acclaimed chef
Paul Minnillo first opened The Baricelli
Inn in December 1985, it was a formal,
fine-dining restaurant serving creative
European-American fare. But in 2007
he decided the times called for something else. It's more of a bistro now with
a selection of affordable options, and
the kitchen spotlights Minnillo's family
heritage and the rustic Italian cuisine
he loves. The menu and the ingredients
are seasonally driven, and local produce
is used when available, including tomatoes Minnillo grows at home and in a
garden plot in a corner of the restaurant
parking lot. No surprise that pasta is a
key element.
There's always some version of ravioli, gnudi (soft little dumplings made
with sheep's milk ricotta), and linguini
available, along with the classic bucatini
all' amatriciana—thick, hollow tubes
of spaghetti, real San Marzano tomatoes, and crispy bits of pancetta. Two
"boards" are ideal for sharing: One features cured meats such as prosciutto,
culatello, and coppa, the other artisanal
cheeses aged on the premises. (Cheeses
can be purchased at the Baricelli Cheese
Shop, listed elsewhere in this chapter.)
Find a bottle of wine to go with them
from the extensive list.

In 1947, Paul's father, the child of immigrants from Abruzzi, opened a small
trattoria and bar in the Cleveland neighborhood known as Little Italy. Young
Paul grew up helping in the kitchen and
went on to become an award-winning
chef who appeared in PBS's *Signature
Chef* series. The Baricelli Inn, which
has lovely overnight accommodations
upstairs, is housed in a turn-of-the-cen-
tury mansion just a few blocks from his
father's old place. There are four "parlor" dining rooms and a fifth on an enclosed porch, ideal for private dinners.
Tables in these charming and intimate
spaces are dressed in white linens and
adorned with sparkling glassware. A
well-trained wait staff is always attentive
and efficient. The secluded garden patio
is one of the city's most lovely outdoor
dining spots. A large lot just for guests
means no need to be concerned about
parking.

## Bovalino's Italian Ristorante

☎ (440) 892-9300

CITY: **Westlake**   AREA: **West Side**
ATMOSPHERE: **Casual**   COST: $$$$$

**ADDRESS:** 27828 Center Ridge Rd.
**HOURS:** Mon–Thu 4–9 p.m., Fri–Sat 4–10 p.m.;
closed Sun; will open for lunch meetings or
parties of 10+ **RESERVATIONS:** Taken, Fri–Sat
until 7 p.m. only **PAYMENT:** MC, VS **BAR:** Beer,
wine, liquor **TAKEOUT:** Yes **ACCESS:** & Full access

A green awning helps you identify this freestanding brick building on a residential stretch of road as a restaurant and not a home. It is an utterly sweet little place, and driving up I had the same feeling I remember from years ago, in Italy, when we'd unexpectedly stumbled upon a delightful restaurant in the middle of nowhere. Inside, green plants hang in leafy profusion from latticework suspended from the ceiling, and it's as though you've come into a garden, an outdoor trattoria perhaps, somewhere in southern Italy.

The town of Bovalino, for which the restaurant was named, is in Calabria, at the southern tip of Italy. Owner Lori Williams uses some of their family recipes. The kitchen turns out more than 60 different Italian dishes that reflect southern and northern cuisine; two additional daily specials might be anything from chicken Milanese to lobster-filled ravioli. Lori is in there every morning, starting the sauces that will simmer all day, and she won't let anyone else prepare them. She also makes fresh pizza dough daily.

Portions are huge, enough for the next day's lunch if you have an average appetite. The menu offers a hand-picked selection of imported and domestic wines, red and white, and an Italian beer. There's room for 40 diners and, in warm weather, additional seating outside in a small fenced-in courtyard adjacent to the parking lot.

## Bruno's Ristorante

☎ (216) 961-7087

CITY: **Cleveland**   AREA: **Near West Side**
ATMOSPHERE: **Casual**   COST: $$$$$

**ADDRESS:** 2644 W. 41st St.
**HOURS:** Mon–Thu 11 a.m.–10 p.m., Fri 11
a.m.–11 p.m., Sat 4–11 p.m., Sun 4–9 p.m.
**RESERVATIONS:** Taken, recommended on
weekends and for groups of 4+ on weekdays
**PAYMENT:** MC, VS, AX **BAR:** Beer, wine
**TAKEOUT:** Yes **ACCESS:** & Full access

Owner Bruno DiSiena, former executive chef for the Cleveland Browns at their Berea facility, knows how to make patrons feel good about dining out and eating with gusto. His motto, printed on the menu, is, "He who eats well is very close to God." His operating philosophy, also on the menu, reads, "Make love to your stomach with these specials." How much more encouragement do you need?

Bruno, an attentive host, can usually be found in the dining room, going from table to table to make sure people are happy and getting all they want. But he always has time to pause among those he knows—and he seems to know many of his customers—to offer handshakes to the men and kisses, on the cheeks of course, to the ladies. This friendly, welcoming atmosphere is echoed in the space itself, which achieves that special combination of cozy and classy. It's a small restaurant, seating about 40 in a single room decorated in contemporary style, using an off-white and maroon color scheme, with dark wood furniture and subdued lighting. There's a beautiful old bar—a part of the original décor that thankfully did not fall victim to the renovation—that gleams with new life and a high gloss, with stools for 12; a comfortable waiting area; a private dining room, and plans for an outdoor patio and installation of a brick oven.

Some of the dishes are familiar, although I must admit I think they sound more glamorous and enticing in Italian, which is how they appear on the menu (with translations and descriptions underneath): I'd rather eat Salciccia Panini than a sausage sandwich, Zuppa di Sposa than wedding soup, and Pesce del Giorno than fish of the day. The kitchen offers a basic selection of the classics: chicken, veal, and eggplant Parmesan; spaghetti; masticoli; ravioli; lasagna; gnocchi; calamari; and pizza, plus some specialties such as vitello ala carciofi (veal and artichokes in marsala cream sauce), Bruno's Famous Fettucini ala Pescatore (pasta with seafood in a marinara sauce), and bistecca al funghetto (filet of beef in a wine sauce with mushrooms). The pepe al banana (a baked hot pepper stuffed with sausage) is a favorite appetizer, though I'd go for the more unusual baked mussels on the half shell every time.

Portions are large enough to make every traditional Italian grandmother happy. Desserts to go along with your cappuccino and espresso don't appear on the menu, but don't let that fool you—just ask your server. Many of the desserts are made by Bruno's mother, who is known for her tiramisu and cheesecake. The wine list offers an interesting variety of reds and whites, and the bar stocks three imported Italian beers.

You can park across the street at a car wash owned by Bruno's brothers. At lunchtime leave the keys and get your car cleaned while you clean your plate. In the evenings the lot is guarded. Bruno's is located in a residential neighborhood, easy to spot by virtue of its brick facade and green awning sporting the place's name. There's a separate entrance near the back of the building

for picking up carryout orders. Full service in-house, and off-premise catering is available.

## Bucci's

☎ (440) 331-5157

CITY: **Rocky River**    AREA: **West Side**
ATMOSPHERE: **Casual**    COST: **$$$**$$

ADDRESS: 19373 Hilliard Rd.
HOURS: Tue–Thu 4–9 p.m., Fri–Sat 4–10 p.m., Sun 4–9 p.m.; closed Mon **RESERVATIONS:** Not taken **PAYMENT:** MC, VS, AX, DIS **BAR:** Beer, wine **TAKEOUT:** Yes **ACCESS:** ♿ Full access

This is the original Bucci's, opened 30 years ago. A small, homey, intimate restaurant seating between 50 and 60 people, Bucci's specializes in central and southern Italian food. The ceiling has exposed beams, and the pastel-toned wallpaper features classic scenes of Italian peasant life: vineyards, farms, and villages. The lighting is pleasantly soft, and candles glow on each table. The bread basket brought to the table by fast and friendly servers includes regular Italian bread, fat-free ciabatta bread, and freshly made garlic butter. Entrées, which are large, come to the table piping hot. There's always a homemade soup of the day, pasta primavera made with angel hair and a light blush sauce, and beef funghetto (tenderloin in wine sauce). They also do pizza and all the classic pasta dishes (with smaller side orders available for children under 12), plus steak, chicken, veal, and seafood. And if you still have room, there's spumoni, homemade cannoli, and tiramisu.

## Bucci's
☎ (440) 826-4500
CITY: **Berea**   AREA: **Southwest**
ATMOSPHERE: **Dressy**   COST: $$$$$

**ADDRESS:** One Berea Commons
**HOURS:** Mon–Thu 11:30 a.m.–10 p.m.,
Fri–Sat 11:30 a.m.–11 p.m.; closed Sun
**RESERVATIONS:** Taken, recommended on
weekends **PAYMENT:** MC, VS, AX, DIS **BAR:** Beer,
wine, liquor **TAKEOUT:** Yes **ACCESS:** ᴛ Limited
*Not recommended for children

Some of the windows of this comfortable, pleasant restaurant overlook the entrance to the Metroparks' Mill Stream Run Reservation. Others look out onto Berea's historic downtown triangle. Wherever the maitre d' seats you, you'll quickly realize that this is the sort of place where you settle back into the quiet, intimate reading-room atmosphere and enjoy the view. Shortly after you're seated, fresh bread and rolls and flavored butter will arrive at the table. The kitchen consistently turns out a good selection of Italian favorites. The ravioli, cavatelli, and gnocchi are homemade. Some of their more unusual offerings include angel hair pasta with baby squid and tricolored peppers, and chicken sautéed with capers and fresh herbs in a brown sauce with balsamic vinegar and lemon. This second Bucci's is more formal than the original. Think of eating here as an occasion, even if you don't have anything special to celebrate. Dress up a bit, let the subdued lighting set the mood, and take your time, because this is a place you choose when you want to appreciate a well-served, well-prepared meal eaten in good company.

## Carrie Cerino's Ristorante
☎ (440) 237-3434
CITY: **North Royalton**   AREA: **Southwest**
ATMOSPHERE: **Casual**   COST: $$$$$

**ADDRESS:** 8922 Ridge Rd.
**HOURS:** Lunch Tue–Fri 11:30 a.m.–2:30 p.m.;
Dinner Tue–Thu 4–9 p.m., Fri–Sat 4–10 p.m.,
Sun 1–6 p.m.; only open on Mon during
December; closed between lunch and
dinner; lounge open until 1 a.m. (appetizers
only) **RESERVATIONS:** Taken, recommended on
weekends **PAYMENT:** MC, VS, DIS **BAR:** Beer,
wine, liquor **TAKEOUT:** Yes **ACCESS:** ᴛ Full access

This has been a family business since it opened in 1962. That's when Carrie Cerino, an immigrant from the Umbria region of Italy, bought the place. Built around 1915 as a home on a country estate, it was later converted into a restaurant by a German family. They gave it a Swiss Chalet look that is still in evidence, along with the original hearth, beams, and stained-glass lighting fixtures. There are three dining rooms that together seat around 235. One features barn wood and fieldstone; another, known as PaPa's Garden, is a bright, window-filled space, once the front porch but now fully enclosed. Banquet facilities were added on in 1972, and eight crystal chandeliers designed by Carrie and made in Italy give the main ballroom a timeless elegance. Downstairs in the basement, reputed to have once housed a speakeasy, is a lounge complete with bar, booths, stage, and dance floor where musicians play every weekend.

This is a "scratch" kitchen, which means they make their own stocks, sauces, and sausage. All the pasta is handmade and hand cut, so even an order of cavatelli or gnocchi is out of the ordinary. Topped with MaMa's famous white sauce, an unbelievably rich combination of whipped butter and

Parmesan cheese, it qualifies as a feast. Italian-menu staples are the heart and soul of the kitchen: wedding soup, fried calamari with spicy marinara, lemony veal piccata, and chicken Marsala. But for something really special, order spaghetti alla carbonara. A masterpiece of simplicity, it's made with guanciale, a unique dry-cured jowl bacon, and eggs from free-range Aracauna chickens raised nearby on Breychak Farms. Raw and intensely flavorful yolks are tossed with the hot pasta, which "cooks" them, along with Romano and Parmesan cheeses to form the ultimate sauce. Other house specialties include artichokes aglio, tenderloin funghetto (beef in a brown mushroom sauce), and Tuscan chicken, featuring caramelized onions and a balsamic glaze. There's also an in-house bakery, which produces all the breads and desserts served in the restaurant.

Unless you live in the area, it takes a special effort to get here. The location is out-of-the-way and near no other entertainment venues. But it's worth the trip. Carrie Cerino would no doubt be proud and pleased to see what her descendents have done with the restaurant and the recipes she created.

## Ferrante Winery & Ristorante

☎ (440) 466-8466

CITY: **Geneva**   AREA: **Farther East**
ATMOSPHERE: **Casual**   COST: $$$$$

**ADDRESS:** 5585 SR 307
**HOURS:** Wed–Thu noon–8 p.m., Fri–Sat noon–10 p.m., Sun 1–6 p.m.; restaurant closed Mon–Tue, open for wine sales 10 a.m.–5 p.m.
**RESERVATIONS:** Not taken **PAYMENT:** MC, VS, AX, DIS, checks **BAR:** Wine **TAKEOUT:** Yes **ACCESS:** ♿ Full access

This is a four-generation story that begins with a woman and a vineyard. Great-grandma Ferrante bought land in Geneva for growing grapes in the early years of the 20th century. Her kids started a winery in Collinwood in 1937, trucking the grapes in from the country. In the '70s, her grandchildren, Peter and Anthony, relocated the winery to the Geneva vineyards. By the 1980s, the family had a little restaurant there, too. Over time, most of Peter's eight kids got involved in the family business. In 1994 a fire destroyed the restaurant, but the disaster was turned into an opportunity. A new, bigger and better restaurant was built, and the winery has been transformed into one of the most beautiful and popular dining destinations in Harpersfield Township. The spacious dining room has high cathedral ceilings, a multilevel design, and huge windows that look out over the vineyards and flood the space with natural light, augmented by clerestory windows on the second floor. At sunset, the room is filled with a golden glow.

The restaurant is comfortable, casual, and affordable. With seating for 200 and numerous semiprivate areas, it's an ideal place for birthdays, anniversaries, reunions, and special events. The Ferrantes treat regulars like family. Acting as hostess, Carmel Ferrante often greets guests with hugs, kisses, and questions about kids and parents. The food is also family-style—antipasto plates (Italian meats, cheeses, and bread) and classics such as lasagna, spaghetti and meatballs, linguine with clam sauce, seafood alfredo, pasta primavera, capellini with pesto, veal with wine and mushrooms, and chicken in a red wine marinara sauce with peppers and cappicola. Specials reflect a more creative approach, especially with fresh fish. The tomato sauce is so tasty you'll be tempted to use your fingers to get the last drops out of the bowl and into your mouth. But such behavior would be forgiven here, and even the kinds of messes kids make are cleaned up with good humor. Portions are large (there is a kids' menu), often leaving all but those with prodigious appetites too full for dessert. But the Italian bread pudding with Riesling wine sauce should not be missed. My suggestion: If necessary quit eating before you've finished, box up your entrée leftovers, and enjoy the *dolce*. A wine suggestion for every entrée is part of the menu, and a separate wine list gives detailed descriptions of each one on their list. Sampler trays offer a variety of vintages.

There are three covered pavilions, a small lake, and seating for 80 outside, where wine is always served. On weekdays, everything on the lunch and dinner menus is available on the patio, but on Fridays and Saturdays, only selected items can be ordered. Bands play in the summer, and there's room for dancing. Another, more intimate garden space is located at the front of the building. It's connected to the gift shop, where wine is sold by the bottle and case. There's also a wine bar and tasting room equipped with a fireplace, small tables, and comfortable chairs. Reservations are not accepted (except for private parties) because people tend to take their time. "Customers," says Carmel, "often come from more than 30 miles away. They're in no hurry to leave because they enjoy themselves so much." Visit yourself, and you'll understand why. Information and directions at www. ferrantewinery.com.

## Frankie's Italian Cuisine
☎ (440) 734-8646
CITY: **North Olmsted**   AREA: **West Side**
ATMOSPHERE: **Casual**   COST: **$$**$$

**ADDRESS:** 4641 Great Northern Blvd.
**HOURS:** Mon–Thu 11 a.m.–11 p.m., Fri–Sat 11 a.m.–midnight, Sun 1–10 p.m. **RESERVATIONS:** Taken, only for groups of 6+ **PAYMENT:** MC, VS, AX, DIS **BAR:** Beer, wine, liquor **TAKEOUT:** Yes **ACCESS:** ☒ Full access

Established in 1967, Frankie's is a midsized restaurant that families flock to because the atmosphere is casual, and the food, served in generous quantities, is the kind almost nobody can resist: veal Parmesan, lasagna, spaghetti with marinara sauce, meatball and sausage sandwiches, and hand-tossed pizza. The garlic bread is worth a special mention. The dishes on this menu are meant to satisfy rather than surprise, and food is prepared and presented "mamma's kitchen–style" without flash or nouveau anything. But the sauce is so popular they sell it by the quart, meatballs by the dozen, lasagna by the tray, and pizzas by the sheet for takeout. The restaurant seats about 95 in a pleasant, modern setting, and the kitchen will cook for private parties in the restaurant in a room that can easily accommodate 10–30. They do off-site catering as well. Jeans are acceptable here, but you wouldn't feel out of place if you dressed up a bit to make your own out-to-eat occasion special. A six-item kids' menu for the under-10 set and some entrées like chicken piccata and veal à la Frankie are geared to those who'd rather eat light.

## Frankie's Italian Cuisine
☎ (440) 892-0064
CITY: **Westlake**   AREA: **West Side**
ATMOSPHERE: **Casual**   COST: **$$**$$

**ADDRESS:** 25939 Detroit Rd.
**HOURS:** Mon 5–10 p.m., Tue–Fri 11 a.m.–10 p.m., Sat noon–10 p.m., Sun 4 p.m.–9 p.m.
**RESERVATIONS:** Taken, only for groups of 6+
**PAYMENT:** MC, VS, AX, DIS **BAR:** Beer, wine, liquor **TAKEOUT:** Yes **ACCESS:** ☒ Full access

The first Frankie's, in North Olmsted, was so successful that in 1986 this second incarnation opened in Westlake's Williamsburg Square Center. (It's a strip mall, so parking is never a problem.)

Easy to reach via I-90 (Columbia Road exit), this Frankie's is a bit larger than the other, comfortably seating up to 150 in a pleasant, well-lit dining room decorated in a contemporary style with plants and wooden ceiling fans. (For more information, see the previous entry for the original Frankie's, North Olmsted.)

## Gavi's

☎ **(440) 942-8008**

CITY: **Willoughby**    AREA: **East Side**
ATMOSPHERE: **Dressy**    COST: **$$$$$**

**ADDRESS:** 38257 Glenn Ave.
**HOURS:** Tue–Fri 11:30 a.m.–10 p.m., Sat 4:30–11 p.m.; closed Sun–Mon **RESERVATIONS:** Recommended **PAYMENT:** MC, VS, AX, DIS, checks **BAR:** Beer, wine, liquor **TAKEOUT:** Yes
**ACCESS:** ♿ Full access

The setting at Gavi's is a great example of the current architectural aesthetic that favors recycling. Once a power house, the 100-year-old building has taken on a new identity as an elegant, upscale, 80-seat restaurant on a side street in the center of downtown. The original interior brick walls and high, wood-beamed ceiling remain, complemented by track lighting, floral carpeting, potted plants, and a pastel color scheme of salmon pink and mint green. Napkins are cloth, upholstered chairs designed for comfort have an opulent look, and ornate pieces of antique furniture function as service stations. All these design elements work together to create a sumptuous backdrop suitable for fine dining.

The kitchen strikes an impressive first note by sending out hot, crusty, homemade bread after you're seated, along with pinzimonio, a bowl of beautifully arranged fresh vegetables. The focus is on country-style cooking, but peasants never had it this good. The offerings, some of which change seasonally, can include imported rack of Australian lamb, a filet mignon of milk-fed veal tenderloin, rosemary-scented fettucine tossed with hot sausage and cannelloni beans, and chicken cacciatore. The chef likes to alter the menu periodically to keep things interesting. If you select a seafood entrée, the fish is likely to have been flown in from Seattle and brought to the restaurant from the airport by courier. If you select cavatelli or caramelli pasta, it will be handmade. The caramelli is filled with a mix of veal, spinach, and mascarpone cheese (a thick, rich, moist cow's milk cream cheese with a consistency that ranges from that of clotted or sour cream to butter) and served with a roasted tomato sauce. The cavatelli is served in a tomato sauce made with ground veal, mortadella dotted with pistachios, and pancetta.

Check out what's happening in the kitchen from a seat at the bar, where you can also order a glass of wine, choosing from the tremendous selection that restaurant owners Mary and David Gromelski have assembled. If you're not schooled in the wine arts, David, a graduate of a sommelier training program, will be glad to advise. In fact, his enthusiasm for wine is the basis of the restaurant's name: Gavi is a major wine-producing town in Italy. The bar area is also a good spot for taking a peek at the desserts, displayed in a refrigerated case located here. A display tray is also brought to your table. Mary's mother, Adele Busetto, who is from Venice, makes the cannoli and the tiramisu, always available, and there's a rotating selection of other lavish pastry confections. Service is accommodating; you can ask for half-size portions or half-and-half combinations of two items that call to your taste buds. November 2005 marked the 10-year anniversary of this popular establishment. A private room is available for parties of up to 40, and the entire place can be reserved for special events on Sundays and Mondays.

## Giuseppe's Ristorante
☎ (330) 467-1108

CITY: **Northfield Center** AREA: **Southeast**
ATMOSPHERE: **Casual** COST: $$$$$

**ADDRESS:** 32 W. Aurora Rd. (Rte. 82)
**HOURS:** Lunch Tue–Fri 11:30 a.m.–3 p.m.;
Dinner Tue–Thu 5–10 p.m., Fri–Sat 5–11 p.m.,
Sun 3–8:30 p.m.; closed Mon **RESERVATIONS:**
Taken, for groups of 5+ **PAYMENT:** MC, VS, DIS
**BAR:** Beer, wine, liquor **TAKEOUT:** Yes **ACCESS:** ♿
Full Access

This is a white-cloth restaurant, even at lunchtime, but prices are less than you'd expect for such fine food and service. Chef/owner Giuseppe Ripa, who hails from Naples, makes everything himself, from the hearty minestrone soup and rich, earthy Sicilian eggplant caponata to the marinara sauce, salad dressings, and cannoli. He has been cooking since he was 14, and worked at a number of local places before opening this one in 2003. He does things the hard way—from scratch—because it's what he was taught and what he knows is right.

Giuseppe and his wife, Rosaria, who handles the dining room, have re-created a comfortable little Neapolitan-style cafe here in this out-of-the-way urban outpost. It's a genuine family business. The couple's son and daughter lend a hand as needed, and whenever Giuseppe's mom comes to visit from Italy she does a turn or two in the kitchen. The dinner menu is focused and ambitious. There are 10 antipasti, among them salmon carpaccio, mussels in garlic oil, white wine, and tomatoes, and a most unusual—and delicious—tender pan-seared calamari steak. The Ripas are proud of every-

thing they make, especially their veal and fish dishes. They consider the seafood risotto their signature dish and say they have a customer who comes once a week, every week, just for that. Also worth noting are the penne alla amatriciana—pasta with bacon, peas, and onions in a roasted tomato sauce; ravioli in walnut cream; linguine with lobster tail and brandy; pork scallopini in vermouth butter; and the seafood stew (cioppino).

An abbreviated version of this menu and smaller portions are available at lunch, along with four sandwiches including one made with prosciutto, mozzarella, and pesto and another with sautéed spinach and portobello mushrooms. The wine list is naturally heavy on Italians and has some good and reasonably priced bottles. They also keep Peroni beer on ice, San Pellegrino water, and two bottled Italian soft drinks—lemon-flavored Limonata and orange Aranciata, both less sweet than the American versions. The main part of the L-shaped, 42-seat dining room is one step up from the entrance. If you need one of the few tables that don't require climbing be sure to reserve it in advance. There's even a tiny four-stool bar tucked away in back where you can wait for a table. The restaurant is located next to a fire station in a small strip of shops with plenty of parking.

## Guarino's Restaurant
☎ (216) 231-3100

CITY: **Cleveland** AREA: **Near East Side**
ATMOSPHERE: **Dressy** COST: $$$$$

**ADDRESS:** 12309 Mayfield Rd.
**HOURS:** Mon–Thu 11:30 a.m.–10 p.m.,
Fri–Sat 11:30 a.m.–midnight, Sun 1–8 p.m.
**RESERVATIONS:** Taken, recommended on
weekends **PAYMENT:** MC, VS, AX, DIS **BAR:** Beer,
wine, liquor **TAKEOUT:** Yes **ACCESS:** ♿ Full access

According to Marilyn Guarino, the restaurant established in 1918 by her father-in-law, Vincenzo Guarino, now claims the honor of being the oldest continuously operating Italian restaurant in town—it celebrated its 50th anniversary in November 1997. It's not unusual for tour buses to stop here. The family used to live above the restaurant; now one floor has become a bed and breakfast, and another is a series of Victorian-style parlors where dinner is served to private parties of 2 to 50 people. For reservations, contact Nancy Phillips, Marilyn Guarino's business partner. Downstairs, the restaurant, which seats between 75 and 90, also has an antique Victorian motif. The food is primarily southern Italian with some northern influence. In addition to the standard selection of pasta dishes with a variety of sauces, the menu includes wedding soup, escargot (snails), saltimbocca (veal with prosciutto ham and cheese), and brasciole (a thin steak stuffed and rolled). The wine list offers a comprehensive selection. In warm weather, there's outdoor dining amid the grape and trumpet-flower vines that Vincenzo Guarino originally brought with him from Sicily. Valet parking available on weekends; otherwise use their lot adjacent to the restaurant.

## Gusto Ristorante Italiano
☎ (216) 791-9900
CITY: **Cleveland**   AREA: **Near East Side**
ATMOSPHERE: **Formal**   COST: **$$$$**$

ADDRESS: 12022 Mayfield Rd.
HOURS: Tue–Thu 5 p.m.–10 p.m., Fri–Sat 5 p.m.–11 p.m., Sun 5 p.m.–9:30 p.m.; closed Mon RESERVATIONS: Recommended PAYMENT: MC, VS, AX, DIS, checks BAR: Beer, wine, liquor TAKEOUT: Yes ACCESS: & None

The name's pronounced goos-toe. It means good taste, and those two words

perfectly describe the aesthetics of place and presentation and the experience of eating here.

The kitchen is animated by a desire to be creative without ever straying too far from the fundamentals of northern Italian cooking. Preparation of familiar dishes raises the bar on simple things. Campanelle pasta is served with walnut pesto; cavatelli with wild boar sauce; and the braciola features moist Bershire pork loins topped with melted Gorgonzola and drizzled with a port wine glaze. Instead of being breaded and fried, calamari are sautéed to a buttery softness and served in lightly herbed Chardonnay reduction sauce that just begs for bread to sop up every drop. Uncommon dishes are nightly fare, so expect such things as veal porterhouse, braised lamb shank, ravioli with a lobster mascarpone filling and a sauce of truffle, tomato, and claw meat. The menu changes periodically, but what won't change is the commitment to regional fare done with flair.

The restaurant is jointly owned and managed by Ricardo Salerno and his son Fabio. After a visit to Verona, Fabio, who also serves as sous chef, told his father that eating there was just like eating back in Cleveland at their place. And it doesn't hurt that many of the waiters are Italian, so they are able to discuss your options, for food that is, with proper pronunciation. Every time one of them says "tortellini in brodo," "osso bucco alla Fiorentino," or "vitello con carciofi e granchio," (veal, artichokes, and crab), it sounds like music.

Speaking of music, Ricardo's nightly stroll with his accordion is an enchanting touch. He's skilled, with a vast repertoire of standards literally at his fingertips, and his enthusiasm is clearly visible. Perhaps he opened a restaurant so he'd have a guaranteed audience. Women, he says, find it romantic, and it's not unknown for dancing to break out spontaneously. That's not easy, as tables are close together, but this intimacy adds to the very European ambience.

The buzz of conversation creates a kind of amiable surround sound, and it feels more like a gathering, a party really, than a disconnected bunch of strangers. If I didn't know better, I'd swear they hire a cast of actors to fill the 14 tables—it's that perfect a mix of couples, families, and friends. The main dining room, a step up from the little bar at the front of the house, is pretty, with walls the color of a Mediterranean sunset, gauzy swags of fabric to help define the space, and murals that seem to bring the outside in. There's a second equally attractive dining room, available for private gatherings and larger groups, and a brick-paved patio in back. Valet parking is a nice amenity. Even nicer are the hearty handshakes, back slaps, and kisses, on both cheeks of course, that Ricardo typically bestows on his guests as they depart.

## Jimmy Daddona's

☎ (440) 248-2444

CITY: **Solon**  AREA: **Farther East**
ATMOSPHERE: **Casual**  COST: **$$$**$$

ADDRESS: 6200 Enterprise Pkwy.
HOURS: Lunch Mon–Sat 11 a.m.–2 p.m.; Dinner Mon–Thu 4–10 p.m., Fri–Sun 4–11 p.m.
RESERVATIONS: Not taken  PAYMENT: MC, VS  BAR: Beer, wine  TAKEOUT: Yes  ACCESS: ♿ Full access

The *Cleveland Ethnic Eats* reader who first recommended this place wrote, "It's a very small restaurant—no reservations accepted. Expect a long wait on weekend evenings, but what better testimony?! Sinfully good."

That was a description of the old place that opened in 1988. Some things have changed since that was written. The restaurant found a bigger home. There are more tables, a patio, a bar,

and a waiting area so guests no longer have to sit in their cars, as they once did, until a spot opens up. Two things are the same. You can't make reservations unless you've got 12 or more in your party, and you may still have to mark time to get a seat, unless you go for a late lunch or an early dinner. The big attraction is the food. The choice is interesting, the flavors as authentic as you can get, and the portions so huge that plates resemble serving dishes. Everyone—those who go beyond full to stuffed, the large-sized, and even self-proclaimed starving teenagers—takes leftovers home. There are all the Italian standards, such as spaghetti, ravioli, lasagna, veal and eggplant Parmigiana, pizza, and chicken Marsala, plus some less common dishes: veal aglio e olio, breaded medallions of meat sautéed in olive oil with garlic, artichoke hearts, mushrooms, roasted red peppers, and spinach; pasta arrabiata, which is linguine topped with fresh tomatoes, capers, and basil; mussels or calamari marinara; and two or three different specials every night. They make their own bread, using their pizza dough and "twisting" it before baking with garlic, olive oil, and spices.

This is an unpretentious place favored by families, and the kitchen accommodates children with half portions. With advance notice, they'll also accommodate those with dietary restrictions. Service is quick and efficient but nonetheless attentive. The restaurant is named for the owner and chef, and most of his staff have been here as long as he has. Parking in the strip mall lot. There is a second location in Westlake at 29580 Center Ridge Road; 440-250-0075.

## Jimmy Daddona's
☎ (440) 250-0075
CITY: **Westlake**   AREA: **West Side**
ATMOSPHERE: **Casual**   COST: $$$$$

ADDRESS: 29580 Center Ridge Rd.
HOURS: Mon–Thu 4–10 p.m., Fri–Sat 4 p.m.–11
p.m. RESERVATIONS: Not taken PAYMENT: MC,
VS BAR: Beer, wine TAKEOUT: Yes ACCESS: &. Full
access

See listing for Jimmy Daddona's on
Enterprise Parkway in Solon for more
information.

## Johnny's Bar
☎ (216) 281-0055
CITY: **Cleveland**   AREA: **Near West Side**
ATMOSPHERE: **Formal**   COST: $$$$$

ADDRESS: 3164 Fulton Rd.
HOURS: Lunch Thu–Fri 11:30 a.m.–2:30 p.m.;
Dinner Mon–Thu 5–10 p.m., Fri–Sat 5–11
p.m.; closed Sun RESERVATIONS: Taken, for
groups of 4+ on Fri, Sat PAYMENT: MC, VS, AX
BAR: Beer, wine, liquor TAKEOUT: Yes ACCESS: &.
Limited *Not recommended for children

The *Zagat* survey described Johnny's, a sumptuous, upscale restaurant
that sits inconspicuously on a corner
in an aging blue-collar neighborhood,
as "outstanding in every way." Cleveland's own food experts and cookbook
authors Fred and Linda Griffith rank it
among the best in town. The place has a
genial, private-club ambience, a unique
and stunning décor, and unforgettable
northern Italian food prepared with an
innovative, continental flair. When the
three Santosuosso brothers took over
the place from their parents, they decided to re-create a bygone era; entering
their restaurant is like going back to the
1930s.
"We wanted a restaurant that looked
like a real restaurant from the old days,"
said Joe Santosuosso, "when food service was at its height and eating out
was an experience. The look is post-
Deco, pre-streamline, the same as New
York's Radio City Music Hall, and we
reproduced everything exactly, down
to the last detail of aging the color of
the wood." Those details include faux–
leopard skin carpeting, crisp linens, fine
china, wood paneling, original murals
painted on the walls, black leather banquettes, and a mahogany bar. There is
both a sense of humor and an elegance
in it all.
The food, however, is serious business, made for people who appreciate
and understand fine dining. The menu is
large, and there are a number of specials
each day featuring fish, veal, and pasta.
The potato gnocchi are made according
to Mamma Santosuosso's original recipe by Joe's aunt, and all the other pasta
is made fresh on the premises, too. In
their book *The Best of the Midwest*, the
Griffiths describe these pastas as "light
as air" and name the pasta puttanesca,
the angel hair with escargot, the mussels
marinara, the baked calamari, and the
veal tenderloin as standouts. In true Old
World style, tomatoes and fresh herbs
are grown out back. The walled-in garden also contains a patio with seven
tables and a bocce ball court.

## Johnny's Downtown
☎ (216) 623-0055
CITY: **Cleveland**   AREA: **Downtown**
ATMOSPHERE: **Dressy**   COST: $$$$$

ADDRESS: 1406 W. 6th St.
HOURS: Lunch Mon–Fri 11:30 a.m.–3 p.m.;
Dinner Mon–Thu 5–10:30 p.m., Fri–Sat
5–11:30 p.m., Sun 4–9 p.m. RESERVATIONS:
Recommended, required for groups of 4+
on Fri, Sat PAYMENT: MC, VS, AX BAR: Beer,
wine, liquor TAKEOUT: Yes ACCESS: &. Full access
*Not recommended for children

The menu at this second Johnny's, opened in 1993, is close to that at the original Johnny's on Fulton Road (see previous description), featuring pasta, veal, and fish. The main difference here is that preparation is less refined, more reminiscent of the rustic cuisine of Tuscany. The setting, however, is not a duplicate of the old place, though it is equally special, evoking images of the once-famous and stately Oak Room in New York's Plaza Hotel. There's plenty of highly polished mahogany; leather; heavy, high-backed, upholstered chairs; and snowy table linens. The handsome barroom, which is often crowded and lively, is separate from the dining room, and meals are served there, too. The dining area is lighter, brighter, and more spacious, offering panoramic views of downtown. The entire setting is sophisticated and chic and attracts a very urbane sort of clientele who come to see and be seen, enjoy the food, and listen to the music. A great place to bring out-of-towners and suburban visitors to give them a taste of just how suave this city can be.

## La Campagna
☎ (440) 871-1771
CITY: **Westlake**   AREA: **West Side**
ATMOSPHERE: **Relaxed**   COST: **$$$**$$

ADDRESS: 27337 Detroit Rd.
HOURS: Tue–Sat 5–9 p.m. RESERVATIONS:
Recommended PAYMENT: MC, VS, checks BAR:
Beer, wine TAKEOUT: Yes ACCESS: ⅗ Full Access
*Not recommended for children

It looks like a gourmet gift shop. Which it sort of is. Except five nights a week it's a 24-seat restaurant. But don't expect a menu. In fact nothing about this special little place is typical, standard, or even predictable. Here's the story. Chef/owner Carmella Fragassi, who learned everything she knows

about Italian cooking from her mother and two grandmothers, had a restaurant, but a fire put her out of business. When she reopened at this shopping mall location, the plan—for reasons too complicated to go into—was to concentrate on catering and gift baskets. But instead her occasional after-hours dinner service took on a life of its own, and so the tables set amid shelves filled with fancy teas, cookies, and vinegars are usually occupied. However, Fragassi doesn't want her creativity stifled by having to make the same thing night after night, so she cooks as the spirit moves her, deciding daily what she'll serve. It might be tomato bisque or a hearty old-fashioned bread and bean soup, plus lemony chicken piccata, stuffed veal scallopini, or a pork tenderloin with Gorgonzola and pears. Then again she could feel like doing her shrimp Orsara, named after the small mountain town near Bari where her family comes from, a three-sauce ravioli, or fresh tuna with pesto and angel hair pasta.

Almost everything, including the pasta, is cooked to order except long-simmering sauces and dishes like osso bucco. This means you have to wait in real time for her real food, so don't plan on a quick in and out. But it also makes it possible to address individual dietary needs or personal preferences. And if you crave something you tried on your last visit and she has the ingredients on hand, she'll be glad to whip it up even if it's not what she had planned. Bread is baked on the premises as are the desserts—traditional cookies, a crustless mascarpone cheesecake, chocolate torte, and tiramisu.

Because this is an unconventional operation, walk-ins, though welcome, are taking a risk. The place may be closed when it's supposed to be open (either somebody took it over for a private party or Carmella and her entire staff are catering an off-site event), or booked solid for the evening. She says reservations are always suggested. I'd say required if you want to avoid disappointment. La Campagna lacks a proper liquor license, so another quirky twist is that wine and beer are available, but only in two-ounce pours. Choose from the interesting international selection of both, buy by the bottle or the glass, and drink as much as you wish, but you must do it in tasting-size increments. Located in a nondescript strip mall, set back from the road, fronted by a field of parking spaces.

## La Gelateria
**☎ (216) 229-2636**
CITY: **Cleveland Heights**    AREA: **East Side**
ATMOSPHERE: **Relaxed**    COST: **$$**$$$

**ADDRESS:** 12421 Cedar Rd.
**HOURS:** Mon–Fri 4–9 p.m., Sat–Sun noon–9 p.m. (Open only Fri–Sat Jan–Mar; expanded hours in spring & summer) **RESERVATIONS:** Not taken **PAYMENT:** Cash only **BAR:** None **TAKEOUT:** Yes **ACCESS:** ♿ None

Ice cream is featured here, but not your ordinary frozen-milk sweet. This is the Italian version, and to my taste buds a far superior rendition of cool and luscious smoothness. And consider this comforting factoid—it's got less fat than its American counterpart. Less air, too. Hence the dense texture and intense flavor. Valerio Iorio, owner and chef at Valerio's in Little Italy and co-owner of Osteria di Valerio & Al downtown (see listings in this chapter), is the man who's made this indulgence available—late into the night, I'm happy to add. He imported the machinery, set up a gelato-making operation in the basement, and opened for business at the top of Cedar Hill in August 2002. He also makes delectable dairy-free sorbet and a sugar-free version.

The changing array of flavors, in both gelato and sorbet, is large and eclectic: fruits dominate, but are kept in their place by the likes of tiramisu, tartuffo (chocolate and hazelnut), zuppa Inglese (English trifle), pistachio, rum crunch, espresso, and stracciatella (think cookies-'n'-cream). In 2007, a wood-burning oven was installed for making Neopolitan-style pizzas (available only after 4 p.m.).

It's an utterly charming—and very blue (you'll see what I mean when you get there)—little spot and unlike anyplace else around. Seating for about 25 downstairs opposite the counter, the same number upstairs in a loft, which can be booked for private gatherings, plus a few outdoor tables and chairs on the sidewalk in good weather. On nice nights the al fresco overflow perches on the steps of adjacent buildings. Weekend nights in the summer often mean lines out the door, but service is swift and the wait never too long. It seems lots of people have been yearning for this Italian treat and didn't even know it. And they're willing to pay—these dips cost more than your average scoop, but as the marketing mantra goes, "You're worth it." More importantly, so's the gelato. Metered parking on the street, if you can find it, and more metered spots in a small garage around the corner. A second location at Legacy Village, 24401 Cedar Road in Lyndhurst; 216-297-9581. No pizza here and open later.

## La Gelateria
**☎ (216) 297-9581**
CITY: **Lyndhurst**    AREA: **East Side**
ATMOSPHERE: **Relaxed**    COST: **$$**$$$

**ADDRESS:** 24401 Cedar Rd.
**HOURS:** Mon–Sun 11 a.m.–10 p.m.
**RESERVATIONS:** Not taken **PAYMENT:** Cash only
**BAR:** None **TAKEOUT:** Yes **ACCESS:** ♿ Full access

See listing for La Gelateria on Cedar Rd. in Cleveland Heights for more information.

## Lago

☎ (216) 344-0547

CITY: **Cleveland**   AREA: **Near West Side**
ATMOSPHERE: **Casual**   COST: $$$$$

**ADDRESS:** 2221 Professor Ave.
**HOURS:** Mon–Thu 5–10:30 p.m., Fri–Sat 5–11:30 p.m., Sun 5–10 p.m. **RESERVATIONS:** Taken, recommended on weekends
**PAYMENT:** MC, VS, AX, DIS **BAR:** Beer, wine, liquor **TAKEOUT:** Yes **ACCESS:** ♿ Full access
*Not recommended for children

Italian came to the Tremont neighborhood in September 2007 with the opening of this pretty and comfortable white-tablecloth spot. It's related by ownership to Gusto! on the East Side. The menu takes its cue from northern cuisine and excels with house-made pasta dishes. Feathery light gnocchi share the plate with lobster, truffles, sweet corn, basil, and roasted tomatoes; farfalle is topped with a spicy marinara, and tagliatelle gets a rustic wild boar sauce. Some classics are given a 21st-century tweak, like pairing puttanesca sauce with halibut; accenting beef carpaccio with marinated fennel and truffle mustard vinaigrette; and seeding an arugula salad with melon, bits of crispy pancetta, and goat cheese. Pork, steak, and veal are also represented with one dish each, and every day features a pasta and risotto special. The all-Italian wine list has some great bargains and uncommon labels. Among management's inducements to get you in the door are weekly vegetarian dinners, a late-night happy hour, and live music on Friday evenings. A small room that holds up to 15 can be booked for private gatherings. While families are certainly welcome, this is a place where adults come to relax and enjoy food, wine, and quiet conversation. Don't bring young children whose behavior is likely to impinge on other guests' ability to do that. Valet parking on weekends eases the stress of finding a place to put your car.

## Leo's Ristorante

☎ (330) 856-5291

CITY: **Warren**   AREA: **Farther South**
ATMOSPHERE: **Casual**   COST: $$$$$

**ADDRESS:** 7042 E. Market St.
**HOURS:** Mon–Fri 11 a.m.–11 p.m., Sat 4–11 p.m.; closed Sun **RESERVATIONS:** Taken, recommended for groups of 8+ **PAYMENT:** MC, VS, AX, DIS **BAR:** Beer, wine, liquor **TAKEOUT:** Yes **ACCESS:** ♿ Full access

Warren, an hour from both Cleveland and Akron, definitely qualifies as off the beaten path for many of us. But Warren is home to Leo's, and that makes it a destination town for food enthusiasts who won't let a few miles get in the way of a good meal.

Owner and chef Leo Delgarbino, Jr. knows what to do with escarole and artichokes, prosciutto and provolone. He takes the lowly fava bean and turns it into pesto, transforms ordinary tomato sauce by adding brandy and cream or basil and vodka. Delgarbino is a graduate of the Culinary Institute of America, but he also has cooking in his blood on both sides, and the kitchen know-how goes back at least three generations. So it's no surprise that he works wonders with eggplant, wrapping slices around a mix of spinach, roasted red peppers, and ricotta; makes a wedding soup that will likely be a contender for the "best-you've-ever-had" award; and redefines pizza with a topping of leeks, portobello mushrooms, and goat cheese.

The menu changes seasonally, with a mix of pasta, poultry, meat, and seafood dishes. Expect creativity with an Italian flourish—veal meatloaf; chicken Tuscan style with rapini and red wine sauce; homemade gnocchi with sausage and fennel. There are also simpler, more familiar entrées: spaghetti and meatballs in a marinara sauce, chicken and veal Parmigiana, and cavatelli. Salads show the same range, from a straightforward tossed version to a mesclun and endive combination, or strawberries with fresh mozzarella dressed in extra virgin olive oil and balsamic syrup. All of the luscious desserts are made on premises. The wine list offers many options, including some of those rare vintages that are kept under lock and key.

With the help of his wife, Lisa, siblings, and a cousin, chef Leo has built up a loyal and enthusiastic following, and the restaurant is something of a local legend. (He still makes the pizzas that made the family's Parkman Road Dairy famous.) Ask anyone in Warren for directions, and they'll point the way. "Everybody knows Leo's," said a young woman at an area gas station. A large, modern facility designed by Leo's uncle, Larry Strollo, was built to replace his parents' original little eatery and pizza parlor on the other side of town, where he started his kitchen career. It seats 225 in the dining room: the space is two stories high with balcony seating available on weekends. There's a three-table area enclosed by glass walls toward the back of the main floor, and a small bar. The décor is tasteful, with paintings, hangings, and shelves holding candlesticks, small pieces of pottery, and antiques. Paper place mats at lunch, linens at dinnertime.

Children are always welcome, and even the pickiest are likely to find something they like on a children's menu for 12 and under. Outside, a canopy-covered patio has room for 60 diners in good weather, and jazz bands play here on Thursday, Friday, and Saturday nights. A banquet center with its own entrance can handle up to 500 people or be divided into three smaller spaces. Photos of the facilities, as well as menus, prices, and more information can be found at www.leosristorante.com.

## Mama Guzzardi's
☎ (330) 499-1247
CITY: **North Canton**   AREA: **Farther South**
ATMOSPHERE: **Relaxed**   COST: **$$**$$$

**ADDRESS:** 1107 N. Main St.
**HOURS:** Mon, Wed–Sun 11 a.m.–9 p.m., Sun noon–7 p.m.; closed Tue **RESERVATIONS:** Taken, recommended for groups of 6+ **PAYMENT:** MC, VS, DIS, checks **BAR:** None **TAKEOUT:** Yes **ACCESS:** ㅎ None

Family-style, no-nonsense Italian food in a "rec room"–style setting. The tablecloths and curtains are regulation red-and-white checkerboard, the walls sport fake wood paneling, and the only artwork is photographs documenting the lives, loves, weddings, christenings, graduations, and other celebrations of three generations of Guzzardis. Frank Sinatra sings softly in the background, and customers call the waitresses by name. It's been like this since 1986, when Mama opened the place. Though she's handed control over to younger members of the clan, "she still comes in," says granddaughter Lori, "to keep us on our toes and be sure we're doing everything right."

Right means Mama's way, which translates into good food, made from scratch using her recipes and served up in generous portions at a reasonable price in a homey atmosphere where people of all ages feel welcome. I ended up in conversation with a group of guys when I was there for lunch, and when they found out I was gathering information for this book, they assured me I'd come to the right place. And they expressed pride that the little North

Canton place they've patronized for years is attracting notice. The waitress, listening in, added that when she wears her Mama Guzzardi's T-shirt out in public, people always stop her to talk about how long they've been eating here and how much they love the food.

At the top of the menu are two classic, heartwarming Italian soups, wedding and pasta fagioli. They do pasta all the ways you'd expect, with cheese, alla marinara, with meatballs, and aglio e olio (garlic and olive oil). Their lasagna, manicotti, and stuffed shells are not for the lactose intolerant. Each day has its own dinner special, from chicken or eggplant Parmigiana to chicken cacciatore and seafood cannelloni. Half portions are available, and garlic bread comes with every entrée. Even the salad dressings are homemade. They also mention that they'll cut up the meatballs in your meatball sub if it's too hard to handle. Can a restaurant get any more friendly and accommodating than that? The restaurant seats about 90 in two rooms. In a small, three-store strip with parking.

## Mamma Santa's
☎ (216) 231-9567
CITY: **Cleveland**   AREA: **Near East Side**
ATMOSPHERE: **Casual**   COST: $$$$$

**ADDRESS:** 12305 Mayfield Rd.
**HOURS:** Mon–Thu 11 a.m.–10 p.m., Fri–Sat 11 a.m.–11 p.m.; closed Sun **RESERVATIONS:** Taken, only for large groups **PAYMENT:** MC, VS **BAR:** Beer, wine **TAKEOUT:** Yes **ACCESS:** & Full access

My husband and I have been eating here since 1971, when we were students down the hill at CWRU and the restaurant was only 10 years old. We liked the casual, friendly, relaxed atmosphere, affordable prices, good taste, and plentiful portions. Decades later, Mamma Santa's still offers all those some qualities, and

now we take our kids there. The restaurant attracts a steady crowd of students, couples, families, and workers whose collars come white, blue, pink, and just about every other color, too—many from the institutions of nearby University Circle. Many have been eating here for years. When it's full, and it often is, the restaurant can serve pizza and pasta to about 120 at booths and tables spread among three rooms.

The cooking is Sicilian-style, and the noodles are all homemade. When you want to try something different from spaghetti with meatballs, order noodles with fagioli (beans), lenticchie (lentils), or ceci (chickpeas). Pizzas are baked to order, so it can take 20 minutes, but you can get an antipasto plate and garlic toast or a side of fried green peppers to hold you. Lights are low, and old wine bottles and pictures of Italy are all the décor you'll find. Seniors get a discount. A limited number of parking spaces in the rear, otherwise you're on your own on the street.

## Maria's
☎ (216) 226-5875
CITY: **Lakewood**   AREA: **West Side**
ATMOSPHERE: **Casual**   COST: $$$$$

**ADDRESS:** 11822 Detroit Ave.
**HOURS:** Tue–Thu 11:30 a.m.–10 p.m., Fri 11:30 a.m.–11 p.m., Sat 5–11 p.m., Sun (Summer) 5–10 p.m., Sun (Winter) 4–9 p.m.; closed Mon **RESERVATIONS:** Taken, for groups of 5+ **PAYMENT:** MC, VS, AX **BAR:** Beer, wine, liquor **TAKEOUT:** Yes **ACCESS:** & Limited

Maria's has been around more than 40 years, by owner Maria Bastulli's reckoning. It's easy to spot—there's a neon version of their logo, a fork and spaghetti-filled pasta bowl, which can be seen from two blocks away. Inside are a pleasant bar and three dining rooms, two handsomely decorated with a flower motif on curtains and wallpaper, one featuring a red-white-and-green awning stretched across the ceiling. Lots of framed photographs of Italy on the walls, with booths and tables for up to 150. Dressings, sauces, and pasta are all made on the premises. Servings are generous, and when the menu says clam sauce it means *clam* sauce: huge meaty chunks plus some still in the shell grace an order here. They serve their own tasty version of garlic bread, called cucina bread, toasted with Parmesan cheese. Pizza, calzone, lasagna, and ravioli are available in addition to classic veal and chicken dishes. There's a two-item children's menu.

Try to leave room for Maria's signature confections, which include white chocolate cheesecake served with raspberry sauce and chocolate salami made with pistachios—voted one of Cleveland's best chocolate desserts by the *Plain Dealer*.

---

## Michaelangelo's
☎ (216) 721-0300
CITY: **Cleveland**   AREA: **Near East Side**
ATMOSPHERE: **Casual**   COST: **$$$$**$

**ADDRESS:** 2198 Murray Hill Rd.
**HOURS:** Mon–Thu 5:30–10 p.m., Fri–Sat 5:30–11 p.m., Sun 5–9 p.m. **RESERVATIONS:** Recommended **PAYMENT:** MC, VS, AX, DIS **BAR:** Beer, wine, liquor **TAKEOUT:** No **ACCESS:** ও Full access

Open since May 2006, this lovely upscale restaurant is a gem. Though all regional styles are represented, most of the food is rooted in Piedmontese culinary traditions. Chef and co-owner Michael Annandono, a born-and-bred Clevelander, lived, studied, and cooked in the northwestern corner of Italy and came back an enthusiast with an expertise in preparing this robust and rustic cuisine. His menu, which changes seasonally, features a daily risotto, pastas in silky cream sauces, and meat and fish flavored with wines. The mix of dishes that show up regularly include a Kobe beef carpaccio with porcini mushrooms and white truffle oil; eggy papardelle noodles with a tomato-Barolo ragu laced with Muscovy duck and guinea fowl; lobster raviolini in vodka-tomato cream; tortellini stuffed with veal and ricotta and tossed with proscuitto, peas, and Parmigiano-Reggiano; potato gnocchi in hazelnut pesto; veal saltimbocca in a citrus wine reduction, and slow-cooked ossobuco. An antipasti cart is always stocked with a selection of cured meats, olives, grilled and roasted vegetables, house-made mozzarella and imported cheeses. The dolci (sweets) are divine, among them panna cotta and tiramisu, and the kitchen creates a different kind of gelato every day.

The glasses and the silver in the dining room are always gleaming; table linens are spotless. In combination with candlelight, fresh flowers, and attentive, polished, detail-oriented service, the experience is elegant. In good weather, a rear deck decorated with potted plants offers a more casual atmosphere.

Michaelangelo's is also a wine bar. The list is 25 percent California, 75 percent Italian, and 100 percent wonderful with bottles ranging from under $30 to more than $400. Staff members know their grapes and can offer descriptions and pairing advice. Tastings are scheduled monthly. The lounge, equipped with a fireplace and some comfy seating as well as a few tables, is an inviting spot for sipping. Dinner is also served in here, and patrons can even eat at the bar. There's live jazz Friday nights. A separate room is available for private parties. Equipped with a wall-mounted flat screen and laptop plug-ins, it's ideal for business meetings.

The restaurant is housed in a stand-alone brick building set back from the street at the end of a driveway. It has its own lot so parking is never a problem—a real plus in this neighborhood.

## Molinari's
☎ (440) 974-2750
CITY: **Mentor**   AREA: **Farther East**
ATMOSPHERE: **Casual**   COST: **$$$$$**

**ADDRESS:** 8900 Mentor Ave.
**HOURS:** Lunch Tue–Sat 11:30 a.m.–2 p.m.; Dinner Tue–Thu 5:30–10 p.m., Fri–Sat 5:30–11 p.m.; closed Sun–Mon **RESERVATIONS:** Recommended **PAYMENT:** MC, VS, AX, DIS, checks **BAR:** Beer, wine, liquor **TAKEOUT:** Yes **ACCESS:** ♿ Full access **OTHER ETHNIC:** International

Molinari's has grown from a small dining area in a market to a 150-seat restaurant set in the midst of a wine shop. The look is sophisticated New York contemporary, and the view into the kitchen from the dining room is a source of entertainment and interest. The menu, which changes seasonally, is northern Italian and northern California. The wine list is not only extensive but full of great values, reflecting retail rather than restaurant pricing.

Owner and chef Randal Johnson specializes in bold flavors and unique, creative presentations: calamari with three-pepper relish; veal slices tossed in a lemon vodka cream sauce; pancetta shrimp; hot peppers stuffed with four cheeses and herbs; balsamic and brown sugar marinated pork tenderloin; and beef tenderloin risotto.

On Mondays, when the restaurant itself is closed, Molinari's hosts special events open to the public, such as wine tastings and cooking classes. The Web site, www.molinaris.com, includes announcements for these events along with the season's new menu and a separate catering menu. A private room,

suitable for business meetings and parties, can hold up to 50 guests.

## Nino's
☎ (440) 353-9580
CITY: **North Ridgeville**   AREA: **West Side**
ATMOSPHERE: **Casual**   COST: **$$$$$**

**ADDRESS:** 32652 Center Ridge Rd.
**HOURS:** Lunch Wed–Fri 11 a.m.–3 p.m.; Dinner Mon–Thu 4–9:30 p.m., Fri–Sat 4–9:30 p.m., Sun 4–7:30 p.m. **RESERVATIONS:** Taken, for groups of 6+ **PAYMENT:** MC, VS **BAR:** Beer, wine, liquor **TAKEOUT:** Yes **ACCESS:** ♿ Full access

A clue that this isn't just another run-of-the-mill Italian restaurant is the appetizer "Nana's pork neck bones." When's the last time you saw neck bones on a menu—Nana's or anybody else's? For an ethnic food writer, that traditional, unglamorous dish and its attribution to Grandma are a dead giveaway that the food here is the real lasagna. That's why Chip Kullik, news director of WMJI, recommended it to me, describing it as a small, hole-in-the-wall kind of place with incredible food.

Other menu items that get my authenticity meter going are smelts, baccala (dried salt cod), bread pudding, and aglio e olio sauce. The recipes for many dishes are family treasures. The food is Calabrian homestyle, nothing fancy, so you'll find pasta e fagioli (pasta and beans), fried escarole, fresh calamari in homemade marinara sauce, and sausage they make on the premises. Other, more elaborate, offerings include cioppino, a fish stew made with shrimp, scallops, mussels, and clams; veal scallopini with red wine sauce and capers; cavatelli bianco with chicken in alfredo basil sauce; and Asiago cheese–stuffed gnocchi. Some of their house specialties are so popular they prepare and sell them by the pound, pint, and quart, including sausage, salad dressing, wedding soup, and a variety of sauces. They also do pizzas and a few sandwiches.

There are no high chairs, and the intimate space is suitable only for well-behaved kids old enough to hold still for the length of a meal and control their personal volume. The restaurant has a slightly Old World look, and only 13 tables: six are booths, but the others can be pushed together for larger parties. There's a view into the kitchen from the lobby—consider it entertainment if you have to wait for a table, as seating is always first come, first serve. An ATM machine is on hand for those who don't arrive prepared with cash. Family photos and pictures of famous Italian Americans grace the walls. The restaurant is in a strip mall with plenty of parking.

## Osteria

☎ (216) 685-9400

CITY: **Cleveland**   AREA: **Downtown**
ATMOSPHERE: **Casual**   COST: **$$$$**$

**ADDRESS:** 408 St. Clair Ave.
**HOURS:** Mon 5–9 p.m., Tue–Wed 5–10 p.m., Thu–Sat 5–11 p.m., Sun 4–8 p.m. only between September and April **RESERVATIONS:** Recommended, especially Fri, Sat **PAYMENT:** MC, VS, AX, DIS **BAR:** Beer, wine, liquor **TAKEOUT:** Yes **ACCESS:** ♿ Full access

The modest-sized menu of classic Italian dishes is augmented with 15 to 20 daily specials that take advantage of whatever ingredients are freshest, best, and most intriguing. You can always get carpaccio (raw sirloin), ribollita Toscana (Tuscan vegetable soup), saltimbocca (veal and prosciutto), osso bucco (slow-roasted veal shank), seafood risotto, and pappardelle pasta in a deep-flavored Bolognese sauce made with duck and veal. Among the most memorable dishes to dig in to are cioppino, a Ligurian seafood stew;

calamari with roasted tomatoes and a reduction of Vernaccia (a famed Tuscan white wine); potato gnocchi in rich and creamy Gorgonzola sauce; pork tenderloin wrapped in proscuitto; and a grilled lamb rack in balsamic vinaigrette. Desserts too feature a few regular items, such as fruity sorbets, and a changing array of pastries—cassata cake, hazelnut torte, and a flourless mint chocolate cake.

Osteria's co-owner, Al Cefaratti, insists on service in the European style. Once your maitre d' has made you comfortable at one of the dining room's 13 tables and told you all about what the kitchen has to offer, he turns you over to the wait staff, all of whom are available to help you. There's no such thing as "your" server.

The restaurant represents a partnership between Valerio Iorio, chef and owner of Valerio's in Little Italy, and Cefaratti, who formerly tended bar there. The two believe in running very hands-on operations with high standards for food and service. The result, here in the Warehouse District location, is a restaurant that is upscale and stylish yet retains the warm, friendly atmosphere of a neighborhood hangout. Cefaratti is a nightly presence, backslapping regulars, personally welcoming newcomers, and making sure customers who have to wait longer than expected for their table get a drink on the house.

The wine list is extensive, focusing on Italian vintages that range in price from $20–$72. Wine bottles are integral to the décor, displayed on shelves lining one wall, in a wine rack on another, and in a glass-fronted cabinet near the entrance. The dining room is actually below street level, and this adds to the "wine cellar" feel of this pleasantly intimate and cozy space.

Subdued lighting, a black-and-white color scheme with maroon accents, and background music that features timeless classics and Sinatra-style crooners augment the sense that you've stumbled on a lovely little secret hideaway. The music is live on Thursday and Friday nights. A head count on a typical night reveals a romantic tête-à-tête in progress at one table, a business meeting at another, a two-couple get-together at a third, and four women celebrating at the back. At the bar men and women in suits sit beside folks in jeans, and the comfortable high-backed stools clearly make it easy to linger.

I would not choose to bring young kids here, but for those who think otherwise there is a high chair stashed in the ladies' room. The front entrance has steps and is not handicapped accessible, but there is a rear entrance with a ramp. Parking does not come easily or cheaply in this part of downtown—you can drive around endlessly in hopes of finding a meter on the street or pay to put your car in one of the numerous lots. Valet parking Thursday, Friday, and Saturday.

## Players on Madison
☎ (216) 226-5200
CITY: **Lakewood**   AREA: **West Side**
ATMOSPHERE: **Casual**   COST: **$$$**$$

**ADDRESS:** 14527 Madison Ave. (at Belle)
**HOURS:** Mon–Thu 5–10 p.m., Fri–Sat 5–11 p.m., Sun 5–9 p.m. **RESERVATIONS:** Taken, between 5–7 p.m. **PAYMENT:** MC, VS, AX, DIS **BAR:** Beer, wine, liquor **TAKEOUT:** Yes **ACCESS:** ♿ Full access

The building's old pressed-tin ceiling, painted white, is still in evidence, and the old wood floors have been sanded to gleaming perfection, but everything else about Players is sleek and contemporary, that uncanny blend of minimal and glamorous. The most interesting illumination I've ever seen in a restaurant: oddly shaped bits of glimmering light hang clothesline-style across the two dining areas. Tables are white cloth under glass; hand-painted ceramic plates and beautiful bottles of herb vinegar decorate the walls. The menu reflects that same panache. Traditional Italian dishes are updated and pizza or pasta can be ordered with a large selection of toppings including roasted garlic, arugula, herbed chicken, smoked mussels, or shiitake mushrooms. But lest you think it's all just too trendy, on one visit I saw two kids happily tucking into platefuls of spaghetti with tomato sauce, with milk chasers. Dine in a Tuscan-style courtyard patio during the summer (seating is on a first come, first served basis).

## Presti Bakery
☎ (216) 421-3060
CITY: **Cleveland**   AREA: **Near East Side**
ATMOSPHERE: **Relaxed**   COST: **$$**$$

**ADDRESS:** 12101 Mayfield Rd.
**HOURS:** Mon–Thu 7 a.m.–7 p.m., Fri–Sat 7 a.m.–10 p.m., Sun 7 a.m.–6 p.m. **RESERVATIONS:** Not taken **PAYMENT:** MC, VS, AX, checks **BAR:** None **TAKEOUT:** Yes **ACCESS:** ♿ Full access

It's a bakery. It's a cafe. It's Presti's.

New and improved, this Presti's, just one door down from the old one, is a place to sit as well as shop. Claudia Presti Di Bartolo and Sheila Presti Gentile, who took over the business from their father, oversaw a two-year renovation project that transformed the long-empty storefront adjacent to the old bakery from an eyesore to a showpiece. Working with local architect Steven Bucchieri, who has made it his personal mission to preserve the historical integrity of the Murray Hill neighborhood, they have managed to strike a balance between tradition and innovation. The result is something timeless and wonderful. The aim was to save as much of the original building and fittings as possible. Behind the counter is a large mahogany cabinet that was once used to display and stack clothes, back when this was Two Sisters Variety Store. The glass doors were removed, the finish restored, and new mahogany shelves were built to show off the bread. The pressed-tin ceiling, much of which had been destroyed by years of leaks and neglect, was pieced together like a patchwork quilt, and old-fashioned schoolhouse-style lights hang down from it. The wood paneling on the walls was left in place but given a fresh coat of paint. Water damage had marred the maple floor beyond repair, but it was replaced with a new one. Tables now sit in the big windows, perfect for watching the street life that is a distinctive feature of this community. Small glass- and marble-topped tables with wrought-iron and bentwood chairs seat about 70, and in good weather tables appear outside on the sidewalk, European-style.

The mix of clientele, from the neighborhood and beyond, reinforces this blend of Old World and new. Consider this grouping spotted one afternoon: at one table a mom with two kids out for a treat orders dishes of spumoni with a cookie, while she chooses coffee and cannoli; youngish arty and college types—their membership in these groups suggested by their affinity for tattoos, piercings, black clothes, and backpacks—fill the window seats and talk with animation and intensity; a lone middle-aged woman in a back corner enjoys a book and a cappuccino; and at another table a large elderly man, his pants held up over his ample belly by suspenders, a 1940s-style felt fedora on his head, reads an Italian-language newspaper while he sips his espresso.

This is an ideal spot for meeting friends, hanging out, catching up, and taking time to enjoy good talk and good eats. Come for breakfast, lunch, a light dinner, and anything in between. There's a soup each day, salads, pasta, sandwiches, pizza by the piece, bruschetta (bread topped with slices of fresh-grilled tomatoes and melted cheese), and meat, vegetable, or spinach-and-cheese stromboli, and spinach or pepperoni bread. The glass-fronted cases of pastry are a feast for the eyes, and the effect is to make any thought of calorie control seem like yesterday's dumb idea. All things good, sweet, and Italian are to be found here (for a more detailed description see the listing for Presti's in the market section of this chapter). Since there's a real shortage of parking around here, consider walking, even if you live a few miles away or have to leave your car somewhere in Cleveland Heights or University Circle. The exercise will make you feel much better about all the cookies and cakes you will feel compelled to consume.

## Ristorante Giovanni's
☎ (216) 831-8625
CITY: **Beachwood**    AREA: **East Side**
ATMOSPHERE: **Formal**    COST: **$$$$$**

ADDRESS: 25550 Chagrin Blvd.
HOURS: Lunch Mon–Fri 11:30 a.m.–2:30 p.m.; Dinner Mon–Fri 5:30–9:30 p.m. (lounge open between lunch & dinner), Sat 5:30–10:30 p.m.; closed Sun RESERVATIONS: Recommended PAYMENT: MC, VS, AX, DIS BAR: Beer, wine, liquor TAKEOUT: Yes ACCESS: ♿ Full access
*Not recommended for children

Established in 1976, Giovanni's specializes in fine northern Italian cuisine and has earned a reputation as one of Northeast Ohio's best restaurants. The wall of the lobby is peppered with awards: the Chefs of America named it one of the nation's finest, *Cleveland* magazine gave it Silver Spoons for both best Italian and best service, the American Automobile Association honored it with four diamonds for exceptional cuisine and service, and *Wine Spectator* called its wine list one of the most outstanding in the world. Located in a stark, modern concrete office building that gives no hint of the plush and sparkling elegance inside, this is a place to enjoy leisurely, sumptuous five-course meals, an appropriate setting for celebrations and special occasions. The dining area is roomy, seating about 90, and the appointments are luxurious; wood gleams, linens are crisp, the copper-and-brass espresso machine is polished to a high shine, and champagne buckets are ready and waiting. The menu features traditional cuisine prepared with a contemporary sensibility: river mussels in roasted tomato broth, fusilli pasta with braised veal, swordfish and calamari diavolo, or a Parmesan-crusted veal chop with tomato concasse.

## 'Stino da Napoli
☎ (440) 331-3944
CITY: **Rocky River**   AREA: **West Side**
ATMOSPHERE: **Casual**   COST: $$$$$

ADDRESS: 19070 Detroit Rd.
HOURS: Tue–Fri 5–9:30 p.m., Sat noon–10 p.m.; closed Sun–Mon RESERVATIONS: Recommended PAYMENT: Checks BAR: Beer, wine TAKEOUT: Yes ACCESS: ⚬ Full access

This restaurant began life as a very tiny eatery with cosmopolitan big-city panache. It functioned primarily as a takeout place, and a very popular one, judging by the size of the crowds that regularly lined up at the counter to collect their orders of Agostino ('Stino) Iacullo's Neapolitan specialties. But the original eight-table space has been expanded, and now there's seating for 50. Whether you choose to take out or eat there, it's an opportunity to sample the fresh, flavorful cuisine of southern Italy: dishes like spaghetti al fumo del Vesuvio (featuring a tomato sauce lightly smoothed with cream and studded with smoked bacon and onions); penne all' Arrabiata (tube-shaped pasta in a spicy tomato sauce); or gnocchi alla Napoletana (hand-rolled potato dumplings baked with mozzarella, ricotta, and Parmigiano cheese). Patrons get so into the food that the servers even have some special stuff on hand for spot-cleaning olive oil and tomato sauce from shirt fronts and cuffs. Cappuccino and espresso are available, as well as Italian desserts like tiramisu and cannoli. Toddlers are as comfortable here as their well-dressed parents, and although it's literally elbow to elbow, with knees touching under the table, everyone seems to manage to make themselves at home. This is, however, probably not the best choice for groups larger than eight. For bigger gatherings, you can always order a full pan of lasagna alla meridionale 24 hours in advance and serve it at home.

## Trattoria Roman Gardens
☎ (216) 421-2700
CITY: **Cleveland**   AREA: **Near East Side**
ATMOSPHERE: **Casual**   COST: $$$$$

ADDRESS: 12207 Mayfield Rd.
HOURS: Mon–Thu 11:30 a.m.–9 p.m., Fri–Sat 11:30 a.m.–10 p.m., Sun 11:30 a.m.–8:30 p.m.
RESERVATIONS: Recommended PAYMENT: MC, VS, AX BAR: Beer, wine, liquor TAKEOUT: Yes ACCESS: ⚬ Limited

A host will seat you, and shortly thereafter you'll be presented with a basket of fresh, crusty Italian bread. The menu features such classic entrées as veal Marsala, chicken piccata, lamb chops Calabrian, cavatelli, ravioli, and gnocchi. There are also pan pizzas and a fair number of choices for vegetarians. Sauces are homemade, as are all the pastas except for the linguine, which is imported from Italy. Cappuccino and espresso are available. The décor is simple but sophisticated: black-and-white checkerboard floor tiles, white walls, white table linens, wood accents, muted lighting, and potted plants. Unspoken convention keeps attire to the casual side of dressy, the ambience is subdued, and the impression is that this would be a good spot for a romantic dinner. At lunchtime, the restaurant attracts businesspeople and hospital staff from University Circle, and the atmosphere is a bit louder and livelier. The bar in front has a few additional tables where food is also served. A basement room, which can be reserved, is ideal for private parties and meetings. If you're not already familiar with the place and its location, beware—there seems to be a bit of an identity crisis going on here. On one exterior wall, the restaurant bills itself as Trattoria on the Hill. The front window, however, flashes the name Trattoria Roman Gardens. I guess you just can't believe everything you read. The restaurant has its own parking lot around back.

## Vaccaro's Trattoria

☎ (330) 666-6158
CITY: **Bath**   AREA: **Farther South**
ATMOSPHERE: **Casual**   COST: $$$$$

ADDRESS: 1000 Ghent Rd.
HOURS: Mon–Fri 11 a.m.–4 p.m. & 5–10 p.m., Sat 5–10 p.m.; closed Sun RESERVATIONS: Recommended PAYMENT: MC, VS, AX, DIS, checks BAR: Beer, wine, liquor TAKEOUT: Yes ACCESS: ら Full access

The minute you walk in, a large photo of Great-grandma Vaccaro greets you. Scattered on the walls are photos of the "our trip to Italy" variety. The front of the menu features a mom-dad-and-the-kids-in-chef-hats photo that's captioned "From our family to yours!" And on the back of the menu, the Vac-

caros include a personal *grazie* for dining with them. Together, these are a tip-off that this is a family-run place that caters to families. In fact, I saw many three-generation groups dining together on a weekend evening, as well as couples young, older, and in between. Though the food is elegantly prepared and served and the atmosphere is classy, children are welcome to draw on the white butcher paper that tops the cloth-covered tables, and neither guests nor staff seem uncomfortable when the kids do creative things with spaghetti. The close-together tables mean there's not much privacy, and it's actually amazing how skillfully the white-aproned servers make their way through, but rather than feel crowded it feels friendly, a big, boisterous party where everyone is welcome. Newly arrived guests are quickly served a basket of salted, crusty rolls redolent of garlic and accompanied by herbed olive oil.

The food is festive, too—edible artwork that is as colorful and dramatic as it is appetizing. The menu features a mix of traditional and creative Italian fare. Eat your way through wedding soup, grilled radicchio and romaine salad, stuffed banana peppers, eight-cheese ravioli, lasagna with meat (beef, veal, and pork) or without, roasted mussel pasta, and cabernet-braised lamb shank. For something very different, try the eggplant stuffed with mushrooms, spinach, zucchini and a cheesy lemon cream.

Desserts, which I can only describe as a carnival on a plate, are made on the premises and are a blend of traditional Italian favorites and some creative variations: tiramisu; Limoncello napolean; donuts called panne fritta; and house-made chocolate biscotti gelati.

The selection of beers is outstanding, including the unusual along with the predictable: Peroni and Moretti, which are Italian brews, Corsendok from Belgium, Younger's Tartan, and Newcastle Brown Ale. Vaccaro's is a *Wine Spectator* award winner; the wine list offers mostly Italian labels plus some French, Australian, and popular American vintages, with 22 different glass wine pours.

There are two dining rooms, which can easily accommodate large groups, done up in shades of grey, white, and mauve with mahogany accents, and a 10-stool bar in the middle, all together seating about 150. The Vaccaros periodically host wine events that include a six-to-eight-course Italian feast. They also run a full catering service with its own phone number: (330) 990-6158. The restaurant, in a newly built shopping plaza, is visible from I-77 and is easily accessed via the Ghent Road exit, exit #138.

## Valerio's Ristorante Cafe & Bar

☎ (216) 421-8049

CITY: **Cleveland**  AREA: **Near East Side**
ATMOSPHERE: **Casual**  COST: **$$$$**

**ADDRESS:** 12405 Mayfield Rd.
**HOURS:** Tue–Fri 5:30–late, Sat 5–late, Sun 5–late; closed Mon; As long as people are there who want to eat, Valerio's kitchen is open. **RESERVATIONS:** Taken, required Fri–Sat **PAYMENT:** MC, VS, AX, checks **BAR:** Beer, wine, liquor **TAKEOUT:** No **ACCESS:** ♿ Full access

Valerio Iorio, trained at the Culinary School of Florence in Italy, where he was born and raised, is more than the owner of this restaurant, more than the chef. He is the quintessential host, devoted to making sure all the guests in this small establishment are comfortable, well fed, and enjoying themselves. That's why his hours read "til late": he won't close as long as someone wants to eat. He likes to emerge from the kitchen and go table to table, meeting his customers and finding out for himself if they're happy. The sense of being a guest in his home is reinforced by his staff. There's none of the typical restaurant pecking order among employees, and you can't tell the maitre d' from the busboy. Everyone, it seems, takes orders, brings bread, refills water glasses, serves food, wishes you "Buon appetito," stops by to ask if you need anything, and clears tables. I overheard one server teaching a child a few words of Italian, and another jokingly chiding a customer for not cleaning their plate. The overall impression is that this group of friends has decided to give a dinner party and you've been invited.

And what a dinner it will be. Valerio is a passionate, principled chef who creates unique dishes inspired by the rich-flavored, herb-scented cuisine of Tuscany, using only the freshest, top-quality ingredients, such as whole sides of genuine Provimi veal and New Zealand lamb that he cuts by hand himself, extra virgin olive oil and balsamic vinegar, the best imported cheeses, and pasta made locally to his specifications. The presentation is elegant without being pretentious: generous portions of food look beautiful on simple white dinnerware.

For those who know wines, he carries a handpicked selection of some very fine and hard-to-get vintages. For those who don't, his menu includes wine recommendations for every entrée. Dinner offerings include nodino al fungo (a grilled veal chop prepared with portobello mushrooms and sun-dried tomatoes); pollo al limon (a lemon chicken in a white wine sauce); risotto; gnocchi with Gorgonzola; and frutti di mare that includes mussels, clams, shrimp, and scallops. The tiramisu dessert is not to be missed.

In early 2009, Valerio's moved up the street from his old location into the lovely modern 55-seat space that was once Battuto Ristorante.

# Mediterranean mix

## Sergio's in University Circle
☎ (216) 231-1234

CITY: **Cleveland**   AREA: **Near East Side**
ATMOSPHERE: **Casual**   COST: **$$$$**$

ADDRESS: 1903 Ford Dr.
HOURS: Lunch Mon–Fri 11:30 a.m.–2:30 p.m.;
Dinner Mon–Thu 5–9:30 p.m., Fri–Sat 5–11
p.m. RESERVATIONS: Recommended PAYMENT:
MC, VS, AX, DIS BAR: Beer, wine, liquor
TAKEOUT: Yes ACCESS: ♿ Limited

Chef Sergio Abramof, who owns the restaurant with his wife, Susan, draws on both his own personal history and his philosophy of cooking for the inspired cross-cultural offerings here. His grandparents were Russian Jews, his father a French citizen, his mother Brazilian. Born in Brazil, Sergio lived in America for much of his life after age seven. A graduate of Cleveland Heights High School, he served as executive chef at Ristorante Giovanni's for 14 years where he mastered Italian cooking. All these influences come into play in this kitchen, now in the care of Ryan Alabaugh, a talented up-and-comer.

In the past the menu leaned heavily towards Brazilian fare. Just a couple of those Latin dishes remain, most notably the prato misto, a wonderful meatless dish of black beans, fried spinach, rice, and carioca tomato relish. Everything changed when Abramof opened Saravá on Shaker Square (see listing in Latin America chapter) in 2007. The focus now is on how food is prepared in Spain, Italy, and along the Mediterranean shores. The kitchen is dedicated to sourcing the most authentic ingredients, and the effort pays off in everything it turns out. The menu changes seasonally, and the very best way to experience it is to order multiple small, medium, and side plates and eat tapas style. This list is only a sample of the possibilities: chorizo sausage simmered in wine; seared tilapia with marcona almonds; scallops with imported Serrano ham in a zesty romesco sauce; chicken with olive tapenade; fennel rice; a baked egg dish called huevos flamencos; and pappardelle pasta with lemon pistachio pesto cream. The international cheese selection is always special. There is no shortage of good things for those who prefer a single entrée-size portion, among them seafood paella, the fisherman's stew known as cioppino, trout basilica, and salmon modo mia defined by a tangy lemon caper butter. Nice line-up of wines and beers to pair with your food.

The small dining room is defined by splashes of bold, primary colors and clean modern lines, with seating for just 46 in close quarters. When deciding whether to bring kids, consider that guests are in close proximity to one another. If you do bring them, Sergio's has some child-friendly options on the menu. During warm weather, there's a 60-seat garden patio complete with potted palms and market umbrellas for outdoor dining. Seating here is on a first-come, first-served basis. Take your chances finding a parking spot or use their valet service. Located in the heart of University Circle, it's within sight of the Cleveland Botanical Garden and the Cleveland Institute of Music, and walking distance from the area's many arts, education, and cultural institutions. Sergio's tapas is also served next door in the lounge at The Glidden House Inn.

# Spanish

## Mallorca Restaurant
☎ (216) 687-9494
CITY: **Cleveland**   AREA: **Downtown**
ATMOSPHERE: **Dressy**   COST: **$$$$**

**ADDRESS:** 1390 W. 9th St.
**HOURS:** Mon–Thu 11:30 a.m.–10:30 p.m.,
Fri–Sat 11:30 a.m.–11:30 p.m., Sun 1–10 p.m.
**RESERVATIONS:** Recommended, Sun–Thu; taken
only for groups of 5+ on Fri, Sat **PAYMENT:** MC,
VS, AX **BAR:** Beer, wine, liquor **TAKEOUT:** Yes
**ACCESS:** ✦ Full access *Not recommended for
children **OTHER ETHNIC:** Portuguese

This 150-seat restaurant opened in
March 1997 in a beautifully remodeled space in the historic Warehouse
District. You can sample classic Spanish dishes such as broiled chorizo sausage, sopa de ajo (garlic soup), paella (a
mix of saffron-seasoned rice, seafood,
sausage, and chicken), and flan (an egg
custard dessert), as well as Portuguese
specialties like baby goat in red wine
sauce, roast suckling pig, and rabbit
prepared with white wine and sherry.
On a Saturday night there may be as
many as 30 specials, and the regular
menu includes a mix of veal, chicken,
beef, and pork. There's also an array of
seafood dishes, so popular in those regions around the Mediterranean, prepared here with a variety of traditional
sauces (green, wine, garlic, and spicy
tomato), and squid is done in a broth
made with its own ink.

Portions are huge, and entrées
come with rice, vegetables, and potatoes sliced thin and fried like chips, all
served family-style. They don't stint on
service either, and it's executed with artful showmanship in the best European
style, where waitering is a profession,
not just a job. You'll have not one waiter
in black tie but a well-trained troop of
six or seven organized to attend to your
every need.

If you order wine or anything from the
bar (thus cueing staff that you consume
alcoholic beverages), they will serve you
a glass of Portuguese almond-flavored
after-dinner liqueur, on the house. If
they don't bring it and you want it, just
ask. Speaking of ordering from the bar,
there's an inviting 12-seater in the front
room (with a TV). The bartender mixes
up pitchers of sangria (wine and fresh
fruit), poured tableside with a special
flourish that makes it an event. The
wine list is large, with many reasonably
priced bottles, and there's also a port
and sherry list.

At night there's a lovely view of lights
twinkling on the Main Avenue Bridge
from the big picture window at the back
of the main dining room, which is done
up in a mix of exposed white-painted
brick, earth and flesh tones, and a few
pieces of contemporary artwork. All is
bathed in the kind of subdued lighting
that makes everyone look a bit glamorous. Customers tend to dress not in
their party best but well and stylishly.
This is a great place for a celebration, an
occasion that mixes business with pleasure, or a romantic rendezvous. There
are both private and city lots nearby as
well as on-street parking.

## Marbella Restaurant
☎ (216) 464-9939
CITY: **Pepper Pike**   AREA: **East Side**
ATMOSPHERE: **Dressy**   COST: **$$$$**

**ADDRESS:** 29425 Chagrin Blvd.
**HOURS:** Mon–Sat 11:30 a.m.–10 p.m., Sun 1–9
p.m. **RESERVATIONS:** Taken, recommended
Sun–Thu **PAYMENT:** MC, VS, AX, DIS **BAR:** Beer,
wine, liquor **TAKEOUT:** Yes **ACCESS:** ✦ Full access
*Not recommended for children **OTHER ETHNIC:**
Portuguese

This is Mallorca's sister restaurant. Both have the same basic menu. (See listing for Majorca for details.) But here, the atmosphere's a bit more casual, prices are a little lower, there's an early bird special between 5 and 6 p.m., and prix fixe lunch.

## MARKETS

# Greek

## Athens Pastries & Imported Foods
☎ (216) 861-8149
CITY: **Cleveland**   AREA: **Near West Side**

ADDRESS: 2545 Lorain Ave.
FOOD AVAIL.: Meat (fresh, frozen), fish (fresh, frozen, dried), grains, beans, flour, rice, baked goods, canned & packaged goods, spices, condiments, beverages, tea, wine, prepared frozen foods, takeout meals HOURS: Mon–Thu 8:30 a.m.–6 p.m., Fri–Sat 8 a.m.–6 p.m.; closed Sun PAYMENT: MC, VS ACCESS: ⚹ Limited

Recorded Greek music is almost always playing softly in the background. Dark roasted coffee beans, spices, and golden baklava pastry dripping honey syrup give off a heady and decidedly non-Midwestern scent. The overall effect upon entering the store is to feel as though you've left Cleveland far behind.

You'll find every sort of Greek delicacy imaginable here—feta cheese; many different kinds of olives; fresh phyllo dough, pastries, and spinach and meat pies; and many brands of olive oil. You'll also find toiletries imported from Greece, kitchenware, religious icons, music tapes, and Greek greeting cards. A 2003 remodeling brought more space, bright lights, wider aisles, and new merchandise, including a world of beers: Dutch, Czech, Jamaican, English, German, Mexican, Italian, Scottish, and of course, Greek. There's also an international selection of wines and bottled water. You might find a jar of Indian chutney among the condiments or Hungarian red pepper spread, but Greek specialties dominate. On-street parking plus a lot parallel to the building.

## Canton Importing Company
☎ (330) 452-9351
CITY: **Canton**   AREA: **Farther South**

ADDRESS: 1136 Wertz Ave. NW
FOOD AVAIL.: Meat (deli), baked goods, canned & packaged goods, spices, condiments, beverages, tea, coffee, wine, prepared frozen foods HOURS: Mon–Fri 9 a.m.–6 p.m., Sat 9 a.m.–5 p.m.; closed Sun PAYMENT: MC, VS, checks ACCESS: ⚹ Full access OTHER ETHNIC: Italian

Mom and Pop Regas started out in downtown Canton in 1960 in a shop that sold only Greek foods. They moved to their present location in 1972, and as the place had formerly been an Italian import store they combined the two cultures and product lines, many of which overlap anyway. Nick Regas, their son, studied to be a lawyer but found his true calling behind the counter and has been running the family business, which is both wholesale and retail, since 1994. Years ago, he explains, when his parents started out, their customers were mostly Greek and then, later, Italian immigrants, but now everybody wants to eat a Mediterranean diet because it's both healthy and delicious.

All kinds of people come in to get things like fresh mozzarella, never-frozen phyllo dough, arborio rice, and polenta. They stock 15 different brands and types of olive oil, Italian cold cuts, pasta, Italian breads, Greek pastries, and some kitchen equipment, including espresso pots, garlic presses, pizelle makers, and an old-style rocking mincer. Cheese and olives are a specialty. There are 12 varieties of olives and four types of feta: domestic (which, I learned from Nick, is made from cow's milk and hence does not have the sharp, tangy flavor of the real thing), Bulgarian, French, and Greek, which is kept in a real wood barrel in the back (only old-timers and connoisseurs can appreciate this). Some of the more unusual and interesting products to be found here are preserves made from quince, sour cherries, rose petals, and figs; wild Greek onions in brine; frozen smelts; a traditional Greek cereal, trahanas, cooked and served like Cream of Wheat; and krithr, a tiny little pasta shaped like orzo. Plenty of free parking on all sides of the blue-and-white building with the eye-catching mural on one side.

This has been a family-run business since 1989. Mike Detorakis is responsible for the wine selection and the on-site state store that stocks ouzo, a licorice-flavored drink, and metaxa, a Greek brandy. Mom's in charge of the baking, turning out specialties like Greek wedding cookies, baklava, and kataife (sweet shredded wheat dough and nuts), and Dad does the customized fruit baskets. And everybody works together to keep the shelves stocked with imported grocery products like grape leaves, feta cheese, and phyllo dough, used to prepare homemade Greek entrées such as spanakopeta (spinach rolls) and tiropeta (cheese rolls), plus pastitsio (similar to lasagna), and moussaka (eggplant casserole). All of these dishes are also sold frozen and ready to bake. They also offer fresh, as distinct from cured, olives. The Detorakis family wants everyone to know that they'll always get a warm, friendly, personal welcome here, and immediate help. Since the store is across the street from the Akron Art Museum, consider making your shopping trip into a full-blown cultural outing by also stopping in there and checking out what's on display. Western Fruit is on a corner in an architecturally interesting older building. Parking available in back.

## Western Fruit Basket and Beverage

☎ (330) 376-3917

CITY: **Akron**   AREA: **Farther South**

**ADDRESS:** 115 E. Market St.
**FOOD AVAIL.:** Produce, beans, baked goods, canned & packaged goods, spices, condiments, beverages, tea, coffee, wine, beer, prepared frozen foods **HOURS:** Mon–Sat 9 a.m.–5 p.m. **PAYMENT:** MC, VS, AX, DIS, checks **ACCESS:** & Full Access **OTHER ETHNIC:** Eastern European mix

# Italian

## Alberini's Cork & More Shoppe

☎ (330) 652-5895

CITY: **Niles**   AREA: **Farther South**

**ADDRESS:** 1201 Youngstown-Warren Rd. (U.S. 422)
**FOOD AVAIL.:** Baked goods, canned & packaged goods, spices, condiments, beverages, coffee, wine, prepared frozen foods, takeout meals **HOURS:** Tue–Sat noon–10 p.m.; closed

Sun–Mon & holidays **PAYMENT:** MC, VS, AX, DIS, checks **ACCESS:** ♿ Full access

The Shoppe is really just another room in the complex of additions that has become Alberini's. Many of the most popular dishes served in the restaurant—including made-from-scratch tomato sauce, wedding soup by the quart, stuffed peppers, meatballs, and pasta dishes—are available in take-home, heat-and-eat versions here. The "halls" are also decked with pepperoni and spinach breads, quiche, pizza, a selection of freshly baked desserts, and a large and stellar array of wines. Gift baskets are a specialty, and gift certificates are available. (For more information about the restaurant, see listing for Alberini's that appears earlier in this chapter.) Ample, convenient parking.

## Alesci's of South Euclid
☎ (216) 382-5100
CITY: **South Euclid**    AREA: **East Side**

**ADDRESS:** 4333 Mayfield Rd.
**FOOD AVAIL.:** Meat (deli), grains, beans, flour, baked goods, canned & packaged goods, spices, condiments, beverages, tea, coffee, wine, beer, prepared frozen foods, takeout meals **HOURS:** Mon–Sat 9 a.m.–6 p.m., Sun 9 a.m.–3 p.m. **PAYMENT:** MC, VS, AX, DIS, checks **ACCESS:** ♿ Full access

This is a 7,000-square-foot gourmet Italian food superstore. Alesci's opened in 1943 and has been at this location since 1957. The selection of prepared foods is just this side of awesome: Italian meatballs, lasagna, subs (one favorite is the "grinder," made of hard-crust Italian bread, salami, cappicola, provolone, and roasted pimientos), and more than 15 different types of pizza sold by the slice, ranging from standard pepperoni to less conventional ones like crabmeat pizza, broccoli pizza, spinach pizza, and pizza bianco (white pizza). There are more than 30 types of salads in the deli, including pasta salads and olive salads, and fresh Italian sausage is available at the deli counter, too. Alesci's prepares 13 varieties of homemade pasta sauces, sold fresh and frozen by the pint or quart. They are famous for their Italian bread and also bake pepperoni bread, sfogliatelli, and breadsticks. Spices, grated Romano cheese, and coffee (38 kinds in bulk) are available. Many brands of olive oils and balsamic vinegar are available in either quart or gallon sizes. They also carry imported pastas, pignoli nuts, confetti candy, polenta, semolina, and couscous.

Delivery service and catering are available. Orders can also be placed online at www.alescifoods.com.

## Baraona's Baking Co., Inc.
☎ (216) 662-8383
CITY: **Maple Heights**    AREA: **Southeast**

**ADDRESS:** 15842 Libby Rd.
**FOOD AVAIL.:** Baked goods **HOURS:** Mon 8 a.m.–4 p.m., Tue–Fri 8 a.m.–5:30 p.m., Sat 8 a.m.–5 p.m., Sun 8 a.m.–1 p.m. **PAYMENT:** MC, VS **ACCESS:** ♿ Full access

Family owned and operated since 1949, Baraona's has built a solid reputation—reaching as far as Mentor and Brunswick—based on their spumoni, gelati, and lemon ice, homemade the Old World way, as well as their large, beautifully decorated cakes, including cassata, for all occasions. They bake a variety of cookies that includes both Italian and other ethnic specialties like kolachies. No bread.

## Casa Dolce Italian Bakery
☎ (440) 473-0697
CITY: **Mayfield Hts.**      AREA: **East Side**

**ADDRESS:** 5732 Mayfield Rd.
**FOOD AVAIL.:** Baked goods, spices, condiments, beverages, tea, coffee, takeout meals **HOURS:** Mon–Sat 7 a.m.–7:30 p.m. **PAYMENT:** MC, VS, DIS **ACCESS:** ♿ Full access

Calling this place a bakery is both misleading and an understatement. It's true that there's a wonderful selection of fresh, baked-on-the-premises traditional sweets, from cassata cakes and cannoli to biscotti and pignoli, along with breads and rolls. But you can buy breakfast, lunch, and dinner here, too. The ever-changing line-up of prepared appetizers, entrées, and side dishes are sold by the piece and the pound— think frittata, veal Marsala, deep-dish lasagna, chicken in pesto, stuffed artichokes, pasta in vodka cream sauce, and eggplant parmesan, all on display in refrigerated cases. It's also a market with shelves of dried pasta, jarred sauces, oils, and vinegars. You could even get away with calling it a cafe, as there are five tables and 20 chairs here if you prefer to order a bowl of Italian wedding soup, a panini, a pizza, or a salad and eat on the spot. Since they also serve gelato, sorbetto, and lemon ice it could even qualify as an Italian ice cream parlor. So what to label this place? It needs a category all its own. I propose "Foodery"—a shopping and dining venue that supplies all sorts of good things to eat in various states of readiness. The pleasant space lets in lots of light through the big windows overlooking the parking lot, and beautiful food provides all that's needed of décor and ambience. It opened at the end of 2004, and the talented Margie Onofrio Axelrod, who has cooked at Sergio's and

the Baricelli Inn, purchased the business in the fall of 2007. She really upped the ante on quality, variety, and creativity, making everything including stocks and breadcrumbs from scratch, slicing turkey off the bone for sandwiches, and offering restaurant-style specials like risotto and lamb shanks. She does offsite catering, party trays, gift baskets, and boxed lunches.

## Colozza's Cakes & Pastries
☎ (440) 885-0453
CITY: **Parma**     AREA: **Southwest**

**ADDRESS:** 5880 Ridge Rd.
**FOOD AVAIL.:** Baked goods **HOURS:** Tuesday 7 a.m.–3 p.m., Wed–Sat 7 a.m.–5:30 p.m., Sun 7 a.m.–2 p.m.; closed Mon **PAYMENT:** MC, VS, DIS, checks **ACCESS:** ♿ Full access

Because Angelo Colozza bakes every day, Clevelanders can take home some very special Italian desserts. There's Santa Lorenzo, alternating layers of puff pastry, raspberry filling, amaretto-soaked sponge cake, and whipped cream topped with shaved chocolate; three-layer glazed fruit tortes; and rum babas. His traditional cassata cake is rum-soaked, ricotta-filled, and studded with chocolate chips and diced fruit. He also makes what he refers to as "American" cassata cake with strawberries and whipped cream, cannoli, and sfogliatelli, a sweet ricotta-filled pastry that looks like a clam shell. Colozza will decorate any of his 30 varieties of tortes (some of which he'll sell by the slice) and cakes to suit any occasion.

## Corbo's Dolceria

☎ (216) 421-8181

CITY: **Cleveland** AREA: **Near East Side**

ADDRESS: 12210 Mayfield Rd.
FOOD AVAIL.: Baked goods HOURS: Tue–Sat 8
a.m.–10 p.m., Sun 8 a.m.–8 p.m. PAYMENT: MC,
VS, checks ACCESS: & Full access

Family-owned and operated since 1958, this is a landmark in Little Italy. In the spring of 2008, the business moved to new digs next door. This much bigger two-room space accommodates a dozen tables with more out front on the sidewalk seasonally. Refrigerated cases are filled with pasta dishes, salads, and sandwiches for eating here or taking out. Though every day brings in regular customers from the neighborhood, people from all over the state also stop in to buy one of their famous cassata cakes (a strawberry-and-cream-filled yellow layer cake) and cannoli. They bake biscotti, totos, piginoci, cuchidoti, and other Italian cookies, breads, and sheet pizzas as well. Staff members scoop gelato and Italian ices and steam up frothy cups of cappucino.

## DeVitis & Sons

☎ (330) 535-2626

CITY: **Akron** AREA: **Farther South**

ADDRESS: 560 E. Tallmadge Ave.
FOOD AVAIL.: Meat (deli), produce, grains, beans, flour, rice, baked goods, canned & packaged goods, spices, condiments, beverages, tea, coffee, wine, prepared frozen foods, takeout meals HOURS: Mon–Fri 8:30 a.m.–6:30 p.m., Sat 8:30 a.m.–6 p.m., Sunday 9 a.m.–1 p.m. PAYMENT: MC, VS, checks ACCESS: & Limited OTHER ETHNIC: Greek

Robert DeVitis likes to say that "Columbus discovered America, Marco Polo discovered spaghetti, and the De-Vitis family discovered a way to bring Italy (and spaghetti) to Northeast Ohio." Frank DeVitis, born in 1900, emigrated here from Italy and opened the store (which sold only produce) in 1940; it's remained a family business. But it's expanded both in size and scope, now offering a large variety of imported Italian staples, deli meats, cheeses, homemade sausage, and Italian salads and entrées in addition to top-quality fresh produce. Heat-and-eat meatballs, lasagna, veal patties, and breaded eggplant are always available, and staff estimate they prepare 300-400 sandwiches to order daily. Sausage comes regular, hot, and Sicilian-style, and to satisfy their customers' changing tastes they now make another version using turkey. Their customers are a loyal band and often know each other. According to Robert, they use the store as a meeting place, so there's a kind of sociable atmosphere. "People come in, see folks they haven't seen in a while, and it's like a reunion or a celebration."

## Dioguardi's Specialty Foods

☎ (330) 492-3777

CITY: **Canton** AREA: **Farther South**

ADDRESS: 3116 Market Ave. N
FOOD AVAIL.: Meat (deli), baked goods, canned & packaged goods, spices, condiments, beverages, tea, coffee, wine, beer, prepared frozen foods, takeout meals HOURS: Mon–Fri 9 a.m.–6 p.m., Sat 9 a.m.–5 p.m., Sun 9 a.m.–midnight PAYMENT: MC, VS, DIS ACCESS: & Full access OTHER ETHNIC: Greek, Middle Eastern mix

A red-white-and-green awning makes this Italian market easy to find for those who don't already know about the place. This is no longer as much of a residential neighborhood as it was when the Dioguardi family erected the small brick storefront in 1920, and a busy four-lane road now runs in front of it. But the original owners still live across the street, just as they did back then. And the store still sells Italian salads, olives, cold cuts, and cheeses, including Calabrese salami, mascarpone (thick, rich, moist cow's milk cream cheese with a consistency that ranges from that of clotted or sour cream to butter), and scamorze (a hard, distinctively flavored cheese). They make their own sausages, sauces, and meatballs. Also on hand are Moretti beer, a large selection of wines, pasta (dried and frozen), spices, and jars of traditional products like peppers in sauce, lupini beans, and marinated mussels. A line of Greek cheeses and grocery items has been added. The selection of wines is extensive, with more than 700 different domestics and imports. You can get sandwiches to go here, party trays, or everything you need to put together a meal at home. Gourmet cooks like this place because the owners are willing to track down whatever special ingredients customers request.

## DiStefano's Authentic Italian Foods
☎ (440) 442-7775
CITY: **Highland Heights** AREA: **East Side**

ADDRESS: 5600 Highland Rd.
FOOD AVAIL.: Flour, baked goods, canned & packaged goods, spices, condiments, beverages, tea, wine, prepared frozen foods, takeout meals HOURS: Mon–Fri 9 a.m.–6:30 p.m., Sat 9 a.m.–5 p.m., Sun 9 a.m.–1 p.m. PAYMENT: MC, VS, AX, DIS, checks ACCESS: & Full access

This is what most grocery stores were like just a generation ago: a family-owned, friendly neighborhood place, not too big or too small, with a regular and familiar clientele. Shoppers will find homemade (on the premises) sausage,

meatballs, lasagna, and chicken cutlets prepared for takeout or heat-at-home, and freshly baked breads (including their famed Calabrese version), pastries, biscotti, and other cookies. Made-from-scratch pizzas can be ordered, and they make one version of focaccia. There's a large selection of imported olive oils, spices, packaged pasta, and imported and domestic wines.

## Fragapane Bakery & Deli
☎ (440) 779-6050
CITY: **North Olmsted** AREA: **West Side**

ADDRESS: 28625 Lorain Rd.
FOOD AVAIL.: Meat (fresh, deli), baked goods, canned & packaged goods, condiments, beverages, tea, coffee, wine, beer, prepared frozen foods, takeout meals HOURS: Tue–Sat 6 a.m.–6:30 p.m., Sun 6 a.m.–4 p.m.; closed Mon PAYMENT: MC, VS, AX, DIS, checks ACCESS: & Full access

This is a bakery, an Italian deli, and an import store. They make the usual Italian-style breads, cakes, cookies, and pastries; pans of lasagna and sheets of pizza; and frozen homemade sauces, garlic bread, sausage, and pasta. They also stock a selection of wines, sauces, peppers, and pasta from Italy. There's a large variety of non-Italian baked goods, too, from croissants to strudel. They have two other locations: in Bay Village and Middleburg Heights (see separate listings for details).

## Fragapane Bakery & Deli
☎ (440) 871-6340
CITY: **Bay Village** AREA: **West Side**

ADDRESS: 650 Dover Center Rd.
FOOD AVAIL.: Meat (fresh, deli), baked goods, condiments, beverages, tea, coffee, prepared frozen foods, takeout meals HOURS: Tue–Sat 6 a.m.–6 p.m., Sun 7 a.m.–3 p.m.; closed Mon

**PAYMENT:** MC, VS, AX, DIS, checks **ACCESS:** ♿ Full access

All the baking is done at the North Olmsted store and delivered fresh to this location each morning. For a description of their stock, see previous listing for Fragapane on Lorain, but be aware that the selection here is smaller.

## Gallucci Italian Food
☎ (216) 881-0045
CITY: **Cleveland**    AREA: **Near East Side**

**ADDRESS:** 6610 Euclid Ave.
**FOOD AVAIL.:** Meat (fresh, frozen), grains, beans, flour, baked goods, canned & packaged goods, spices, condiments, beverages, tea, wine, prepared frozen foods, takeout meals
**HOURS:** Mon–Fri 8 a.m.–6 p.m., Sat 8 a.m.–5 p.m.; closed Sun **PAYMENT:** MC, VS, AX, DIS, checks **ACCESS:** ♿ Full access

The Gallucci family has been selling Clevelanders Italian specialty foods since 1912. Current manager Ray Gallucci Jr., the third generation to be involved in this importing and retailing business, goes "shopping" in Italy every year. Because they buy directly from producers themselves, they're able to pass the cost savings on to their customers, a loyal and devoted breed. It's not uncommon for second- and third-generation customers to frequent Gallucci's, following them from the original downtown location to the current Euclid Avenue store.

The space is large, modern, and convenient, and the selection of everything Italian is huge. I've never seen so many different kinds of olive oils and vinegars in one place. Some of the pasta and olive oils are packaged so attractively that I buy them to give as gifts. Gallucci's offers customers a number of noteworthy products: a grilled artichoke that comes from Italy in a large vacuum-sealed tray;

mascarpone, a thick, rich, moist cow's milk cream cheese used in traditional desserts like tiramisu; polenta prepared in a refrigerated roll; their own brand of extra virgin olive oil; and a ham from Parma, only recently allowed into this country, called Parmacotto, that is cooked instead of cured like the famous prosciutto from the same region.

The store is often packed on Saturdays with many shoppers driving in from distant suburbs, but it's a congenial kind of crowd. You might have to take a number and wait in line at the counter if you want a hunk of Parmigiano-Reggiano, antipasto salad, or some pancetta (an herb-flavored smoked bacon). The prepared food counter offers a variety of hot and cold Italian dishes, pizza, and sandwiches. The wine department was expanded in 2002; it now features an even larger selection of imported and domestic bottles than before—many not available elsewhere in the state—and several wines imported by Gallucci's directly from Italy. The store has its own parking lot (enter either from Euclid Avenue or Carnegie Avenue, and staff will even help shoppers get their purchases packed into the car. Their Web site, www.tasteitaly.com, offers online shopping, recipes, party tray descriptions and prices, and the lunch menu.

## Giganti's Imported Foods
☎ (440) 546-4455
CITY: **Broadview Heights**    AREA: **Southeast**

**ADDRESS:** 9198 Broadview Rd.
**FOOD AVAIL.:** Meat (fresh, deli), grains, beans, flour, baked goods, canned & packaged goods, spices, condiments, wine, takeout meals **HOURS:** Mon–Thu 9 a.m.–6 p.m., Fri 8 a.m.–6 p.m., Sat 9 a.m.–5 p.m., Sun 9 a.m.–1:30 p.m. **PAYMENT:** MC, VS, AX, DIS, checks **ACCESS:** ♿ Full access

In September 1996 the old Giganti's on Broadway, in Maple Heights, closed, and in March 1997, a new and better Giganti's opened in the Center, a new retail complex. The Giganti family continues to bake bread as well as Italian-style pastries seven days a week. They've added a deli counter in the middle of the store and feature, as they always have, a very large selection of olive oils and vinegars. The shelves are filled with a variety of canned imports, including tuna, sardines, olives, and peppers. They have coffee from Italy, too. Specialty takeout items available daily include Italian subs, cavatelli, rigatoni, stuffed mushrooms, and marinated artichokes. They will gladly prepare party trays and order spices in bulk. Fax your order to 440-546-9045 and it will be ready for pickup when you arrive.

## Giovanni's Meats & Deli

☎ (440) 442-8440

CITY: **Lyndhurst** AREA: **East Side**

**ADDRESS:** 5716 Mayfield Rd.
**FOOD AVAIL.:** Meat (fresh, deli, frozen), fish (fresh, frozen), canned & packaged goods, spices, condiments, beverages, tea, coffee, wine, takeout meals **HOURS:** Mon, Tue, Thu & Fri 9 a.m.–6 p.m., Sat 8 a.m.–6 p.m.; closed Wed & Sun **PAYMENT:** MC, VS, AX, DIS, checks **ACCESS:** ♿ Full access

Joseph Castrataro came from Italy, started this business in 1968, and his son John took over when Joseph retired in 1980. He's managed to keep a sense of neighborliness and European style that makes shopping here a pleasure. That leads to this riddle: How can a butcher shop be like a bar? Or why is Giovanni's like *Cheers* of TV fame? Answer: because everybody knows your name. Once you're a regular like I am, expect to walk in the door and be greeted with a warm, friendly, and very personal hello from John (Giovanni, in Italian) and all his staff. You can chitchat about the kids and the weather if you've got the time, get good advice about how best to prepare the pork scallopini or veal brisket, and have one of the guys help you carry your packages to the car. You can phone your order in, just like in the good old days gone by, and it will be ready for pickup when you arrive. You may have to take a number on Saturdays and before holidays, because this market is a popular stop for those who care about what they put on the table.

I buy all my meat and poultry here—not just Italian specialties—because once I tasted the fresh Amish-raised chickens, milk-fed veal, Black Angus beef, and spring lamb that John stocks, I was no longer willing to eat the stuff they wrap in plastic and keep on the shelves of the supermarket. But it is a great source of things Italian. They're known for their fresh, homemade sausage (hot and mild), but many customers—the older, the old-fashioned, and the culinarily intrepid—prefer to prepare their own, and it's not unusual to wait in line behind someone requesting 50 pounds of ground pork and a quantity of sausage casings. John carries fresh pasta, frozen homemade meatballs and sauce, frozen pizza dough, a variety of olives, mortadella, Genoa salami, prosciutto, and pancetta. There's a good selection of cheeses imported from Italy, including some uncommon and delicious ones made from sheep's milk, and they'll grind Romano and Parmesan to order. These are also mounds of fresh ricotta. Floor-to-ceiling shelves—and all available floor space—are filled with imported olive oil; wines; tomato products; dried pasta; spices and herbs; breadcrumbs; cornmeal for polenta; canned products, like tuna in olive oil, caponata, marinated artichoke hearts, and roasted red peppers; espresso; and household essentials (if you're a make-it-from-scratch type) like meat grinders, tomato strainers, and pizelle irons.

Party trays and custom cutting are available. The shop is located in a little strip beside the larger plaza known as the Greens of Lyndhurst, just east of Brainard Road, with ample parking.

## Molisana Italian Foods
☎ (440) 526-4141
CITY: **Broadview Heights**   AREA: **Southwest**

ADDRESS: 8037 Broadview Rd.
FOOD AVAIL.: Meat (deli), beans, flour, baked goods, canned & packaged goods, spices, condiments, beverages, tea, coffee, wine
HOURS: Tue–Fri 9 a.m.–6 p.m., Sat 8:30 a.m.–4 p.m.; closed Sun–Mon  PAYMENT: MC, VS
ACCESS: & Full access

The two women who started this business took its name (though they feminized it) from the Molise region of Italy on the Adriatic coast. They aim to offer traditional Italian foods in a modern, upscale European-style setting, complete with marble countertops, custom-made cabinetry, and ceramic floor tiles. There's a varied and interesting selection of deli meats and cheeses, which they use for made-to-order sandwiches on their freshly baked breads and authentic crusty little bread rolls called panini. They also do red focaccia pizza, anise and lemon flavored cookies called ToTos, and prepare party trays. Lots of interesting imports available, including Italian wines and aperitifs, and they'll assemble unusual food gift baskets, incorporating some of the kitchenware they carry. And while you're trying to decide what to buy, you can sample a cup of their espresso or cappuccino from the coffee bar.

## Ninni's Bakery
☎ (330) 634-0060
CITY: **Akron**   AREA: **Farther South**

ADDRESS: 1155 E. Tallmadge Ave.
FOOD AVAIL.: Baked goods, beverages  HOURS: Tue–Sat 9 a.m.–5 p.m., closed Sun–Mon
PAYMENT: MC, VS, DIS  ACCESS: & Full access

Anthony Ninni and his son Aric are proud that their family has been seeing to it that Akronites have cannoli since 1926. On my visit here with fellow food writer Jane Snow, we discovered that we share a passion for them. Our nonstop conversation went on pause while we gobbled up every last delicious crumb and licked the perfectly sweet ricotta cream from our fingertips. Using family recipes that came to this country at the turn of the century with Antonio Ninni, who had a bakery in New York City, they prepare traditional cookies like fig bars, tadole, biscotti, pisselli, and pignoli, which are available by mail order for shipping anywhere in the country; pasticciotti, a pastry "cup" filled with custard; neopolitans; sfogliatelle; rum baba sponge cakes; and torroni nougat candy. They also bake crusty breads and are famous for their beautiful and tasty wedding cakes.

There are three tables inside where you can lick lemon ice or dig into a piece of tiramisu. A few shelves display Italian-themed gift items, like a sign that reads "Parking for Italians Only," T-shirts, imported candies, and pretty bottles of olive oil. This isn't the original location of the family's business, but the old sign still hangs in the window. A nice place to shop or hang out with no-problem parking.

## Presti Bakery
☎ (216) 421-3060
CITY: **Cleveland**   AREA: **Near East Side**

ADDRESS: 12111 Mayfield Rd.
FOOD AVAIL.: Baked goods, beverages, tea, coffee, takeout meals HOURS: Mon–Thu 7 a.m.–7 p.m., Fri–Sat 7 a.m.–10 p.m., Sun 7 a.m.–6 p.m. PAYMENT: MC, VS, AX, checks ACCESS: ♿ Full access

In its third generation as a family business, Presti's is a Little Italy fixture, but the bakery relocated to bigger, better quarters next door just as we were about to slip into the new century. Much has changed along with the address, but the crusty preservative-free Italian breads for which they have long been known are still baked fresh daily. They come in many shapes—some are still molded by hand, just as they were when Grandma and Grandpa Presti were doing the baking at the original place on Coltman Road back in the 1920s. Their granddaughters, Sheila Presti Gentile and Claudia Presti Di Bartolo, run the place now, and Claudia's son Michael does much of the specialty baking, after having been trained by a New York pastry chef flown in for the purpose, who shared some of his own traditional Italian recipes.

The large kitchen and storefront have allowed them to go beyond bread, and they now offer a mouthwatering array of cakes and pastries. There are Italian classics like tiramisu (sponge cake soaked in coffee and Marsala wine combined with sweet mascarpone cheese and chocolate); cannoli, mini-cannoli, and chocolate-dipped cannoli; a veritable army of biscotti flavored with cinnamon, almond, lemon, anise, and hazelnut; sweet ricotta–filled sfogliatelle; and cassata cake. You'll also find some more unusual but nonetheless traditional desserts: casatini (a little sponge cake with cannoli filling wrapped in almond paste); buccelati (once you taste these fig-filled cookies you'll never be happy with a Fig Newton again); pignoli (an almond paste and pine nut cookie) and pizzicotti (an almond paste and cinnamon-flavored cookie); and ricotta pie.

They also prepare pizza, which is sold by the slice, pepperoni and spinach breads, focaccia, stromboli (stuffed breads) and bruschetta, as well as soups, sandwiches, and salads: all can be purchased ready to eat or for heat-and-eat at home. Gelato and Italian ices are also on the menu and my must-have list. The lines get long around lunchtime on Saturday and Sunday after Mass.

## Rito's Italian Bakery
☎ (440) 845-9414
CITY: **Parma**   AREA: **Southwest**

ADDRESS: 10551 W. Pleasant Valley Rd.
FOOD AVAIL.: Meat (deli), fish (frozen), baked goods, canned & packaged goods, coffee, wine, beer, prepared frozen foods, takeout meals HOURS: Mon–Fri 8 a.m.–7 p.m., Sat 8 a.m.–6 p.m., Sun 8 a.m.–3 p.m. PAYMENT: MC, VS, AX, DIS, checks ACCESS: ♿ Full access

A family business since the mid-1970s, Rito's specializes in Sicilian- and Neapolitan-style foods. They are especially proud of their almond paste cookies and sfogliatelli, a cheese-filled pastry. They also prepare lasagna and eggplant Parmesan, sheet pizzas, and homemade breads and rolls. The deli counter maintains a nice selection of meats and cheeses, and sandwiches are made to order. They also carry a selection of non-Italian cookies and donuts, and bake cakes for all occasions. Parking is available in lot next to bakery.

## The Stone Oven Bakery Cafe
☎ (216) 932-3003
CITY: **Cleveland Heights**   AREA: **East Side**

**ADDRESS:** 2267 Lee Rd.
**FOOD AVAIL.:** Baked goods, beverages, tea, coffee, takeout meals   **HOURS:** Mon–Thu 7 a.m.–9 p.m., Fri 7 a.m.–10 p.m., Sat 8 a.m.–10 p.m., Sun 8:30 a.m.–8 p.m.   **PAYMENT:** MC, VS, AX, DIS   **ACCESS:** ⅃ Full access

Opened in 1995, Stone Oven is the brainchild of Tatyana Rehn, a Russian immigrant and former engineer. But it's traditional Italian, not Russian breads, that she hand shapes and bakes in small batches in stone-lined ovens that give the place its name and the bread its distinctive crust. It all began when she tasted bread freshly made by an Italian chef at her former brother-in-law's New York restaurant. It was, she recalls, the first good bread she'd had since leaving Russia, and she decided to perfect her own baking skills at home. At her bakery, where the only piece of kitchen machinery she'll allow is a mixer, she and her staff prepare traditional focaccia loaves, Siciliano and Pugliese bread, and others scented with rosemary or flavored with olives, cheese, or nuts. She does a large wholesale business, supplying many area restaurants and grocery stores. Italian desserts like tiramisu and biscotti are also available along with bread pudding, tea biscuits, fruit tarts, and European style cakes. There are about 60 seats in this spacious cafe, plus more outside on the patio in back, where you can enjoy homemade soups, salads, sandwiches, or a piece of gourmet pizza, as well as espresso, cappuccino, and dessert. On-street parking and additional parking in a city lot at the back.

# EUROPE EAST OF
# THE DANUBE

Europe east of the Danube River includes newly emerging and re-emerging nations, groups engaged in fierce struggles to redefine both their borders and their identities. Some of the countries whose names I learned in grade school no longer exist, and places I never knew existed, long lost in the no-man's-land of the Soviet bloc, now proclaim themselves nations. So it is problematical even to begin with a simple list of countries whose heritage is reflected in this chapter. Perhaps it is more accurate to focus on the people rather than the places, for it is through their lives that traditions endure. Czech, Slovak, Lithuanian, Croatian, Polish, Slovenian, Serb, Hungarian, Byelorussian, and Ukrainian immigrants all left the land they knew for a new start in Cleveland, transplanting their cultural and food traditions in the process.

A local newspaper editorial written in 1851 urged immigrants to immediately become "Americanized" by "casting off" their European "skins." It was advice few could really follow, needing that sense of national identity to see them through the hardships of being strangers in a strange land, often engaged in grueling, mind-numbing labor. Most stuck close to their own kind, finding comfort and protection in the proximity of their countrymen.

This was especially true for those of Eastern European descent, and they formed distinct ethnic corridors throughout the city, with nationality neighborhoods growing around the various industries and factories where the men earned their hourly wage.

As the century came to an end, each of the various Slavic groups had formed its own self-help societies, social clubs, schools, and religious congregations based on ethnic affiliations. Singing societies, sports clubs, and dance groups created a sense of solidarity that has endured, even as following generations left the old neighborhoods, moved to the suburbs, and became fully assimilated into an American lifestyle.

These are heritages difficult for an outsider to fully understand, and I admit my shortcomings here. There are at least 12 different so-called Slavic nationality groups. "Historically, as well as in the present," explains Algis Ruksenas, executive director of Cleveland's International Services Center, "there has been a tendency to homogenize the various Eastern European peoples, to bunch them together and see them as a single entity. Immigration officials used to mistakenly log newcomers in as Russians when in fact they may have been from Poland, Lithuania, Latvia, or Estonia. Each nationality is a distinct cultural group, as different as an Italian from a Frenchman, though both are from what's called Western Europe."

Czechoslovakia as a state was a modern political entity representing an affiliation of Czechs and Slovaks. Cleveland's Czech community is one of its oldest and largest. The Slovaks are a separate immigrant group, and in the early 1900s the Cleveland area was home to the largest number of Slovaks in the world. Poles, too, came in great numbers. The Association of Polish Women in the USA chose Cleveland as the site for their first annual convention in February 1913. In a 1930 census, 32,688 people named Poland as their country of origin.

At one time, only Hungary itself had more Hungarians than Cleveland, and we still rank fourth in this country in the number of Croatians living here. Greater Cleveland's Lithuanian community is one of the most active outside of Lithuania itself. It's hard to identify the numbers of Russians who have come here because there has always been a question about what the word actually means. Under that umbrella might be included Byelorussians, Carpatho-Russians, Great Russians, and Ukrainians. And Jews from all these Eastern European homelands formed yet another separate, distinctive subset of immigrant Americans (see American Regional chapter).

What all this really means is that, collectively, the people of Eastern Europe have had a profound effect on the development of Cleveland, significantly impacting what this city has become. Ruksenas, himself an immigrant from Lithuania, calls them "the quiet influence," for they interacted with the city from the bottom up. They were the muscle that provided the infrastructure for a growing Cleveland.

Years ago there were countless restaurants and boardinghouses all around the city where the foods beloved by these Slavic groups could be had. Now there are relatively few. But there remain a surprisingly large number of shops, bakeries, and butchers that cater to these ethnic groups—tangible evidence of their long-standing presence and deep roots in the community. Many of the stores have been run by one family for generations or have been in the same location for half a century or more. There a visitor today will encounter the timeless aroma of pickles and paprika, kielbasa and kraut. The sight of mounds of potato-filled pierogies, slices of liver sausage, and strips of flaky strudel tell a story of day-to-day life that perennially unfolds around the table. In their own way, these stores are windows looking back into the lives of all those Eastern European immigrant families. Though culturally diverse, they have always shared a taste for many of the same foods and a common style of preparing them.

Eastern and Central European cooks traditionally make hearty, filling food rich with the taste of butter, cottage cheese, and sour cream. The cuisine depends upon potatoes, cabbage, beets, mushrooms, peppers, noodles, and dumplings seasoned with dill, caraway seeds, onions, garlic, and parsley as well as paprika.

All varieties of meat and poultry are used in soups and stews laced with root vegetables. Pickling is the favored way to handle garden produce. Sausage-making is an art, and the variety is almost endless; the same could be said of their traditional pastries, cakes, and cookies, many made with fruit such as apples, cherries, and plums.

"People who have Americanized," said Ruksenas, who was seven when he arrived in Cleveland with his parents as a World War II refugee, "can recapture their heritage with a recipe, which is literally and figuratively palatable. Often that's all that remains of their cultural legacy. While I think it's terribly important to understand that the sum and substance of each of these Old World cultures is much more than sausage and sauerkraut, food is without a doubt a basic, concrete connection to one's own history, and menus hearken back to a deeper, more abstract cultural wealth."

Every Clevelander with Eastern European roots I've ever spoken with insists that nobody makes dishes as good as their own grandmother's, but nonetheless they can all be depended upon to do justice to a plateful of stuffed cabbage or a brimming bowl of goulash, no matter who prepared it. "For Eastern Europeans," explained Chris Jagelewski, whose grandparents came from Poland, "eating is a social occasion, and social occasions always include eating. When I was growing up, friends and relatives regularly gathered around the kitchen table to eat, talk, and laugh. My mother and my grandmother always had something extra ready to serve to unexpected guests. There's an old Polish housewives' saying that goes, 'If you have no leftovers, tomorrow will be a beautiful day.' I think it means that when people come together and enjoy your food, it's a good thing."

## RESTAURANTS

# Croatian

### Dubrovnik Garden Restaurant
☎ (440) 946-3366
CITY: **Eastlake**   AREA: **Farther East**
ATMOSPHERE: **Casual**   COST: $$$$$

**ADDRESS:** 34900 Lake Shore Blvd.
**HOURS:** Lunch daily 11 a.m.–2:30 p.m.; Dinner daily 4:30–10 p.m.; closed between lunch & dinner **RESERVATIONS:** Recommended **PAYMENT:** MC, VS, AX, checks **BAR:** Beer, wine, liquor **TAKEOUT:** Yes **ACCESS:** ♿ Full access

Coming here is more than going out to eat—it's a cultural event. That's because this restaurant is located inside the American Croatian Lodge, which also houses the Croatian Heritage Museum, Library, and Gift Shop (usually open on Friday and Saturday nights, Sunday afternoons, and by appointment). The lobby, too, always has some interesting historical or craft exhibits on display. The restaurant itself feels like a private club, but all are welcome. You step up into the dining room, which has tables down the center and booths on the sides, and step down to the bar. The walls feature paintings of Croatian cities done by a local artist, as well as carved

wooden plates and other pieces of folk art and craft. The back of the menu is a full-page history of the ancient seaside town of Dubrovnik.

There are four traditional Croatian entrées: the Dubrovnik Grill, which includes raznici (pork and veal kebabs) and cevapcici (a blend of beef, pork, and veal); the Croatian Dish, made with raznici, cevapcici, pork chops, and chicken; and the Chef's Specialty of sauerkraut, sausage, smoked pork chop, and bratwurst. The rest of the menu is pure Ohio, an eclectic mix of spaghetti, steak, and a dish called Chicken American. Whatever you choose to eat for your main course, try to leave room for their palacinke, a light and delicate dessert.

# Czech

### Marta's
☎ (216) 731-9596
CITY: **Euclid**   AREA: **East Side**
ATMOSPHERE: **Relaxed**   COST: $$$$$

**ADDRESS:** 800 E. 222nd St.
**HOURS:** Mon–Sat 4–9 p.m.; closed Sun
**RESERVATIONS:** Taken, only for groups of 6+
**PAYMENT:** MC, VS, AX **BAR:** Beer, wine, liquor
**TAKEOUT:** Yes **ACCESS:** ♿ Limited **OTHER ETHNIC:** German, Hungarian, Polish

Located in a neighborhood of small shops and neat little houses fronted by carefully tended lawns, Marta's offers real home cooking, if your home or your ethnic roots are Bohemian. In this country just 16 years, Marta Runza calls herself a newborn American. She perfected her traditional cooking skills before emigrating from Prague, learning to cook by watching her mother, and as a young bride. The first inkling she had that she enjoyed feeding a crowd was when she prepared meals for all the workmen who helped her and her husband build a house. That experience led her to jobs in restaurant kitchens in Cleveland, including the Czech Inn, and finally to owning her own restaurant, which she runs with the help of her family. "Business has been good, knock on wood," she says. In the first weeks after the *Plain Dealer* review came out, she and her daughter Lenka served about 300 meals a day . . . quite a lot for a restaurant with just eight tables and 18 bar stools.

It's what they serve that makes their customers so happy: roast pork loin so tender you can cut it with a fork; tangy sauerbraten; Wiener schnitzel; crispy-on-the-outside, tender-on-the inside roast duck; beef goulash; chicken paprikash; Czech bread dumplings; and spaetzle, those little noodly drops that are good gravy's perfect mate. One story she tells is of a 94-year-old man who came in looking for kidney stew. He was quite disappointed when he discovered this dish was not on the menu, but when told that she does make liver dumpling soup, he visibly brightened and announced, "I'll be back!" And he has been, along with a host of other regulars from nearby and as far away as Bay Village and Akron.

Dinner portions must be described as huge; younger children could easily share an entrée. There are also a few kid-sized meals on the menu and a choice of American-style appetizers, salads, and lunchtime sandwiches and burgers. Virtually everything they serve, including the salad dressings, the real mashed potatoes, and the strudel, is made from scratch in their own kitchen. Marta also prepares palacinka, a crepe filled with fresh fruit and topped with whipped cream.

There's a simple sweetness to the place, which still maintains the feel of the cozy tavern it once was, despite the lace curtains at the windows, the cloth flowers on the tables, the white paper napkins banded with burgundy paper rings, and the Czech folk music playing softly in the background. Czech beer is available. Marta's is easy to find: the place has a distinctive black-and-white diner-style exterior, with an awning. Parking in back.

## Old Prague Restaurant

☎ (440) 967-7182

CITY: **Vermilion**  AREA: **Farther West**
ATMOSPHERE: **Dressy**  COST: **$$$**$$

**ADDRESS:** 5586 Liberty Ave.
**HOURS:** Jun–Oct: Mon–Fri 4–10 p.m., Sat–Sun noon–10 p.m.; Nov–Feb: Fri 4–10 p.m., Sat noon–10 p.m., Sun noon–9 p.m.; Mar–May: Wed–Fri 4–10 p.m., Sat–Sun noon–10 p.m.
**RESERVATIONS:** Taken, recommended on weekends **PAYMENT:** MC, VS, DIS **BAR:** Beer, wine, liquor **TAKEOUT:** Yes **ACCESS:** ♿ Limited

Set in the heart of Vermilion's historic harbor district, the place looks like a European mountain chalet. It's definitely a "destination restaurant," and patrons consider it well worth the 45-minute trip from downtown Cleveland, a drive many of the area's Czech Americans make regularly. The Lich family, who has owned the place for decades, and the chef are from the former Czechoslovakia. In 2004, Vera Lich handed off ownership and responsibilities to her son Michael. Del Donahoo has visited here, and Dick Feagler is a regular.

The most popular dishes are shishki, a spicy meat-stick appetizer; roast duck with sauerkraut and dumplings; roast pork; Wiener schnitzel; chicken paprikash; Bohemian goulash; and sauerbraten. It's the kind of food you keep on eating even when you know you're full. They bake all their own pastries, including melt-in-your-mouth strudel and palacinkas. There are also some simple American items on the menu, like steak and seafood (including fresh Lake Erie perch). There is a meatless paprikash entrée option for vegetarians, plus some other vegetarian dishes. They carry wines and beers made in the Czech Republic, including the famous Pilsner Urquell. The size of the place is modest, the ambience warm and comfortable in the Old World style, with Czech crystal and folk art on display.

# Eastern European mix

## Al's Corner Restaurant
☎ (330) 753-7216
CITY: **Barberton**   AREA: **Farther South**
ATMOSPHERE: **Relaxed**   COST: $$$$$

**ADDRESS:** 545 W. Tuscarawas Ave.
**HOURS:** Mon–Fri 11 a.m.–2 p.m.  **RESERVATIONS:** Not taken  **PAYMENT:** Checks  **BAR:** None
**TAKEOUT:** Yes  **ACCESS:** & Full access

Barberton is a working-class town with strong Eastern European roots, so it's surprising that no local restaurant was dishing up ethnic food on a daily basis. People had such a craving for it that they begged Tim and Jeanette Eberhardt, who sold homemade sausages and fresh heat-'n'-eat cabbage rolls at their butcher shop, to start offering hot lunches. (For more information about the butcher shop, see listing for Al's Market in the market section of this chapter.) Jeanette heeded the call and decided to open a restaurant, but her mantra is "Keep It Simple." She makes only five different entrées and serves them on disposable plates that customers carry to the tables themselves.

Here "simple" also means delicious. There's chicken paprikash with fluffy, melt-in-your mouth dumplings that are also paired up with cabbage; stuffed cabbage rolls with a dense meat filling that you can order with a side of real mashed potatoes; potato and cheese pierogies sautéed in butter with onions; and Slovenian and Hungarian sausages, made by the Eberhardts themselves, with sauerkraut. And if that doesn't leave you feeling full, they make their own strudel and cheesecake.

The restaurant is located in a building Tim already owned, a few doors away from the butcher shop. He and his father did the remodeling themselves, leaving the old tin ceiling intact, and re-creating the look of a '50s luncheonette, using a counter and red swivel stools from an old Woolworth's store and booths from a long-gone area restaurant. The interior is painted a sunny yellow. The midweek lunch line was out the door, and Jeanette has told me that it's not unusual for her to serve 144 meals in three hours. Not bad for a little place that doesn't even have a phone. (If you must reach the restaurant, use the number for the butcher shop, 330-753-7216, and Tim will walk over there the first chance he gets to deliver the message. Likewise, although credit cards are not accepted at the restaurant, in a pinch or for very large orders Jeanette will run over to the butcher shop and use the machine there.) Apparently there was a need—or should I say an appetite—for a place like this, and Jeanette's happy to serve up a hearty, homestyle solution.

## Marie's Restaurant

☎ (216) 361-1816

CITY: **Cleveland** AREA: **Near East Side**
ATMOSPHERE: **Casual** COST: **$$**$$

**ADDRESS:** 4502 St. Clair Ave.
**HOURS:** Mon–Sat 11 a.m.–9 p.m.; closed Sun
**RESERVATIONS:** Taken, recommended evenings
**PAYMENT:** Checks **BAR:** Beer, wine, liquor
**TAKEOUT:** Yes **ACCESS:** & Full access **OTHER ETHNIC:** Croatian

. . . . . . . . . . . . . . . . . . . . . . . . . .

Marie's is definitely the sort of place you'd have to know about before choosing it. A storefront amid mostly commercial buildings, it offers little to attract a passerby (the area would never be mistaken for a restaurant row). But once you do know about it, there's every reason to get yourself there because of the made-from-scratch food Mila Sabljic prepares each day. Born and raised in the former Yugoslavia, Mila makes stuffed cabbage, chicken paprikash, stuffed peppers, beef goulash, schnitzel, and dumplings the Old World way. She also prepares cevapi (a grilled Croatian sausage), and if you call a few days in advance she'll make roast lamb or pork for a large group.

The effort here is on the food and not the atmosphere. There are two small rooms; the front section handles the takeout business. The rooms have high, old-fashioned ceilings of pressed tin, wood paneling, and fresh carpeting. Tables wear white cloths. One patron described the place as 15 degrees shy of comfortable but nonetheless a good place to eat, and regulars call it warm and welcoming. I'd have to agree, and so would my three sons, who found the hefty portions and informal, friendly atmosphere much to their liking. The prices make it possible for a family like mine to eat well without having to take out a second mortgage on the house.

The place is often busy at lunch with a downtown business crowd, but the dinner hour seems to draw fewer people, mostly folks from the neighborhood.

## New Era Cafe

☎ (330) 784-0087

CITY: **Akron** AREA: **Farther South**
ATMOSPHERE: **Relaxed** COST: **$$**$$

**ADDRESS:** 10 Massillon Rd.
**HOURS:** Mon–Thu 11 a.m.–9 p.m., Fri–Sat 11 a.m.–10 p.m., Sun 11 a.m.–8 p.m.
**RESERVATIONS:** Not taken **PAYMENT:** MC, VS, DIS, checks **BAR:** Beer, wine, liquor **TAKEOUT:** Yes
**ACCESS:** & Full access

. . . . . . . . . . . . . . . . . . . . . . . . . .

This former tavern opened in 1937. These days Mary Lekic is in charge, along with her husband Milos, aka Mitch, who mans the bar, and her mother, Lucija Strebick, who cooks everything from scratch, six days a week, no small accomplishment for a woman in her 80s. She's been doing it since her cousin, the restaurant and bar's original owner, brought her over from the former Yugoslavia in 1960s to help in the kitchen, having heard that Lucija was a really hard worker. That's an understatement. I once overheard this small, gray-haired dynamo, who still stretches her strudel dough by hand (no premade sheets of filo dough allowed here), tell a customer that she was beginning to feel her age. So she goes home for a few hours between the lunch and dinner hours to give her tired legs a little rest.

The rest of the time she—and her helpers—have plenty to do. There's chicken paprikash and dumplings to make; the dinner includes a side dish and a piece of her strudel at a steal of a price, with a smaller portion at an even lower price for kids. The meat is so fall-off-the-bone tender that the only thing you need a knife for is to push it onto the fork. Her version, however, is a dish best eaten with a spoon, in my opinion, so you can scoop up all the good paprika-red gravy and onions, too. The paprikash and the strudel, served warm, are the only obviously ethnic items on the regular menu. But specials that change daily give her a chance to show off her heritage in the form of entrées such as stuffed cabbage, stuffed peppers, ham and cabbage, or chicken livers. She does duck on Fridays, and goulash every Saturday. Although the remainder of the menu is standard tavern fare, Mrs. Strebick, who is originally from a region near the Adriatic Sea, has her own distinctive way of preparing such dishes as pork chops; meatloaf; and chicken noodle, potato, vegetable, or bean soup, so popular that they're available by the quart for carryout. Whole and half strudels can be ordered in advance, and traditional sour cream kifle cookies are sold by the dozen.

In 2005 the old cinderblock building came down and a much larger and nicer one was erected on the same spot. Now, there are two rooms, one for drinkers and smokers, a waiting area, and more booths and tables. It's bright, it's white, and unfortunately it lacks all the character of its predecessor, now sporting the generic look common to many midpriced chain restaurants. But the New Era remains an Akron landmark, frequented by politicians, professionals, and celebrities, as well as everybody else. T-shirts, jeans, and work-stained coveralls predominate, but nobody will look twice if you're wearing a suit. The place has its own parking lot. It's located in a not-so-pretty industrial part of town, easily accessed from I-76 or East Market Street.

# Hungarian

## Balaton Restaurant

☎ (216) 921-9691

CITY: **Cleveland**   AREA: **East Side**
ATMOSPHERE: **Casual**   COST: **$$$**$$

ADDRESS: 13133 Shaker Square
HOURS: Tue–Thu 11:30 a.m.–9 p.m., Fri 11 a.m.–9 p.m., Sat 1 p.m.–9:30 p.m., Sun 1 p.m.–8 p.m.; closed Mon; closes an hour earlier each day Jan–Mar RESERVATIONS: Recommended PAYMENT: MC, VS BAR: Beer, wine TAKEOUT: Yes ACCESS: ♿ Full access

Originally located in an aging building on Buckeye Road, this is Cleveland's oldest Hungarian restaurant. The kitchen's gift with classic entrées like becsiszelet (a thin boneless breaded veal cutlet), goulash, chicken paprikash with dumplings, stuffed cabbage, and palacsinta (crepes) has received high marks and praise from *Where to Eat in America*, *Bon Appétit*, *Gourmet*, *Cleveland* magazine, *Northern Ohio Live*, *Ohio* magazine, the *Cincinnati Enquirer*, and out-of-state newspapers as far afield as Florida, New Jersey, and Kansas.

Owner Louis Olah closed the old place down after 33 years, only to reopen a larger, lovelier version on Shaker Square in the fall of 1997 with the help of new partners George and Christina Ponti. Olah's mother, Theresa, used to do all the cooking herself, but she's been training Erika Nagy, who was born and raised in Budapest, since 1992 and can now leave the kitchen in her more than capable hands. "But Grandma Olah," George Ponti assured me, "is still our official taster and critic."

The food is as fine as ever, most served in huge portions (half portions are available on many entrées) and for a moderate price. The menu has expanded, and the new additions include a seasoned Hungarian feta cheese appetizer called korozott; lecso, a tomato-based stew made with peppers and smoked sausage (also available in a vegetarian version); a pork cutlet gypsy-style served in a paprika cream sauce with fried onion rings; skewers of cubed pork, Hungarian bacon, and sausage; tenderloin of Budapest, a fillet mignon made according to a recipe that's several hundred years old; and roast duck with red cabbage on the first Saturday of each month and on certain selected holidays. The Wood Platter for two offers a selection of different entrées and side dishes served on a beautiful handcarved serving dish, a feast that just "begs" for a good Hungarian wine, says George Ponti, to accompany it—which Balaton now offers by the glass and the bottle. To cater to a wider variety of tastes and needs, they also offer three lighter entrées of broiled or grilled fish and chicken. Every day has its own soup and special, and non-meat eaters can make a great meal out of side orders of potato pancakes or dumplings paired with a cucumber, beet, or tomato-pepper salad. It is this eater's considered opinion that the wise diner will leave room for dessert: strudel, a napolean (layers of flaky pastry alternating with custard and whipped cream), rum raisin cake, or Dobos torte (a multilayer cake).

The two spacious and nicely appointed dining areas offer more in the way of comfort and ambience than the Balaton of before. The Pontis have recreated the look and feel of a Budapest restaurant circa 1920–1930, and they had the perfect space—the building first opened for business in 1928 as a men's clothing store. They tried to restore as much of the original structure and fittings as possible and replaced, when necessary, with reproduction-quality materials and fixtures. The ceilings are high, the floors are natural wood, and the walls are white. The curtains on the large storefront windows are made with fabric imported from Hungary. The lights, which are reminiscent of gas fixtures from the 19th century, give off a soft, pleasant glow. There are fresh flowers on the tables and soft music in the background. Parking on the Square or follow the signs to a municipal lot.

## Helen and Kal's Kitchen

☎ (440) 934-5194

CITY: **Avon**   AREA: **Farther West**
ATMOSPHERE: **Relaxed**   COST: $$$$$

**ADDRESS:** 36795 Detroit Rd.
**HOURS:** Tue–Sat 11 a.m.–8 p.m.; closed Sun–Mon **RESERVATIONS:** Not taken **PAYMENT:** MC, VS, AX, checks **BAR:** Beer **TAKEOUT:** Yes
**ACCESS:** ċ Full access **OTHER ETHNIC:** German

Helen Birkas left Hungary with her parents in 1956. If you're still here after the dinner rush has died down, she may come out of the kitchen to say hello. And if you ask the right questions, she'll tell you about her experiences as a child during World War II, describe life under Communist rule, and give you the story of her family's escape to America.

You can also get her talking about the delights of Hungarian food. Helen, who learned to cook from her mother, likes to say, "You have to eat what your mother cooked for you." But if your mother was neither Hungarian nor a good cook, you can dip into the Birkas tradition instead. In the kitchen of her small storefront restaurant, which she runs with her son, Kal, she prepares homemade soups, beef goulash, dumplings, stuffed cabbage, veal and chicken paprikash, and Wiener schnitzel. But hers is by no means a strictly ethnic restaurant. She also turns out simple, American-style staples: ribs, breaded fish, steaks and burgers, sandwiches, spaghetti and meatballs.

This is a homey place, decorated with knickknacks, curios, paintings. Located in the French Creek district, in a shopping strip across from the Avon fire department and the city hall, it's a popular stop-in spot for the antique hunters who frequent the area on Saturdays and during festivals held three or four times a year.

## Hungarian Business and Tradesman Club
☎ (216) 587-3773
CITY: **Maple Heights**   AREA: **Southeast**
ATMOSPHERE: **Relaxed**   COST: **$$**$$

ADDRESS: 15805 Libby Rd.
HOURS: Tue–Fri 11 a.m.–2 p.m.; closed Sat–Mon RESERVATIONS: Not taken PAYMENT: Cash only BAR: None TAKEOUT: ACCESS: ఉ Full access

There's no better food deal in town. This is a private club, originally formed in the 1920s and still going strong, but they open the dining room to the public four days a week for lunch. Don't expect a menu—each day features a single soup and an entrée—but count on large portions of traditional Hungarian fare at the bargain price of $6. Your money buys you a bowl of thick, hearty soup (chicken noodle, mushroom, vegetable, potato, or perhaps liver dumpling) and a plate of roast pork or duck, chicken or veal paprikash, Wiener schnitzel, or goulash—all of which are likely to come with a side of those little melt-in-your-mouth dumplings that do such an admirable job of soaking up gravy, pierogies, stuffed peppers, or stuffed cabbage. The bread is from a bag, and the salad is a chunk of iceberg with a few carrot shreds soaked in bottled dressing, but it's hard to care about those shortcomings when the rest of the food is so satisfying. "Lunch to go" can be dinner at home—one man told me he comes in a few days a week, eats just the soup, and takes home the rest of his meal along with a second one that he buys for his wife because they both work and have no time to cook. "And the food here," he says, "is just one step away from your own grandma's kitchen."

Tables are large, and strangers, as well as friends, sit together. It's a big space with a party-room atmosphere, because it *is* a party room—the club's an all-purpose social hall, complete with a dance floor and a small, raised platform for the band—and it can be rented. The club offers a catering service, too. Nothing fancy here (this is a hangout, not a destination)—it's a place where members come to see friends, play cards, shoot pool, and celebrate milestones. And all the rest of us are welcome to join them for lunch. Find it next to a bowling alley, between Lee and Broadway, with plenty of parking in an adjacent lot.

# Polish

## Babushka's Kitchen
☎ (330) 468-0402
CITY: **Northfield Center**   AREA: **Southeast**
ATMOSPHERE: **Relaxed**   COST: **$$**$$

ADDRESS: 9199 Olde Eight Rd.
HOURS: Tue–Thu 11:30 a.m.–7 p.m., Fri 11:30 a.m.–8 p.m., Sat 1–7 p.m. RESERVATIONS: Taken PAYMENT: MC, VS, DIS BAR: None TAKEOUT: Yes ACCESS: ఉ Full Access

Whether your heritage includes a golabki-making grandma (that's Polish for stuffed cabbage) or not, you'll feel right at home here, because hominess—that special quality that combines cozy domestic comfort with simple hospitality—is the defining ingredient of the food, the room, and the people behind the counter. Caterers Nancy and David Abramowski are re-creating the meals that are part of their family heritage— kielbasa with kraut, roast pork, and of course handmade pierogies, prepared on the premises daily from an award-winning, and secret, recipe—so secret that only one person is allowed to prepare the dough. There are 54 different sweet and savory fillings. Not all are available every day, but the lineup usually includes potato in various combinations, farmer's cheese, which they also make themselves, and fresh cabbage. The cream cheese pastries known as kolachy are also homemade, with a variety of fillings including poppy seed, cheese, and fruit.

Don't come expecting fancy surroundings or tuxedo-wearing waiters. The draw is double-basted meatloaf with gravy, buttery mountains of mashed potatoes, and specials such as stuffed peppers or chicken paprikash, not atmosphere or service. Portions of everything are generous, prices are reasonable. The day's menu is posted up front. Many customers come in for takeout. But if you're eating here, place your order at the counter. The dining room seats about 44, and recorded polka music provides a soundtrack.

Most of the warehouse-sized space is devoted to a commercial kitchen, where white-coated cooks are visible rolling dough and stirring pots. Pierogies are also sold cold by the dozen, and with 24 hours' notice they'll prepare trays of sauerkraut and dumplings, cabbage and noodles, and entrées from the menu. The restaurant is one of a brace of businesses, set back from the road and fronted by a parking lot. The entire place can be reserved for private parties on selected Sundays. Learn more about what's going on here at www.babush-kafoods.com.

## Little Polish Diner
☎ (440) 842-8212
CITY: **Parma**   AREA: **Southwest**
ATMOSPHERE: **Relaxed**   COST: $$$$$

ADDRESS: 5772 Ridge Rd.
HOURS: Tue–Fri 11 a.m.–7 p.m., Sat 11 a.m.–6 p.m.; closed Sun–Mon   RESERVATIONS: Not taken   PAYMENT: MC, VS, DIS   BAR: None
TAKEOUT: Yes   ACCESS: ⚐ Limited

Sophie Hart emigrated from Poland in the early 1990s and brought with her an expertise in making galumpki (cabbage rolls) and chicken paprikash. She prepares those dishes and a short list of other Polish specialties for her customers. Be prepared for close quarters as you slurp borscht or chow down on smoked kielbasa, sauerkraut, and pierogies. The dining area is smaller than many suburban kitchens with shoulder-to-shoulder seating for 22, including six stools at the counter. It's a plain, narrow space with a few pieces of traditional arts and crafts on the wall for decoration. The atmosphere is friendly, and regulars are treated with an extra helping of sociability. Hart and her partner John Holt also operate a small party center in the same building, and they'll gladly provide a traditional Eastern European menu for event guests. There is a parking lot behind the restaurant.

## Polish American Cultural Center
☎ (216) 883-2828
CITY: **Cleveland**   AREA: **Near East Side**
ATMOSPHERE: **Relaxed**   COST: $$$$$

ADDRESS: 6501 Lansing Ave.
HOURS: Sep–Jun Sun only 11 a.m.–1 p.m.
RESERVATIONS: Not taken   PAYMENT: Checks   BAR: None   TAKEOUT:   ACCESS: ⚐ None

Real Polish food made by real Polish, and Polish-American, people. In keeping with this private club's mission to preserve and promote their cultural heritage, members prepare traditional dishes and serve them buffet style once a week, nine months of the year, in the social room of their facility, located in the heart of Cleveland's Slavic Village. Each Sunday lunch features a soup; two different main dishes; potatoes, noodles, dumplings, or pierogies; salad; and dessert. Expect large portions of things like kielbasa and other varieties of Polish sausage, stuffed cabbage, bigos (stew), goulash, and paprikash. It's always fixed price and always inexpensive. The atmosphere is friendly, welcoming, and clubby. Many diners will know each other, but newcomers quickly feel at home. A step at the entrance, another down into the hall, and short few leading to the restrooms make this a poor choice for the handicapped or elderly who may have difficulty going up and down. For a little culture with your cabbage, visit the heritage museum next door.

## Sokolowski's University Inn
☎ (216) 771-9236
CITY: **Cleveland**    AREA: **Near West Side**
ATMOSPHERE: **Casual**    COST: $$$$$

ADDRESS: 1201 University Rd.
HOURS: Lunch Mon–Fri 11 a.m.–3 p.m.; Dinner Fri 5–9 p.m., Sat 4–9 p.m.; closed between lunch & dinner; open for private parties & catering on Sat, Sun & weeknights
RESERVATIONS: Taken, only for large groups
PAYMENT: MC, VS, checks BAR: Beer, wine, liquor TAKEOUT: Yes ACCESS: ⅙ Full access

This cafeteria, Cleveland's second-oldest family owned and operated restaurant, is popular with the downtown business crowd for lunch, began as a tavern that Mike and Bernie Sokolowski's grandfather opened in 1923. In the 1950s, their parents turned it into a restaurant, and Mrs. Sokolowski cooked hearty meals for the men who worked at the nearby steel mills. Now the restaurant has expanded and serves a group that includes judges, truckers, and everybody in between. It fills three rooms and a kitchen, added on in 1979. One room has a wood-burning fireplace, old trestle tables, and gorgeous copper pots that were used long ago at Cleveland's Leisy Brewery. An expansion connected and converted the garage next door, a huge place where dragsters were once built.

They offer live piano music here all day on Fridays and on Saturday evenings. In a 2001 remodeling of the landmark, the small wood-paneled bar at the back was turned into a dining area, and a 30-seat bar with a spectacular view of downtown was installed where it had originally been located back in the 1920s, at the front of the building. The food line offers homestyle Ohio cooking plus the same Polish specialties they've been serving up for more than 40 years: stuffed cabbage with mashed potatoes, stuffed peppers, award-winning pierogies, fresh bratwurst, smoked kielbasa, and chicken paprikash on Friday and Saturday nights. An outdoor patio is open May through October.

# Slovenian

## Frank Sterle's Slovenian Country House
☎ (216) 881-4181
CITY: **Cleveland**    AREA: **Near East Side**
ATMOSPHERE: **Casual**    COST: $$$$$

ADDRESS: 1401 E. 55th St.
HOURS: Tues–Wed 11:30 a.m.–2:30 p.m. (also open for dinner if they have a party of 45

or more), Thu–Fri 11:30 a.m.–9 p.m., Sat 4:30–9 p.m., Sun 11:30–7 p.m.; closed Mon **RESERVATIONS:** Taken, recommended for groups of 5+ **PAYMENT:** MC, VS, AX, checks **BAR:** Beer, wine, liquor **TAKEOUT:** Yes **ACCESS:** ♿ Full access

Sterle's began life as the Bonner Cafe, a bar with some food that opened for business in 1960. When Frank Sterle bought the place it was just one small room, but like Topsy, it just grew and grew. Now the huge space, which can handle as many as 300 people, is a landmark and a tourist destination, attracting suburban visitors and out-of-town guests who want to get a taste of Cleveland's ethnic past. It begins at the parking lot, a large enclosed area that you enter through an impressive, decorative gateway, like the entrance to a castle. The leitmotif, inside and out, is a European mountain chalet, with all the accompanying Old World warmth and hospitality. Waitresses wear a version of Slovenian traditional dress, much like a German dirndl, and many have worked here for years. And they're adept at managing the heaping plates full of roast pork, stuffed cabbage, Wiener schnitzel, and paprikash. There's always a selection of American standbys, like meat loaf and roast chicken, and some so-called European favorites (mostly Italian-style), but the really interesting part of the menu is Slovenian: kidney or tripe stew, jeterca (liver with onions), klobase and zelje (sausage and sauerkraut), and segedin goulash. Family-style dinners offer a combination of entrée items and side dishes. There's a large bar in front and a separate room for meetings and private parties. Live music on Friday nights, from 6 to 9 p.m., and Saturday from 8 p.m. to midnight. The kitchen closes at 9 p.m.

# MARKETS

# Czech

## Bohemian Hall
☎ (216) 641-9777
CITY: **Cleveland**  AREA: **Near East Side**

**ADDRESS:** 4939 Broadway Ave.
**FOOD AVAIL.:** Baked goods, prepared frozen foods **HOURS:** n/a **PAYMENT:** Checks **ACCESS:** ♿ Full access

The female members of the Sokol Greater Cleveland (a Czech athletic club) raise money by preparing traditional Czech dumplings, which they sell frozen year-round on Wednesdays and Saturdays. They also hold a Christmas bake sale featuring homemade strudel and raisin-and-almond bread and another at Easter when they offer raisin-filled sweet breads. Prices are always reasonable. Caraway seed, barley, Czech mushrooms (when available), and imported gifts are also available for purchase by the general public. They have their own cookbook for sale that contains tried-and-true Czech recipes for breads, soups, dumplings, and main course dishes. Call for information. You can ask to be put on their mailing list.

# Eastern European mix

## Al's Quality Market
☎ (330) 753-7216
CITY: **Barberton**   AREA: **Farther South**

ADDRESS: 563 Tuscarawas Ave.
FOOD AVAIL.: Meat (fresh, deli), canned &
packaged goods, spices, condiments,
beverages HOURS: Tue–Fri 9 a.m.–5:30 p.m.,
Sat 8 a.m.–4 p.m. PAYMENT: MC, VS ACCESS: &
Limited OTHER ETHNIC: Italian

There once was an Al, and he opened
this butcher shop when he came back to
Cleveland after serving in World War II.
Tim and Jeanette Eberhardt have owned
it since March 1999, and they're com-
mitted to continuing what he started,
making traditional Hungarian, Slovenian, Slovakian, Polish, and Italian sausages by hand, the old-fashioned way.
They also prepare head cheese, cabbage
rolls, Hungarian bacon, and salami. In
addition, this is a full-service butcher
shop offering fresh meat and hand-cut
steaks, plus lard and suet, both hard to
find and essential in some recipes. He
also grinds his own poppy seed.

The wood-floored shop was also
once home to one of the earliest Acme
grocery stores, and a few shelves remain
stocked with homemade noodles from
Richfield; hot pickled peppers from a
Suffield, Ohio, company; and convenience items like chips, napkins, sugar,
and ketchup.

There's an out-of-time feel in here,
a sense of small town friendliness and
personal service that's getting harder
and harder to find.

Tim, a man with a quick and ready
smile, is usually behind the counter, and

a chat with him is sure to make shopping more fun.

## Buettner's Bakery
☎ (216) 531-0650
CITY: **Cleveland**   AREA: **Near East Side**

ADDRESS: 704 E. 185th St.
FOOD AVAIL.: Baked goods HOURS: Tue–Fri 7
a.m.–4:30 p.m., Sat 8 a.m.–4:30 p.m., Sun 9
a.m.–12:30 p.m.; closed Mon PAYMENT: Checks
ACCESS: & Full access OTHER ETHNIC: Croatian,
German, Hungarian, Polish

There's been a family-owned bakery at
this spot since the late 1920s, according
to the current manager, who has been
there many decades herself. They still
use old-fashioned gas ovens with rotating shelves, and the products they turn
out are not quite like their counterparts
made in more modern stoves. In fact,
in a tradition that hearkens back to a
time when the baker's oven was used by
the entire community, Buettner's makes
these special ovens available to the public at holidays and roasts whole pigs
and lambs for various ethnic celebrations. Swedish limpa bread is available
at Christmastime and Irish soda bread
around St. Patrick's Day. The rest of the
year they make a variety of Polish, Slovenian, Hungarian, and Croatian specialties, including kuchens, strudels, nut
and poppy seed rolls, and kolachy, plus
a variety of non-ethnic breads, Danish,
pies, and donuts.

## European Food Market
☎ (440) 884-1800
CITY: **Parma**   AREA: **Southwest**

ADDRESS: 5745 Chevrolet Blvd.
FOOD AVAIL.: Meat (deli), produce, grains,
beans, baked goods, canned & packaged
goods, spices, tea, coffee, wine, beer HOURS:

Mon–Sat 10 a.m.–8 p.m., Sun 11 a.m.–6 p.m.
**PAYMENT:** MC, VS **ACCESS:** & Full access

The store serves a primarily Russian, Ukrainian, and Polish clientele, catering to their taste in cured meats, sausages, smoked fish, and pickled vegetables. So shoppers are sure to find Moscow dry salami, buzhenina, a salted and smoked pork loin, and veal roll. But the selection of Eastern European edibles also includes cheeses from Lithuania, Hungarian salami, and a big selection of imported packaged sweets. The market's owner, Taras Sharanevych, also does catering and operates a party center, so you can add some ethnic flavor to your celebrations.

## Gertrude Bakery
☎ (216) 641-7582
CITY: **Cleveland** AREA: **Near East Side**

**ADDRESS:** 6506 Gertrude Ave.
**FOOD AVAIL.:** Baked goods, takeout meals
**HOURS:** Tue–Fri 7 a.m.–6 p.m., Sat 7 a.m.–5 p.m., Sun 7 a.m.–4 p.m.; closed Mon **PAYMENT:** Checks **ACCESS:** & Limited

Although ownership has changed multiple times, this little neighborhood bakery has been in existence since the 1920s. And what always stays the same are the traditional handcrafted products customers have come to know and love, generation after generation. The bakery continues to turn out homemade Eastern European specialties such as Polish sweet breads, paczki, strudel, and kolaczki, along with French and Italian pastries. Shelves are also filled with loaves of rye, ienna, and pumpernickel bread, baked daily, as well as cookies, Danish, donuts, and cakes. Be sure to pick up some of their homemade pierogi.

## International Foods
☎ (216) 932-5000
CITY: **Cleveland Heights** AREA: **East Side**

**ADDRESS:** 2078 S. Taylor Rd.
**FOOD AVAIL.:** Meat (deli), fish (deli, dried), grains, baked goods, canned & packaged goods, beverages, tea, wine, beer, prepared frozen foods, takeout meals **HOURS:** Wed 10 a.m.–6 p.m., Thu–Sat 10 a.m.–5 p.m.; closed Sun–Tue **PAYMENT:** Checks **ACCESS:** & None **OTHER ETHNIC:** Polish, Russian

This small store is part deli, part grocery, and the best of what they have to offer is in the glass case filled with one of the biggest selections of smoked fish anywhere in town, including sable and lox, and both black and red caviar. Prepared Jewish and Eastern European specialties are available for takeout: gefilte fish, blintzes, pierogies, and pelmeni (a Russian dumpling stuffed with meat, potato, or cheese). They also stock 20 varieties of herring, 60 different kinds of Old World prepackaged cakes and cookies, and 25 different types of chocolate candy. Beer, wine, and mineral water available. Party trays made to order with meats, fish and fish salads, and baked goods.

## K & K Meat Shoppe
☎ (216) 662-2644
CITY: **Maple Heights** AREA: **Southeast**

**ADDRESS:** 6172 Dunham Rd.
**FOOD AVAIL.:** Meat (fresh, deli, frozen), fish (frozen), cheese, baked goods, canned & packaged goods, condiments, beverages, tea, takeout meals **HOURS:** Mon–Fri 9 a.m.–6 p.m., Sat 9 a.m.–5 p.m., Sun 9 a.m.–2 p.m. **PAYMENT:** MC, VS, DIS, checks **ACCESS:** & Full access **OTHER ETHNIC:** Polish, Slovenian, Western European mix

The claim to ethnic fame at this full-service meat market is their homemade fresh and smoked kielbasa and Eastern European specialties, including Polish-style hurka (with rice); paprika bacon and Bohemian kizka and jaternice sausages; and sekanice (Easter loaf). Family owned and operated for three generations, they also offer an array of ethnic specialties including stuffed cabbage, roast pork and sauerkraut, and chicken paprikash, plus party trays and made-to-order sandwiches. A selection of imported items that complement their meats, such as pickles and mustards, are also on hand. The Kolars have a second location at 10682 Main Street in Mantua; 330-274-5322.

## K & K Meat Shoppe
☎ (330) 274-5322
CITY: **Mantua**   AREA: **Farther East**

ADDRESS: 10682 Main St.
FOOD AVAIL.: Meat (fresh, deli, frozen), fish (frozen), baked goods, canned & packaged goods, condiments, beverages, tea, takeout meals HOURS: Mon–Fri 9 a.m.–6 p.m., Sat 9 a.m.–4 p.m., Sun 9 a.m.–2 p.m. PAYMENT: MC, VS, checks ACCESS: & None

See description for K & K Meat Shop in Maple Heights.

## Kathy's Kolacke & Pastry Shop
☎ (440) 835-6570
CITY: **Westlake**   AREA: **West Side**

ADDRESS: 24961 Detroit Rd.
FOOD AVAIL.: Baked goods, beverages, coffee HOURS: Tue–Fri 8 a.m.–5:30 p.m., Sat 9 a.m.–4 p.m.; closed Sun, Mon PAYMENT: MC, VS, checks ACCESS: & Full access OTHER ETHNIC: Hungarian, Polish

This bakery is best known for its kolacke. The Polish version of this tra-ditional pastry is light, flaky, and filled with fruit and nuts. The Czech form is soft, sweet, and stuffed with meat. Kathy Schriner runs this one-woman business that was named "Best Ethnic Bakery" in the Cleveland Sweet Revenge contest. She also makes Hungarian nut and poppy seed rolls, a cheesecake that's been featured on Del Donahoo's television show, and a large variety of non-ethnic cookies, cakes and cupcakes, brownies, and muffins.

## Lviv International Food
☎ (440) 887-1199
CITY: **Parma**   AREA: **Southwest**

ADDRESS: 5689 State Rd.
FOOD AVAIL.: Meat (fresh, deli, frozen), fish (fresh, frozen, dried), produce, grains, beans, baked goods, canned & packaged goods, spices, condiments, beverages, tea, coffee, prepared frozen foods, takeout meals HOURS: Mon–Sat 9 a.m.–8 p.m. PAYMENT: MC, VS ACCESS: & Limited OTHER ETHNIC: Polish, Russian, Ukrainian

Hunting for bags of frozen pelmeni, cans of cod liver, jars of borscht concentrate, or a nice smoked fish? Look no further. There's a large selection of foods here for anyone with a taste for the delicacies and staples of the Ukraine, Russia, Poland, and the rest of Eastern Europe. Coolers are filled with imported butter, yogurt, and sour cream. A deli case has a variety of cured meats, and fresh cakes and pastry fill another glass-fronted display case. Bazar is a store within the store offering Ukrainian handicrafts, Czech glass, and other gift items. A parking lot is adjacent to the building, which is located across the street from St. Josaphat Ukrainian Catholic Cathedral near the intersection with Brookpark Road.

## Perla Homemade Delights
☎ (216) 741-9222
CITY: **Parma**  AREA: **Southwest**

**ADDRESS:** 5380 State Rd.
**FOOD AVAIL.:** Meat (deli), baked goods, beverages, tea, coffee, takeout meals **HOURS:** Mon–Fri 10 a.m.–7 p.m., Sat 10 a.m.–6 p.m.
**PAYMENT:** MC, VS, AX, DIS **ACCESS:** ♿ Full access
**OTHER ETHNIC:** German, Polish, Ukrainian

If pork kotlets, borsch soup, and Dobos torte sound like good eating, then make your way to this little oasis of Eastern European prepared foods and sweet treats. The Serban family, originally from Romania, opened this combination prepared-foods market and bakery in May 2006 in an area that's been designated Ukranian Village. Ana and Constantin cook and bake, son David is the general manager, and his brother Daniel helps whenever they need a hand. On the heat-and-eat side, the options include both Ukranian- and Romanian-style cabbage rolls, cabbage and noodles, chicken paprikas, fried fish, meat-filled pilmeni and a Ukranian version of these dumplings stuffed with mushrooms called *vushka* or "little ears." Nadiya Denysyuke, from the Ukraine and known as the resident pierogi specialist, prepares eight versions of these traditional dough pockets, all sold by the dozen, and if you order ahead she'll do some with prune or apricot filling. But it's the pastry case that really catches your eye and sets the mouth watering when you walk in the small, brightly lit shop. On the shelves sit trays of strudel, poppy seed and nut rolls, fat squares of cremsnit (the Romanian version of a napoleon), and rows of golden savarines, which are something like cream puffs soaked in rum. If you need an immediate infusion of food, there are three small tables where you can sit and enjoy your purchases. The store is in a small strip mall with parking out front.

## Raddell's Sausage Shop, Inc.
☎ (216) 486-1944
CITY: **Cleveland**  AREA: **East Side**

**ADDRESS:** 478 E. 152nd St.
**FOOD AVAIL.:** Meat (fresh), grains, baked goods, canned & packaged goods, spices, condiments, tea, coffee **HOURS:** Mon–Sat 8 a.m.–5 p.m.; closed Sun **PAYMENT:** MC, VS, DIS, checks **ACCESS:** ♿ Full access **OTHER ETHNIC:** German, Lithuanian, Slovenian

Specializing in the traditional foods of Slovenia, Lithuania, Croatia, and Germany, Raddell's is in its third generation of family ownership. It's best known for the large variety and Old World quality of its meats and sausages. According to Tom Radell, people come from all over just to buy their sausage. "The homemade rice-and-blood sausage and the Slovenian smoked sausage are among our best sellers, and customers even ask us to UPS our ethnic specialties out of state." They also offer imported chocolates, noodles, jams and jellies, pickles, cookies, and European mineral waters. Located in a freestanding building with its own parking area.

## State Meats
☎ (216) 398-0183
CITY: **Parma**  AREA: **Southwest**

**ADDRESS:** 5338 State Rd.
**FOOD AVAIL.:** Meat (fresh, deli) **HOURS:** Mon–Wed 9 a.m.–6 p.m., Thu–Fri 8 a.m.–8 p.m., Sat 8 a.m.–6 p.m. **PAYMENT:** MC, VS **ACCESS:** ♿ Full access **OTHER ETHNIC:** German

Bite into the German-style bratwurst, fresh kielbasa, Slovenian sausage, or Hungarian salami sold here and you taste a family tradition. George Salo owns the business in partnership with his mother Marie, who grew up on a farm where sausage making was an annual event. The son has picked up where his father left off when he died. George Sr. was Ukrainian. He came to the United States in the 1950s as a teenager, worked for a meat packer, and eventually went out on his own. He set up shop at the current location in 1974, building two old-style gravitational block smokehouses behind the store. This is where George Jr., using his father's recipes, cures cottage hams, bacon, pork chops, and the meats he grinds, seasons, and stuffs into casings. The coolers are filled with his version of kishka, rice rings, and head cheese. A small selection of nonmeat products is available, including hunks of brinza, a salty sheep's milk cheese similar to feta; herring; homemade pierogi, potato pancakes, and beet horseradish; bags of noodles; and jars of pickles. The store has a pleasant out-of-time charm and is located on a two- mile stretch of State Road that has been designated Ukrainian Village by city officials.

and rice rings. He's got a big smoker out back for his bacon, cottage hams, pigs' feet, ham hocks, pork loins, and racks of ribs. The man also makes traditional cured meats, including zelodec, Polish krakova, headcheese, and sunkarica. His wife Carol keeps the freezers stocked with stuffed cabbage, stuffed peppers, and strudel. Fresh custom-cut meat is available only Thursday–Saturday. A few shelves line the walls of the tiny shop, and they're filled with jars of sour turnips and pickles, packages of soup and sauce mix, plastic bags of buckwheat groats and millet, and bottles of imported sparkling water and sour cherry syrup (a tasty and refreshing combination). Walk through the door and you're sure to be greeted by three things: a wonderful, sweet, smoky smell, a friendly smile, and two glass cases brimming with the good things that the Zukaks have made. A parking lot fronts the squat little stand-alone building located across the street from the Beachland Ballroom in the Collinwood neighborhood. Joe still calls it the Croatian Hall, but that venue gave way to the concert club in 2000.

# Eastern European

## R & D Sausage Company
☎ (216) 692-1832
CITY: **Cleveland**   AREA: **East Side**

**ADDRESS:** 15714 Waterloo Rd.
**FOOD AVAIL.:** Meat (fresh, deli), grains, baked goods, spices, condiments, prepared frozen foods **HOURS:** Tue–Sat 8 a.m.–5 p.m. **PAYMENT:** Cash only **ACCESS:** ⅃ Full access

Joe Zuzak learned to be a chef back in Croatia. He's been the master of this kitchen since 1984. His specialty is turning ground pork into all kinds of sausage: Slovenian, Hungarian, bratwurst,

# Hungarian

## Farkas Pastry Shoppe
☎ (216) 281-6200
CITY: **Cleveland**   AREA: **Near West Side**

**ADDRESS:** 2700 Lorain Ave.
**FOOD AVAIL.:** Baked goods **HOURS:** Wed–Fri 9 a.m.–4 p.m., Sat 9 a.m.–2 p.m.; closed Sun–Tue **PAYMENT:** Cash only **ACCESS:** ⅃ Full access

Atilla Farkas, who had been baking and selling Hungarian pastry in Ohio City for almost 40 years, sold his business to Ed Kroeger in 2000. Farkas fans need not fear that this means the pastry party's over. Attila's staying on as baker-in-chief. He also trained Kroeger, who plans to continue making traditional Dobos, hazelnut, and chocolate tortes; nut, poppy seed, and fruit squares; napoleons (a personal favorite); and zserbo. The only advertising this business has ever needed is the reputation of their products, and that's not likely to change under the new management either. What is different is the shop's address. Still within shouting distance of the West Side Market, the store relocated to more spacious quarters. The old place was little more than a kitchen. Now that the bakery actually has a storefront, more people are likely to find it. Get there early if you want to have a selection, or call to place an order in advance.

## Kaczur Meats

☎ (440) 232-6556

CITY: **Bedford** AREA: **Southeast**

**ADDRESS:** 712 Broadway Ave.
**FOOD AVAIL.:** Meat (fresh, deli), baked goods, canned & packaged goods, spices, condiments, beverages **HOURS:** Tue–Sat 9 a.m.–6 p.m.; closed Sun & Mon **PAYMENT:** Checks **ACCESS:** ⅙ Full Access

This old-fashioned butcher shop, sans sawdust on the floor, draws customers from all around the state and country. Some walk in the door. Others ask to have their orders shipped to them. All are fans of the traditional, made-on-the-premises Hungarian specialties: flavorful dry-cured cottage hams with no water added; fresh, smoked, or spicy 100%-pork kolbasz sausage; hurka—a rice-and-liver sausage; kocsonya—pigs' feet in their own gel (available from October until Easter); and head cheese. *Szalonna* means bacon in Hungarian, and a number of different kinds are of-fered here: garlic; garlic and paprika; a fattier version used in a Hungarian specialty made with drippings, bread, and grilled vegetables; and abalt szalonna, a boiled bacon with the rib bones attached that can be sliced and used without further cooking. They also make their own cracklings, some of which go into the pogacsa (buns) they sell.

Everything is prepared using traditional techniques and ingredients, and the current owner, Brad Miller, is proud to be keeping alive a dying, labor-intensive art. He bought the business when former owner and lifelong friend Robert Kaczur died suddenly in 2005. His wife was going to liquidate the business but Miller, with a culinary school degree, stepped in. "I grew up eating this food," says Brad, "and couldn't bear to see all this knowledge and expertise just disappear." He has the few recipes Robert wrote and is recreating others through trial and error with lots of input from his customers.

The store also carries Hungarian-style salamis, imported pickles, noodles, a small selection of spices and seasonings, dry aged beef and farm fresh pork, both cut to order.

## Lucy's Sweet Surrender

☎ (216) 752-0828

CITY: **Cleveland** AREA: **East Side**

**ADDRESS:** 12516 Buckeye Rd.
**FOOD AVAIL.:** Baked goods, coffee **HOURS:** Mon–Fri 7 a.m.–4 p.m., Sat 7 a.m.–4 p.m., also open by appointment. **PAYMENT:** MC, VS, AX, checks **ACCESS:** ⅙ Limited

Michael Feigenbaum and his wife, Marika, who is from Transylvania, are the current owners of this bakery (which dates back to the 1950s and was formerly known as Lucy's Hungarian Strudel), and they are dedicated to continuing the tradition of making unique, authentic Eastern European specialties. The women who prepare the strudel dough each morning have been stretching it by hand the old-fashioned way for just a few years less than the shop's been open, and this is still a cut-no-corners, everything-from-scratch operation. Michael even buys the apples they use for strudels and pies fresh from local growers.

This is one of the few places that still bakes zserbo, layers of crisp dough alternating with raspberry preserves, hazelnuts, and chocolate; grillazs, a "lace" cookie filled with chocolate cake and chocolate butter cream and decorated with chocolate sprinkles; pogacsa, a flaky layered biscuit seeded with bits of bacon that's like a meal you can hold in your hand; and krupli, yellow cake with chocolate cream inside, a marzipan coating on the outside, and a dusting of powdered sugar and cocoa that leaves it looking a bit like a potato, only better. Lucy's also offers kolac, a braided yeast bread with golden raisins, Dobos torte, cream cheese and sour cream cookies filled with fruit, and nut and poppy seed rolls. Also available are other types of European-style cakes and pastries, muffins, bread, doughnuts, and pies. Michael also specializes in creating unusual customized, made-to-order chocolate mousse, cassata, and Dobos torte wedding cakes.

The couple of tables and chairs, plus the availability of coffee by the cup and Hungarian-language newspapers, makes this an informal, impromptu gathering place for Hungarians from all around town, as well as anyone else interested in soaking up the atmosphere and the goodies. If you'd rather order from home, go to the store's Web site, www.lucyssweetsurrender.com, where you'll find pictures of wedding cakes and pastry trays, and a handy online shopping cart just waiting to be filled. Parking lot adjacent to the store.

## Mertie's Hungarian Strudel Shop
☎ (216) 362-0012
CITY: **Middleburg Heights**   AREA: **Southwest**

**ADDRESS:** 6606 Smith Rd.
**FOOD AVAIL.:** Baked goods **HOURS:** Tue–Fri 8 a.m.–5 p.m., Sat 8 a.m.–4 p.m.; closed Sun–Mon **PAYMENT:** Checks **ACCESS:** ♿ Limited

Mertie Rakosi has done all the baking herself, from scratch for decades, both here and at a bakery on Buckeye. The variety of strudels is almost endless: apple, cherry, cheese, apricot, blueberry, poppy seed, lemon, raspberry, and peach. She also prepares some sugar-free versions. Ethnic goodie seekers will be happy to find tortes—Dobos, double chocolate, Black Forest, strawberry, lemon tortes, and potica (nut roll) too.

## Tommy's Pastries
☎ (216) 521-4778
CITY: **Lakewood**   AREA: **West Side**

**ADDRESS:** 14205 Madison Ave.
**FOOD AVAIL.:** Baked goods, beverages **HOURS:** Mon–Sat 6 a.m.–7 p.m.; closed Sun **PAYMENT:** Cash only **ACCESS:** ♿ Full Access **OTHER ETHNIC:** Eastern European mix, Western European mix

The owners and the baker are from Hungary, and when you taste their strudel, Dobos torte, pogacsa (a bun made with bacon), and kolache, you can be sure you're eating the real thing. They also offer Linzer tortes, croissants, a variety of muffins, and European-style pastries, scones, and pies. Staff can chat and answer your questions comfortably in English or Hungarian. It's a little shop, with easy access from I-90 using the Bunts Road exit. Metered parking available out front.

# Polish

## Jaworski's Meat Market & Deli
☎ (440) 260-9788
CITY: **Middleburg Hts.** AREA: **Southwest**

ADDRESS: 7545 Pearl Rd.
FOOD AVAIL.: Meat (fresh, deli, frozen), takeout meals HOURS: Tue–Fri 8:30 a.m.–6 p.m., Sat 8 a.m.–5 p.m.; closed Sun–Mon PAYMENT: MC, VS, DIS, checks ACCESS: ♿ Full access

After 69 years in the Slavic Village neighborhood, Jaworski's relocated to Middleburg Heights in 2005. They still make their trademark ethnic specialties, including fresh and smoked kielbasa sausage. Stuffed cabbage and pierogies as well as hard-to-find Polish delicacies are also prepared on the premises, including flaczki (tripe) and czarnina (duck) soups; bigos, a stew of sauerkraut, kielbasa, tomatoes, and mushrooms; head cheese; and kabanose, a dried smoked sausage made with pork and garlic. There's a full deli with pierogies, cold cuts, and salads. Overstuffed sandwiches are made to order. The meat cases hold cuts of fresh beef, pork, and chicken.

## Krusinski Finest Meat Products
☎ (216) 441-0100
CITY: **Cleveland** AREA: **Near East Side**

ADDRESS: 6300 Heisley Ave.
FOOD AVAIL.: Meat (fresh), beverages, tea, wine, takeout meals HOURS: Mon, Tue, Thu, Fri, Sat 8 a.m.–5:00 p.m.; closed Wed & Sun (open Wed the week before a major holiday) PAYMENT: MC, VS ACCESS: ♿ None

This classic old-fashioned butcher shop in the heart of Slavic Village has been around since the 1950s and is still owned and operated by the Krusinski family. A wide variety of pierogies are made fresh daily, including potato, cheese, potato and cheese combination, kraut, and fruit. Helen Krusinski and her staff also prepare smoked and fresh kielbasa, potato pancakes, blintzes, stuffed cabbage, and stuffed peppers. Other Polish specialty items include jeternice (liver puddings); hurka, a rice and liver ring; and krakowska, a lean-meat cold cut similar to salami. They also sell all types and cuts of meat, deli meats, and cheeses.

## Peter's Market
☎ (216) 341-5910
CITY: **Garfield Heights** AREA: **Southeast**

ADDRESS: 4617 Turney Rd.
FOOD AVAIL.: Meat (fresh), produce, grains, beans, flour, baked goods, canned & packaged goods, condiments, beverages, tea, coffee, wine, beer, prepared frozen foods, takeout meals HOURS: Mon–Thu 8:30 a.m.–6 p.m., Fri 8:30 a.m.–6:30 p.m., Sat 8:30 a.m.–6 p.m. PAYMENT: Checks ACCESS: ♿ Full access

Peter's is a neighborhood meat market and grocery, with an emphasis on Eastern European foods and a good reputation that's grown by word of mouth. They carry cottage hams, head cheese, a variety of sausages and kielbasa, and canned and packaged products from Poland. There's a small selection of kitchen staples, plus deli meats. But the pierogies are the real specialty here. The little dough pockets come filled with potatoes, potatoes and cheese, sauerkraut, mushrooms, vegetables, apples, apricots, and prunes. They are prepared fresh on Friday only (from 11 a.m. to 6:30 p.m.) at Sophie's Cafe, a carryout food operation located within the market. Yes, there is a real Sophie, and she also makes traditional Polish homemade favorites to go, including soups, dumplings, blintzes, stuffed cabbage, potato pancakes, and fruit and vegetable crepes.

## Samosky Home Bakery
☎ (440) 845-3377
CITY: **Parma Heights**   AREA: **Southwest**

ADDRESS: 6379 Pearl Rd.
FOOD AVAIL.: Baked goods, beverages, coffee
HOURS: Tue–Sat 7 a.m.–4 p.m.; closed Sun & Mon PAYMENT: MC, VS, AX, DIS, checks ACCESS: & Full access

Decorated to resemble an Old World bake shop with antique display cases, Samosky's has been in existence since 1910. And during that time they've continuously done what they do best: make traditional European baked goods, including hoska (a Polish bread traditionally served at Easter), paczki (donuts), and kolacky. They also make a variety of cookies, cakes, and pies, strudel, Hungarian nut and poppyseed rolls, angel wings, plus brownies, Danish, ladylocks, and Russian tea biscuits. They also carry old-fashioned jellies, candies, and novelty gift items.

## Seven Roses Delicatessen
☎ (216) 641-5789
CITY: **Cleveland**   AREA: **Near East Side**

ADDRESS: 6301 Fleet Ave.
FOOD AVAIL.: Meat (deli), baked goods, spices, condiments, tea HOURS: Mon–Sat 8 a.m.–8 p.m., Sun 9 a.m.–3 p.m. PAYMENT: Cash only ACCESS: & Limited

The only American thing in sight is the daily paper. Otherwise this specialty food store is pure Polish, from the kielbasa and head cheese in the cooler to the jars of kraut and pickles on the walnut floor-to-ceiling shelves that date from the time when hardware was sold here. The sliding rail ladders remain too, and the hardwood floors have been refinished to a golden glow. The place looks and feels like it's been around for a hundred years. That's the feel owner Tina Tyl was going for when she opened in 2004, and her little cafe market definitely has lots of old-fashioned charm, complete with lace curtains in the front window. Four tables are tucked in back, amid the imported teas, candy, jam, and boxes of dumpling mix. There's also a baby grand piano—perhaps prompting patrons to impulsively pound out a polonaise or mazurka—and an easy chair. A display of porcelain teapots fills a glass case. Everywhere else it's food: cured meats, cheeses, freshly baked poppy seed rolls, tortes, paczki, and sweetbreads. There's a short menu of huge sandwiches—don't miss the Polish Cristo featuring ham, cheese, and onions—and prepared dishes to eat in or take out. Daily homemade specials include soup—the cabbage is outstanding—pierogies, potato pancakes, and blintzes. Everything but soup is served on disposable plates. Located in the heart of the historic Slavic Village neighborhood. Free and metered parking on street.

# Russian

## Gorby Grocery Store
☎ (216) 382-3006
CITY: **South Euclid**   AREA: **East Side**

ADDRESS: 4004 Mayfield Rd.
FOOD AVAIL.: Meat (deli), fish (deli), produce, grains, beans, flour, baked goods, canned & packaged goods, spices, condiments, beverages, tea, prepared frozen foods HOURS: Mon–Sat 10 a.m.–7 p.m., Sun 11 a.m.–4 p.m. PAYMENT: MC, VS, DIS, checks ACCESS: & None

This mini-market at the corner of Mayfield and Warrensville Center roads is almost invisible; it shares an entryway with the bar next door, and it's beside a fast-food franchise. But there's a lot of food packed in this small space, a cornucopia of Russian delicacies and imports from other parts of Eastern Europe. There are bags of pelmeni (a potato-filled "ravioli") and blintzes in the freezer; soft white farmer cheese with raisins and a large variety of pickles, mustard, and horseradish in the refrigerator case; smoked fish, sausages, and salami at the deli counter; and big bowls full of candy on every available surface. On the shelves, you might find jars of vegetable spread from Bulgaria, sweet pepper relish from Slovenia, fruit jam from Poland, and seven different kinds of honey. There are bags of poppy seeds, buckwheat groats, millet, and barley, and a limited selection of fresh vegetables and fruits. If you're not fluent in Russian, you probably won't be interested in the Russian-language newspapers for sale or all the announcements posted on the bulletin board, but it's clear that the Russian immigrants who shop here find these worth their attention. Convenient parking in front.

is clearly meant to serve the Russian immigrant community. The front windows display posters in Russian announcing upcoming events. There's the requisite small table with a few chairs, which provides a place for Russian men, who always seem to be wearing black leather jackets no matter what the weather, to gather, talk, and observe. Open bins are filled with the brightly wrapped hard candies and chocolates Russians favor. And the shelves and refrigerated cases are stocked with the foods they were familiar with back home—pickles and pickled vegetables, barley, buckwheat groats, pear preserves and gooseberry jam, sunflower seeds, smoked fish, and farmers' butter. There are usually at least seven versions of salamis, and the labels, in Russian and English, reveal regional preferences, historical influences, and the sometimes humorous realities of modern life: there's Estonsky salami (think Estonia) and others called, respectively, Kievsky, Minsky, Vienskaya, Hungarian, German, and the one I personally find intriguing—Tourist salami. They also offer caviar in white, red, and black, homemade dumplings, Russian-style cakes, and prepared salads.

## Yeleseyevsky Deli
☎ (440) 605-0907
CITY: **Mayfield Heights**   AREA: **East Side**

ADDRESS: 5832 Mayfield Rd.
FOOD AVAIL.: Meat (deli), fish (deli), produce, grains, beans, flour, baked goods, canned & packaged goods, condiments, beverages, tea, coffee, prepared frozen foods, takeout meals HOURS: Mon–Sat 10 a.m.–8 p.m., Sun 11 a.m.–6 p.m. PAYMENT: MC, VS, DIS, checks ACCESS: & Full access OTHER ETHNIC: Eastern European mix

Tucked back in a strip mall behind the Mayland Shopping Center, this store

# Slovenian

## Patria Imports
☎ (216) 531-6720
CITY: **Cleveland**   AREA: **East Side**

ADDRESS: 794 E. 185th St.
FOOD AVAIL.: Meat (deli), canned & packaged goods, beverages, wine, beer HOURS: Mon–Sat 9 a.m.–5 p.m; closed Sun PAYMENT: MC, VS, checks ACCESS: & Full access OTHER ETHNIC: Croatian, German, Polish

This is a fairly small store located in Cleveland's Old World Plaza shopping district. They carry imported cheeses, canned fish, sprats (a smoked fish similar to sardines), chocolates, cookies, jams, and preserves. Some household products and convenience items. Parking lot in back.

## Rudy's Quality Meats
☎ (440) 943-5490
CITY: **Willowick**   AREA: **East Side**

ADDRESS: 31728 Vine St.
FOOD AVAIL.: Meat (fresh), fish (frozen), canned & packaged goods, spices, condiments, prepared frozen foods HOURS: Mon–Thu 9 a.m.–6 p.m., Fri 9 a.m.–6 p.m., Sat 8 a.m.–6 p.m.; closed Sun PAYMENT: Checks ACCESS: ᕍ Full access OTHER ETHNIC: Hungarian, Italian, Polish

. . . . . . . . . . . . . . . . . . . . . . .

Rudy came to America from Slovenia just as the First World War ended, and in 1928 he opened a butcher shop on Superior Avenue in Cleveland. In 1937, he died in a car accident, and his wife Agnes took over the business with the help of their three sons. By 1955 there was a second store on East 67th and St. Clair, and a third opened in Willowick in 1963. The family sold the two Cleveland locations, and now Agnes's sons Rudy and Karl, and grandsons David and Tom, run the remaining suburban store. They are convinced that the success of the family business is tied to the uniqueness and quality of their products and the personal service they provide. "A supermarket can't offer what we do," says Dave, "and our customers know it." They prepare zelodec (a rarely found type of large-sized cooked Slovenian sausage that can be sliced and used like lunch meat), regular Slovenian smoked sausage, blood sausage, and rice sausage using their own cherished recipes; they also offer Polish, Hungarian, and Ital-

ian sausage, Mexican chorizo, and hot Cajun Andouille sausage. Nothing is prepackaged—meat is cut fresh every day, and cut to order—and the staff is friendly and knowledgeable. The shop is in a four-store strip with plenty of parking.

## Wojtilas Bakery
☎ (216) 731-7080
CITY: **Euclid**   AREA: **East Side**

ADDRESS: 897 E. 222nd St.
FOOD AVAIL.: Baked goods, beverages, coffee, takeout meals HOURS: Tue–Sat 6 a.m.–3 p.m., Sun 7 a.m.–noon; closed Mon PAYMENT: Checks ACCESS: ᕍ Full access

. . . . . . . . . . . . . . . . . . . . . . .

Using family recipes his father brought over from Czechoslovakia, Donny Wojtilas and his wife Barb prepare a variety of traditional Slovenian pastries daily, including potica (a nut bread), flancete (often called angel wings), and krofe (a sort of donut). They also offer a selection of non-Slovenian fresh breads, muffins, cookies, cakes, wedding cakes, and party trays. They opened the bakery with the idea of re-creating the kind of neighborhood shop Donny recalled from his childhood.

## Wojtilas Bakery
☎ (440) 352-7311
CITY: **Painesville**   AREA: **Farther East**

ADDRESS: 15 S. St. Clair St.
FOOD AVAIL.: Baked goods, beverages, coffee, takeout meals HOURS: Tue–Sat 6 a.m.–3 p.m., Sun 7 a.m.–noon; closed Mon PAYMENT: Checks ACCESS: ᕍ Full access

. . . . . . . . . . . . . . . . . . . . . . .

See Euclid listing for description.

# EUROPE WEST OF
# THE DANUBE

For the purposes of this book, Western Europe includes Ireland and the
United Kingdom, France, Germany, and Scandinavia. Grouping these countries together, even from a culinary point of view, is problematical, for they are
all as different as the languages they speak. But one thing they hold in common is a connection to Cleveland, both past and present.

It has been estimated that by 1860, 45 percent of the city's population was
foreign born, with the majority of immigrants coming from Germany, Ireland,
England, Scotland, and Wales. They were poor, usually uneducated, and forced
to accept backbreaking jobs at the bottom of the economic pyramid. So they
labored to build canals and railroads, worked in the quarries, the steel mills,
and at the docks, and manned the growing number of factories that trans-

formed Cleveland from a rural outpost to an industrial metropolis. Swedes followed in the 1870s, and then the Danes and Finns. The French, however, came one by one, as traders in the 1700s, nuns in the 1850s, and the brides of American servicemen after World War II. While the flow of immigrants from most other Western European nations tapered off, Germans continued to settle here in significant numbers well into the 20th century. Many were skilled craftsmen: jewelers, tailors, musical instrument and cabinetmakers, and machinists.

Over the years, these nationality groups quietly transformed themselves from immigrant outsiders to mainstream Americans. The Irish, especially, were eager to put aside all that reminded them of the poverty and despair that most had left behind. But what was kept by all were the rich folk traditions of their homelands, traditions that lived on in music, dance, storytelling, and, of course, food.

Though Ireland is renowned more for starvation than feasting, and for a cuisine of potatoes and boiled meat, those who know the food well insist that it is in its own way memorable. "I grew up on a little farm in County Mayo," said Celine O'Leary, who came here in 1952 at the age of 20. "Vegetables grew in our garden, and my grandfather was a butcher, so we always had some meat. There were griddle cakes made over an open fire, soda bread, and scones with whole milk and fresh butter. We'd roast lamb or beef in a cast-iron pot oven. It would cook on hot peat coals in the hearth. And of course we ate plenty of potatoes and turnips. Our food was plain and nourishing, but now when I think of the things we ate, I think how good they were."

The British and the Irish eat much the same way. Bacon, oats, root vegetables and cabbage, dairy products and seafood are basic, along with tea, toast, and marmalade. Traditionally, cooking is done simply, and food is seasoned with a light hand. Pies filled with meat, rolls stuffed with sausage, and eggs with bacon may not be haute cuisine, but they are invariably satisfying.

Equally satisfying are the substantial dishes of old-fashioned German cooking, a genuine meat-and-potatoes cuisine. Good, hearty breads, cheeses, wurst (cold cuts), sausages of all kinds, sauerkraut, and pickles are characteristic. Braten (roasted meat) is the national dish, and pork, both cured and fresh, is the favored meat. "Our food," explained Dr. Robert Ward, a third-generation German American, "is so much a part of the American way of eating, that most people don't even know they're enjoying German food. It was Germans, for example, who introduced Americans to sauerkraut and beer." In the 1850s, he continues, there were gasthauses (taverns) and outdoor beer gardens like those in Europe in neighborhoods located all over the city, and each one brewed its own beer.

The cuisine of the Scandinavian countries warrants little exposition here because there are no longer any restaurants that serve it; only a few stores sell some of their imported products or bake traditional breads. Like the other nationalities that make up this chapter, they use potatoes and pork extensively.

Fish and cheese also dominate their table. Dill is the herb of choice, as it is for the Germans.

And then, at last, there is French food, a cuisine that has had an influence on fine dining far out of proportion to the number of French people who have come to America. French cooking at the professional level has long set the standard for chefs and gourmets in this country, and the precise techniques and methods of preparation they've perfected form the foundation of a good culinary education.

"French cuisine is organized and unified with a great respect for the character of each ingredient," said chef and teacher Donna Adams. "Once you've got the basics, they can be expanded in so many ways."

A well-stocked French larder includes butter, wine, cream, mustard, onions, garlic, shallots, leeks, potatoes, and wild mushrooms. Bay leaves, chervil, bouquet garni, tarragon, and parsley are favored herbs. Root vegetables, green beans and peas, fresh fruit, nuts, and cheeses are also important.

"Real French cooking," said Jeanine Mihallek, who came here from Paris in 1946, "is about the art of beautiful simplicity. We like to know what we are eating, and waste nothing. Even leftovers can look and taste like a feast. But we need our bread; good bread is everything."

Luckily for Jeanine and the rest of us, good French bread is indeed available in Cleveland, along with some other authentic examples of the French culinary art of beautiful simplicity.

## RESTAURANTS

# British

### The Lobby Lounge on 6 at the Ritz-Carlton Hotel
☎ (216) 902-5255
CITY: **Cleveland**   AREA: **Downtown**
ATMOSPHERE: **Casual**   COST: **$$$**$$

**ADDRESS:** 1515 W. 3rd St.
**HOURS:** Sat–Sun noon–4 p.m. (last seating at 2:30) **RESERVATIONS:** Recommended **PAYMENT:** MC, VS, AX, DIS **BAR:** Beer, wine, liquor
**TAKEOUT:** No **ACCESS:** ♿ Full access

Choose this place when you want to put a little British in your weekend, make an Anglophile happy, or pretend to be an extra in a movie based on a Brontë book. You'll feel quite grand sitting in comfortable, high-backed chairs, sipping Earl Grey tea poured from a bottomless silver pot by an attentive server, and nibbling little cakes. It reminds me of playing "Ladies" when I was a little girl, only better because the food is real. The Lounge is a beautiful room, with large windows, a fireplace, and consistently stunning arrangements of fresh flowers on a table in the center. The full afternoon tea includes elegant finger sandwiches and a three-tiered dessert tray that comes with a bowl of thick, sweet Devonshire cream. Light tea is the same, without the sandwiches. A children's tea provides hot chocolate and Shirley Temples for the younger set. Bringing kids is a great opportunity to have them dress up and experience what it's like to eat in a civilized manner. Tell them to think of it as a sort of off-season Halloween. There's a small full-service bar for those not thoroughly into the etiquette of tea. Before arriving, practice crooking your little finger while holding a china cup. Park in Tower City's lot and walk through the mall to the entrance on the upper level, or drive to the front entrance of the hotel on West Third and have your car parked by a valet.

# French

### Chez Francois
☎ (440) 967-0630
CITY: **Vermilion**   AREA: **Farther West**
ATMOSPHERE: **Formal**   COST: **$$$$$**

**ADDRESS:** 555 Main St.
**HOURS:** Tue–Thu 5–9 p.m., Fri–Sat 5–10 p.m., Sun 4–8 p.m. In warm weather months, patio opens at 2 p.m. on Sat–Sun; restaurant closed Dec 31–Mar 14 **RESERVATIONS:** Recommended, required for Fri, Sat evenings and patio
**PAYMENT:** MC, VS, AX, checks **BAR:** Beer, wine, liquor **TAKEOUT:** No **ACCESS:** ♿ Limited
*Not recommended for children

Vermilion was once a fishing port, and long ago sails were made and nets were stored in the building that now houses this restaurant. The original hand-carved beams and exposed-brick floors and walls create a rustic ambience countered by coral-colored table linens and a classic French menu. Chef John D'Amico, who owns the place along with partner and maitre d' Matthew Mars, uses reduction sauces made with cream, butter, and stock and tends toward grilling and poaching his meat, poultry, and seafood. "In keeping with contemporary tastes," he explained, "I try to make my sauces lighter than the traditional version, and flavor with fresh herbs that I buy from local farmers along with their fresh produce. Much of what I use is organically grown." At a customer's request, John will gladly prepare dishes with no saucing at all and can compose interesting offerings for vegetarians with some advance notice. All the desserts, from napoleons to sorbets, are made in his kitchen, too.

In business since 1987, Chez Francois relies primarily on word of mouth to attract diners, many of whom willingly travel over an hour (it's a 45-minute trip from downtown Cleveland) for the experience. The patio garden overlooks the Vermilion River, and diners here sit amid greenery under an awning. A few tables inside share this lovely view. At least eight times a year there are scheduled events, such as wine tastings, Mother's Day celebrations, and clam bakes. Get on the mailing list to receive newsletters announcing these special activities.

## L'Albatros Brasserie and Bar
☎ (216) 791-7880
CITY: **Cleveland**   AREA: **East Side**
ATMOSPHERE: **Casual**   COST: $$$$$

ADDRESS: 11401 Bellflower Rd.
HOURS: Mon–Wed 11:30 a.m.–11 p.m.,
Thu–Sat 11:30 a.m.–midnight **RESERVATIONS:**
Recommended **PAYMENT:** MC, VS, AX, DIS **BAR:**
Beer, wine, liquor **TAKEOUT:** Yes **ACCESS:** ♿ Full
access

As 2008 drew to a finish, this new restaurant debuted in what had been

That Place on Bellflower for decades. The interconnected carriage houses on the alley in University Circle were completely and beautifully renovated. Original exposed brick walls and woodwork remain, but the warren of small, intimate rooms are sleekly stylish with modern white tabletops, and banquettes upholstered in a pale opalescent material. The atmosphere includes plenty of nooks that are just right for private conversations. One space has a fireplace; others are outfitted with cozy booths; and most offer a view of the enclosed courtyard patio. The overall effect nicely balances the inherent charm of the old with a contemporary minimalist sensibility and a casual ambience. The look, like the menu, reflects the vision of chef and owner Zach Bruell, a longtime and highly regarded player on the Cleveland restaurant scene.

In true brasserie style, you can eat and drink here from midday to midnight and dine hearty or light. Graze on a charcuterie platter or an appetizer of chicken and fois gras mousseline while sipping French champagne by the glass. Share a late-night bottle of white burgundy or an absinthe cocktail and a few hors-d'oeuvres, perhaps the pork and veal terrine, escargot, and braised leeks in Dijon mustard sauce. Drawing inspiration from time spent in Paris, Bruell created a list of entrées that feature a selection of classic dishes: an Alsatian choucroute garni (pork and kraut), mussels and pommes frites, skate in brown butter, and a cassoulet made with white beans, lamb, duck confit, and sausages that's served in a skillet. Ordering the cheese plate is a not-to-be-missed experience. The on-staff fromage expert brings the day's selection arrayed on a big wooden board to you, describes each one, and offers personalized suggestions for finding just the right combination of flavors to start or finish a meal. For those who prefer sweeter endings, there's a Grand Marnier soufflé, pineapple tart tatin, and mocha pot de crème.

This brasserie and bar, conveniently located in the midst of the Case Western Reserve University campus, is close to all the area's educational and cultural institutions. Parking is available in a pay-to-park lot in front of the building.

## Le Petit Triangle Café
### ☎ (216) 281-1881
CITY: **Cleveland**   AREA: **Near West Side**
ATMOSPHERE: **Casual**   COST: **$$$**$$

ADDRESS: 1881 Fulton Rd.
HOURS: Tue–Thu 11 a.m.–10 p.m., Fri–Sat 11 a.m.–11 p.m., Sun 10 a.m.–3 p.m.; closed Mon RESERVATIONS: Taken, recommended for groups of 6+ PAYMENT: MC, VS, DIS BAR: Beer, wine, liquor TAKEOUT: Yes ACCESS: ⟁ None
*Not recommended for children

This is the second time the old Ohio City storefront has been chosen as the setting for the re-creation of a Paris café. In this go-round, neighborhood residents and Francophiles Tom and Joy Harlor are in charge of this mom-and-pop shop. The couple, who operated a deli and ran a catering business in the past, took over in the spring of 2007, and their goals were to create a friendly day and night hangout with European attitude and French-inspired food. They've succeeded on all counts.

The freshly flipped crepes, a carry-over from the former tenants, are wonderful. You can order them savory or sweet. The make-a-meal versions have fillings such as ham and double cream brie; chevre, spinach, and tomatoes; and mushrooms, Roquefort, and eggs. Seven sweet dessert versions are made with dark chocolate, fruit preserves, whipped cream, or Grand Marnier.

Also on the menu is an assortment of classic dishes: smoked trout and lentil salad, dense chicken liver paté, a cheese plate, onion soup with a cap of melted Gruyère, a daily quiche, cassoulet, salad Niçoise, omelets, and croissant sandwiches. If you're really hungry you can get steak au poivre with a side of ratatouille. Amazingly, all this appears out of an open kitchen barely big enough to turn around in. For liquid refreshment, there's a small selection of white, red, and sparkling wines by the glass and bottle, boutique beers, cocktails, and coffee drinks.

The tiny space with the floor plan of a pie wedge seats only 20. More tables appear on the sidewalk when the sun shines and the temperatures are mild. Friendly takes on nuances of meaning here, applying to diners as well as hosts. Tables are in such close proximity that it's almost like eating en famille; cross-party conversations spring up easily and with regularity.

Unless you're dining outside this isn't the best place to bring kids, especially the fussy kind or those incapable of sitting still for any length of time. Not good for large groups either. But it's absolutely perfect for romance, foursomes, and singles looking for a nice spot to enjoy a solitary meal, a meal that just might end up as a tête-a-tête with the person seated nearby. The restaurant can be booked for private parties.

# German

## Das Schnitzel Haus
☎ (440) 886-5050
CITY: **Parma**   AREA: **Southwest**
ATMOSPHERE: **Casual**   COST: $$$$$

**ADDRESS:** 5728 Pearl Rd.
**HOURS:** Mon–Thu 11 a.m.–9 p.m., Fri–Sat 11
a.m.–10:30 p.m., Sun 1–8 p.m.   **RESERVATIONS:**
Taken, for groups of 4+ **PAYMENT:** MC, VS,
AX, DIS **BAR:** Beer, wine, liquor **TAKEOUT:** Yes
**ACCESS:** ♿ Limited

In 1951 "Come On-A My House" was a hit. The smooth-voiced Rosemary Clooney sang about all the good things you'd get to eat if you came over to her place. Goran and Branka Djurin want everyone to come on-a their Haus for good eats the German way. The food here is the absolute opposite of trendy. No experimenting with ingredients from other cultures. No garnishing with microgreens. Tradition rules when it comes to dishes such as schnitzel, roast duck, potato pancakes, and sauerbraten. The bratwurst and knockwurst pair up perfectly with the many German beers. Sides of sauerkraut, tangy red cabbage, and spaetzel turn every meal into a hearty one. Strudels say dessert in Deutsche, and the wine list is mostly German.

There are two dining rooms, but only one is handicapped accessible. The carpet throughout is industrial strength, the tableware sturdy, and the "look" isn't likely to win any decorating awards, but the serviceable no-frills approach makes for the kind of place where you'll feel comfortable no matter how you're dressed or what kind of a hair day you're having. It's a good choice for families with young kids—there is a section of the menu for the 12 and under crowd. In an effort to please everybody, the kitchen also turns out pasta dishes, burgers, salads, and sandwiches.

The 90-seat restaurant opened in June 2004 under different ownership. There's a 12-seat bar and lounge, and the TV is usually tuned to sports. A covered patio beer garden, complete with fireplace, offers outdoor seating with high wooden walls so you don't have to look at the surrounding parking lot. It can be booked for private parties.

## Der Braumeister
☎ (216) 671-6220
CITY: **Cleveland**   AREA: **Near West Side**
ATMOSPHERE: **Casual**   COST: $$$$$

**ADDRESS:** 13046 Lorain Ave.
**HOURS:** Mon–Sat 11 a.m.–10 p.m. (bar open
until midnight); closed Sun **RESERVATIONS:**
Taken **PAYMENT:** MC, VS, AX, DIS **BAR:** Beer,
wine, liquor **TAKEOUT:** Yes **ACCESS:** ♿ Full access

The décor is German *gasthaus* cum American rustic, and the atmosphere is warm, comfortable, and friendly. Many patrons are regulars and address each other, as well as the servers, by name. The 100-seat dining room works as a setting for a drink and a quick, light meal or a place to linger over a four-course dinner, and the Castle Room, which seats up to 75, is a popular venue for club meetings or private parties. The menu is a mix of German specialties like schnitzel (a thin veal cutlet) and schweinsbraten (braised pork roast), and American-style dishes such as pan-fried walleye and roast duck. Portions are large. Appetizers, soups, salads, and snacks also reflect the blend of traditional German and thoroughly American favorites. There is a selection of German sausages and cold cuts for sandwiches and side dishes like pickled cucumber salad and potato dumplings. German beers are on tap, and imported wines are available by the glass or bottle. Easy to find with convenient parking on the well-lit side street and in the rear. A small German deli operates under the same name and roof (see market listings in this chapter for more information).

## Donauschwaben German American Cultural Center

☎ (440) 235-2646

CITY: **Olmsted Twp.**   AREA: **West Side**
ATMOSPHERE: **Relaxed**   COST: **$$**$$

ADDRESS: 7370 Columbia Rd.
HOURS: Tue–Fri 11 a.m.–2:30 p.m., Sun 11 a.m.–2:30; closed Sat & Mon RESERVATIONS: Taken, only for groups of 6+ PAYMENT: Checks BAR: Beer, wine TAKEOUT: Yes ACCESS: よ Full access

Go German for lunch at Leanu Park. Following a talk I gave at Fairview Park Library, a member of the audience (you know who you are . . . unfortunately, I don't, but I owe you a thank-you) told me about it. In 2002, this private club decided to open up to the public in a small way. Executive chef Steve Weiss prepares a variety of traditional entrées and side dishes including sauerbraten, wiener schnitzel, chicken paprikash, bratwurst, potato pancakes, and sauerkraut, with the menu changing every few months. Food is served in the small bar area and main lobby. Large groups and private parties can also be accommodated in the main dining room. It's very informal, kids are welcome, and casual attire is fine, although the Sunday-after-church crowd is generally well dressed.

## Heimatland Restaurant

☎ (330) 220-8671

CITY: **Brunswick**   AREA: **Farther South**
ATMOSPHERE: **Casual**   COST: **$$$**$$

ADDRESS: 3511 Center Rd.
HOURS: Tue–Thu 11 a.m.–2 p.m., Fri 11 a.m.–9 p.m., Sat 8 a.m.–9 p.m., Sun 8 a.m.–7 p.m.; closed Mon RESERVATIONS: Taken, for groups of 6+ PAYMENT: MC, VS, DIS BAR: Beer, wine, liquor TAKEOUT: Yes ACCESS: よ Full access

"This," said one diner, "is some serious grub. I left the table in a delightful food coma." He went with a friend, whose father is from Germany, and his official word was that the *Deutsche* part of the menu is the genuine article. The folks in the kitchen have genuine German roots, so they've got the right credentials when it comes to preparing spaetzle, tangy sweet and sour potato salad, and potato pancakes from scratch to serve with knockwurst and bratwurst. The schnitzel rates high on the ethnic Richter scale, as does the red cabbage side dish. Serious sampling can be done by visiting at lunchtime Tuesday–Friday, when a buffet is set out from 11 a.m.–2 p.m.

There are other European dishes on the menu, many of which are featured on the buffet, a section for kids, and numerous non-German dishes that range from grilled chicken breast to chef's salad. An ever-varied selection of European-style desserts is available. Breakfast, served only on Saturday and Sunday mornings, is American style bacon and eggs plus A.M. specials. The building was designed to resemble a mountain chalet. The main dining room is narrow and deep, decorated with hand-painted murals that depict various Bavarian cities, European scenes, and distinctive town crests.

The restaurant seats about 60. Service is that nice combination of friendly and efficient. *Herzlich willkommen*, they write on the menu: "With a warm heart, we welcome you." And they do.

## Henry Wahner's Restaurant & Lounge
☎ (330) 678-4055
CITY: **Kent**   AREA: **Farther South**
ATMOSPHERE: **Casual**   COST: **$$$$**$

ADDRESS: 1609 E. Main St.
HOURS: Tue–Thu 4–8:30 p.m., Fri–Sat 4–9:30 p.m.; closed Sun–Mon  RESERVATIONS: Not taken  PAYMENT: Checks  BAR: Beer, wine, liquor  TAKEOUT: Yes  ACCESS: ♿ Full access

. . . . . . . . . . . . . . . . . . . . . . . . . .

This family restaurant is well known and loved by the German American community. The two sisters who own the place will often stop by tables to chat with diners, comfortable in either English or German. Many people have been coming here for years to celebrate their high-water marks—birthdays, anniversaries, and graduations—and the staff, too, have almost all worked here for a long time. Mixed in with a standard selection of steaks, chops, and seafood are some German classics: sauerbraten, rouladen, schnitzel, and kassler rippchen (smoked pork chops). Spaetzle, potato pancakes, German potato salad, and sauerkraut are also available, and the "Deutsche combination plate" offers a selection of German house specialties including homemade sausage.

Portions are enormous. There is a children's menu, and half portions (which still tend to fill the plates to overflowing) are available during the early-bird-special hours between 4 and 6 p.m. The dining room is wood paneled, the carpeting looks well used, and the place doesn't offer much in the way of ambience or décor. Nonetheless, it attracts a crowd and it's easy to find, a freestanding building surrounded by a parking lot just past the Kent State University campus.

## Kuhar's Carry Out & Catering
☎ 440-951-1000
CITY: **Mentor**   AREA: **Farther East**
ATMOSPHERE: **Relaxed**   COST: **$$**$$$

ADDRESS: 8030 Broadmoor Rd.
HOURS: Mon–Sat 11 a.m.–8 p.m.; closed Sun
RESERVATIONS: Not taken  PAYMENT: Checks  BAR: None  TAKEOUT: Yes  ACCESS: ♿ Full access

. . . . . . . . . . . . . . . . . . . . . . . . . .

You can't sit down here, but you can take home a complete German lunch or dinner and hardly notice the cost. Very reasonable prices and very traditional recipes lend appeal to this otherwise inconspicuous and informal takeout and catering operation. If you're a fan of things like sauerbraten, rindsrouladen (stuffed and rolled steak), roast pork, and stuffed cabbage, you'll be tempted to call in an order often. They prepare veal schnitzel four different ways—in wine sauce with peppers, onions, and mushrooms (natur); sautéed in butter (Paris); breaded and fried (Wiener); and stuffed with ham and Emmenthaler cheese (St. Moritz). All just beg for sides like cucumber salad, potato pancakes, or dumplings and should be followed by by the housemade strudel. The kitchen also does Hungarian goulash, chicken paprikash, and a Slovenian smoked-sausage sandwich.

The Old World meets the new here because the menu includes fried chicken, burgers, and assorted sandwiches. They bake their own bread and offer a daily soup special. Phone ahead to have your food ready when you arrive.

# Irish

## Flannery's Pub
☎ (216) 781-7782
CITY: **Cleveland**　AREA: **Downtown**
ATMOSPHERE: **Casual**　COST: **$$$**$$

**ADDRESS:** 323 Prospect Ave.
**HOURS:** Mon–Thu 11:30 a.m.–9 p.m., Fri 11 a.m.–midnight, Sat 11:30 a.m.–midnight, Sun 11 a.m.–midnight.; bar open daily until 2 a.m.; late night menu avail. **RESERVATIONS:** Taken **PAYMENT:** MC, VS, AX, DIS **BAR:** Beer, wine, liquor **TAKEOUT:** Yes **ACCESS:** ら Full access *Not recommended for children **OTHER ETHNIC:** British, Scottish

It's a bar, it's a restaurant, it's a concert hall; it's all three rolled into one. The bar is long—24 seats with the requisite wall-mounted televisions that are always tuned to people chasing various sorts of balls, most often European soccer and rugby matches. Nearby are four round, tall tables with stools and a ledge along the front window that's at just the right height for resting a beer or an elbow.

In addition to all your common brews, they have a selection of Irish and British Isle ales, lagers, and stouts, including Guinness, Beamish, Harp, Newcastle Brown, and Old Speckled Hen—my personal favorite for both name and taste. When it comes to "sippin'" whiskey, the choice of single-malt scotches is large and the brand names lilting: Glenfiddich, Bunnahabain, Glenmorangie, Craggamore, Glenronach, Dalwhinnie, Glenkinchie.

The restaurant serves up some traditional pub food and Irish fare, including fish and chips, steamed mussels, Irish beef and lamb stew with parsnips, shepherd's pie, cottage chicken pie, boxty, potato and cheese soup, and colcannon, a flavorful, stick-to-your-ribs portion of mashed potatoes with cabbage, carrots, and scallions. The menu also offers a selection of sandwiches, steaks, and salads.

There is seating for over 300 people, divided into two main dining areas (one is a completely separate room that can be reserved for private parties), plus some absolutely intriguing secluded little rooms just big enough for a couple or a foursome who want to sit up close and personal. There's also a pool room complete with fireplace. This spot has a true pub look, though on a somewhat grander and larger scale, all done up in foresty green, rich red woods, and well-polished brass. The bands, who make music Friday and Saturday nights between 9:30 p.m. and 1 a.m. on a built-in stage specially designed to accommodate them, are mostly Irish and local original jazz, folk, and rock groups. The pub is housed in a beautifully restored brick building on the corner of East Fourth and Prospect, across from the Quicken Loans Arena. A late-night menu kicks in after 9 p.m., until midnight Monday through Thursday, and until 1 a.m. on Friday and Saturday.

## The Harp
☎ (216) 939-0200
CITY: **Cleveland**　AREA: **Near West Side**
ATMOSPHERE: **Casual**　COST: **$$$**$$

**ADDRESS:** 4408 Detroit Ave.
**HOURS:** Mon–Thu 11 a.m.–10 p.m., Fri–Sat 11 a.m.–11 p.m., Sun 11 a.m.–9 p.m.
**RESERVATIONS:** Taken **PAYMENT:** MC, VS, AX **BAR:** Beer, wine, liquor **TAKEOUT:** Yes **ACCESS:** ら Full access

The signpost reads, "Carr Chlos, Oilean Acla, Dueige [pronounced Dooega]," but your feet are firmly planted on Detroit Avenue. The question for today's geo-quiz is, Where are you? The answer is The Harp, a place to eat and drink that is so thoroughly Irish you might think the Emerald Isles had been relocated to the Erie shores. Two of the signs out front once pointed the way to the small village in County Mayo where Mike O'Malley, the father of Harp owner Karen O'Malley, was born and raised, and to nearby Achill Island. (The third, Carr Chlos, in case you're curious, means parking lot.)

O'Malley built this brick-and-stucco building for his daughter from the ground up, and his fine craftsmanship is visible in the wooden moldings and millwork. The Harp was designed by a prominent Irish architectural firm to resemble the pubs found in Dublin and Galway. There's a stone hearth, inviting nooks, and comfy benches. All the furniture's from Ireland, too, and the beautiful murals were painted by a Dublin artist. Big windows frame a stunning view of the lake and the city skyline. A deck that seats 115 is open during good weather. The bar is a beauty, backed by stained-glass windows from an old Woodland Avenue church that was demolished.

Karen is usually found at the front door, greeting her customers and making them feel like they've just arrived at her house for a party. The music's Irish on Wednesday, Friday, and Saturday nights. The atmosphere is as relaxed and sociable as you'd find in a real pub, too. The 20-ounce imperial pints of Guinness, Harp Lager, Smithwick's, and Boddington are as Irish as you can get for slaking your thirst. For those who prefer Irish whiskey, the barkeep pours Jameson's, Bushmills, Tullamore Dew, and Middleton Rare and makes a drink dubbed James Joyce Hot Whiskey. For something nonalcoholic, try Barry Irish Teas by the pot.

Over the years the Irish fare has diminished to very few dishes: fish and chips, boxty (potato pancakes); a shepherd's pie that's first-class comfort food, and sides of colcannon. Soda bread, dense without being heavy, rich-flavored and studded with raisins, is made from Grandma's recipe, and it's so popular they sell it by the loaf. For sweets, consider the bread pudding, a luscious Guinness ice-cream sundae, or a hot toddy made with whiskey, lemon, sugar, and cloves. There's a kids' menu, on- and off-site catering services, special dinners, and month-long festivities in honor of St. Patrick's Day.

## Nighttown
☎ (216) 795-0550
CITY: **Cleveland Heights**  AREA: **East Side**
ATMOSPHERE: **Casual**  COST: **$$$$$**

**ADDRESS:** 12387 Cedar Rd.
**HOURS:** Mon–Thu 11:30 a.m.–midnight, Fri–Sat 11:30 a.m.–1 a.m., Sun 10 a.m.–midnight
**RESERVATIONS:** Taken, recommended Thu–Sat nights, especially before Cleveland Orchestra concerts **PAYMENT:** MC, VS, AX, DIS **BAR:** Beer, wine, liquor **TAKEOUT:** Yes **ACCESS:** ♿ Full access *Not recommended for children **OTHER ETHNIC:** British

A literary education lets you in on the meaning of the name and logo, explaining why this place looks like a cross between an early-20th-century bawdy house, a British Isles pub, and a piano bar. In his book *Ulysses*, James Joyce calls the district in Dublin frequented by women of ill repute and their customers Nighttown, the after-dark world of food, drink, music, and other assorted entertainments.

This Nighttown offers has a clubby feel—darkish, comfortable, and eccentric, with an abundance of gleaming wood, stained and etched glass, mirrors, and dim lighting from gas lamp look-alikes—and is frequented by a loyal coterie of regulars. There are two bar and four dining areas, and each has its own distinctive and eclectic, tongue-in-cheek décor. An altar and pews were used for one of the bars, and a marble slab that once graced a public men's room is used for the other. There are mounted elk heads; memorabilia from the days of trolley cars and straw boaters; vintage photos; a portrait of Joyce; posters and prints, including one of a creature that's half naked woman, half chicken; a tavern clock made in London in the 1700s; and, on the wall in the men's room (don't ask how I know), an old, framed menu from the Blazes Boylan Grill Room in Bloom's Hotel, Ireland. There are spaces for large groups and private twosomes. A lovely and delightful outdoor bar and dining area, protected from the elements, is called Stephen's Green (another Joyce reference).

The menu is a mix of upscale standards—shrimp cocktail, Caesar salad, steaks and prime rib (all beef is certified Angus)—and some classic Irish and English dishes, among them bangers and mash (sausages with cabbage, and mashed potatoes); Mayo lamb stew; fish and chips; and apple bread pudding with bourbon crème Anglaise. One of the kitchen's specialties is "Dublin Lawyer," a combination of lobster meat, mushrooms, and scallions in cream sauce spiked with Irish whiskey.

Harp and Guinness are on tap, and there are 10 classic single-malt whiskeys aged 8 to 12 years, nine premium single-malts, aged 10 to 18 years, and seven brands of port. Cafe Ulysses is a drink that blends coffee with Jameson's Irish Whiskey, Bailey's Irish Cream, Frangelico liqueur, and whipped cream. The wine list is comprehensive in both choice and cost, and well organized to make selection easier. (Bottles are available for sale to go at carryout prices.) The cellar reserve or "Captain's List" offers extraordinary vintages that go for anywhere from $83 to $133 a bottle.

A brunch, offering five specials like eggs Benedict and quiche, plus the regular lunch menu, is served every Sunday from 10 a.m. to 3 p.m. The last Sunday night of each month is reserved for the Irish, a regular event that features a special menu and live Irish folk music, everything from lyric ballads to lewd bar tunes: make reservations, it's always a sellout. On other nights jazz performers entertain. Get on the mailing list to stay up to date about visiting artists as well as scheduled wine tastings, champagne brunches, and cigar dinners. Rooms for parties and meetings can be reserved.

This is primarily a place for adults, a spot to talk business, hold hands, or confess transgressions while indulging in the pleasures of good food, fine drink, and excellent music.

## Sullivan's Irish Pub and Restaurant

☎ (216) 529-8969

CITY: **Lakewood** AREA: **West Side**
ATMOSPHERE: **Relaxed** COST: **$$**$$$

**ADDRESS:** 13368 Madison Ave.
**HOURS:** Mon–Thu 5 p.m.–midnight, Fri 5 p.m.–1:30 a.m., Sat noon–1:30 a.m., Sun noon–9 p.m.; kitchen closes at 11 p.m. nightly
**RESERVATIONS:** Not taken **PAYMENT:** MC, VS, AX, DIS **BAR:** Beer, wine, liquor **TAKEOUT:** Yes
**ACCESS:** ♿ Full access

Patrick Sullivan had a dream. The culinary school graduate had an idea for a restaurant that would be a friendly, welcoming place, the kind of place that encouraged lingering and sociability, where people would gather with friends and family to lift a glass and fill a hunger for good food and good company. The kind of place that would be just the right setting to celebrate everything from birthdays and anniversaries to the end of a hard day or a long week. So he set out to re-create an Irish pub. He thought Lakewood was the right location, and since he opened the doors in March 2003, the public has heartily embraced the concept.

Sullivan went all out to make it real, hiring a Dublin-based firm to design the spacious interior, which looks as though it has been there for a century or more. The woodwork and stained glass were crafted in Ireland. The taps, from which flow Guinness, Beamish, Murphy's Red, Bass, Boddington's, Harp, two English ales and an amber lager, and Bulmer's cider, maintain the requisite ratio of $CO_2$ to nitrogen. Beer's served in proper pint glasses.

The menu features Irish smoked salmon, steamed mussels, corned beef, battered cod, fish and chips, shepherd's pie, lamb stew, boxty, and the house special all-day breakfast that's a dead ringer for an Emerald Isle staple, consisting of fried eggs, rashers (bacon) and imported Irish sausage, and black and white "puddings," which are actually a mix of ground pork, oatmeal, and some other ingredients better left unnamed, with a consistency like polenta. Although many items on the menu don't qualify as traditional—steak sandwich, Gorgonzola and sun-dried tomato salad, and filet mignon—the kitchen works with an Irish-inspired market basket whenever possible. The apple cider chicken and the pork chops come with carrot parsnip mash; the house salad features Irish cheddar and bacon; the barbecue sauce is made with Guinness and the cheesecake with Bailey's. The Irish cheddar appetizer is a lovely thing—a bowl of warm melted cheese with triangles of boxty for scooping it up. There's vinegar on the tables for the fries, and the barkeep pours Bushmills, Tullamore Dew, and Glenfiddich on request.

Once a boat propeller repair shop, the pub's divided into a collection of discrete sections: one has the look of a library in an old manor; another, with

low four-legged stools, hearth, and cast-iron stove, evokes images of a country cottage. Bring a date, your pals, your kids, or your mum. Can't miss it as the trim on the brick building is bright blue. Parking in a lot at the rear or on the street. And if ever you feel a head cold coming on, my advice is to stop in immediately for Sullivan's hot toddy, made with Jameson's whiskey, lemon, and cloves.

# MARKETS

## French

### The Baricelli Cheese Company
☎ (216) 791-6500
CITY: **Cleveland**   AREA: **Near East Side**

**ADDRESS:** 2203 Cornell Rd.
**FOOD AVAIL.:** Cheese **HOURS:** Call for info/ appointment. **PAYMENT:** MC, VS **ACCESS:** ♿ Full access **OTHER ETHNIC:** American Regional, Italian, Western European mix

Located inside the lobby of the beautiful Baricelli Inn in Little Italy, this cheese boutique is little more than a walk-in refrigerator, but it's no ordinary one. This is a glass-walled affinage cooler specially designed for properly maturing and "blooming" artisan cheeses made from raw, unpasteurized cow, sheep, and goat's milk. Most come from

France, a few from Italy, and a handful from small American dairy farms. The taste of these hunks of epoisse, camembert, reblouchon, and chevre, and the approximately 30 to 40 other rare varieties is astonishing and worlds apart from the mass-produced plastic-wrapped products sold in the supermarket. There are some so ripe and runny, they're eaten with a spoon. They come in wheels, wedges, four-sided pyramids, and wrapped in dried herbs. Paul Minnillo, chef, owner of the inn, and cheese importer, wholesaler, and retailer, is the cheese master, and he's eager to educate the public about what he has to offer. As this is not a shop, in the ordinary sense of the word, hours for retail sales are irregular. It's best to call ahead and even make an appointment to get the benefit of his advice about pairing wines, foods, and cheeses. Thanks to Minnillo's passion and his 42-square-foot temperature- and moisture-controlled cooler, Northeast Ohio residents can experience and enjoy cheese as the Europeans do.

## On the Rise—Artisan Breads and Pastries
☎ (216) 320-9923
CITY: **Cleveland Heights**   AREA: **East Side**

ADDRESS: 3471 Fairmount Blvd.
FOOD AVAIL.: Baked goods, tea, coffee HOURS: Tue–Fri 7 a.m.–6 p.m., Sat 8 a.m.–5 p.m., Sun 8 a.m.–2 p.m; closed Mon PAYMENT: MC, VS, checks ACCESS: ᕹ Limited OTHER ETHNIC: Italian

The old world meets the new at this bakery specializing in handcrafted European baked goods. Owners and bakers Adam and Jennifer Gidlow opened for business in December 2001. The husband-and-wife team show real talent when it comes to scones, biscotti, and fruit tarts. And their raspberry chocolate truffle torte deserves a mention too. But it's bread making that really defines their mission and their passion. "The ingredients are simple," says Adam, "but are made special by process and time—the unique flavor and texture come from slow fermentation." The entire place smells yeasty, and the air in the bakery, which also has a few tables and chairs, is warm. Bread comes out of the oven twice a day, as it does in France, so the loaf you take home at 5 p.m. is truly fresh—baked in the afternoon and not the early morning hours. French baguettes and epi loaves that are shaped like a stalk of wheat; pain de mie (Pullman sandwich loaves); sourdough; and rustic Italian, focaccia, and Italian olive bread are always available. Daily specials include scali (a white Italian bread with sesame seeds), golden fruit tea bread (Saturday only), and challah.

It's worth a visit for the setting alone—makes you feel like you've had a lovely outing and not merely run a food errand. The place is charming—walls are bright yellow and peach, a small marble-topped antique buffet holds self-serve hot coffee and tea, and the counter is an old, stripped wooden sideboard; free samples are always offered on a tasting board. Coffee beans are sold by the pound. On street parking.

# German

## Der Braumeister Deli
☎ (216) 671-6220
CITY: **Cleveland**   AREA: **Near West Side**

ADDRESS: 13046 Lorain Ave.
FOOD AVAIL.: Baked goods, canned & packaged goods, spices, condiments, beverages, tea, wine HOURS: Tue–Fri 11 a.m.–6 p.m., Sat 3–8

p.m.; closed Sun & Mon **PAYMENT:** MC, VS, AX, DIS **ACCESS:** &. Limited

. . . . . . . . . . . . . . . . . . . . . . . . .

This well-stocked deli is located inside Der Braumeister restaurant. It carries a variety of German food imports and many of the most popular German brands and products. Imported biscuits and cookies, mustards, jelly and jam, and pickles can be found here. There's a good selection of German wines and beers and a deli counter with traditional favorites such as head cheese, leberwurst, blood tongue, and other cold cuts. (See restaurant listing under same name in this chapter.)

## Hansa Import Haus
☎ (216) 281-3177
CITY: **Cleveland**   AREA: **Near West Side**

**ADDRESS:** 2701 Lorain Ave.
**FOOD AVAIL.:** Meat (deli), baked goods, canned & packaged goods, spices, condiments, beverages, tea, coffee, wine, beer **HOURS:** Mon–Sat 9 a.m.–5:30 p.m.; open Sun in December only, 1–4 p.m. **PAYMENT:** MC, VS, checks **ACCESS:** &. Full access

. . . . . . . . . . . . . . . . . . . . . . . . .

You can't miss this place. Built to resemble a Bavarian mountain chalet complete with white stucco and exposed wood beams, it's a standout in its West Side neighborhood. The Hanseatic League, from which this store gets its name, was a medieval trading association of merchants from northern Germany and neighboring areas, and like its namesake this store does a brisk business buying and selling German imports. They stock a variety of packaged breads, cakes, cookies, and Swiss as well as German chocolates and maintain a good selection of beers and wines, and the deli counter offers traditional German cold cuts, sausages, and cheeses. In addition to food products, the store has

a large number of German-language magazines and tapes, toiletries, and gift items such as nutcrackers, beer steins, and wall plaques. At Christmastime, they also stock traditional German tree lebkuchen.

## Michael's Bakery
☎ (216) 351-7530
CITY: **Cleveland**   AREA: **Near West Side**

**ADDRESS:** 4478 Broadview Rd.
**FOOD AVAIL.:** Meat (fresh, deli), baked goods, beverages, tea, takeout meals **HOURS:** Mon–Fri 7 a.m.–6 p.m., Sat 7 a.m.–4 p.m.; closed Sun **PAYMENT:** MC, VS, AX, DIS, checks **ACCESS:** &. None

. . . . . . . . . . . . . . . . . . . . . . . . .

Best known for their baked goods made from authentic Old World recipes, Michael's also offers a nice selection of other foods, imported primarily from Germany, including pickles, peppers, and juices. They ship their heavy dark rye, German rye, crusty Vienna, and other old-fashioned European breads all over the country. The deli counter prepares sandwiches to order on this same freshly baked bread. A variety of tortes like mocha, chocolate, and rum are available as well as cookies, poppy seed and nut rolls, Danish, and donuts. Michael's has a second location at the West Side Market that's open Wednesdays, Fridays, and Saturdays; for further information, call 216-351-7530. (Also see listing for West Side Market in chapter 8.)

## Old Country Sausage
☎ (216) 662-5988
CITY: **Maple Heights**   AREA: **Southeast**

**ADDRESS:** 15711 Libby Rd.
**FOOD AVAIL.:** Meat (fresh), baked goods, canned & packaged goods **HOURS:** Tue & Wed

9 a.m.–5 p.m., Thu 9 a.m.–6 p.m., Fri 9 a.m.–7 p.m., Sat 9 a.m.–5 p.m.; closed Sun & Mon **PAYMENT:** Checks **ACCESS:** ♿ Limited

Some of their customers come from the other end of the state—or another state altogether—just to get their genuine German-style meats and sausages. When the Neiden family took over the business in 1982, they brought in a German *metzger* (butcher) to teach George Neiden how to make sausages the Old World way. Now one of only a few stores left in Cleveland that actually prepare these products themselves, Old Country offers 40 different kinds of sausage and wursts including bratwurst, liver paté, mettwurst (a spread made with smoked meats), and rohschinken (a smoked, aged ham similar to Italian prosciutto). They also stock a selection of cheeses, candies, packaged cookies and pickles from Germany, imported sauerkraut and red cabbage, and mixes for potato pancakes, dumplings, and spaetzle. "We're considered an authentic source of German food," says George, "even by people visiting Cleveland from Germany. Our spicings and flavorings are just like what you'd find there." Their meat products can also be found at the West Side Market at Stand G8; 216-579-0233. (For information about the West Side Market see listing in the market section in the International chapter).

## Reinecker's Bakery
☎ (330) 467-2221
CITY: **Macedonia**    AREA: **Southeast**

**ADDRESS:** 8575 Freeway Dr.
**FOOD AVAIL.:** Baked goods **HOURS:** Call first: hours vary. Generally, Mon–Fri 9 a.m.–4 p.m.; closed Sat–Sun **PAYMENT:** MC, VS, checks **ACCESS:** ♿ Full access

Three remaining members of the Reinecker family run this business, which is primarily a wholesale operation. They've been supplying area grocery stores with German-style baked goods since 1959. But if you're willing to make the trip to their place, they're happy to sell smaller quantities to individuals, too. They specialize in breads—rye is their particular triumph—and all five types of bread that they bake are natural whole-grain products with little sugar or fat. They are preservative-free, and most are made from recipes the family says are over 300 years old. Reinecker's is one of the only bakeries in the country to make these types of bread, and even their baking equipment is from Germany. They also make Christmas stollen, nut and poppy seed potica, and a variety of tortes. Note: there's no storefront to speak of. Heidi Reinecker, who says the casual, family-like atmosphere of the place means that most of their retail customers feel like old friends, suggests people use the back door.

## Sachsenheim Hall
☎ (216) 651-0888
CITY: **Cleveland**    AREA: **Near West Side**

**ADDRESS:** 7001 Denison Ave.
**FOOD AVAIL.:** Meat (fresh) **HOURS:** Two times a year (one day in Dec, & Feb); must place order a month in advance. **PAYMENT:** Checks **ACCESS:** ♿ Full access

The exact date varies from year to year, but annually in December traditional bratwurst, made with and without garlic, is offered for sale. In February, there's liver sausage as well. They're prepared by hand by members of the Alliance of Transylvanian Saxons on a Wednesday and sold the next day. Call about one month in advance to find out the precise date. Orders must be placed about two weeks ahead. The freshly made sausages can be purchased in bulk and frozen. German dinners are served here once a month. Reservations are required. Enter the Hall from the side door. There's a 300-car parking lot adjacent to the building.

## The Sausage Shoppe
☎ (216) 351-5213
CITY: **Cleveland**   AREA: **Near West Side**

**ADDRESS:** 4501 Memphis Ave.
**FOOD AVAIL.:** Meat (fresh, deli), baked goods, beverages **HOURS:** Wed 11 a.m.–5 p.m., Thu 10 a.m.–5 p.m., Fri 9 a.m.–6 p.m., Sat 9 a.m.–4 p.m.; closed Sun–Tue **PAYMENT:** MC, VS, checks **ACCESS:** ₺ Full access

The *Cleveland Ethnic Eats* reader who brought this establishment to my attention told me that the liverwurst made here is the best she's ever tasted. And no wonder: master sausage maker Norm Heinle, who owns and operates the market with his wife, Carol, has been practicing and perfecting his craft for 40 years. The shop was originally opened by Hans Kirchberger, a German immigrant who brought with him many of the Old World recipes still used here today. Norm was 13 when he started working for Herr Kirchberger, and since then he's added a few recipes of his own to the shop's repertoire.

Like his predecessor, Norm does not use any MSG, preservatives, additives, or fillers in the meat products he makes, which include a large selection of fresh sausages; 15 varieties of bratwurst; regular kielbasa plus a special holiday version made with wine and garlic, available now at Christmas, New Year's, Easter, Memorial Day, Fourth of July, Labor Day, and Thanksgiving; proski (a garlic-flavored pork-based cold cut); and leberkasse (literally translated as "liver cheese"). Irish potato sausage, made from the original Kirchberger recipe is a March special. Chef Parker Bosley

has described Norm's award winning paté as "customer friendly" because it's sold in containers rather than unappetizing casings and attractively topped with chives, peppercorns, or five other garnishes. Bosley calls the shop "a one-stop sandwich-maker's paradise." Bread from three different bakeries is also sold, two made locally and one from Canada. There are lunchmeats and cheeses, and a small selection of imported pickles, sauerkraut, and candy.

Their catalog and information about seasonal specials are available on their Web site, www.sausageshoppe.com The store is one block south of the Cleveland Zoo in Old Brooklyn and close to three major highways—I-71, I-90, and I-480—and parking is convenient. During the summer months, Norm and Carol fire up a grill on the front patio and cook weiners and "the brat of the day." For those who want to dig right in, there are picnic tables in the backyard. If you're in a hurry, call 10 minutes before you get there and your food will be ready for pick-up. Call or check the Web site for grill hours.

# Irish

## Casey's Irish Imports
☎ (440) 333-8383
CITY: **Rocky River**   AREA: **West Side**

**ADDRESS:** 19626 Center Ridge Rd.
**FOOD AVAIL.:** Meat (frozen), canned & packaged goods, condiments, beverages, tea **HOURS:** Mon–Wed & Fri 10 a.m.–6 p.m., Thu 10 a.m.–8 p.m.; Sat 10 a.m.–5 p.m.; closed Sun; extended hours during the Christmas holiday season and for St. Patrick's Day **PAYMENT:** MC, VS, AX, DIS, checks **ACCESS:** ₺ Full access

Vera Casey, who hails from County Mayo, and husband, Tom, of County

Galway, emigrated from Ireland with their three young daughters and one son in the '70s. Every time they went home for a visit, friends here asked them to bring things back. Eventually these "favors" turned into a business, one that involves the entire family. Now both friends and strangers can easily get Irish teas, cookies, candy, biscuits, oatmeal, jams, black/white pudding, packaged soups, sausage, bacon, and steak sauces. "Some people come in daily," says Patricia Casey-Lowery, "for their bit of Irish candy. It's a taste of home for them." Freshly baked Irish soda bread is available by special order. The shop, which is easily identified by the large attractive window displays of Irish china, crystal, and gifts, also stocks silver and gold Irish-themed jewelry, Aran knit sweaters, CDs, and books.

## Gaelic Imports
☎ (216) 398-1548
CITY: **Cleveland**    AREA: **Near West Side**

**ADDRESS:** 4882 Pearl Rd.
**FOOD AVAIL.:** Meat (frozen), baked goods, canned & packaged goods, condiments, tea, prepared frozen foods **HOURS:** Tues–Sat 10 a.m.–5 p.m., Sun 1–5 p.m; closed Mon **PAYMENT:** MC, VS, DIS, checks **ACCESS:** ♿ Limited **OTHER ETHNIC:** British

The shelves here are well stocked with foods imported from Scotland, Ireland, Wales, and England. Products whose brand names are music to the ears of those who know them well include Bovril, Marmite, Branston Pickles, H.P. Sauce, and Cadbury Candies. There's a good selection of marmalades and teas. The store's own sausage is available frozen. Homemade meat pies, Cornish pasties, and sausage rolls are available, too. Also made on the premises are black-and-mealy pudding and haggis (a dish you must have grown up

with to fully appreciate, as it consists of minced calf innards mixed with barley and oatmeal boiled together). Baked goods are fresh, too, and include tarts, shortbread, scones, and biscuits. Some gift items are available, including tartan accessories, made-to-order kilts, music, and jewelry. Parking is available in the rear or on the street.

# Swedish

## Swedish Pastry Shop
☎ (440) 993-6702
CITY: **Ashtabula**    AREA: **Farther East**

**ADDRESS:** 5713 Main Ave.
**FOOD AVAIL.:** Baked goods **HOURS:** Mon–Fri 6 a.m.–5:30 p.m., Sat 6 a.m.–5 p.m.; closed Sun **PAYMENT:** Cash only **ACCESS:** ♿ Full access **OTHER ETHNIC:** Finnish

Fans of Scandinavian baked goods have been asking me where to go for years. I didn't have anyplace to send them until 2002, when a reader told me about this 51-year-old shop in Ashtabula. Owner and baker Bill Murphy continues the business his father started. It may strike you, as it did me, that Murphy doesn't sound like much of a Swedish name, and lead you to doubt the authenticity of his product. But have no fear. Murphy's mother was from Sweden, and she supplied the recipes for skorper (toasted sweet bread), apple cake, nissua (cardamom braid), and limpfa (rye bread) that are the bakery's specialty. Bill, who starts his day at midnight, bakes till dawn, and makes deliveries in the afternoon, also prepares Finnish rye bread and Danish pastries. The shop is a popular stop for area tours; 20 to 30 groups a year come by the busload to meet Bill, get a walk-through, a talk, and a taste.

# Swiss

## Zoss The Swiss Baker
☎ (216) 368-4055
CITY: **Cleveland Heights**  AREA: **East Side**

ADDRESS: 12397 Cedar Rd.
FOOD AVAIL.: Baked goods, beverages, coffee
HOURS: Tue–Fri 7:30 a.m.–6:30 p.m., Sat 7
a.m.–4 p.m.; closed Sun & Mon PAYMENT:
Checks ACCESS: ♿ Full access OTHER ETHNIC:
French, Italian

We're very lucky that Barbara Zoss is from Cleveland Heights. Because when she and her husband, Kurt, a baker from Switzerland, decided to leave Zurich and come to America with their children, they also decided to open their bakery in her hometown. That's provided us with a unique opportunity to sample the kinds of breads and pastries the Swiss have traditionally enjoyed.

With skills honed over several decades, starting with an apprenticeship that began when he was a teenager in Zurich and augmented by a stint on the West Coast, where he learned about San Francisco sourdough techniques, Kurt creates an array of Swiss/European specialties rarely, if ever, available in this area. Since the spring of 1996, the shop has been offering Zurcherbrot, a crusty loaf with a chewy interior texture; Tessiner, a softer crusted bread typically found in the Italian region of Switzerland; Zopf, an egg bread often eaten for Sunday breakfast in Switzerland; and Swiss farmer bread. There are also a variety of baguettes, some laced with herbs or flavored with roasted garlic, brioche (slightly sweet and egg-yellow), and all sorts of flavorful little rolls. Some of the more unusual and outstanding sweets include zimblatt, a chocolate frosted cookie and flaky prussiens.

Only unbleached flour, filtered water, and fresh best-quality ingredients are used. You can watch the bakers at work through a small window in the shop that looks into the large work room, with the kneading table, cooling racks, and steam-injected stone-deck oven. Many items are available every day the bakery's open, others only when posted on a board or as listed in their product handout sheet. The shop is set back from the street, with limited parking in front but more in the back, which can be accessed via a driveway that is just past Nighttown.

# Western European mix

## Charles Peters Bake Shop
☎ (216) 641-6887
CITY: **Garfield Heights**  AREA: **Southeast**

ADDRESS: 4608 Turney Rd.
FOOD AVAIL.: Baked goods HOURS: Call for hours.
PAYMENT: Checks ACCESS: ♿ None OTHER ETHNIC:
Eastern European mix

Only three different owners have run this bakery since it opened in 1929. The shop features specialties that span the European continent: Polish sweet bread and paczki (donuts) and Bohemian rye bread. Everything is baked in a brick oven. Professional baker Jeff Stadnik prepares authentic made-from-scratch rolls, Danish, strudel, kuchens, cookies, and pastries daily. Miniature pastry party trays and decorated cakes available with two days' notice.

## Rudy's Strudel & Bakery
☎ (440) 886-4430
CITY: **Parma**   AREA: **Southwest**

**ADDRESS:** 5580 Ridge Rd.
**FOOD AVAIL.:** Baked goods, coffee, prepared frozen foods, takeout meals **HOURS:** Tue–Fri 7 a.m.–6 p.m., Sat 8 a.m.–5 p.m.; closed Sun–Mon **PAYMENT:** MC, VS, AX, DIS, checks **ACCESS:** ♿ Full access

Sweet strudel, both fresh and frozen, has long been the signature product of this business, started in 1948. The bakers fill them with apple, cherry, cheese, poppy seed, nut, pineapple, blueberry, apricot, and peach. More recently they began preparing gourmet dinner strudels—layers of flaky dough alternating with cabbage, spinach, and mozzarella; mushroom and onion; or potato, onion, and bacon. Their line of prepared takeout foods, called "Flavor of Europe," also features cababbage and noodles, stuffed cabbage, and 15 varieties of pierogi. Other desserts made here includee Dobos, Sacher, and Black Forest tortes and kolachky. Everything is all-natural and without preservatives. Sugar-free versions of strudel and cookies are also available (call ahead). Muffins, breads, Danish pastry, crepes, and a variety of cakes are made fresh daily. Parking available.

# LATIN AMERICA

Culinary practices form a living historical record, reflecting the political and economic events that have generated cultural exchange. Nowhere is this more apparent than in Latin America and the island nations of the Caribbean, represented in the Cleveland food community by Mexico, Brazil, and the countries of Central America, as well as Jamaica, Puerto Rico, and Cuba. For centuries these countries played host to pirate brigs and trading ships, slaves from Africa, conquistadors and explorers, expatriates from the far reaches of the British Empire, and immigrants from the war-torn nations of Western Europe. Over time, the foods of indigenous tribal peoples merged with the products and techniques these outsiders brought with them.

"How we Mexicans eat," explains Maria Galindo, a member of Cleveland's Hispanic Cultural Center, "reflects much of our history. You cannot separate the two. We were invaded, conquered, and colonized. And these people gave us language, religion, and culture. But behind that are the influences of our ancient ancestors which we never gave up, and it is from them we got the tortilla, the tostada, and our taste for hot and spicy food made with the hundreds of different types of chilies that grow here."

Chris McLaughlin, who is from Jamaica, tells the same story about her own country. "Our food is a mix of cultures and flavors, telling all about the people who've come to the islands. You can taste Africa, India, and China, mixed in with what is native to the region."

So Jamaicans use ackee, a fruit first brought by a slave ship from West Africa; allspice and Scotch bonnet chilies, which grow there in abundance; and curry, which they think of as their own national dish. Mexicans eat flan, a custard dessert that came with the Spanish, and make moles using cocoa, an ingredient rooted in their Aztec past, which they serve with rice, a food that was introduced to them by Asian sailors and merchant ships.

Most of the Caribbean island nations work with similar ingredients, which appear in the cuisines of Central and South America, too. Rice, beans, garlic, onions, citrus fruits, thyme, and both sweet and hot peppers are widely used throughout these regions. Where seafood is plentiful, it is an important part of the cuisine. Fruits like papaw (another name for papaya), mangoes, bananas, and coconuts are important ingredients in many dishes.

But there are obvious differences, too. Jamaicans tend to cook with allspice, curry powder, and ginger, while Mexicans more often use cilantro, cinnamon, and cacao. For Brazilians, manioc flour made from cassava is a staple and, seasoned, it's a standard table condiment. Jerked meat is a strictly Caribbean specialty. A rich, fiery version of barbecue, it's said to have originated when escaped slaves, hiding in the jungle, survived by pit-roasting wild pigs and flavoring the smoked meat with the herbs and spices they learned to use from the local Arawak Indians. The addition of salt helped preserve the meat for long periods.

The people of Mexico and South America use tomatoes and corn in much of their cooking. According to Salvador Gonzalez, a Mexican of Indian descent who has lived here for many years, each area of his country has its own way of preparing tostadas, tamales, and tortillas. "Tortilla making by hand is an art," he says, "and they taste nothing like the packaged variety available in this country. In my family, they were made fresh every day."

The largest group of Spanish-speaking people for whom Cleveland is home are Puerto Ricans, followed by those from Mexico. Many make their home on Cleveland's West Side, where numerous Hispanic restaurants and markets are to be found. Like other immigrant groups past and present, people from Latin America have come to Northeast Ohio to escape political instability and pursue economic advancement. They have filled the ranks of industrial and agricultural workers, and increasingly in recent years have been attracted here by the wealth of educational opportunities.

The Club Azteca, a local Mexican social organization begun in 1923, now includes members from many different Latin American nations. "We try not to focus so much on where we've come from," explained Zulema Carreon, an active member for many years, "but on the fact that we all want to work together to share our cultures with Cleveland. We are proud of our pasts and don't want to lose what is our own. But it's also important to learn about one another. I get so excited when I have a chance to experience other people's ethnic customs, and I want them to feel the same about my heritage."

# RESTAURANTS

## Brazilian

### Brasa Grill

☎ (216) 575-0699

CITY: **Cleveland**   AREA: **Downtown**
ATMOSPHERE: **Casual**   COST: $$$$$

**ADDRESS:** 1300 W. 9th St.
**HOURS:** Mon–Thu 4–10:30 p.m., Fri–Sat
4–11:30 p.m., Sun (brunch) 10 a.m.–2 p.m.
(dinner) 4–10 p.m. **RESERVATIONS:** Taken,
recommended on weekends; required for
groups of 5+ **PAYMENT:** MC, VS, AX, DIS **BAR:**
Beer, wine, liquor **TAKEOUT:** Yes **ACCESS:** ᕫ Full
Access *Not recommended for children

Brasa Grill offers a unique eating experience that combines Latin American flavor with the North American appetite for vast quantities of food. For a flat fee, diners eat until they can't eat anymore, and the meal includes an endless parade of rotisserie-cooked meats plus unrestricted access to a lavish buffet. But this warehouse-district destination is by far the swankiest all-you-can-eat restaurant you'll ever encounter.

Billing itself as a churrascaria-style steakhouse, Brasa is defined by its distinctive way of preparing and serving meat, a practice that originated in the Pampas region of southern Brazil in the early 19th century. Sixteen different cuts and kinds—ranging from sausages and short ribs to chicken, turkey, ham, and a special Brazilian top sirloin called picanha—are cut off long skewers at the table by a specially trained wait staff who are experts at using their knives to make picture-perfect slices of leg of lamb, pork tenderloin, and bacon-wrapped filet mignon. One of my regular eaters, who boasts of never being bested by a meal, made it through only 11 varieties before throwing in his napkin. Self-control is key. Every diner, equipped with a small plastic disk, is personally in charge of his or her intake. One side is red and the other green. As long as the green side is face up, waiters appear to carve another delicious portion. But as soon as the red side appears, they know you've had your fill or need a break.

In addition to the steady supply of things carnivorous, dinner here includes sides of fried bananas, rice, and polenta plus a dish of farofa, toasted flour made from the yucca plant and meant to be lightly dusted on the meat to enhance its flavor. A dangerously delicious basket of crusty cheese-laced rolls arrives shortly after guests are seated—consume too many of those and you'll have to take a pass on much of what's to come. An "island" buffet offers multiple choices, and the selection could easily constitute a complete meal for vegetarians. Shrimp, mussels, green beans with sesame seeds, couscous, Waldorf and Caesar salads, artichoke hearts, and Asian noodles show up regularly. Among the traditional Brazilian items are hearts of palm, chicken cilantro salad, and fish in coconut sauce. On weekends there's feijoada, the country's national dish made with pork and black beans. The bar mixes tropically inspired drinks. Request tableside preparation of a caipirhina (Brazilian rum or vodka, fresh lime juice, and sugar over ice) or a mojito (clear rum, fresh mint leaves, and sugar). The wine list emphasizes bottles from Brazil, Chile, and Spain. The large dining room comfortably accommodates big groups, and the upscale décor is a nice backdrop for special events.

There is no menu so ordering is easy, and with two prix fixe options—one for the salad bar only and the other for the complete dog-and-pony show. Tables appear outside during Ohio's heat wave season. Pricey lots, valet service, and meters on the street.

## Saravá

☎ (216) 295-1200

CITY: **Cleveland**    AREA: **Near East Side**
ATMOSPHERE: **Casual**    COST: **$$$**$$

**ADDRESS:** 13225 Shaker Square
**HOURS:** Mon–Thu 5–10 p.m., Fri–Sat 5 p.m.–midnight, Sun 5–9 p.m. **RESERVATIONS:** Taken **PAYMENT:** MC, VS, AX, DIS **BAR:** Beer, wine, liquor **TAKEOUT:** Yes **ACCESS:** ♿ Full access **OTHER ETHNIC:** International

Sergio and Susan Abramof, who own and operate Sergio's in University Circle (see listing in Mediterranean chapter) wanted to make their second restaurant more than just a place to eat dinner. They're aiming to be a neighborhood hangout and a part of the community, a gathering spot where friends can meet up and relax in a sociable, party atmosphere that is oh-so-Brazilian. That's why they made a long and inviting bar the centerpiece of the big space, surrounded it with lots of small tables and comfortable seating, and included a raw bar beside it where you can nibble fresh chilled oysters and middleneck clams by the dozen. The large dining area, beautifully conceived by architect Joe Hanna, is broken into many discrete and intimate sections, with cozy little nooks, booths, and living-room style arrangements. There's even a corner for lounging next to the fireplace. The patio out front, linked to the interior by French doors and big windows, is a gateway to the activity on the Square. It extends half the block, with seating for 100, and live music is a regular side dish in the summer.

The Abramofs have created what they call a "street plate" menu, offering a selection of light, inexpensive, tapas-style finger foods meant to be shared: artichoke fritters, crispy fried smelts with chile dipping sauce; spicy shrimp; puffs of cheesy bread called pão de queijo in Portuguese; and salgadinhos, an ever-changing mix of snacks like those found in São Paulo and Rio de Janeiro. All pair up perfectly with caipirinhas, a drink made with crushed limes and cachaça. But diners with heartier appetites are not neglected. There's more substantial fare among the regular entrée offerings: xim xim, a fiery dish of chicken, shrimp, coconut milk, and malaguetta pepper; prato misto, a traditional meatless mix of black beans, rice, farofa (browned cassava flour), and a carioca tomato relish; bouillabaisse; grilled skirt steak; and feijoada, a rich stew filled with linguiça sausage, bacon, ham, and pork loin. Daily specials tend toward more cross-cultural and Mediterranean-style presentations. Wrap up the meal—or the night—with churos, warm, freshly-made donuts; coconut butter cake; or tropical fruit, and a cup of sweet, press-pot café Brasil Santos. The wine list is organized in a wonderfully helpful and informative way, grouping vintages by description from "bright, crisp whites" to "big, bold reds," with suggestions about how to match each category with food.

The restaurant is gorgeous—spare with a clean, minimal contemporary look and at the same time sensuous and inviting, with splashes of lush color, curving banquettes, and dramatic spot lighting. Decorative metalwork, natural plant materials, and paintings provide visual interest. With a samba beat in the background the overall effect is hip, stylish, and sexy. And yet, somehow, the scene also seems to accommodate a multigenerational crowd, couples are at ease bringing their kids, and card-carrying AARP members won't feel the least bit out of place.

Two areas available for private parties. Parking is free in the lot behind the restaurant. Metered spots available on the street and valet service nightly.

# Caribbean

## Bratenahl Kitchen
☎ (216) 383-1875
CITY: **Cleveland**   AREA: **East Side**
ATMOSPHERE: **Relaxed**   COST: **$$**$$

ADDRESS: 14002 Lake Shore Blvd.
HOURS: Mon–Sat 10:30 a.m.–11 p.m.
RESERVATIONS: Not taken PAYMENT: Cash only
BAR: None TAKEOUT: Yes ACCESS: ♿ Full access

Chef and owner Richard Dawkins brings more than 25 years in food service to the little place he launched in 2006. For the first two years, there was only a single table inside, so fans of his curry shrimp and jerk chicken had to rely on the takeout service. Now, during the summer—when the weather cooperates—seating is available on the back deck. He also caters for all occasions. A Jamaican transplant, Dawkins cooks island versions of beef patties, gumbo, oxtails, stew, pepper steak, rice and beans, and bread pudding. The menu in this no-frills operation is posted behind the counter. Call ahead to request vegetarian or special diabetic preparations.

# Jamaican

## Dailey's West Indian Food Mart
☎ (216) 721-7240
CITY: **Cleveland**   AREA: **East Side**
ATMOSPHERE: **Relaxed**   COST: **$$**$$

ADDRESS: 3019 E. 116th St.
HOURS: Mon–Thu 8 a.m.–midnight,
Fri–Sat 8 a.m.–1 a.m., Sun 8 a.m.–midnight
RESERVATIONS: Not taken PAYMENT: MC, VS,
AX, DIS BAR: Beer, wine, liquor TAKEOUT: Yes
ACCESS: ♿ Limited *Not recommended for children

This come-as-you-are Jamaican eatery does not have a particularly inviting exterior, and even after you enter you'll think you made a wrong turn somewhere and ended up in a mini-mart. Orders are placed at the takeout counter in the rear of the store, where you can see the food that's been freshly prepared that day by Chris McLaughlin, who learned the art of Caribbean cooking from her grandmother when she was a girl living on a farm in Clarendon Parish on the island of Jamaica. Then you take a seat in a dining area at the back that looks rather like a windowless family rec room, usually populated with West Indians who are eating, visiting, hanging out at the small bar, or watching television.

The menu is surprisingly varied, each day featuring a different mix of selections. Some dishes are quite alien to the American palate: cowfoot and tripe, salt fish and ackee (cod stewed with fruit, onions, and other vegetables), beef skin, and oxtail (they're just what the name implies). But those who grew up on this food say it's got the real taste of home. More popular with native Clevelanders are jerk (spicy barbecued) chicken wings, curried chicken, fried snapper, rice with gungo (pigeon) peas, and peppered shrimp. There's a soup a day, and the variety is wide—from chicken and beef to conch, red pea, and mutton. One diner reports that this is not a place for the timid: unless you're West Indian or live in the neighborhood, both the food and the location demand a certain adventuresome spirit.

## Island Style Jamaican Cuisine
☎ (216) 851-4500
CITY: **East Cleveland**   AREA: **East Side**
ATMOSPHERE: **Relaxed**   COST: **$$**$$

ADDRESS: 2144 Noble Rd.
HOURS: Tue–Thu 11:30 a.m.–8 p.m.;
Fri–Sat 11:30 a.m.–9 p.m., closed Mon–Sun
RESERVATIONS: Not taken PAYMENT: Checks BAR:
None TAKEOUT: Yes ACCESS: ♿ Full access

Isolene Burke opened her tiny eatery in March 1997, in the same location as the L & R Tropical Food Store listed in the first edition of *Cleveland Ethnic Eats*. She gave the place a fresh coat of paint, took out the old counter and stools and put in a steam table, installed new shelving for the bottles of imported pepper and jerk sauce she carries, and remodeled the kitchen and the bathroom. It's still a simple, laid-back place where connoisseurs of Caribbean cookery can indulge their taste for jerk chicken, curried chicken, curried goat, and rum cake. With the help of her daughter, Ms. Burke, who is from Kingston, Jamaica, also prepares her version of stewed beef and stewed chicken, beans and rice, dumplings, fried plantains, and banana bread according to treasured family recipes. They also make gingery coconut drops, a special candy from home, and roti, a pita-like bread that came to the Jamaican table by way of India with the immigrants from the subcontinent who ended up on the islands. Packing up takeout orders is a big part of her

operation because the restaurant only seats 15–20 diners.

Though she has plans to expand the line of Caribbean groceries and produce she stocks and sells, Ms. Burke wants her business to stay small and feel friendly. She likes getting to know her customers and says, "People seem to like us just the way we are, so why change when things are going good!"

## Rachel's Caribbean Cuisine
☎ (216) 382-6952
CITY: **South Euclid**   AREA: **East Side**
ATMOSPHERE: **Relaxed**   COST: **$$$**$$

ADDRESS: 14417 Cedar Rd.
HOURS: Tue–Thu 4–10 p.m., Fri–Sat 4–11 p.m.; closed Sun–Mon RESERVATIONS: Taken, recommended for large groups PAYMENT: MC, VS, AX BAR: Beer, wine, liquor TAKEOUT: Yes ACCESS: ♿ Full access OTHER ETHNIC: Caribbean

In my version of the old Tony Bennett tune, "If I Ruled the World," every day would be the first day of spring . . . and every chef would be as inspired as David Sterling. He came to Cleveland by way of Jamaica, culinary school, and years spent in the kitchens of cruise ships and area restaurants. Since November 2000 everything he learned along the way has been coming together here. The food is wonderful to look at and to eat.

The menu is concentrated: it features six appetizers, two soups, three salads, four sandwiches, 12 entrées, six sides that could be meals unto themselves, especially for vegetarians, and three desserts labeled Rachel's Finale that just might bring you to your feet for a standing ovation. Standouts include conch fritters; seafood chowder; rice and beans; fried plantains; jerked marinated halibut crowned with pineapple mango salsa; jerk chicken; chicken curry; coconut bread pudding; and David's Island Touch carrot cake with spiced-rum cream cheese frosting. Jamaican honey biscuits come with all the house specialties. Other dishes, such as grilled salmon in a lobster cream sauce; cilantro shrimp; hickory smoked baby back ribs; or a marinated, aged New York strip steak and garlic mashed potatoes, are not, strictly speaking, Caribbean, but they are made with the same distinctive care and flair.

The presentation is meticulous and lovely—not what you'd expect in a reasonably priced and relaxed place like this. Even something as simple as a club sandwich gets upgraded with cilantro aioli in place of mayonnaise, and a Caesar salad goes tropical with the addition of jerk chicken breast or blackened salmon.

Because he loves to create as well as cook, Sterling's menu periodically changes. That's part of the excitement of eating at a one-of-a-kind place like this rather than a chain. David admits that having his own place and doing everything the way he thinks it should be done requires long hours and hard work. At least he has his family to keep him company. His wife, Rachel, in whose honor the restaurant is named, runs the front of the house, and the couple's daughters pitch in when needed along with Rachel's sister and niece. Rachel makes it her business to court and coddle customers, and she's very good at it, convincing one hesitant drinker to try a Shandy Caribe (lager beer spiked with ginger), and a regular to order something different than their usual.

The couple has done a nice job decorating the small, narrow space, painting the upper half of the walls a shade of blue that seems to be a reflection of sea and sky and bleaching the wood paneling on the lower half to sandy white. Tables are covered in white cloths under glass. There's an eight-stool bar near the entrance that pours Jamaican Red Stripe

beer, and a waist-high partition down the center separates the booths on one side from the tables and chairs (which can be pushed together for groups of more than four) on the other. Recorded reggae is likely to be playing softly in the background. It's low key, welcoming, and pleasant. The combination of food and atmosphere attracts a laid-back, interracial, intergenerational crowd. None of this ambience is even hinted at from the outside: the restaurant is located behind an uninviting facade in an equally uninviting strip that, to its credit, offers ample free parking. It's an unlikely location for food of this high quality. But now that you know, there's no excuse not to go. Or have David bring his culinary magic to your house or event—he does catering.

# Latin American mix

## Lelolai Bakery & Cafe
☎ (216) 771-9956
CITY: **Cleveland**   AREA: **Near West Side**
ATMOSPHERE: **Relaxed**   COST: $$$$$

ADDRESS: 1889 W. 25th St.
HOURS: Mon–Wed 9 a.m.–5 p.m., Thu–Sat 9 a.m.–6 p.m.; closed Sun **RESERVATIONS:** Not taken **PAYMENT:** MC, VS, DIS **BAR:** None **TAKEOUT:** Yes **ACCESS:** ♿ Full access **OTHER ETHNIC:** Spanish

Another contender in the bakery-cafe combo category. Come to shop, come to eat, or stop trying to choose and do both. Caribbean is the culinary theme and carries over into the ambience—the walls are white with bright, bold color accents. Seating for about 22 at small tables of wrought-iron and glass—the sort you'd find in a garden—that fill up the front half of the store. More tables and chairs appear outside when the weather is inviting. This is especially nice as the city has invested in an overhaul of the street to make it more pedestrian friendly. The menu is short, but there's no shortage of good things to eat. Sandwiches are made on a slightly sweet kind of bread called pan criollo. Wrap your hands around a Cubano, a Miami-style Cuban, or the Caribbean—all featuring roast pork that can also be purchased by the pound—or one made with Spanish sausaage. Other options include octopus salad, chicken or beef empanadas, and garlic-laced yucca. Finish up with a pastelillos, quesito, or flan, and a cup of cinamon-topped café con leche. Lelolai earned a spot in *Gourmet* magazine's 2002 Guide to America's Best Restaurants, as a neighborhood gem. (For more information see Lelolai's listing under markets.)

# Mexican

## El Charro Restaurante
**☎ (440) 237-6040**
CITY: **North Royalton**   AREA: **Southwest**
ATMOSPHERE: **Casual**   COST: **$$**$$$

ADDRESS: 13570 Ridge Rd.
HOURS: Mon–Sat 3 p.m.–11 p.m.; closed Sun
RESERVATIONS: Taken, for groups of 6+ **PAYMENT:** MC, VS, AX, DIS, checks **BAR:** Beer, wine, liquor
TAKEOUT: Yes **ACCESS:** ♿ Full access

The Mexican portion of the menu has no big surprises, offering a selection of crowd-pleasing favorites from tacos to chiles rellenos, and some Tex-Mex standards. But there are some intriguing Nuevo Latino options, defined as modern renditions of traditional Latin American dishes. Here they add flavor twists with chimichurri, tequila, mojo, and margarita sauces. There's a children's menu for the younger set. The

menu explains that foods are prepared with flavorful spices and are never hot unless you add the heat yourself. Service is fast and friendly, portions are substantial, and nachos with hot and mild sauce are complimentary. The bunuelo (light, fried dessert pastries with cinnamon and sugar) are a special after-dinner treat, because they are traditionally served only at New Year's. Park in the small lot out front or in the additional spaces in the rear.

## El Rincon Mexican Restaurant
**☎ (330) 497-2229**
CITY: **North Canton**   AREA: **Farther South**
ATMOSPHERE: **Casual**   COST: **$$**$$$

ADDRESS: 720 South Main St.
HOURS: Mon–Thu 11 a.m.–10 p.m., Fri–Sat 11 a.m.–10:30, Sun 11 a.m.–9 p.m.
RESERVATIONS: Taken **PAYMENT:** MC, VS, AX, DIS
BAR: None **TAKEOUT:** Yes **ACCESS:** ♿ Full access

Mexican knickknacks provide the visual theme, inside and out. In front of the building, which looks like it was once home to a pancake or steak house, are ceramic burros and little guys in sombreros and serapes. The walls in the dining room are decorated with scenes from Mexico, and festive piñatas hang from the ceiling.

The food is straight-ahead Mexican with no surprises—tacos, enchiladas, burritos, tostadas, fajitas, quezadilla (their spelling), chalupas, chiles rellenos, and carne asada. The menu is chatty and shows a sense of humor, with the following announcement from "The Boss": "Due to inflation and everything else you already know, we are not allowed to accept Mexican pesos" (probably a lot of those floating around North Canton). He also promises that "brave amigos" who want their food hot need only ask. There's also a description of Mexican dishes, but I must admit they go a bit overboard as I doubt there's anyone around who needs a definition of nachos. Chips and salsa are available in take-home portions.

A second El Rincon is located in Akron, at 1485 South Arlington Street; 330-785-3724.

## El Tango Taqueria
**☎ (216) 226-9999**
CITY: **Lakewood**  AREA: **West Side**
ATMOSPHERE: **Relaxed**  COST: $$$$$

**ADDRESS:** 14224 Madison Ave.
**HOURS:** Mon–Sat 11 a.m.–10 p.m.; closed Sun **RESERVATIONS:** Not taken **PAYMENT:** MC, VS, AX, DIS **BAR:** None **TAKEOUT:** Yes **ACCESS:** ♿ Full access **OTHER ETHNIC:** Caribbean, Central American, South American

Antonio Carafelli is not a modest guy. He's absolutely certain that his tacos and burritos are the best in the world! How's that for confidence? Bite into one of his creations and decide for yourself. The baked grande version is certainly among the largest I've run across—the burrito might be considered a piece of carry-on luggage if you were to board a plane with it in hand.

As his name suggests, Carafelli does not have Mexican roots, but Antonio has had a long-standing passion for all things Mexican and edible. He has studied Mexican cooking; lived in Santa Fe, New Mexico, and San Antonio, Texas, where he learned how good Mexican food should taste; and honed his skills at a number of other restaurants. My own internal taco tester tells me Antonio knows what he's doing. His roast chicken with an Oaxacan mole sauce and the enchiladas rojas (beef with a red chili sauce) are outside the box of standard Mexican fare. There are four versions of salsa, all made on the premises: two mild blends, pico de gallo and poblano tomatillo verde; a medium-hot smoked

cinnamon chipotle combination; and the hot Tango special. The outstanding tamale pie, rarely found in these parts, is made with layers of chicken, cheese, and corn tortillas baked together with a spicy chili cascabel sauce and salsa. Nachos go beyond the ordinary—they come in a "grande" portion topped with beans, poblano sauce, cheese, and fresh salsa. Since I first visited, the menu has been expanded to include dishes from all of Latin America. There's Cuban grilled red snapper, barbecued pork Mayan style, Venezuelan roasted beef and potatoes, and Guatemalan chicken made with honey and cinnamon. The dining room seats 25, and the custom-made wooden tables, a warm red-and-yellow color scheme, and Antonio's paintings set a tone evoking a country hacienda in central Mexico or Spain.

Part of the storefront space is geared for takeout, with a low, tiled counter and four stools in the window. The kitchen, wide open and visible from the customer side of the counter, dominates the room. It's also a classroom for Carafelli's cooking classes. Call for information about upcoming sessions. El Tango is located in a brick building with plenty of on-street parking in front.

## La Fiesta
**☎ (440) 442-1445**
CITY: **Richmond Heights**  AREA: **East Side**
ATMOSPHERE: **Casual**  COST: $$$$$

**ADDRESS:** 5115 Wilson Mills Rd.
**HOURS:** Lunch Mon–Fri 11:30 a.m.–2:30 p.m.; Dinner Mon–Sat 5–10 p.m.; closed Sun & most holidays **RESERVATIONS:** Taken, recommended for groups of 6+ **PAYMENT:** MC, VS, AX, DIS **BAR:** Beer, wine, liquor **TAKEOUT:** Yes **ACCESS:** ♿ Full access

Antonia Valle began serving Mexican food to Clevelanders in 1952. Using many of the same family recipes,

Antonia's children and grandchildren continue the tradition in a restaurant that features the cuisine of the central Mexican region of Michoacan, the area south of Guadalajara where Antonia came from. Diners will find many familiar Mexican dishes on the menu, including tacos, enchiladas, burritos, and tamales, but the flavor is different from the Tex-Mex most Americans are used to. There are also some more unusual offerings like lomo de cerdo con chipotles y ciruelas (roast pork loin stuffed with chipotle peppers and prunes and topped with orange gravy) and shrimp chipotle. Sea bass Veracruz is a special on Friday and Saturday nights. Servers, who are knowledgeable about the food, are glad to explain and advise. There's a large selection of items for vegetarians and special children's platters, too. The walls are peach-colored stucco, the floors are clay tile, and the overall effect is attractive and comfortable. Located in a retail strip adjacent to Richmond Mall, this is a relaxing place to eat and socialize.

## Luchita's Mexican Restaurant
☎ (216) 252-1169
CITY: **Cleveland**   AREA: **Near West Side**
ATMOSPHERE: **Casual**   COST: **$$$**$$

ADDRESS: 3456 W. 117th St.
HOURS: Lunch Tue–Fri 11 a.m.–2 p.m.; Dinner Tue–Thu 5–10 p.m., Fri–Sat 5–11 p.m., Sun 5–9 p.m.; closed Mon RESERVATIONS: Not taken
PAYMENT: MC, VS, AX BAR: Beer, wine, liquor
TAKEOUT: Yes ACCESS: & Full access

A friend who has spent considerable time in Mexico says that a bite of Luchita's food transports her back there. The Galindo family has been preparing authentic regional dishes from central Mexico since 1981, and the only modification they make to traditional recipes is to substitute vegetable oil for

lard. The menu, with glossary, explains what goes into each dish. There are some rarely encountered sauces such as mole (rich with cocoa), suiza (tomatillos and cheese or sour cream), and pico de gallo (a sweet and sour salsa made with sugar and vinegar); unusual appetizers like ceviche (a tomato dish made with lime-flavored shrimp, onions, and cilantro), corn masa turnovers stuffed with chicken and Chihuahua cheese and topped with marinated cabbage, and sopes de chorizo ("boats" made of corn masa filled with black beans, spicy sausage, anejo cheese, and guacamole).

Specialties offered change every three months both to take advantage of what's in season and to feature specific regional cuisines. So you might find puerco potosino, a simmered pork; pollo sinaloa, a stew of chicken, potatoes, onions, and cactus; pescado pibil, a fish fillet marinated in achiote orange salsa and wrapped in banana leaves; empanadas con mole Amarillo, a filled flour-dough turnover in a mole typically made in Oaxaca; or tinga de pollo, shredded chicken prepared with homemade Mexican cream and a tomato-based salsa of chipotle peppers and tomatillos. Of course, there are always burritos, enchiladas, tacos, and flautas (a stuffed tortilla rolled and deep fried). There is a good selection for vegetarians.

The world beyond Cleveland is more familiar with this place than locals; its praises have been sung in airline magazines and international dining guides. But despite its fame, the atmosphere here is low-key, friendly, and comfortable. Both the bar, which serves Bohemia beer, a brand popular in Mexico, plus top-shelf tequilas, and the 80-seat dining room are often populated by regulars. The building is vintage 1930s and, inside, the simple stucco walls accented with Mexican ceramics, artwork, and figurines form an ideal backdrop for the food, which is the real attraction here.

Luchita's locations are multiplying rapidly. The family now has four: see the following listings.

## Luchita's Mexican Restaurant
☎ (440) 743-7650
CITY: **Parma**   AREA: **Southwest**
ATMOSPHERE: **Casual**   COST: **$$$**$$

ADDRESS: 7431 Ridge Rd.
HOURS: Lunch Tue–Fri 11 a.m.– 2 p.m.; Dinner Tue–Thu 5–10 p.m., Fri 5–11 p.m., Sat 4–11 p.m.; Sun 4–9 p.m.; closed Mon **RESERVATIONS:** Not taken PAYMENT: MC, VS, DIS BAR: Beer, wine, liquor TAKEOUT: Yes ACCESS: ♿ Full access

This is the largest restaurant in the family's group, and Adrien Galindo's baby. He's put his own stamp on the look of it, going to Mexico for tiles and furnishings, and selecting a sun and moon motif, vivid colors, and a hacienda style décor.

The bar and main dining room are on the first floor. A room for private parties that holds up to 60, complete with its own bar, is in the basement. The menu is a duplicate of those at all the other Luchita locations. See listing for Luchita's on West 117th Street. One added feature here is a Sunday liquor license here. Look for a freestanding white building with a green awning and a big parking lot.

## Luchita's Mexican Restaurant
☎ (440) 365-0094
CITY: **Elyria**   AREA: **Farther East**
ATMOSPHERE: **Casual**   COST: **$$$**$$

ADDRESS: 1134 North Abbe Rd.
HOURS: Tue–Thu 11:30 a.m.–10 p.m., Fri 11:30 a.m.–11 p.m., Sat 4–11 pm; Sun 4–9 p.m.; closed Mon RESERVATIONS: Taken PAYMENT: MC,

VS, DIS BAR: Beer, wine, liquor TAKEOUT: Yes ACCESS: ♿ Full access

Menu here is the same at other locations. See previous listing for Luchita's on West 117th Street.

## Luchita's Mexican Restaurant
☎ (440) 205-5966
CITY: **Mentor**   AREA: **East Side**
ATMOSPHERE: **Casual**   COST: **$$$**$$

ADDRESS: 8870 Mentor Ave.
HOURS: Mon–Thu 11:30 a.m.–2:30 p.m., 5–9:30 p.m.; Fri–Sat 11:30 a.m.–10 p.m., Sun noon–9 p.m.; closed Mon RESERVATIONS: Taken, for groups of 6+ PAYMENT: MC, VS, AX BAR: Beer, wine, liquor TAKEOUT: Yes ACCESS: ♿ Full access

See listings for other Luchita's locations.

## Marcelita's Mexican Restaurant
☎ (330) 656-2129
CITY: **Hudson**   AREA: **Farther South**
ATMOSPHERE: **Casual**   COST: **$$**$$$

ADDRESS: 7774 Darrow Rd. (SR 91)
HOURS: Tue–Thu 11 a.m.–9:30 p.m., Fri–Sat 11 a.m.–10:30 p.m.; closed Sun and Mon; Happy Hours in "La Cantina" Tue–Fri 3–7 p.m., Sat 11 a.m.–4 p.m. RESERVATIONS: Taken, for groups of 6+ PAYMENT: MC, VS, AX, DIS BAR: Beer, wine, liquor TAKEOUT: Yes ACCESS: ♿ Full access

Marcelita, who hails from Mexico City, husband Jack, and sister-in-law Jeanne have been helping, in their own words, "to stamp out gringo food" since 1978. The crowds have grown larger every year, so they've had to keep breaking through walls and adding space. First the original one-room restaurant got a new kitchen, foyer, and spacious cantina (bar) plus greenhouse. In 1992 came the garden room, a bright, cheery, tropical-feeling place, even in the dead of an Ohio winter. The restaurant can now accommodate about 200 diners, in four rooms, each one with a different color theme and distinctively decorated with traditional pottery and pieces of whimsical folk art the family has brought back from their many trips to Mexico. The two-section middle room is composed of the original low-ceilinged dining area and foyer. It has a darkish intimacy, brightened by candles on the tables and a mural of a window with flowers on the sill. The former kitchen is now a small, separate dining area perfect for private parties. The sunny, yellow garden room is all blond wood, big windows, plants, and ceramic birds.

The 75-seat cantina is reminiscent of a log cabin, and is usually filled with people who are easing the wait for a table (typically 15–30 minutes on the weekend) by enjoying complimentary chips and sauces and sipping one of the many types of "Marvelous Margaritas" the restaurant is famous for, a Mexican or microbrewed beer, or a shot of tequila. The menu offers enchiladas; burritos; tostadas; tacos; chiles rellenos; chimichangas; steak, chicken, and vegetarian fajitas; and a traditional "pepita" salad made with roasted pumpkin seeds. Desserts include homemade flan, ice cream nachos, and a house special coated ice cream ball.

This is a family restaurant in every sense—it's run by a family, much of the wait staff is like family (many having been with Marcelita's for 10 or more years), and it's genuinely kid friendly with a fleet of boosters and high chairs. A room is available for private parties. They boast a Triple-A Three Diamond rating. There's a large parking lot surrounded by a thick backdrop of trees.

## Mexican Village Restaurante y Cantinas

☎ (216) 661-3800

CITY: **Parma**   AREA: **Southwest**
ATMOSPHERE: **Casual**   COST: **$$$**$$

ADDRESS: 1409 Brookpark Rd.
HOURS: Mon–Thu 11:30 a.m.–10 p.m., Fri 11:30 a.m.–10 p.m.; Sat 4–10 p.m.; closed Sun RESERVATIONS: Taken, recommended on weekends for groups of 5+ PAYMENT: MC, VS, AX BAR: Beer, wine, liquor TAKEOUT: Yes ACCESS: ὅ Full access

The building appears small from the outside, but inside there's actually room for up to 200 diners. The décor is traditional and attractive: tile floors, stucco walls decorated with masks, pottery, and blankets from Mexico, and arched tile-trimmed doorways. There's a separate barroom with a few tables. Established in 1962 and still family owned, the Village features both traditional northern Mexican specialties and those Mexican-style dishes, like fajitas and chimichangas, found only on this side of the border. They offer tacos American-style or a more Mexican version. There's something to please those who crave Tex-Mex or those in search of truly regional dishes—like enchiladas in a mole or a tomatillo sauce, chorizo con huevos (sausage and eggs served with beans, rice, and tortillas), and chiles rellenos (poblano peppers stuffed with Mexican cheese). There are three classic desserts: flan, fried ice cream, and sopapillas (fried dough flavored with honey, sugar, and cinnamon).

Downstairs is a special Fiesta Party Center for private parties of 50–150 people (call 216-661-3800 two weeks in advance); they'll prepare a Mexican buffet and decorate appropriately for the occasion. The exterior of the building was recently remodeled to give it a Spanish/Mediterranean look that features a red clay tile roof with real beams protruding from the building, stucco walls with arches, and ornate Spanish lanterns.

## Mi Pueblo

☎ **(216) 671-6661**

CITY: **Cleveland**   AREA: **West Side**
ATMOSPHERE: **Relaxed**   COST: **$$**$$

ADDRESS: 12207 Lorain Ave.
HOURS: Mon–Thu 9 a.m.–10 p.m., Fri–Sat 9:30 p.m.–midnight., Sun 9 a.m.–10 p.m.
RESERVATIONS: Taken PAYMENT: MC, VS, DIS BAR: None TAKEOUT: Yes ACCESS: ♿ Full access

. . . . . . . . . . . . . . . . . . . . . . . . . . .

This combination restaurant and market is a convenience concept whose time has come, and one sure way to avoid the well-known dangers of grocery shopping on an empty stomach. (For more information about the market, see Mi Pueblo's market listing further on in this chapter.) Informal simplicity is the standard here—food is served in plastic baskets, napkins are found in table dispensers. But there's no scrimping on quality or quantity. Portions are huge and just as big on taste. The menu offers a choice of tacos, burritos, and tortas (sandwiches) with a variety of fillings, and all are so big and overstuffed that an average appetite is challenged. And the fillings bear no resemblance to the bland ground beef or beans that most Americans expect: there's spicy Mexican sausage, diced skirt steak, roasted barbecued pork, steamed beef, avocado, and lengua (artfully translated on the menu as "Mexican delicacy" to avoid the off-putting reality of tongue, which is what it is). The kitchen also turns out enchiladas, tamales, and flautas. Daily specials might be chiles rellenos, chicken mole, or tamales. On Saturdays and Sundays only, because they are so time-consuming to prepare, menudo (tripe soup) and birria (goat stew) are

added to the menu, and the demand for these flavorful and rarely encountered dishes is so great that they're available in take-home gallons. A complimentary relish tray of pickled carrots and jalapeno peppers, red tomato pepper sauce, and green tomatillo sauce arrives at your table shortly after you sit down. From your booth or table you can see the open kitchen and grill where pork cooks slowly on a spit. Entrées can be accompanied by an intriguing array of drinks: orchata (rice water, a concoction that is like a liquid version of rice pudding); tamarindo (a soft drink made from tamarind fruit); freshly made natural fruit juices; and malteadas, malts so thick, sweet, and special that they can double as dessert, made by blending milk, ice, sugar, and fresh fruit. For breakfast, consider huevos rancheros, a combination of eggs and salsa, warm tortillas, beans, and chorizo sausage.

Though the four owners—two sets of brothers—and staff are originally from Mexico, and much of the taqueria's clientele is Spanish-speaking, the menu is easy for everyone to read, with English-language descriptions to accompany dishes listed by their Spanish names. The CD jukebox contains only Spanish and Mexican selections, from traditional folk music to popular singers, and a disc is almost always playing. Sometimes staff sing along. On a wall near the entrance is a large hand-painted mural of a Mexican village scene. Carved wooden miniatures depicting traditional 19th-century Mexican kitchens and some wooden plates of the type used in Mexico in the 1800s decorate the other walls. There is a lightness and brightness here that adds to the tropical, far-from-the-steel-mills feel; walls are orange, floor tiles are red, and light pours in from the big plate-glass storefront windows. A major expansion in 2004 added more tables (seating now for 120) and a cantina with bar service so you can enjoy a margarita or a cerveza (beer) with your meal. The atmosphere, as well as the food, is so decidedly un-Cleveland that coming here is like taking a trip out of town. In addition, the place is very kid friendly, so a visit can serve double duty as a family outing—throw in a stop at the grocery and you've accomplished three things at once!

## Mi Pueblo

☎ (216) 791-8226

CITY: **Cleveland**   AREA: **Near East Side**
ATMOSPHERE: **Casual**   COST: **$$$**$$

**ADDRESS:** 11611 Euclid Ave.
**HOURS:** Mon–Thu 11 a.m.–10:30 p.m., Fri–Sat 11 a.m.–2:30 a.m., Sun 11 a.m.–10:30 p.m.
**RESERVATIONS:** Taken, recommended for groups of 4+ on weekends **PAYMENT:** MC, VS, AX, DIS
**BAR:** Beer, wine, liquor **TAKEOUT:** Yes **ACCESS:** &
Full access

Mi Pueblo took on a whole new identity when it migrated east. This location, which opened late in 1998, is a larger, prettier, dressed-up version of the original West Side taqueria, but the food has retained all its authenticity and flavor. Plates of chiles rellenos (stuffed poblano peppers), enchiladas, and shredded beef tortas prepared in the culinary tradition of the central regions provide a taste-bud ticket to the heartland of Mexico. You get the same ride when you spoon up some caldo de pollo (cilantro-spiked chicken soup) or take a mouthful of guacamole con tostaditas. There's a good selection of dishes familiar to fans of the burrito and the taco, and some more unusual preparations made from seafood, beef, chicken, and pork. Portions are always generous, and most entrées come with rice and beans. It's unlikely you'll leave with that empty feeling, especially if you freely indulge in the on-the-house corn chips (freshly made and served in a basket that is constantly refilled), salsa (red and green), and pickled carrots before your meal. The margaritas, prepared in the cantina at the front of the restaurant, can also fill you up as they come in various sizes, one as big as a punch bowl (42 ounces of liquor-laced liquid), and the same is true for glasses of sweet orchata. (For more information about food and drinks, see previous listing for the original Mi Pueblo).

Like the food, the décor honors tradition. At the entrance are a 100-year-old wooden butcher's block and a stone grinder. Stucco walls, tile work, masks, murals, and brightly colored paper flowers all evoke a sense of place . . . and that place is Mexico, not Cleveland. The same care and attention that go into preparing each dish are evident in the imported hand-carved chairs. On Friday and Saturday from 6 to 9 p.m., a pair of strolling musicians sings Mexican favorites—if you're with that special someone and the time is right, request a love song (and don't hesitate to show your appreciation with both applause and cash). Although I'd say this is a fine choice for the romantically inclined, the place draws diners of all ages and types. Part of its charm is the mix—AARP members and those almost old enough to vote; the well-dressed and the should-have-dressed-better; students and staff from Case Western Reserve University, the Art Institute, and the Cleveland Institute of Music; families from Cleveland and Shaker Heights with kids ranging from the high-chair set to the body-pierced; Latinos who talk to the servers in Spanish; and a varied assortment of folks who could be on their way to or from the Art Museum, University Hospitals, the Garden Center, the oh-so-funky Euclid Tavern next door, or the nearby the Food Co-op. With space for about 40, it's also available by reservation for private parties. The restaurant also does off-site catering, but heed this word of caution—my husband and his partner had them prepare the food for a party at their photography studio, and it was so good that nobody wanted to leave, nor were they content to nibble politely, and halfway through the event I had to make a run to the restaurant for more! Two very small lots in front of and behind the restaurant, and on-street parking.

## Nuevo Acapulco
☎ (440) 734-3100
CITY: **North Olmsted**   AREA: **West Side**
ATMOSPHERE: **Casual**   COST: **$$$**$$

**ADDRESS:** 24409 Lorain Rd.
**HOURS:** Mon–Thu 11 a.m.–10 p.m., Fri–Sat 11 a.m.–11 p.m., Sun noon–10 p.m. **RESERVATIONS:** Taken, Mon–Thu only; recommended for lunch **PAYMENT:** MC, VS, AX, DIS **BAR:** Beer, wine, liquor **TAKEOUT:** Yes **ACCESS:** ♿ Full access

Opened in 1994, Nuevo Acapulco, located close to Great Northern Mall, bills itself as a Mexican restaurant for families. There are American steaks, hamburgers, and chicken dishes on the menu for those family members who'd rather not come face to face with a plate of camarones a la diabla (prawns and mushrooms in a spicy red sauce) or quesadillas (flour tortillas stuffed with cheese, tomatoes, and chilies). Entrée choices reflect cuisine from many regions of the country, and the explanations on the menu will help even novices to understand what they're choosing. Staff, who greet guests in Spanish, are friendly and helpful. A dish of complimentary salsa arrives at the table before diners even place their order, and rice and beans (your choice of refried or cholesterol-free beans) come with most main dishes. The large, bright, colorful, open space seats about 130 and features beautiful murals and artwork with a Mexican motif.

## Nuevo Acapulco
☎ (440) 234-2500
CITY: **Berea**   AREA: **Southwest**
ATMOSPHERE: **Casual**   COST: **$$$**$$

**ADDRESS:** 804 Front St.
**HOURS:** Mon–Thu 11–9 p.m., Fri–Sat 11–10 p.m., Sun noon–9 p.m. **RESERVATIONS:** Taken, Mon–Thu only; recommended for lunch **PAYMENT:** MC, VS, AX, DIS **BAR:** Beer, wine, liquor **TAKEOUT:** Yes **ACCESS:** ♿ Full access

See listing for Nuevo Acaplco on Lorain Rd. in North Olmsted for more information.

## Rancheros Taqueria
☎ (330) 510-2110
CITY: **Akron**   AREA: **Farther South**
ATMOSPHERE: **Relaxed**   COST: **$$**$$$

**ADDRESS:** 286 E. Cuyahoga Falls Ave.
**HOURS:** Tue–Thu 11 a.m.–9 p.m., Fri–Sun 11 a.m.–10 p.m.; closed Sun in summer; closed Mon **RESERVATIONS:** Not taken **PAYMENT:** Cash only **BAR:** None **TAKEOUT:** Yes **ACCESS:** ♿ None

This is a joint, in the best sense of the word—small, inexpensive, and with a no-fuss, no-frills atmosphere that comes from being itself with no apologies or excuses. "You pays your money" (cash only)—and you get really good, really authentic Mexican food in return. That's it. Places like this are a dime a dozen in Austin, Texas, but rare in these parts. When former *Akron Beacon Journal* food editor Jane Snow and I walked in, early in the day before the lunchtime crowd appeared, chef, owner, and sometime server David Soreque already had a pot of stock simmering, evidence that everything here is made from scratch, just as his mother taught him back in

Michoaca, a little town east of Mexico City where he has born. Although there are some Tex-Mex items available, what makes his menu special is the more traditional preparation of things like tamales, enchiladas, and quesadillas. Tortillas are top quality. Tacos, filled with cubes of spiced pork, chicken, steak, chorizo sausage, or tongue, are fried twice and topped with grilled onions, a squeeze of lime, and a sprinkling of cilantro. According to David, the Mexican dishes most popular in the U.S. would be considered merely appetizers in a proper meal. So on the weekends, he cooks more complicated, time- and labor-intensive specials—mole, chiles rellenos, or a dish made with pork and nopales (cactus)—because he wants to give Americans a taste of what he describes as "the true Mexican cuisine," adding, "that's why lots of Mexicans come here. It's real home cooking to them." Seating is limited to an eight-stool counter and three four-top tables, plus a couple more outside in good weather.

## Tlaquepaque Restaurant

☎ (330) 649-9109

CITY: **Canton**    AREA: **Farther South**
ATMOSPHERE: **Relaxed**    COST: **$$**$$

**ADDRESS:** 4460 Dressler Rd.
**HOURS:** Sun–Thu 11 a.m.–10 p.m., Fri –Sat 11 a.m.–11 p.m. **RESERVATIONS:** Taken, recommended for large groups **PAYMENT:** MC, VS, AX, DIS **BAR:** Beer, wine, liquor
**TAKEOUT:** Yes **ACCESS:** ♿ Full access

As I pulled into the big parking lot of this stand-alone stucco building, my first thought was that I'd arrived in the Mexican neighborhood at Disney World. The place has a look that is loosely (very loosely) connected to pueblo-style architecture, but it's a cartoon fantasy version of the real thing. I didn't have high hopes for what I'd

find on the other side of the door, but although the look is still kitschy, it's also pleasant, and the large dining area (seats 200) is divided by half walls into cozy, comfortable sections with a mix of tables and booths. Owner Rafel Madragal and his family opened the restaurant in 1998 and have already garnered many regulars. Standard, familiar Mexican dishes fill the menu, with variations coming mostly in the form of fillings, combinations, and quantity, but the preparation, according to Madragal, is rooted in old family recipes. The kitchen does like to play with beef tips (you may like to eat them, but how many of you actually know just where the cow's tips are?): you'll find them in chile Colorado; Tlaquepaque (with rice and beans); and the Special La Casa (with burritos and melted cheese). The menu includes a pronunciation guide as well as a glossary, so you can perfect your ability to order correctly: say, "Chelays Ray-ya-nos" and "En-chie-lah-das." I left humming that great old tune, "I say Tah-mah-lays and you say . . ." The bar at the front near the entrance pours Mexican beer, sangria, and margaritas. There's a patio with seating for about 70 that is relatively sheltered from the parking area.

## Villa Y Zapata

☎ (216) 961-4369

CITY: **Cleveland**    AREA: **Near West Side**
ATMOSPHERE: **Relaxed**    COST: **$$**$$

**ADDRESS:** 8505-09 Madison Ave.
**HOURS:** Mon–Fri 11 a.m.–11 p.m., Sat 4–11 p.m., Sun noon–10 p.m. **RESERVATIONS:** Taken
**PAYMENT:** MC, VS, AX, DIS **BAR:** Beer, liquor
**TAKEOUT:** Yes **ACCESS:** ♿ None

There's no sign outside, but the building is easily identifiable by the tricolor paint job: the red, white, and green bands represent the Mexican flag. Inside it's friendly, functional, and un-adorned with the look and feel of an old neighborhood hangout, with a vaguely '50s-era sensibility. The restaurant seats about 75 at tables and booths, in two rooms. Neon-colored margaritas are available by the pitcher and are a great drink deal. House-made tortilla chips arrive at the table with salsa. The menu is made up of homestyle recipes, mostly from southern Mexico. There are plenty of American favorites—burritos, chiles rellenos, enchiladas, and fajitas. But what really makes this place worth a visit are the less familiar choices—dishes such as shredded chicken in chipotle and tomato sauce; pork simmered in green sauce; guisado de bistek (beef cooked with cactus, potatoes, and jalapenos); and sopes, small corn-dough cakes filled with chicken, beans, and anejo cheese. The chicken soup served with pico de gallo and avocado is a satisfying bowlful for lunch or dinner. Easy access to this West Side venue from I-90. Parking lot at the rear.

# Puerto Rican

## El Taino Restaurant

☎ (216) 621-4888

CITY: **Cleveland**   AREA: **Near West Side**
ATMOSPHERE: **Relaxed**   COST: $$$$

ADDRESS: 3038 Scranton Ave.
HOURS: Mon–Thu 11 a.m.–8 p.m.; Fri, Sat 11 a.m.–9 p.m.; closed Sun RESERVATIONS: Taken
PAYMENT: MC, VS, AX, DIS, checks BAR: None
TAKEOUT: Yes ACCESS: & None

I learned about this place, formerly called Lincoln Deli, in my favorite way—from a satisfied customer and fan. I was sitting in another small West Side ethnic restaurant and fell into conversation with the man at the next table.

I told him about my ongoing search for authentic ethnic eateries, and he told me to visit El Taino. It's not the sort of place that advertises, but even so, it attracts a crowd, and not just people who have grown up eating tostones (plantains) and bacalaito (dried, salted cod). Their clientele is international, but Spanish is the first language here. The list of daily specials may require translation. Once my server, afraid her English wasn't good enough for us, sent a manager over to help. The small storefront restaurant, which takes its name from the island's indigenous people, offers home cooking Puerto Rican–style. There's goat stew (cabro en fricasse), fried pork (chicharrones), chicken stew (pollo guisado), chuleta (pork chops), and pescadilla (fish). Most dishes include arroz (rice) and habichuelas (beans) or gandules (pigeon peas). Green bananas are a staple—combined with shrimp you get mofongo con camarones; with octopus, mofongo con pulpo; and with lobster, mofongo con langosta. Stuff them with ground beef, and they become alcapurria; with a pork filling, they're pasteles. Not every item on the menu is available every day. Expect a relaxed, congenial atmosphere, a Latin beat to the background music, in a plain and simple setting. Parking is on the street.

## Rincon Criollo

☎ (216) 939-0992

CITY: **Cleveland**   AREA: **Near West Side**
ATMOSPHERE: **Relaxed**   COST: $$$$

ADDRESS: 6504 Detroit Ave.
HOURS: Mon–Sat 7 a.m.–7 p.m.; closed Sun
RESERVATIONS: Taken PAYMENT: MC, VS, DIS BAR: None TAKEOUT: Yes ACCESS: & Full access

Same name, different location. Rincon Criollo, listed in the 2002 edition of *Cleveland Ethnic Eats*, disappeared from the 2003 volume while they were moving from the old space on St. Clair to their current home in a double storefront in the Detroit-Shoreway neighborhood. It's still the same laid-back, family-run place with a friendly atmosphere and Caribbean accents. The menu is a short list of Latin comfort foods—meat pies, chicken and vegetable soup, stewed pork chops, banana and potato balls, crispy chicarrones (fried pork), rice, and beans. Specialty of the house is the Jibarito sandwich, Rincon's equivalent of a hamburger, made with steak tips served between two slices of plantain. Owner Felix Ocasio told my son Nathan, who had never tasted one, that he'd love it. Felix was right, as evidenced by the purring sound, punctuated by words like "wow" and "yum," that escaped from Nathan between bites. For dessert, he had flan, and he commented, "This alone is worth the trip across town. If we weren't out in public, I'd be licking the bowl." I felt the same about my pescao encebollado en salsa (fish in red sauce). Puerto Ricans call their cuisine "cocina criollo." Like the restaurant's name, which translates as "Creole corner," it refers to the blend of foodstuffs and cooking cultures that characterizes their dishes. Each of the different nationality groups that have populated the island has left its culinary mark, including the native Taino Indians, the Spanish and other Europeans, Africans, Asians, and Cubans. That mix is reflected in the highly spiced, but not spicy, dishes that Rincon Criollo has to offer: Ensalada de Pulpo (octopus salad); stews made with beef, goat meat, or tripe; steak in an onion and vinegar sauce; vianda con bacalao (cod with root vegetables); and Monfongo, "bowls" made with mashed plantain that can be filled with shrimp, pork, octopus, or fish. Not every dish is available every day—one or two are featured as specials each weekday, with a larger selection on Fridays and Saturdays. Plants

in the windows, soothing colors, table-cloths under glass, and photos of Puerto Rico combine to create a pleasant setting. Rincon Criollo does a brisk take-out business, and there are two counter seats where you can wait for your order. Kids are more than welcome, and high chairs are available. Judging from all the Spanish-language notices on the bulletin board, I'd say much of the clientele is Hispanic. Easy to find—look for the green awning.

# Salvadoran

## La Brasa
☎ (216) 319-0500
CITY: **Cleveland**   AREA: **Near West Side**
ATMOSPHERE: **Relaxed**   COST: $$$$$

ADDRESS: 6110 Denison Ave.
HOURS: Mon, Wed–Sun 11 a.m.–10 p.m.;
closed Tuesdays RESERVATIONS: Not taken
PAYMENT: Cash only BAR: None TAKEOUT: Yes
ACCESS: ⅖ None OTHER ETHNIC: Central
American

This is one of those no-frills, off-the-eaten-path places. And even after you've made your way here, the bars on the doors and windows and nondescript storefront could prompt you to keep on going. But don't be put off because good eating awaits. Claim one of the five tables in the brightly colored room, place your order at the counter, and then dig in to chicken cooked on an indoor charcoal grill, beef and potato stew, empanadas, papusas (a cornmeal pouch filled with beans or squash and cheese), tamales, and sides of pigeon peas or red beans with rice, fried plantains, pickled cabbage, and fresh salsas. In the Old Brooklyn neighborhood, the restaurant is easily accessible via I-71, the Jennings Freeway, and I-480. It's near the zoo, so you could easily plan a day of food and fun.

## La Casa Tazumal

☎ (216) 688-1803

CITY: **Cleveland** AREA: **Near West Side**
ATMOSPHERE: **Relaxed** COST: **$$**$$

ADDRESS: 3260 W. 105th St.
HOURS: Tue–Sat 11 a.m.–8 p.m., Sun 11 a.m.–7:30 p.m.; closed Mon RESERVATIONS: Not taken PAYMENT: Cash only BAR: None TAKEOUT: Yes ACCESS: & None

Although the names of some things on the menu may seem familiar, this food is not like the Mexican cuisine many of us know. The tamales are made with a cornmeal and chicken-broth batter and filled with chicken, carrots, and potatoes. Pastales con carne are fried flour tortillas encasing a mixture of ground meat, carrots, green beans, and potatoes. Instead of chiles rellenos, you'll find Rellenos de Guisquil, cheese-filled chayote squash dipped in an egg batter, fried, and topped with tomato sauce. Horchata, a version of the chilled rice drink called orchatta, is similar to chai or iced coffee, with an intriguing and unique flavor that comes from morro seeds, which come from the calabash squash. The true centerpiece of this culinary culture is the pupusa. It's as common in El Salvador as hamburgers are in the U.S. Pupusas look like big raviolis or pierogies. The dough that forms the exterior is made with cornmeal, but it's thicker and chewier than a tortilla. Inside there's meat, cheese, and beans. The stuffed "pocket" is fried and served hot with cold pickled cabbage salad and a sweet/hot red sauce on the side, the Central American equivalent of coleslaw and ketchup. Instead of french fries to go with it, you can get platanos fritos con frijoles o crema—fried plantains with beans and sour cream. Main-dish selections include bistec encebollado (grilled steak and onions), pescado frito boca colorada (fried red snapper), stew, and pollo asado (broiled chicken). On Fridays and Saturdays only Doña Maria Martinez, who owns the place, cooks two different kinds of beef soup. Everything is made from scratch.

This is the second incarnation of a Salvadoran diner in this 32-seater location just south of Lorain Avenue. Spanish is the first language spoken here, but the menu has subtitles, and even though your waitress, who may be Doña Martinez herself, says "muchas gracias" instead of "thank you," the smile that comes with it will communicate better than words. The dining room is nothing fancy, but it's maintained with loving care. The walls are painted the color of sunset. Green plants crowd the front window, and pretty cloths covered with plastic are on the tables. The unadorned flat-fronted brick building is not exactly inviting, but once you walk through the door the message is *bienvenidos*— "welcome." One person who recommended this place to me said that it's like you're in Maria's kitchen when you eat at her restaurant. No matter how long it takes you to get here, I think her home cooking will leave you feeling that it was well worth the trip. On-street parking is available.

# MARKETS

# Jamaican

## Dailey's West Indian Food Mart
☎ (216) 721-7240
CITY: **Cleveland**    AREA: **East Side**

ADDRESS: 3019 E. 116th St.
FOOD AVAIL.: Meat (fresh, frozen), fish (fresh, frozen), produce, grains, beans, flour, baked goods, canned & packaged goods, spices, condiments, beverages, tea, wine, prepared frozen foods, takeout meals HOURS: Mon–Thu 8 a.m.–midnight, Fri–Sat 8 a.m.–1 a.m., Sun 8 a.m.–midnight PAYMENT: MC, VS, AX, DIS ACCESS: ♿ None

From the outside, this looks like a typical little neighborhood grocery. But inside it's filled with exotic, imported Caribbean foods, such as cans of pigeon peas or callalou (a Jamaican spinach), jars of guava jelly, soursop nectar (a fruit pulp), Pickapeppa sauce, and many varieties of bottled jerk (a spicy barbecue sauce). Dailey's also stocks many different types of hot peppers, including the hard-to-find fiery Scotch bonnets; unusual species of fish like conch and Caribbean snapper, plus dried salted codfish; and a large selection of fresh specialty produce, including chocho (a root vegetable that resembles a tur-

nip), huge yams, coconuts (as well as canned coconut milk), and plantains, those hard green bananas so good for cooking. Traditional Jamaican foods like fried plantains, mutton soup, spiced shrimp, and jerk chicken are prepared fresh every day, and you can purchase a complete meal or just a single item ready to eat on the spot or take home. Irish moss, a seaweed used to make a sweet, invigorating drink that's reputed to be especially good for giving a guy's engine a jump start, is sold dried in bags. There are also tropical fruit drinks and Jamaican sodas and freshly baked rum cake.

# Latin American mix

## Azucar Bakery
☎ (216) 281-7516
CITY: **Cleveland**    AREA: **Near West Side**

ADDRESS: 6516 Lorain Ave.
FOOD AVAIL.: Baked goods, coffee, prepared frozen foods HOURS: Mon–Sat 8 a.m.–7 p.m.; closed Sun PAYMENT: Cash only ACCESS: ♿ Limited

Signs of ethnic credibility are obvious upon entering this modest little store on the near West Side, from the barrage of unfamiliar sounds and smells to a menu written in both Spanish and English. Nestled in the heart of one of Cleveland's Latino neighborhoods, Azucar dishes up a short list of local favorites from the Caribbean and Central and South America. There are potato rolls; Mexican breads; sandwiches made with steak or pork, among them an Ecuadoran ham and cheese "con heuvo" (with a fried egg); and a variety of confections. The churros (the long, thin Hispanic version of fried dough or elephant ears) are as sweet as the name of the bakery implies (azucar is Spanish for sugar), and the same can be said of the three-milk cake (dulce de tres leches), rice pudding, and budin de pan (bread pudding). One of my trusted, well-traveled, and unpaid helpers who has been to that part of the world, commented that the warm empanadas (pastry filled with either beef, chicken, ham and cheese, or guava and cheese) were just like the ones he'd had in South America. Pupusas, the Salvadoran equivalent of a hamburger, is a stuffed tortilla topped with marinated cabbage and salsa. It is offered here with a variety of fillings: cheese, pork, beans, or a flower blossom called loroco. Another Salvadoran specialty on the menu is a quesadilla made from rice flour.

The Bakery's owners are two couples, one from Guatemala and the other from El Salvador. I would travel to the other side of the world just for their flan, but fortunately I only have to get myself to West 65th. A stop here during the work week for a Cubano with a quesitos chaser (cream cheese pastry) could reinvent the idea of lunch to go. Free parking on street.

## Dave's Supermarkets
☎ (216) 961-2000
CITY: **Cleveland**   AREA: **Southwest**

ADDRESS: 3565 Ridge Rd.
FOOD AVAIL.: Meat (fresh, frozen), fish (fresh, frozen), produce, grains, beans, flour, rice, baked goods, canned & packaged goods, spices, condiments, beverages, tea, wine, prepared frozen foods HOURS: Mon–Sat 7 a.m.–10 p.m., Sun 7 a.m.–8 p.m. PAYMENT: MC, VS, checks ACCESS: & Full access

This full-service grocery store caters to the Hispanic community, and just about anything you need for Latin cookery can be found here. They stock Goya, La Proferita, and Vita Rose brand canned goods; rice in 20-pound bags; salted codfish; Mexican cheeses like panela, manchego, ranchero, anejo, asadero, and chihuahua; chipotle chiles en adobo (dried smoked jalapenos in sauce); and a large selection of fresh produce, including plantains, fresh chilies, tomatillos, and uncommon root vegetables. Produce specifically from the West Indies, such as malanga and breadfruit, is also in evidence, and there are unusual colas and fruit drinks from the islands. If you don't see what you want, ask for it; if they don't have it, they'll try to get it. Renovation on the building that now houses the store was completed in 1993. It's spacious, modern, and convenient, with plenty of free parking. Dave's on Carroll in Ohio City and Dave's on Payne also carry these products. For more information on the Payne Avenue store, see listing in chapter 7. For more information about Dave's in Ohio City, see next listing.

## Dave's Supermarkets
☎ (216) 274-2940
CITY: **Cleveland**   AREA: **Near West Side**

ADDRESS: 2700 Carroll Rd.
FOOD AVAIL.: Meat (fresh, deli, frozen), fish (fresh, frozen), produce, grains, beans, flour, rice, baked goods, canned & packaged goods, spices, condiments, beverages, tea, coffee, wine, beer, prepared frozen foods, takeout meals HOURS: Mon–Sat 7 a.m.–9 p.m., Sun 7 a.m.–8 p.m. PAYMENT: MC, VS, DIS, checks ACCESS: & Full access OTHER ETHNIC: African-American/Southern, Asian, Mediterranean mix

This 35,000-square-foot full-service store opened in the summer of 1997 in Ohio City. For information about products stocked, see listing for Dave's on Ridge Road (above), and Dave's on Payne Avenue (see chapter 7). They also carry some ethnic foods that are considered more gourmet than traditional, including imported cheeses, Italian-style hams and salami, and Greek olives.

# Mexican

## La Borincana Foods
☎ (216) 651-2351
CITY: **Cleveland**   AREA: **Near West Side**

**ADDRESS:** 2127 Fulton Rd.
**FOOD AVAIL.:** Meat (fresh, frozen), fish (fresh, frozen), produce, grains, beans, flour, rice, baked goods, canned & packaged goods, spices, condiments, beverages, tea, coffee, wine, beer, prepared frozen foods, takeout meals **HOURS:** Mon–Fri 10 a.m.–7 p.m., Sat 9 a.m.–7 p.m., Sun 9 a.m.–5 p.m. **PAYMENT:** MC, VS, checks **ACCESS:** ⅖ Full access **OTHER ETHNIC:** African, Brazilian

. . . . . . . . . . . . . . . . . . . . . . . . .

If you want to eat as they do in the Caribbean, Central America, or South America, then shop here. This is the city's most concentrated selection of foodstuffs from Barbados, Trinidad and Tobago, Jamaica, Guyana, Puerto Rico, Honduras, the Dominican Republic, El Salvador, Guatemala, Mexico, Columbia, Peru, Argentina, Uruguay, and Venezuela, Haiti, Ecuador, Ghana, and Nigeria. Products are neatly organized according to nationality. This makes it easy to zero in on what you want, but random browsing is much more fun, a virtual tour via box, jar, bag, and can. Whether your recipe calls for Salsa Lizano sauce, masa harina, achiote, pickled pig snouts, breadfruit, bacalao, plantains, cassava root, Scotch bonnet peppers, or mountain parsley, the chances of getting it here are high. If his Ohio City market doesn't have it, insists owner Ricky Muniz Jr., he will find it and order it for you. The place has the feel of a neighborhood "corner store," also stocking Spanish-language newspapers, magazines, cards, tapes, and CDs.

## La Michoacana
☎ (330) 864-0565
CITY: **Akron**   AREA: **Farther South**

**ADDRESS:** 1448 Copley Rd.
**FOOD AVAIL.:** Produce, grains, beans, baked goods, canned & packaged goods, spices, condiments, beverages, tea, coffee **HOURS:** Mon–Sat 10 a.m.–9 p.m., Sun 10 a.m.–7 p.m. **PAYMENT:** MC, VS, AX, DIS, checks **ACCESS:** ⅖ None

. . . . . . . . . . . . . . . . . . . . . . . . .

This is the only Mexican grocery store in the Akron area, and it's easy to spot. The exterior of the building is decorated with a mural painted in bright colors. The images of food on the outside only hint at the wealth of stuff on the inside. The market is spacious, well organized, and full of surprises. This is a Mexican cook's paradise. In addition to all the predictable items from tortillas to tomatillos, there's a really impressive assortment of more esoteric ingredients—Mexican-style sour cream, dried tamarinds, pasilla and arbol peppers, guajillo paste, masa, dried corn husks for wrapping tamales, fresh chayote squash, cans of cajeta, a thick syrup made from caramelized sugar and milk, and a crate filled with the green cactus "pads" called nopales. For those in search of culinary shortcuts, there's a good selection of jarred mole and adobo sauces, and owner Evelia Gudino, who opened for business in September 2002, makes her own tamales and sells them by the dozen. Easy parking right in front.

## Mi Pueblo
☎ (216) 671-6661
CITY: **Cleveland**   AREA: **West Side**

**ADDRESS:** 12207 Lorain Ave.
**FOOD AVAIL.:** Meat (fresh), fish (fresh), produce, grains, beans, flour, rice, baked goods, canned & packaged goods, spices, condiments, beverages, coffee, takeout meals
**HOURS:** Daily 9 a.m.–9 p.m.   **PAYMENT:** MC, VS, AX, DIS  **ACCESS:** ♿ Full access  **OTHER ETHNIC:** Latin American mix, Puerto Rican

. . . . . . . . . . . . . . . . . . . . . . . . . . . .

This is a combination taqueria (a place for tacos) and supermercado (supermarket). I love the idea; you can even get some shopping done while waiting for your food to be served. You enter the market and the restaurant through the same door leading into a vestibule. Market and restaurant are mutually visible through a large glass wall. If you're inspired to try preparing the food you eat on one side, the store on the other sells all the ingredients they use. (See Mi Pueblo's other listings in this chapter.) The market offers a large variety of salsas, moles (a type of sauce), butcher-prepared beef and pork featuring the types of cuts necessary for preparation of traditional Mexican and Latin dishes, fresh produce of both the American and the more tropical South American variety, and ready-made specialties like guacamole, ensalada de nopales (made with cactus, peppers, and tomatoes), carnitas (cooked pork) on weekends, and pan dulce (Mexican sweet bread). There's an extensive selection of chili peppers, spices, and cheeses. The owners, originally from Mexico, pride themselves on being a source for Latin American products not typically found in other markets. Parking available on the street and across the street in a lot with 20-25 spaces.

# Puerto Rican

## Caribe Bake Shop
☎ (216) 281-8194
CITY: **Cleveland**   AREA: **Near West Side**

**ADDRESS:** 2906 Fulton Rd.
**FOOD AVAIL.:** Meat (deli), grains, beans, flour, baked goods, canned & packaged goods, spices, beverages, tea, takeout meals  **HOURS:** Mon–Sat 7 a.m.–7 p.m., Sun 7 a.m.–5 p.m.
**PAYMENT:** MC, VS  **ACCESS:** ♿ Full access

. . . . . . . . . . . . . . . . . . . . . . . . . . . .

In 2006 Luis and Sandra Burgos took over this Puerto Rican bakery from the Morales family, who first opened it in 1969. They continue to offer freshly baked breads and traditional sweets, such as bread pudding, coconut candy, flan, and guava-filled turnovers, but they have expanded the menu to include a variety of other prepared Caribbean specialties and added a few tables, so if you can't wait until you get home (or at least into your car) to dig into your empanada (a meat-filled pastry they describe as a "Caribbean pierogi"), fried plantain, tostomes, Cuban sandwich, or potato balls, you can sit down and eat on the spot. Chicken is available by the piece and by the pound, fried, roasted, and barbecued, and roast pork can also be purchased as a single serving or in quantity. Green bananas or yucca come stuffed with meat, or you can go for the yucca with escabeche (poached or fried fish in a flavorful marinade). Different rice, meat, and bean combinations are available daily. There are also some grocery items: canned products, seasonings, and packaged goods to stock an authentic Puerto Rican pantry. Catering service.

## Lelolai Bakery & Cafe
☎ (216) 771-9956
CITY: **Cleveland**   AREA: **Near West Side**

ADDRESS: 1889 W. 25th St.
FOOD AVAIL.: Baked goods, takeout meals
HOURS: Mon–Wed 9 a.m.–5 p.m., Thu–Sat 9
a.m.–6 p.m.; closed Sun PAYMENT: MC, VS, DIS
ACCESS: ♿ Full access

Alma Alfonzo was born and raised in Puerto Rico, but she's lived in Cleveland since the 1980s. In 2001, she opened this bakery near the West Side Market. It's a lovely place to shop—light, bright, and spacious. The Hispanic- and Spanish-inspired desserts that come out of the kitchen are attractively displayed in glass-front cases. Choose from pastelillos (flaky crust turnovers) with fillings of mango, strawberry, apple, and pineapple; tropical fruit cheesecakes; guava pound cake; polvorones (almond cookies); flans flavored with almonds, coconut, or vanilla; and mallorcas (warm buttered buns made of sweetened bread dough), a popular breakfast food on the island. I can't resist the coconut bread pudding. Cakes can be purchased whole or by the slice. Everything is prepared from scratch daily using fresh fruits and quality ingredients. A small selection of sandwiches is available, prepared Carribean–style: After they pile on combos like ham and cheese or turkey and Swiss and add a special, well-seasoned sauce, the sandwich is put in a hot press that's like a waffle iron with a smooth rather than a ridged surface.

The bakery will do special custom orders and prepare party trays of bite-size portions. I went to an opening that featured a variety of sweet eats, and Lelolai's flan was the first to disappear! I heard some guests whimpering for more. (There is some seating. For more information see Lelolai's listing under restaurants.)

## Supermercado Rico
☎ (216) 631-1156
CITY: **Cleveland**   AREA: **Near West Side**

ADDRESS: 4506 Lorain Ave.
FOOD AVAIL.: Meat (frozen), fish (frozen), produce, grains, beans, flour, rice, canned & packaged goods, spices, condiments, beverages, coffee, wine, beer, prepared frozen foods HOURS: Mon–Sat 9 a.m.–8 p.m., Sun 9 a.m.–6 p.m. PAYMENT: MC, VS, AX, DIS, checks ACCESS: ♿ Full access OTHER ETHNIC: Caribbean, Mexican

The scale of this market hearkens back to the time before grocery shopping meant places as big as warehouses with carts large enough to hold a steamer trunk, to stores that could be staffed by just two or three people. The décor is strictly utilitarian, and there are no carefully calculated displays promoting sales. The result is a shopping environment that has a sort of sweetness to it, a simplicity and human appeal.

The store is well stocked despite the fact that the shelves are not mile high. The selection of fresh produce, including plantains, bito (sweet potatoes), and malaga (a potato-like vegetable), is displayed in cardboard boxes rather than sleek metal crisper cases. There are interesting products imported from all over Latin America and the Caribbean: soursop syrup, pounded yam flakes, red and yellow hot pepper sauce, chorizo sausage, dried chilies, plantain chips, coconut water, tamarind soda, passionfruit nectar, and bacalao (salt fish). Of course, you'll also find a large variety of rice, beans, and cornmeal.

Spanish is spoken here by staff who also speak English, and by most of the clientele as well. A fenced parking lot is adjacent to the brick building, which is easily identified by the wood-shingle awning out front.

# AMERICAN REGIONAL

This is a short chapter, and the title is somewhat misleading. There are just three distinct food cultures included in this section, and only two, Louisiana Cajun/Creole and Southern soul, are actually tied to a specific geographic section of this country. The third, Jewish-style, is as placeless as, historically, the people who claim it as their own. But each represents a way of eating that has become identifiably American, a blend of regionalism and ethnic roots, combined with a hodgepodge of influences from around the world that could only happen in the United States. You could say that they are the best of what was once called, before it became politically incorrect, the melting pot.

The idea of one homogenous blend has been put aside. Now the dominant motif is a mosaic. Diversity is the buzzword, and celebrating it has become the new American way. Acknowledging our social and historical singularities is a way to express enthusiasm about one's own particular way of fitting into the big picture, and it's more than just fashionable. It speaks of how we are redefining who we are as a culture and a country.

The word "ethnic" evokes images of folksy people in quaint costumes from a bygone era. And even though that view is outmoded, it does not seem out of place when applied to the cultures of other countries. It makes sense to us to go to restaurants and see waitresses in Tyrolean dirndls or Japanese kimonos. But in fact, the word really connotes any racial, religious, or social group with a common culture. So while they are neither exotic nor old-fashioned, existing very much in this time and place, the three groups assembled under this heading are also very definite and distinct ethnic entities. And their food, whether you view it as what comes from the melting pot or the tossed salad result of diversity, contributes to this city's cultural and culinary wealth.

The terminology can be perplexing. Should hoppin' John (black-eyed peas with rice) and sweet potato pie be called African-American, Southern, or soul? As far as many people are concerned, when you're talking about food, there's not much difference. "Compare what are called soul food cookbooks with Southern cookbooks, and you'll find that they are pretty much the same," said Dr. Lolly McDavid. "White women of means didn't do their own cooking, and many cherished southern recipes were actually created by the black women who cooked for them. And while the two races were segregated in their lives and lifestyles, they both ate the same things for Sunday dinners and celebrations. Even for blacks like me who have lived our entire lives in the North, home food, traditional food, is still what you'd call Southern food."

"My father grew up on a farm where all the women cooked," she continued. "He met my mother at college, and he had no idea she didn't know her way around the kitchen. It never even occurred to him. When he discovered that she couldn't cook, he sent her down to his family in Alabama so she could learn. The story goes that she followed the women around with a notebook, wanting to write down all their recipes."

But there were no recipes to write down. And an old expression explains why: "Frying pork chops is like drinking water—you either know how or you don't."

But Southern cooking is much more than fried chops and chicken. Cooks in the coastal states have countless ways to prepare seafood. Beaten biscuits, country ham, pan gravy, and stewed tomatoes are dinnertime favorites, along with cornbread and corn cooked any other way you can think of. Grits, greens, beans, and yams are staples. Echoes of a long-forgotten African past crop up in the way many dishes are prepared, and some scholars suspect that seeds of okra and sesame, which are not native to the area, came here with the slaves.

Much of what came out of the black kitchens of the South is inextricably linked to a culture of slavery and discrimination. Rice was originally viewed as poor folks' food, unfit for higher society, and chitterlings, which have now acquired a certain down-home panache, were used because they were the leftovers that nobody else wanted. Once, you could get them by the bucketful for free. Now, even people who can afford prime rib eat them because they are a treasured taste from childhood.

Black families have been a presence in Cleveland since the settlement's earliest days, increasing in numbers gradually over the years: 1,300 in 1870, 3,000 in 1890, 8,500 in 1910. Most came from the South, and by 1930 they accounted for the majority of the population in many of the inner-city neighborhoods once filled with immigrants from Europe. During the World War II years, many more came, lured by the opportunities in the city's expanding industrial economy.

As people migrated north, their cooking style was transformed in the context of an urban and often poverty-stricken environment. It came to be associated with salty, greasy dishes, but true African-American cooking is neither. True Southern cooking was both healthy and economical. Cooks could make a little bit of meat or poultry go a long way by adding grains, beans, and vegetables. Meals were built around fresh natural foods from the garden: tomatoes, onions, sweet peppers, corn, okra, and cucumbers.

Whether it's called Cajun, Creole, or New Orleans–style, the purely Louisiana way of eating is a kissing cousin to Southern cuisine. Cajun food is actually a very old form of French country cooking that came to the region with the Acadians of Canada, adapted to make use of all the game and wild foods indigenous to the area, like alligator and tabasco peppers. The result is étouffe (a sort of stew), jambalaya, and boudin (pepper hot sausage). Creole cooking is more citified, the New Orleans version of Cajun with its own unique accent that came from the variety of people who gathered there. Gumbo, for example, is an African word, and the file it's made with (the powdered leaves of the sassafras tree) was introduced to the Acadians by Choctaw Indians. After the Civil War, Greek, German, and Italian immigrants added to the culinary mix. So you can get a mufalletta (an Italian-inspired sandwich unique to New Orleans), oyster loaves and shrimp po' boys, bouillabaisse and crawfish bisque, and praline pudding.

You can find a few of these dishes on some Cleveland restaurant menus, but it must be understood up front that little of it can hold a candle to what you might encounter—if you were lucky—down in Bayou Lafourche or the French Quarter. That said, it's still an experience worth having if you want to learn something about hot sauce, 'gator, or red beans and rice.

In his book about Southern food, which explores the particularities of African-American and Louisiana kitchens, writer John Egerton sums up the heart and soul of it all this way: "Fix plenty, make it good, share it around."

As a motto, that's too homespun and folksy to be a good fit for the Cleveland Jewish community of today, but the same sentiments still apply. That sense of plenty coupled with a voluble sociability characterizes the Jewish-style delis listed in the following pages. All serve sandwiches almost too big to get your mouth around, a smear of cream cheese equals a mountainous slather, and the bowls of pickles on the tables seem bottomless.

What most of us think of as Jewish-style is actually very European. Jews from Morocco eat quite differently from those whose roots are in Hungary. The Jews of Europe didn't eat bagels and lox, but we think of that as typically Jewish. The kind of deli food familiar to Clevelanders is actually Eastern European Jewish by way of New York. So how to define Jewish food?

"There's really no such thing as Jewish cooking," insists Cleveland rabbi Daniel Schur. "Jews have lived in various countries, a minority among a majority, and historically, we have always adapted, and adopted new ways of cooking. What makes food Jewish is the fact that it's kosher, prepared according to precise and ancient dietary laws."

In the early part of the 19th century, the largest number of Jews arriving in Cleveland were from Germany. But by 1870, they were emigrating from Poland, Hungary, Romania, and Russia. Between 1905 and World War I, the flow became a flood as Jews from other parts of the area known as the Pale—Latvia, Lithuania, and Estonia—struggled to escape the pogroms. In recent years, there has been another flurry of immigration by Jews from the former Soviet Union. Though they may have come from different countries, Jews have always been, and to a great extent continue to be, an ethnically cohesive community because of their shared values, ideas, and practices, which spring from their religious traditions.

Historically, Jews have always incorporated aspects of the food culture wherever they settle, and then they take it with them wherever they go. Each country where Jews have made their home has contributed to what is known as "Jewish cuisine." In Cleveland, most Jewish people are of Eastern European descent, so the local delis and stores with a large Jewish clientele are filled with foods such as pickled herring, matzo ball soup, kugels and kreplach, borscht and blintzes.

# RESTAURANTS

## African-American/ Southern

### Angie's Soul Café

☎ (216) 426-8890

CITY: **Cleveland** AREA: **Near East Side**

ATMOSPHERE: **Relaxed** COST: **$$**$$$

**ADDRESS:** 7804 Carnegie Ave.
**HOURS:** Mon–Wed 9 a.m.–6 p.m., Thu–Fri 8 a.m.–8 p.m., Sat 8 a.m.–6 p.m. **RESERVATIONS:** Not taken **PAYMENT:** MC, VS **BAR:** None
**TAKEOUT:** Yes **ACCESS:** ♿ Full access

Southern home cooking, Angie's style, has been part of the local dining scene since the 1960s. Akin Affrica takes up where his mother Angie Jeter, now retired, left off. He opened his own place in the fall of 2008, using her recipes for made-from-scratch soul food along with a few of his own. The mouthwatering line-up includes smothered pork chops, fried chicken, oxtails, macaroni and cheese, candied yams, collard greens, and corn bread. Specials might be BBQ one day, meatloaf the next. For a sweet finish, try one of the fruit cobblers, sweet potato pie, or red velvet cake. The café is spacious, the WI-FI access is free, and light pours in from the big windows that face the street. The emphasis is on carry out, but there are five tables and a pair of long counters outfitted with a dozen stools where you can sit down and dig in. A small gas fireplace in the center of the room and a couple of armchairs make a nice spot to hang out with a cup of coffee and slice of pound cake. A parking lot is adjacent to the building. Disabled and elderly patrons can call ahead for curb service.

### The Lancer Steak House

☎ (216) 881-0080

CITY: **Cleveland** AREA: **Near East Side**

ATMOSPHERE: **Casual** COST: **$$$**$$

**ADDRESS:** 7707 Carnegie Ave.
**HOURS:** Mon–Sat 11 a.m.–2:30 a.m., Sun 1 p.m.–2:30 a.m. **RESERVATIONS:** Taken
**PAYMENT:** MC, VS, AX **BAR:** Beer, wine, liquor
**TAKEOUT:** Yes **ACCESS:** ♿ Limited

The city's oldest black-owned and -operated restaurant, Lancer's is tantamount to a landmark. The original restaurant, started by Fleet Slaughter in the 1950s at this location, had another name. Back in those days, when every black celebrity who came to town came to Lancer's to see and be seen, the waiters wore tuxedos. Over the years, the place has grown considerably more casual. The restaurant is still a watering hole for well-known athletes, performers, and politicians, but the not-so-rich-and-famous are right at home here too. Everybody table hops, glad-handing and backslapping friends and making new ones. The place feels like a private club, though if you're not a "member" you can still drop by for a heaping plateful of perch, catfish, or pork chops and cole slaw. In the South, frogs are abundant in the freshwater ponds and rivers, and frogs' legs are considered by some to be a true delicacy. Which must be why they appear on Lancer's menu.

Mr. Dixon, whom I overheard hailed by patrons as "King George," regally presides over his boisterous domain. Sometimes he's the host, other times you'll find him in cook's whites manning the kitchen. His operating philosophy is "I do whatever it takes to make it all work." The round-the-clock party atmosphere must mean he's doing it right. Parking available in the rear.

# Cajun/Creole

## Battiste & Dupree Cajun Grille

☎ (216) 381-5338

CITY: **South Euclid**   AREA: **East Side**
ATMOSPHERE: **Relaxed**   COST: $$$$$

ADDRESS: 1992 Warrensville Center Rd.
HOURS: Mon 5–9 p.m., Tue–Sat 4 p.m.–10:30 p.m. (kitchen); 4 p.m.–1 a.m. (bar); closed Sun
RESERVATIONS: Not taken  PAYMENT: Checks  BAR: Liquor  TAKEOUT: Yes  ACCESS: ё Limited

Junior Battiste has a culinary dream team in his bloodlines, with a family tree that includes Italians, Germans, French folks, and a great-granddaddy from Lafayette, Louisiana, also known as the capital of Cajun country. He combined that natural bent toward good cooking with professional training, and he's been dishing up top-notch food in a small strip mall storefront since February 2005. Junior's cooking earned him awards three years running in the Taste of Cleveland competition. His gumbo, studded with chunks of chicken and sausage, has just the right amount of spice; the jambalaya packs an authentic punch; and the shrimp étouffée is nothing short of sublime. He also prepares

sides of Creole green beans; po' boy sandwiches; deep fried wings; and his own desserts—pecan pralines, pound cake, bread pudding, sweet potato pie, and upside-down cake. All-you-can-eat Mondays are devoted to Cajun fried chicken, and Fridays feature fried fish.

What's truly astonishing about this place is the level of care and attention that goes into everything. It's not what you'd expect from such a pared-down venue, which features just five tables, a couple of short counters with stools, and New Orleans Jazzfest posters for décor. It looks like a burger joint, with a view right into the working kitchen, but the plates "read" like an upscale restaurant—stylish, brightly colored dishes with orders attractively presented. You'll miss this if you get takeout, but with such limited seating, reservations are required to eat in. Another distinctive feature is the choice of high-end ingredients and creative, made-from-scratch preparations. The salad includes field greens, walnuts, raisins, and a basil balsamic dressing. The brochette appetizer features slices of fresh French bread topped with herb butter and honey.

There's a full service bar with a selection of Big Easy beers.

## Fat Fish Blue

☎ (216) 875-6000

CITY: **Cleveland**   AREA: **Downtown**
ATMOSPHERE: **Casual**   COST: $$$$$

ADDRESS: 21 Prospect Ave.
HOURS: Mon 11:30 a.m.–10 p.m., Tue–Thu 11:30 a.m.–11 p.m., Fri 11:30 a.m.–1 a.m., Sat 11 a.m.–1 a.m., Sun 3 p.m.–9 p.m. (may open at 10 a.m. for games and downtown events; call to verify times)  RESERVATIONS: Taken, for groups of 8+  PAYMENT: MC, VS, AX, DIS  BAR: Beer, wine, liquor  TAKEOUT: Yes  ACCESS: ё Full access

Come for the food and stay for the music. Or come for the music, but be sure you have an appetite. Their motto is "food, fun, and music," and owner Steven Zamborsky and his staff like to think that a visit here is a total experience, more than just eating a meal or listening to some music. They work with a year-round Mardi Gras mentality, Northern Ohio–style. The crowds and the energy help make it so. It all happens downtown, at the corner of Prospect and Ontario, within shouting distance of Progressive Field and the Quicken Loans Arena, in a former tire store and parking garage that's been rehabbed, retooled, and redecorated with warehouse chic and Cajun accents (and parking still available in the garage above the restaurant).

Windows dominate the large space, and inspirational concepts like "Laissez les bons temps rouler" are part of the wall art, along with their signature fish graphics. Eye-pleasing curves and multiple levels break up the big room, and a large bar opposite the small stage is the centerpiece. Some tables are ideal for watching the performers, while others put you out of the way and at a distance that brings with it fewer decibels. The tunes tend to be blues, jazz, Latin licks, zydeco, and swing blues.

Wherever you sit, you need to give some of your attention to the menu—a mouthwatering mix of Louisiana Creole artistry and Southern charm. Choosing is no easy thing. The appetizers alone are enough to overwhelm: honey-grilled Cajun shrimp and sausage, fried green tomatoes with collard greens, crawdaddy tails in hot sauce or crawfish in shrimp sauce, crab and bluefish fritters fried crispy and doused with New Orleans–style cream sauce, praline duck tenders that are made with ground pecans in place of bread-crumbs, shrimp remoulade, and oysters either fried Delta-style or swimming in shrimp sauce. Jambalaya and gumbo are available in both appetizer and entrée portions.

If it's a sandwich you want, there's muffaleta, made with olive paste, cheese, meats, lettuce, and tomatoes; pulled pork; and po-boys in fried oyster, shrimp, catfish, chicken, or Andouille sausage versions. Main courses bring you Southern-fried chicken; étouffé made with crawfish, chicken, or shrimp cooked in brown gravy and served over rice; pecan chicken juiced with Jack Daniels; boiled crawfish; catfish, pan-fried, beer battered, broiled, or blackened; and specials like 'Nawlins barbecued shrimp, soft shell crabs, and a blackened Delmonico steak. Sides stay true to the theme too: grits, cornbread, and rice and beans. They've earned a following for their coffee, made with chicory, and their desserts: bread pudding with Jack Daniels cream sauce, pecan pie, beignets (otherwise known as fried dough), and bananas Foster (the lowly fruit raised to new heights with caramelized butter and sugar, rum, and vanilla ice cream). Lunch is strictly "bidness"—the business of eating that is.

Music is served up in the evenings, every night except Mondays. Tuesday through Thursday there's usually no cover, and local acts are featured. Wednesdays are reserved for the Robert Lockwood Jr. All-Star Band, who pay weekly homage to Cleveland's king of the blues. Fridays and Saturdays you pay at the door to see big names and nationally touring artists. The restaurant hosts its own parties to celebrate holidays and CD releases, and they'll be glad to host your party, too. They'll give you a room (holds around 40), and you can use their standard menu or customize your selections. Information about planning an event, plus directions, a calendar of events, and menu are available at www.fatfishblue.com.

## Russo's

☎ (330) 923-2665

CITY: **Peninsula**   AREA: **Farther South**
ATMOSPHERE: **Casual**   COST: $$$$$

**ADDRESS:** 4895 State Rd.
**HOURS:** Lunch Tue–Sat 11 a.m.–3:30 p.m.; Dinner Tue–Sat 5 p.m.–closing **RESERVATIONS:** Taken **PAYMENT:** MC, VS, AX, DIS **BAR:** Beer, wine, liquor **TAKEOUT:** Yes **ACCESS:** ♿ Full access **OTHER ETHNIC:** Italian, Southern U.S.

For fans of Cajun food and Southern-style cooking, reading the menu is enticing. There's gumbo, shrimp remoulade, fried catfish and oysters, pulled pork, jambalaya, seafood Creole, and chicken étouffée.

The bottles of house-made hot sauce on the table suggest that the words "hot and spicy" are taken seriously here. The smells that waft through the dining room are even more promising. But it's tasting what chef/owner Dave Russo and his team of talented kitchen staff serve up that gets his customers hooked and coming back for more.

Russo learned his stuff working at some of the most renowned restaurants in New Orleans, including Galatoire's and Commander's Palace, and with Louisiana culinary luminaries Paul Prudhomme and Emeril Lagasse. After many years in the Big Easy, he came home, bringing with him a head full of recipes, like one for shrimp uggie, a zesty shrimp and potato appetizer from Uglesich's, in his opinion the best restaurant in New Orleans. But he still likes to prepare some roots food, which in his case means Italian, the cavatelli, marinara sauce, and ravioli he was raised on. So since he's the boss, the eclectic offerings at his restaurant feature what he describes as his two favorite kinds of eating.

And you can watch it all being prepared. Step inside and you get a full frontal of the kitchen: flames leaping up from the grill, chefs on the move, and pans almost flying through the air when it's busy. Plenty of area restaurants have such open kitchens, but this is the only one I know of that has a wraparound counter on three sides where diners can watch the action while enjoying the results. The rest of the space is quietly contemporary and designed to make you feel at home. White cloths on the tables are topped with white paper so you don't feel self-conscious when you drip olive oil or some Cajun beef gravy with debris (so called because it contains the bits of meat that fall off the roast).

Details worth noting: baby changing stations in men's room as well as ladies; closing time is when the last customer leaves; and space and staff available for private parties Sundays and Mondays. If you like a party, mark your calendars for February. They throw an annual Mardi Gras bash complete with beads and a special menu. My guess is that breast-baring is optional. Freestanding building with ample parking, on the border between Peninsula and Cuyahoga Falls, near Routes 8 and 303.

## The Savannah

☎ (440) 892-2266

CITY: **Westlake**   AREA: **West Side**
ATMOSPHERE: **Casual**   COST: $$$$$

**ADDRESS:** 30676 Detroit Rd.
**HOURS:** Mon–Fri 11 a.m.–2 a.m., Sat–Sun 8 a.m.–2 a.m. **RESERVATIONS:** Taken, recommended for dinner **PAYMENT:** MC, VS, AX, DIS **BAR:** Beer, wine, liquor **TAKEOUT:** Yes **ACCESS:** ♿ Full access **OTHER ETHNIC:** Southern U.S.

The Savannah warrants an ethnic food category all its own; let's call it blues cuisine. Bands play seven nights a week with a heavy emphasis on 8-bar and 12-bar groans, moans, and wails, and the standard bar-food menu is highlighted by some dishes deeply connected to places that nurtured this music: New Orleans, St. Louis, and Delta juke joints. There's gumbo, so thick you can stand a spoon in it; Cajun catfish and Cajun spiced fries; blackened fish and blackened prime rib; barbecued ribs St. Louis–style; some serious Southern-fried delicacies that include the unlikely but amazing fried dill pickles; garlic shrimp with rice; and dessert specialties made by the Sisters of the Savannah Soul Kitchen.

But we are, after all, in Cleveland, where polka was once king, and the restaurant does try to showcase local and regional talent. So in a nod to the hometown, they also offer potato/cheese pierogies daily and the occasional Eastern European–style special. On a less ethnic note, there are always assorted sandwiches; pasta, steak, and chicken entrées; salads; and a pint-size kids' menu. Drinking is as important as eating and listening here, so the beer list—featuring reasonably priced domestics and more pricey microbrews, imports, and seasonal varieties—is long. It's okay to take it straight from the bottle, though wine sippers are also welcome and get their beverage of choice served in a proper, stemmed glass.

Expect a truly eclectic crowd that morphs nightly depending on the music, which is a mix of blues, jazz, R&B, and Motown. You're just as likely to find guys in golf shirts and black leather jackets, women in jeans or straight-from-work dress-for-success suits. There are folks with walkers and crowds of college kids, all-female groups and families celebrating birthdays. To get a good read on the Savannah crowd, check out the variety of messages emblazoned on T-shirts. On a single night, I saw the following: "Joe Boxer," "Go Tribe," "Blues Project," "Phunk Junkeez," "Ameritech," "Rock Your World," "Ohio State," and "Calvin and Hobbes."

The miniature dance floor accommodates those who want to get up and shake it. Some are more skilled than others, and the mix is usually an entertaining floor show. Even when the band's not playing on the stage up front, the place is lively and buzzing, full of talk, laughter, and high-fiving. There are tables—good for four and easily pushed together for more—booths, a bar, and some small, high pedestal tables with stools.

All this action lurks behind a staid exterior in a generic shopping plaza that gives no hint of how pleasant and almost old-fashioned the place is inside. The kitchen does on- and off-premises catering. A 1,200-square-foot party room has its own entrance and can accommodate up to 75. Large, well-lit parking lot. For detailed information about everything they've got going go to www.thesavannah.com.

# Jewish

## Corky and Lenny's

☎ (216) 464-3838

CITY: **Woodmere Village**    AREA: **East Side**
ATMOSPHERE: **Casual**    COST: **$$$**$$

**ADDRESS:** 27091 Chagrin Blvd.
**HOURS:** Sun–Thu 7 a.m.–9 p.m., Fri–Sat 7 a.m.–10 p.m. **RESERVATIONS:** Taken, only for groups of 8+ **PAYMENT:** MC, VS, AX, DIS **BAR:** Beer, wine, liquor **TAKEOUT:** Yes **ACCESS:** ♿ Full access

The first thing you see when you walk in is the mouthwatering display of brownies, cheesecakes, and rugelach (little pastries). Then the eye moves on to the deli counter packed with pickled herring, gefilte fish, huge hunks of corned beef, and long salamis. Behind this counter are the deli men, trained professionals who understand that making a real sandwich is an art. The menu here is almost big enough to be a room divider and features every kind and combination of deli food ever imagined. You can eat light—a bagel with lox and cream cheese or a fruit platter, indulge in house specials like beef and latkas (corned beef stacked on potato pancakes) or "Three Little Tootsies" (corned beef, chopped liver, and hot pastrami on small rolls), or go the whole nine yards with beef flanken (potted short ribs) or roast stuffed kishkas (don't ask what it is, you're better off not knowing, and as any traditional Jewish grandma would say, "Just taste it").

*Northern Ohio Live* magazine readers rated this the best deli in 1996. It has an intergenerational mink-coat-to-jeans clientele—sometimes mink coats *with* jeans. Grateful parents will find an ample supply of boosters, pull-up-to-the-table high chairs, and even hook-onto-the-table seats for the very youngest diners. There is a kids' menu, dairy specials, daily specials, seafood, and burgers. Located in the Village Square shopping plaza.

## Goodman's Sandwich Inn
☎ (216) 398-6885
CITY: **Old Brooklyn**   AREA: **Near West Side**
ATMOSPHERE: **Casual**   COST: **$$**$$

ADDRESS: 5164 Pearl Rd. (at Brookpark)
HOURS: Mon–Sat 8:30 a.m.–4 p.m.; closed Sun
RESERVATIONS: Not taken PAYMENT: Checks BAR: Beer TAKEOUT: Yes ACCESS: ♿ Limited

Goodman's, which opened in 1950 and is still owned and operated by the

Goodman family, may be one of the few delis left in town that still hand cuts its corned beef. Though its small, narrow space seats only 31, and its menu is equally abbreviated, the place draws those in the know who visit Cleveland, including movie and sports stars, and it's not unusual to see a limo or a motorcade parked out front. Adult patrons often tell Dennis Goodman they remember coming in as kids with their parents. The lure is the corned beef, brisket, and pastrami sandwiches (hot or cold), which, according to one patron who's been a regular for 40 years, "are the finest deli sandwiches, bar none, anywhere in this city, even the country." Worth a mention, too, are the egg specials: they're prepared, pancake-style, with corned beef, pastrami, or salami. The biggest part of the business is takeout. Located in the Pearl-Brookpark Shopping Center, so parking is easy.

## Jack's Deli & Restaurant
☎ (216) 382-5350
CITY: **University Heights**   AREA: **East Side**
ATMOSPHERE: **Casual**   COST: **$$$**$$

ADDRESS: 14490 Cedar Rd.
HOURS: Mon–Sat 7 a.m.–9 p.m., Sat 8 a.m.–8 p.m. RESERVATIONS: Taken, for groups of 8+
PAYMENT: MC, VS, DIS BAR: Beer, wine, liquor
TAKEOUT: Yes ACCESS: ♿ Full access

The original Jack's is no more. The owners literally turned a corner in 2005, relocating to bigger, less cluttered, more contemporary digs on Cedar Road. The space is certainly easier on the staff, as the kitchen and deli counter are now adjacent to one another instead of at opposite ends of the dining room. But many people will likely miss the old place, because this generic-looking Jack's lacks character and originality.

Despite the changed décor, the waitresses still call you "Dear," and the many regulars who frequent this place continue to feel right at home. The white-haired "boys" still arrive before the doors open and re-create the atmosphere that's always made this place feel like a private club. Happily for them and the rest of us, the same traditional Jewish dishes of the Eastern European school are still served. There's borscht (beet soup) with sour cream, blintzes (thin pancakes rolled around a cheese or fruit filling), potato pancakes, noodle kugel (pudding), lox and smoked white fish, and deli sandwiches—corned beef, Reuebens, steak pastrami, turkey (roasted in-house and sliced off the bone), and pickled tongue. You can even order your already-thick sandwiches extra large. A bowl of pickles and pickled tomatoes is part of the standard table setting, like napkins and forks. Alvie Markowitz, son of the real Jack, says they also make the best-looking deli trays in town but admits he may not be totally objective on this point since he assembles them himself. The good news is you no longer have to wait for a bar mitzvah or a funeral to graze these platters of assorted meats—now they make them for one and you can have it delivered right to your table along with a bowl of rich, noodley chicken soup. Breakfast is served anytime, as is standard fare such as hamburgers, onion rings, and salads. There's a kids' menu for those under 12 who can't handle the regular hefty portions. Located in a brace of stores with ample parking. Entrance on the side of the building.

## Slyman's Deli
☎ (216) 621-3760
CITY: **Cleveland**   AREA: **Downtown**
ATMOSPHERE: **Casual**   COST: $$$$$

**ADDRESS:** 3106 St. Clair Ave.
**HOURS:** Mon–Fri 6 a.m.–2:30 p.m.; closed Sat–Sun **RESERVATIONS:** Not taken **PAYMENT:**

MC, VS **BAR:** None **TAKEOUT:** Yes **ACCESS:** & Full access

This is not a place you'd choose for either the décor or the ambience. But even so, the line is usually out the door between 11 a.m. and 1 p.m., both for tables and takeout, because the deli-style sandwiches are awesome. A Slyman's sandwich is so big that average eaters simply cannot get their mouths around one, and the place is best known for its unbelievably huge corned beef on rye. This small luncheonette, located in an industrial area near the Inner Belt, has a counter and tables that seat only about 46, and serves a clientele that runs the gamut from be-suited business folks to the truck drivers who like to come in early for their eggs and coffee.

# Southern U.S.

## Henry's at the Barn
☎ (440) 934-6636
CITY: **Avon**   AREA: **Farther West**
ATMOSPHERE: **Relaxed**   COST: $$$$$

**ADDRESS:** 36840 Detroit Rd.
**HOURS:** Tue–Thu 4:30–10 p.m., Fri–Sat 4:30–11 p.m.; closed Sun and Mon **RESERVATIONS:** Recommended **PAYMENT:** MC, VS, AX, DIS
**BAR:** Beer, wine, liquor **TAKEOUT:** Yes **ACCESS:** & Limited

Chef and owner Paul Jagielski grew up in Elyria, but his culinary passions were shaped in Myrtle Beach. That's where his family vacationed when he was a child. Later he developed his professional chops at culinary school in Charleston. In 2006, he opened his own restaurant in this far western suburb, named after a beloved dog. Here he serves the Low Country cuisine he learned to love. The menu, which changes seasonally, is all about what's good to eat South Carolina style. Expect shrimp, oysters, she-crab soup, sweet chow-chow relish, creamy grits, buttermilk fried chicken, braised pork belly, pecan rice, okra, collards, and all manner of things prepared in a cast iron skillet. Everything stays true to its roots, but that doesn't mean these dishes don't show some personal flair. The chef makes his hush puppies with Andouille sausage and crab; his succotash with caramelized onions, pears, and potatoes; and reinvents red-eye gravy as a demiglaze for beef tenderloin. Every dinner starts with good bread and three irresistible things to slather on it, including the house's signature spicy pimento cheese spread.

Henry's is housed in a 19th-century barn painted a lovely shade of grayish blue. It was lifted off its foundation, moved down the road, and installed in Olde Avon Village, a shopping center pretending to be a town. Inside there's a snug and comfy bar with a stone hearth—surely the coziest watering hole to be found in the area on a winter night. The bar itself as well as the foot rail are made of driftwood from Lake Erie. A charming second-floor room in what was once the hayloft is furnished with leather couches, wing chairs, antiques, Oriental rugs, and a big supply of atmospheric charm. If the room is not booked for a private gathering, guests can bring their cocktails up here or have dinner served on the coffee table. The 80-seat dining room, not formal but certainly somewhat genteel, was added on to the original structure. French doors open onto a delightful patio surrounded by trees and shrubs. Big striped market umbrellas create shade, and parents are welcome to park strollers beside their tables. A gas-fed fire pit glows after dark, and blankets are available for those who want to hang out despite a chill in the air. A warm, gregarious guy, Chef Paul is likely to make an appearance in any of these venues, greeting the regulars with hugs and getting acquainted with newcomers. His wait staff is equally friendly but not quite so demonstrative.

The restaurant is not visible from the road, so if you haven't been here before, the place can be hard to find. Look for a small sign that marks the entry to the Village, turn off Route 254 (Detroit Road), and follow the road to reach the complex of restored 1800s-era buildings.

The kitchen caters events on and off site.

# MARKETS

# African-American/ Southern

## Dave's Supermarkets
☎ (216) 361-5130
CITY: **Cleveland**   AREA: **Near East Side**

**ADDRESS:** 3301 Payne Ave.
**FOOD AVAIL.:** Meat (fresh, frozen), fish (fresh, frozen), produce, rice, baked goods, canned & packaged goods, spices, condiments, beverages, tea, coffee, wine, prepared frozen foods **HOURS:** Daily 7 a.m.–9 p.m. **PAYMENT:** MC, VS, AX, DIS, checks **ACCESS:** ♿ Full access

This is one of the few really large

supermarkets within the city limits, and it's been around since 1932. In the mid-'90s they expanded to stretch the entire block and can now provide plenty of parking, too. Over the years their stock has changed to serve the needs of the changing ethnic makeup of the community. Currently they carry everything for Southern and soul-food cooking, including a large selection of smoked meats and hams; fresh salted ham hocks, pigs' feet, hog maws, pork brains, neck bones, and chitterlings; fresh greens; and a variety of barbecue and hot sauces. They carry the full line of Glory Foods, canned and packaged Southern soul-food products. The heat-and-eat dishes, created to make it quick and easy to serve traditional (and labor-intensive) favorites, include kale; collard, mustard, turnip, and mixed greens; field and black-eyed peas; beans; sweet potatoes; and okra. There are also mixes for homestyle cornbread and corn muffins.

The store used to have many items used in Latin American and Caribbean cooking and still maintains a small selection at this location, but since the store on Ridge Road was opened, and another in Ohio City, most of those products are stocked there. The result has been that this Dave's is less crowded and cramped than it used to be, and there's a shorter wait in the checkout lines.

## Dave's Supermarkets
☎ (216) 441-0034
CITY: **Cleveland**    AREA: **East Side**

**ADDRESS:** 7422 Harvard Ave.
**FOOD AVAIL.:** Meat (fresh, deli, frozen), fish (fresh, frozen), produce, baked goods, canned & packaged goods, spices, condiments, beverages, tea, coffee, wine, beer, prepared frozen foods, takeout meals **HOURS:** Mon–Sat 7 a.m.–9 p.m., Sun 7 a.m.–8 p.m. **PAYMENT:**

MC, VS, DIS, checks **ACCESS:** ⚹ Full access
**OTHER ETHNIC:** Asian, Eastern European mix, Jamaican, Mexican

For information about the Southern-style and African-American products stocked, see description for Dave's on Payne.

## Dave's Supermarkets
☎ (216) 486-6458
CITY: **Euclid**    AREA: **East Side**

**ADDRESS:** 15900 Lake Shore Blvd.
**FOOD AVAIL.:** Meat (fresh, deli, frozen), fish (fresh, frozen), produce, baked goods, canned & packaged goods, spices, condiments, prepared frozen foods, takeout meals **HOURS:** Mon–Sat 7 a.m.–9 p.m., Sun 7 a.m.–8 p.m. **PAYMENT:** MC, VS, DIS **ACCESS:** ⚹ Full access

See description for Dave's on Payne.

# Jewish

## Boris's Kosher Meat
☎ (216) 382-5330
CITY: **University Heights**    AREA: **East Side**

**ADDRESS:** 14406 Cedar Rd.
**FOOD AVAIL.:** Meat (fresh, frozen), fish (fresh, frozen), baked goods, canned & packaged goods, beverages, wine, beer, prepared frozen foods, takeout meals **HOURS:** Mon–Wed 8 a.m.–6 p.m., Thu 8 a.m.–7 p.m., Fri 8 a.m.–2 p.m., Sun 8 a.m.–1 p.m.; closed Sat **PAYMENT:** MC, VS, checks **ACCESS:** ⚹ Full access

Boris's is primarily a meat market but does carry some of its own prepared Jewish-style specialties. Take home chicken or mushroom barley soup, stuffed cabbage, matzo balls, potato kugel, kreplach, and chicken roasted and stuffed or cut up into cutlets, breaded, and fried. Salami, smoked turkey, Romanian-style pastrami, and a jerky-like South African–style beef called bitong are made on the premises. In the freezer you'll find gefilte fish and blintzes. They also stock a small line of canned and packaged goods—basics that you might pick up to complete a meal, plus wine and beer, mostly imports, including some from Israel. They also have some baked goods from Unger's. (See entry for Unger's in this section.) Convenient parking in the strip.

## Lax & Mandel Kosher Bakery
**☎ (216) 382-8877**
CITY: **South Euclid**   AREA: **East Side**

ADDRESS: 14439 Cedar Rd.
FOOD AVAIL.: Baked goods, beverages HOURS: Mon–Wed 7 a.m.–7 p.m., Thu 7 a.m.–8 p.m., Fri 7 a.m.–3 p.m., Sun 8 a.m.–2 p.m.; closed Sat. PAYMENT: MC, VS, DIS, checks ACCESS: ⅙ Full access

This is the third home for the kosher bakery since it was opened by Shimon Lax and Burt Mandel in 1956. The cases still hold loaves of the same Jewish rye (which happens to be fat- and cholesterol-free) the shop's been making for decades, along with French, garlic, and potato breads; Russian raisin pumpernickel; bagels and onion rolls; and challah (including one that's cholesterol-free). A wonderful dense, chewy corn rye is available only on Sunday. They also bake rugelach, Russian tea biscuits, tortes, custom-made cakes, and a variety of cookies, donuts, and Danish. The store stocks a small selection of kosher grocery items, including Dougie's Barbecue, straight from New York, and frozen ready-to-eat meals, some nonperishables, and dairy products. The coffee's always hot and ready to go. Head-in parking spaces front the strip mall store.

## Pincus Bakery
**☎ (216) 382-5120**
CITY: **University Heights**   AREA: **East Side**

ADDRESS: 2181 S. Green Rd.
FOOD AVAIL.: Baked goods, beverages, coffee HOURS: Daily 6 a.m.–8 p.m. (closed some holidays) PAYMENT: Checks ACCESS: ⅙ Full access OTHER ETHNIC: British, French, German, Hungarian, Italian

This is the kind of Jewish bakery I grew up with in New York City and its environs. Though it's located in a thoroughly contemporary strip mall (the Cedar-Green Shopping Center), there's something timeless about this place. Customers are typically greeted by name, totals are figured by adding up columns of figures penciled on bags or boxes, and the egg kichel (sweet little biscuits), mandelbrot (almond cookies), and large loaves of dark, raisin-studded pumpernickel bread look exactly as I remember them from my childhood. Owner and baker Steven Pincus is a member of the Bread Bakers Guild of America, and a sign above the counter identifies him as The Artisan Baker. What all this means is that bread, cake, and pastry are taken seriously here and handcrafted the Old World way. Traditional Jewish products such as egg and water challah bread, corn rye, and honey cakes are available as well as European-style specialties such as Hungarian strudel, baguettes, biscotti, scones, focaccia bread, rugelach, cheesecake, and Russian tea biscuits.

## Tibor's Quality Kosher Meat Market

☎ (216) 381-7615

CITY: University Heights    AREA: East Side

ADDRESS: 2185 S. Green Rd.

FOOD AVAIL.: Meat (fresh), grains, beans, baked goods, canned & packaged goods, spices, condiments, wine, prepared frozen foods, takeout meals HOURS: Mon–Wed 8 a.m.–6 p.m., Thu 8 a.m.–7 p.m., Fri 8 a.m.–3 p.m., Sat–Sun 8 a.m.–1 p.m. PAYMENT: MC, VS, checks ACCESS: & Full access

Tibor Rosenberg, once an Altman's employee, is now the owner of what used to be Altman's Quality Kosher Meat Market. Originally located on Chagrin Boulevard, Altman's was in business 45 years, and at the present location since 1968. The current owner has given the place a new name but continues to offer all the same items, including many Jewish-style foods prepared on the premises according to old Eastern European recipes. One longtime customer, now in his 70s, told me that going here takes him back 60 years, because the food tastes just like the kind he grew up eating. There's chicken soup, matzo ball soup, kreplach (the Jewish version of ravioli) in soup, mushroom barley soup, roast chicken, brisket, potato and noodle kugels (puddings), stuffed cabbage, and potato latkes (pancakes). Among the cold items are chopped liver, gefilte fish, potato salad, cole slaw, and pickles. They make their own salamis and hot dogs, including unusual veal and turkey dogs. Zucchini kugels and zucchini latkes are two of their own modern versions of traditional delicacies. The baked goods are from Unger's, and challah is delivered every Friday. Recent additions to Tibor's selection of kosher meats are cold cuts, wieners, and corned "beef" made from bison meat, and beef and turkey jerky—perfect he says, for those who go into the woods where kashrut has not gone before.

The store has its own parking lot. Jack's deli is only a few doors away, so before you head home with dinner in a bag, you might want to stop off there for a "nosh."

## Unger's Kosher Bakery & Food Shop

☎ (216) 321-7176

CITY: Cleveland Heights    AREA: East Side

ADDRESS: 1831 S. Taylor Rd.

FOOD AVAIL.: Meat (fresh, deli, frozen), fish (fresh, deli, frozen), produce, baked goods, canned & packaged goods, spices, condiments, beverages, tea, coffee, wine, beer, prepared frozen foods, takeout meals HOURS: Mon–Wed 6 a.m.–8 p.m., Thu 6 a.m.–11 p.m., Fri open 6 a.m., Sun 6 a.m.–6 p.m. closing time varies (call for information); closed Sat (sometimes open Sat night, after sunset; call to confirm) PAYMENT: MC, VS, AX, DIS ACCESS: & Full access

Unger's is a bakery and a supermarket, with a deli counter that also features a selection of ready-to-eat entrées like kishka, roast chicken, and stuffed cabbage, plus cole slaw and other salads. I like to buy pickles, an essential part of a deli meal, here because they have both sour and half-sour, and pickled red peppers like those found on New York's Lower East Side. Fresh-baked breads include Jewish rye, challah, and pumpernickel, plus onion rolls and bagels, cinnamon-raisin bread, and croissants. A variety of cakes, pies, Danish, donuts, and cookies are available, but Unger's is known mainly for true Jewish-style treats (some of which bear a strong resemblance to those of Eastern Europe) such as Dobos torte, kichel, honey and sponge cakes, Russian tea biscuits, cinnamon-, nut-, or chocolate-laced coffee cakes called babkas, and Hungarian nut slices. On the shelves, along with regular grocery store items, are food imports from Israel and packaged Israeli-style salads. The store is bright and modern. They've got their own parking lot.

# INTERNATIONAL

There is no historical lead-in appropriate for this chapter, no groups of people to write about or "palette" of ingredients to explain. This section is devoted to restaurants and markets that defy a single, simple ethnic definition yet still have some definite ethnic characteristics.

Included are restaurants that successfully prepare a variety of dishes from many different food traditions, while staying true to the origins of each. There are only a few, but they do what they do so well that they deserve a place of their own in this book.

Interest in ethnic ingredients is growing rapidly, and those ingredients are assuming an increasingly prominent role in contemporary American cooking. The markets listed in this section are important resources. They offer convenience, variety, and a global array of choices so busy shoppers can get what they need to stock a multicultural kitchen at a single location.

Restaurants and markets with an international flair reveal our current preoccupation with diversity, pluralism, and what has been called our "tossed salad" society, a recently coined term meant to replace the old "melting pot" concept. The idea is that as a society we no longer want to see ourselves as a bland, homogenized American whole but instead wish to keep what is our own and strive for an interesting, eclectic, all-inclusive mix.

At a time when borders are changing rapidly and national allegiance can be a highly charged issue, restaurants and markets whose offerings transcend the divisions of geopolitics are a sort of cultural oasis, a metaphor for peaceful coexistence.

# RESTAURANTS

## International

### Johnny Mango
☎ (216) 575-1919
CITY: **Cleveland**   AREA: **Near West Side**
ATMOSPHERE: **Relaxed**   COST: **$$$**$$

**ADDRESS:** 3120 Bridge Ave.
**HOURS:** Mon–Thu 11 a.m.–10 p.m., Fri 11 a.m.–11 p.m., Sat–Sun 9 a.m.–11 p.m.; the bar is open Mon–Sat until 1 a.m., Sun & holidays until 10 a.m. **RESERVATIONS:** Taken, only for groups of 8+ **PAYMENT:** MC, VS, AX **BAR:** Beer, wine, liquor **TAKEOUT:** Yes **ACCESS:** ♿ Limited **OTHER ETHNIC:** Jamaican, Mexican, Thai

Owners Shelly Underwood and Gary Richmond refer to their place as a world cafe and juice bar. They offer a small but eclectic selection of dishes, drawing their inspiration from the Pacific Rim, the Caribbean, and Central America, which have cuisines that traditionally emphasize grains and vegetables. They also feature New Age–style drinks made from the likes of carrots, cucumbers, apples, melons, yogurt, and soy milk. If this makes you think it's a health-food restaurant, you're right, but that's only half the story. It's a health-food restaurant that goes the extra mile to try to make everybody happy. So you can get a burrito filled with beef or grilled veggies; a cup of coffee or a "morning after" (a blend of freshly juiced tomatoes, carrots, celery, scallions, green peppers, and garlic); fried tofu or french fries (made, it should be noted, with plantains rather than potatoes). The ethnic menu mix includes Jamaican jerk chicken and Bangkok barbecued chicken, Cambodian-style fried rice, Thai noodles, and Mexican black bean quesadillas. Produce comes fresh from the nearby West Side Market, and when it's available Underwood and Richmond favor organically grown stuff.

Depending on your point of view, some aspects of the Mango modus operandi are either too cute for comfort or tongue-in-cheek amusing: legumes are dubbed "Happy Beans" (presentation changes daily); extras for the burritos are listed under the heading "Merry Add-ins"; and the carrot and apple juice combo is known as a "Fruity Wabbit."

The décor is equally whimsical—colors are tropical; artwork on the walls, done by local Tremont artist Chris Demkow, has a "primitive" look; the pressed-tin ceiling is painted sky blue and dotted with clouds and glow-in-the-dark stars; and wood-slatted window blinds draped with ragged-edge fabric and rope seem meant to create a beach-shack ambience. Servers dress to express themselves and tend to be the sort who favor combat boots with shorts. It's a hip sort of hangout with a decidedly youngish feel that can accommodate vegans and unrepentant carnivores; light eaters and self-described gluttons; clean-living food purists and the persistently sinful who still indulge in animal flesh, alcohol, and sugar.

The restaurant is not large, accommodating about 35 diners. Tables have tile tops and each one displays a different design. The blond wood bar seats

10. It's located at the corner of Bridge, Fulton, and West 32nd, in an unusual triangular-shaped building of orange-yellow brick. Brunch is served on Saturday and Sunday from 9 a.m. to 2 p.m. and includes Vietnamese rice crepes, huevos rancheros, whole-wheat waffles, and omelettes. The regular menu kicks in at 11 a.m. Plenty of free parking on the adjacent streets.

## Loretta Paganini School of Cooking

☎ (440) 729-1110

CITY: **Chester Township** AREA: **Farther East**
ATMOSPHERE: **Casual** COST: **n/a**

**ADDRESS:** 8613 Mayfield Rd.
**HOURS:** Mon–Sat 9 a.m.–5 p.m. (open until 9 p.m. if there's an evening session); closed Sun **RESERVATIONS:** Required **PAYMENT:** MC, VS, DIS, checks **BAR:** None **TAKEOUT:** **ACCESS:** ♿ Full access *Not recommended for children

· · · · · · · · · · · · · · · · · · · · · · · · ·

Technically speaking, Paganini's is a cooking school, not a restaurant, but each year the school sponsors a series of ethnic dinners prepared both by staff and visiting chefs. One calendar, for example, highlighted the foods of Bohemia in Central Europe, Brazil, Italy, the American Southwest, Poland, Scandinavia, and Japan. The dinners are not exactly workshops, but they're definitely not your regular out-to-eat experience. Each features the cuisine of a different country or region, and diners learn a bit about the area, discuss recipes, and actually watch the meal being prepared. Although it is not really meant to be a hands-on event, sometimes the chef invites participation. The evening takes place in the school's large and comfortable classroom *cum* dining area. The room is brightly lit, and a mirror hangs over the stove and work area so that no matter where you sit you can see what's going on. Long tables seat six or more. To attend, you must sign up beforehand and pay in advance. Call for more information.

A second building has been added that includes a large kitchen and a wood-paneled dining area with a fireplace. The space is used for "cooking with a partner" classes—couples prepare a meal with a chef's supervision and then eat what they've made.

## West Point Market

☎ (330) 864-2151

CITY: **Akron** AREA: **Farther South**
ATMOSPHERE: **Casual** COST: **$$**$$

**ADDRESS:** 1711 W. Market St.
**HOURS:** Store: Mon–Sat 8 a.m.–6:30 p.m., Sun 10 a.m.–4:30 p.m.; Tearoom: Fri 11 a.m.–3 p.m., Sat 11 a.m.–5 p.m. **RESERVATIONS:** Taken, for tearoom **PAYMENT:** MC, VS, AX, DIS, checks **BAR:** Beer, wine **TAKEOUT:** Yes **ACCESS:** ♿ Full access

· · · · · · · · · · · · · · · · · · · · · · · · ·

The cafe is a spacious, bright, informal in-store eatery with seating for 75. Diners can look into the kitchen and watch the chefs at work. The menu changes seasonally, and diners choose from a selection of sandwiches, salads, and soups, plus specials the chefs are preparing that day. Items are also available to heat-and-eat at home. Making use of the array of international ingredients featured in the store, offerings are an eclectic mix of regional cuisines and flavors. Tables accommodate patrons in wheelchairs and high chairs. It's a popular spot with busy executives, harried shoppers, and parents with children. They do catering with 24 hours' notice. In addition, there's a 45-seat British style tearoom called Mrs. Ticklemore's offering teas, cakes, and savories.

# MARKETS

• • • • • • • • • • • • • •

# International

## Chandler and Rudd
☎ (216) 991-1300
CITY: **Shaker Heights**   AREA: **East Side**

**ADDRESS:** 20314 Chagrin Blvd.
**FOOD AVAIL.:** Meat (fresh, deli, frozen), fish
(fresh, deli, frozen, dried), produce, grains,
beans, flour, rice, baked goods, canned
& packaged goods, spices, condiments,
beverages, tea, coffee, wine, beer, prepared
frozen foods, takeout meals **HOURS:** Mon–Sat
9 a.m.–6:30 p.m.; closed Sun **PAYMENT:** MC, VS,
checks **ACCESS:** & Full access

The almost windowless brick facade
of this market facing Chagrin at Warrensville is less than eye-catching and
gives no hint of what's inside. Parking
is in a lot off Lomond (a side street), at
the rear, and entering through that back
door is a revelation. The supermarket
is large, with wide, easy-to-negotiate
aisles, well lit and well organized, and
loaded with attractively displayed food
products from around the world.

Whether you're hankering for di-
gestive biscuits from England, Swedish gingersnaps, Dutch cocoa, Indian
chutney, or Southern-style chow chow

relish, you'll find it here. There are
many popular brand-name packaged
products from Europe, and the ingredients for almost any cuisine you care,
or dare, to prepare. Under this one roof
you can find such specialty items as
vanilla sugar, Euro-style butter (which
contains less water than what we're used
to), almond paste, handmade pastry
shells from Belgium, French chestnut
puree, the short-grain sticky rice used
in Japanese sushi preparation, Chinese
cellophane noodles, and jars of Mexican
mole sauce. There's also a large selection of mixes that make international
cookery simple, everything from Scottish oat scones, Italian risotto, and German cakes to New Orleans–style dirty
rice and Moroccan couscous. The array
of specialized imported condiments,
sauces, mustards, vinegars, oils, jams,
and jellies is huge, perfect for spicing
up ordinary dishes. Imagine a simple
roast chicken made new with mango
chutney; done-in-a-minute Uncle Ben's
transformed by a topping of peanut
sauce; a relish tray saved from medioc-
rity by the addition of okra pickles and
piccalilli.

This is a great place to buy food
gifts—there are a variety of wines to
choose from, imported chocolates in
lovely tins, specialty candies like lico-
rice drops and butter rum toffees, and
many unique, prettily packaged gourmet items. Of interest to vegetarians
and anyone else who cares to eat something different and tasty are a number
of meatless vegetable pates. Also, this is
a full-service market, so there is a selection of non-ethnic foods and prepared
meals. Shopping here combines all the
advantages of a global perspective on
eating, modern convenience, and the
cozy, intimate feel of an almost extinct
type of market that existed before mega-
retailing was the norm.

## Chef's Choice Meats
☎ (440) 234-3880

CITY: **Berea**   AREA: **Southwest**

**ADDRESS:** 127 West St.
**FOOD AVAIL.:** Meat (fresh, deli), fish (fresh), produce, spices, condiments, tea, coffee, wine, beer, takeout meals **HOURS:** Tue–Fri 10 a.m.–7 p.m., Sat 9 a.m.–7 p.m., Sun 10 a.m.–5 p.m. **PAYMENT:** MC, VS, DIS **ACCESS:** & Full access

Kris Krieger, a trained chef, runs a very special butcher shop. Taste his weisswurst, sopressata, pastrami, liverwurst, and peppered bacon and you'll know what I mean. His spicy tasso ham is a gem, and perfect for gumbo or jambalaya. That's because he makes it all himself on the premises. He does dry curing, hot and cold smoked meats and even a few cheeses, mixes up his own spice blends, and at last count prepares 60 different kinds of sausage from kielbasa, hruka, kiska, and Italian to a coarsely ground Cuban chorizo, Jaternice Bohemian, and a rustic Portuguese linguisa flavored with lots of garlic, crushed red pepper, cider vinegar, and red wine. His works of culinary art age on shelves and racks in the back—there are slabs of prosciutto and pancetta, hunks of Gouda and cheddar, links of frankfurters and knockwurst, and Genoa salamis almost as big as baseball bats. Cottage hams soak in tubs of brine. "The only way I could put more from scratch into what I do would be to raise the animals myself," he said.

The store, a market since 1906, is in a residential neighborhood. Kreiger singlehandedly resurrected it. Besides his charcuterie, and cases of fresh high-quality, hand-cut, Ohio-raised meats and poultry, and his own house-made prepared foods—a menu that includes cabbage rolls, spaetzle, potato pancakes, a Tuscan chicken—the little place is packed with local artisan and imported products and bottles of wines. There are even a few tables. It's one-stop shopping for heat-and-eat stuffed peppers, pulled pork, an expertly trimmed beef tenderloin, pasta from Italy, and farm-fresh butter from Hartzler Dairy, plus a bowl of a soup and a fat sandwich lunch.

## Cleveland Food Co-op
☎ (216) 791-3890

CITY: **Cleveland**   AREA: **Near East Side**

**ADDRESS:** 11702 Euclid Ave.
**FOOD AVAIL.:** Meat (fresh, frozen), fish (fresh, dried), produce, grains, beans, flour, rice, baked goods, canned & packaged goods, spices, condiments, beverages, tea, coffee, prepared frozen foods, takeout meals **HOURS:** Mon–Sat 9 a.m.–8 p.m., Sun 10 a.m.–6 p.m. **PAYMENT:** MC, VS, DIS, checks **ACCESS:** & Full access

It started on our front porch and in our living room on Hessler Road in the '70s. My husband and I were among the founding members of the Food Co-op, a bunch of people, many with neither cars nor much cash, looking for a source of wholesome, interesting, and inexpensive food. We banded together, as folks so readily did back in those days, with others of our kind and formed a buying club. Members would take orders over the phone all week, then take turns going down to the Food Terminal in the dawn hours, using a borrowed and barely running old van, to pick up crates of fresh produce, wheels of cheese, and 50-pound bags of rice and flour. The demand kept growing, and the operation expanded, relocated multiple times, and ultimately became what it is today—a large, bright, pleasant, full-line, full-service grocery store.

The co-op is a not-for-profit operation, just as it was when it began, owned and staffed by members. The focus is on natural, healthy foods. Vegetarians form an important subset of the store's clientele. Much traditional ethnic food is also good for you and ideal for those who don't eat meat. So it should come as no surprise that the co-op is a wonderful source of products from around the world and a good place to find the unusual ingredients used in a wide variety of distinctive regional cuisines. It is especially well stocked with Indian, Asian, and Middle Eastern items. Expect to find curry pastes, ghee (clarified butter), chutney, canned Indian dishes like saag (mustard spinach), chole (hot and spicy chickpeas), matar paneer (peas and cheese), and heat-and-eat curry entrées; Japanese miso soup, sheets of dried seaweed, umeboshi plum paste, and noodles made from buckwheat, lotus root, or wild yams; Chinese rice sticks, tamari soy, hoisin, sweet and sour sauces, fresh bean sprouts, sesame oil, and egg-roll skins; coconut milk for Thai cooking, noodles for pad Thai, and peanut sauce; pita bread, spinach pies, containers of hummus or, for making it yourself, cans of chickpeas and jars of tahini (sesame paste), goat's milk cheese, and freshly prepared tabbouleh salad and baba ghanouj.

For those who want to eat well and eat ethnic without hours invested in cooking, there are mixes for everything from pilaf and felafel to polenta and risotto. They also give a nod to American regional specialties, providing Jewish holiday foods and black-eyed peas, greens, and grits for Southern-style dishes. To add ethnic flair to just about anything you serve, they offer jars of Greek Kalamata olives and roasted red peppers, pickles and sauerkraut from Poland and Hungary, and Mexican green and red salsas, jalapeno peppers, and green chilies. Spices and herbs of every description, as well as teas, are available in bulk,

so you can measure out as much or as little as you need. Grains like buckwheat groats and bulgur wheat, as well as many different types of rice, barley, and pasta, are available the same way. A large variety of beans, nuts, and seeds can be found on the shelves.

Both co-op members and non-members are welcome to shop here, but membership, which comes with payment of a fee, brings special benefits and extra cost savings. Those who choose to put in volunteer hours earn additional discounts. Get information about joining and working at the front desk. Parking is available both in front of and behind the building.

## Leach's Meats and Sweets

☎ (330) 825-6400

CITY: **Barberton**    AREA: **Farther South**

**ADDRESS:** 256 31st St. SW

**FOOD AVAIL.:** Meat (fresh, deli), produce, grains, beans, baked goods, canned & packaged goods, spices, condiments, beverages, tea, coffee **HOURS:** Mon–Fri 9 a.m.–6 p.m., Sat 9 a.m.–5 p.m.; closed Sun; bakery opens at 7 a.m. Mon–Sat. **PAYMENT:** MC, VS, checks **ACCESS:** ♿ Full access

Don't be surprised if you have to take a number on Saturday to get service. The low-slung stand-alone building houses a grocery, full-service butcher, deli where sandwiches and salads are sold, and bakery counter. *Akron Beacon Journal* food writer Jane Snow says they have the area's largest selection of homemade ethnic sausages including Italian hots, Mexican chorizo, Cajun andouille, Hungarian smoked, German bratwurst, Polish kielbasa, and Slovenian zelodec (only on holidays). The bakery offers European-style pumpernickel, Jewish rye, kolachi cookies, and sweet paska loaves at Easter. Leach's also does catering. Being unfamiliar with greater

Akron, I had a hard time finding the store until I discovered that Cleveland-Massillon Road turns into 31st Street. A big, tall sign makes it easy to spot from the road. The big lot makes it easy to park.

## Loretta Paganini School of Cooking

☎ (440) 729-1110
CITY: **Chester Township**   AREA: **Farther East**

ADDRESS: 8613 Mayfield Rd.
**FOOD AVAIL.:** Grains, canned & packaged goods, spices, condiments, tea, coffee **HOURS:** Mon–Fri 10 a.m.–5 p.m., Sat 10 a.m.–4 p.m., also during class; closed Sun **PAYMENT:** MC, VS, DIS, checks **ACCESS:** & Full access

This is an all-gourmet specialty store housed in a cozy, converted old home fondly known as the Gingerbread House. It offers a large and eclectic selection of imports and hard-to-find items. The stock of merchandise changes regularly: You might find vanilla sugar and almond paste from Germany, cannoli forms from Italy, and cloves from Madagascar on the shelves one month and pickled ginger, chestnut honey, and a tortilla press the next. A selection of gourmet oils, vinegars, spices, pastry supplies, and professional quality cookware and utensils are always on hand. Everything is personally selected by owner, chef, and cooking-school teacher Loretta Paganini. There are also many ethnic and international cookbooks for sale, and sometimes authors visit and the shop hosts book signings. Everything is neatly crammed together in a very small but nonetheless delightful space at the front of the Paganinis' cooking school, with lace curtains at the window, an Oriental rug on the floor, a stereo in the fireplace, and china from England gracing the old wooden mantel. (For more information about this

location see listing under the same name in the restaurant section of this chapter.)

## Mediterranean Imported Foods

☎ (216) 771-4479
CITY: **Cleveland**   AREA: **Near West Side**

ADDRESS: 1975 W. 25th St.
**FOOD AVAIL.:** Grains, beans, flour, rice, baked goods, canned & packaged goods, spices, condiments, beverages, tea, coffee, prepared frozen foods **HOURS:** Mon 9 a.m.–4 p.m., Wed 8 a.m.–4 p.m., Fri 8 a.m.–6 p.m., Sat 7 a.m.–6 p.m.; closed Sun, Tue, Thu **PAYMENT:** MC, VS, checks **ACCESS:** & Full access

Your first impression on entering Maria and Costa Mougianis's store is that they've tried to stock this small place with everything from everywhere, and that's not too far from the truth. This tiny corner shop, which can be entered either from within the West Side Market building itself or off West 25th Street, is crammed with an almost all-world selection of food: there's candy from England, chocolate from Belgium, saffron from Spain, coffee from Turkey, beans from Jamaica, rice from India, and tinned fish from Norway. A deli case is packed with a variety of Greek and Italian cheeses and olives. Shoppers will find imported mustard, jam, sauces, and honey; black, blossom, and herbal teas; a wide selection of gourmet oils, including walnut, hazelnut, almond, and rapeseed, as well as safflower and olive, and almost as many vinegars; dried fruits and mushrooms; pasta; canned salmon, caviar, and herring; crackers, biscuits, breads, and cookies. Rice, bulgur wheat, buckwheat groats, barley, chickpeas, and oatmeal are available in bulk quantities. And still, that's not all. There are meat grinders, tomato strainers, cheese graters, and coffeemakers, too. A visit here isn't just a shopping trip, it's an education. Metered parking on the street or use the market lot, which is a good city block away at the opposite end of the market building.

## Miles Farmers Market

☎ (440) 248-5222

CITY: **Solon**   AREA: **Farther East**

**ADDRESS:** 28560 Miles Rd.
**FOOD AVAIL.:** Meat (fresh, deli), fish (fresh), produce, grains, beans, flour, rice, baked goods, canned & packaged goods, spices, condiments, beverages, tea, coffee, wine, beer, prepared frozen foods, takeout meals
**HOURS:** Mon–Fri 9 a.m.–8 p.m., Sat–Sun 9 a.m.–6 p.m. **PAYMENT:** MC, VS, AX, DIS, checks
**ACCESS:** ⅊ Full access

Known among the cooking cognoscenti as "The Place to Shop" if you're searching for the freshest, most exotic gourmet foods or hard-to-find imported ingredients, Miles Farmers Market is a huge, bright, noisy specialty grocery store packed with products from around the world.

It's a place with a history. The store began as an open-air roadside produce stand in 1971, run by the Cangemi family. It's still family owned and operated, and Frank Cangemi, the man who started the business, runs things now. His VP and general manager, David Rondini,who used to cut the grass for Frank's dad, has been involved in the business since 1972. Produce manager Joe DeGaetano has been overseeing the gorgeous displays of fruit and vegetables since 1985. Many people come here for an outing, and the notion that shopping is a leisure-time activity is reinforced by the freshly-ground serve-yourself coffee that's just inside the door.

The selection of produce is vast, and it's not uncommon to see such exotica as Asian pears, star fruit, or papayas, morels, and fiddlehead ferns. An olive, pickle, and salsa bar, set up like a salad bar, allows shoppers to select and package their own combinations. The variety of beans is staggering: French flageolet, calypso, tongues of fire, giant limas, five different kinds of lentils, plus all the more standard sorts like garbanzo, fava, pinto, and black. There's an equally large variety of nuts and dried fruits. The cheese department has a stunning selection of almost 400 varieties. The full-service bakery offers a country Italian loaf, a French pain au levain, a Jewish rye, an Italian chocolate bread with the musical name of pane alla cioccolata, and much more. In Miles Hidden Cellars, shoppers will find wines and beers from around the world. There are at least 100 different brands and types of salsa, 40 versions of hot sauce, and 30 different kinds of barbecue sauce. It's impossible to list all the products Miles stocks, but rest assured that whether you need crumpets or grape leaves, pickled peppers or pasta, an estate-bottled olive oil, balsamic vinegar or butter from Europe, sausage or salsa, you'll surely find it here.

For take-home meals, the prepared food department also features an international selection: each day has a special, and it could be anything from bruschetta pasta salad or chicken Marsala to roast pork with dumplings and sauerkraut, fried chicken, ribs, and freshly made sushi. And if your salivary glands just can't take all the stimulation, there are even a few booths available where you can sit down and eat some of their prepared foods. The Market does catering and assembles gift baskets, a service developed by Frank's son Sebastian. For more information, check out the store's Web site www.MilesFarmersMarket. com

## Old World Meats

☎ (216) 383-1262

CITY: **Euclid**   AREA: **East Side**

ADDRESS: 651 East 185th St.
FOOD AVAIL.: Meat (fresh), prepared frozen foods, takeout meals HOURS: Mon–Sat 9 a.m.–6 p.m., Sun 9 a.m.–1 p.m. PAYMENT: MC, VS ACCESS: ＆ Full access

Owner and butcher-in-chief Ed Jesse has been cutting and preparing meat since 1978. He finally opened his own shop in 2001 and takes full advantage of the smokehouse out back. Jesse makes his own smoked Slovenian and Hungarian sausages, kielbasa, pork loins, cottage hams, and Cajun tasso. He also does fresh versions of kielbasa; Slovenian and Hungarian sausages; sweet, hot Italian, and Sicilian sausages; and bratwurst. The selection of cold cuts includes his own Polish krakowska and head cheese, plus mortadella, soppressatta, cappicolla, and prosciutto from other sources. Shoppers can also take home his Polish-style stuffed cabbage or grab a sausage sandwich to go. In addition to being able to buy steaks, roasts, chicken thighs, and pork chops, shoppers will find locally made pierogies, chicken soup, and packages of noodles. The counter help is friendly, the prices are good, and the parking lot is convenient.

## Pat O'Brien's of Landerwood

☎ (216) 831-8680

CITY: **Pepper Pike**   AREA: **East Side**

ADDRESS: 30800 Pinetree Rd.
FOOD AVAIL.: Meat (fresh, deli, frozen, dried), fish (frozen), beans, flour, rice, baked goods, canned & packaged goods, spices, condiments, beverages, tea, coffee, wine, beer, prepared frozen foods HOURS: Mon–Sat 9:30 a.m.–6 p.m.; closed Sun PAYMENT: MC, VS, AX, DIS, checks ACCESS: ＆ Full access

Pat O'Brien has been in business since the 1970s as a supplier of unusual, exotic, imported gourmet foods, wines, and spirits. The store received *Cleveland* magazine's Silver Spoon award in 1998, 1999, 2000, 2002, 2004, and 2005. Shoppers will find a large and interesting selection of cheeses, many air-shipped from France; olive oils; vinegars; pasta; sauces; caviar; Scottish smoked salmon; tapenades; bottled pickles, olives, peppers, and steaks. There are many brands of jam and jelly from around the world plus cookies, crackers, biscuits, imported chocolates, and candy. They also carry an extensive selection of teas and fresh-roasted coffees. Food items can be selected and assembled into custom-made gift baskets. Some nonfood items, such as French wine accessories, Reidel glassware, Spiegelau crystal, wine racks, and pretty-to-look-at napkins are also sold. Delivery available nationwide.

## West Point Market

☎ (330) 864-2151

CITY: **Akron**   AREA: **Farther South**

ADDRESS: 1711 W. Market St.
FOOD AVAIL.: Meat (fresh), fish (fresh), produce, grains, beans, flour, baked goods, canned & packaged goods, spices, condiments, beverages, tea, coffee, wine, prepared frozen foods, takeout meals HOURS: Mon–Sat 8 a.m.–7 p.m., Sun 10 a.m.–5 p.m. PAYMENT: MC, VS, AX, DIS, checks ACCESS: ＆ Full access

This is a full-service grocery store for adventurous cooks. The focus is on specialty gourmet products from all over the country and the world. Shoppers will find most everything available in a regular grocery store—and then some. So when looking for rice you can choose from white, wild jasmine, or Indian basmati rice. There may be only one brand of paper towels on the shelves but at least 50 different olive oils from France, Italy, Greece, and Spain. The market hosts international food promotions throughout the year that highlight a country and its cuisine with lectures, cooking demonstrations, and tastings. They regularly stock hard-to-find products like Devonshire clotted cream, piccalilli, and treacle from England; Swedish crispbreads and Scandinavian lingonberries; wine kraut from Germany; and the rose and orange waters used in Greek and Middle Eastern cookery. Uncommon produce is common here, and fresh herbs are available year round. Bakers come in at midnight to prepare made-from-scratch Old World breads. With over 4,000 labels in stock, they boast the largest selection of premium imported wines in the state, and the choice of cheeses is equally impressive: imports like Italian Parmigiano-Reggiano, French triple Brie, Dutch Gouda, Greek feta, and English Lancashire, plus products from small American regional cheesemakers.

Using an international array of ingredients, the kitchen, staffed by eight chefs, prepares a variety of entrées to take home or enjoy in the market cafe. (For more information about dining in, see West Point's listing in the restaurant section of this chapter.) There are always samples of new and unusual food products for tasting, and a newsletter, published monthly, lets you know about upcoming events. Visit their Web site, www.westpointmarket.com, to find out more about tastings, cooking demonstrations, and special buys. The site also lets you shop online, read recipes and cookbook reviews, and get directions to the market.

## The West Side Bakery

☎ (330) 836-4101

CITY: **Akron**   AREA: **Farther South**

ADDRESS: 2303 W. Market St.
FOOD AVAIL.: Baked goods, beverages, tea, coffee, takeout meals **HOURS:** Mon–Fri 7 a.m.–7 p.m., Sat 8 a.m.–5 p.m.; closed Sun
PAYMENT: MC, VS, AX, checks **ACCESS:** ♿ Limited

The husband-and-wife team of Barbara and Steve Talevich whip up a whole world of sweet things here at Pilgrim Square. The pretty little bake shop produces long, crusty French baguettes and buttery croissants; Hungarian walnut tortes and slabs of strudel ; Italian cassata cakes and crunchy biscotti; English-style scones; and traditional German, Greek, and Eastern European cookies. Tables and counter service make it possible to enjoy a coffee and a crème brûlée or pastry on the spot, along with a small selection of salads, sandwiches, soup, and other light foods. They're well known for their colorful and beautifully decorated cakes.

## West Side Market

☎ (216) 664-3387

CITY: **Cleveland**   AREA: **Near West Side**

ADDRESS: 1979 W. 25th St.
FOOD AVAIL.: Meat (fresh, deli, frozen, dried), fish (fresh, frozen, dried), produce, grains, beans, flour, rice, baked goods, canned & packaged goods, spices, condiments, beverages, tea, coffee, wine, takeout meals **HOURS:** Mon & Wed 7 a.m.–4 p.m., Fri–Sat 7 a.m.–6 p.m. **PAYMENT:** Cash only **ACCESS:** ♿ Limited

Back in the 1860s this corner was known as Market Square, a place where farmers brought their produce and city dwellers came to shop. The present building on this spot, dedicated in 1912, is an architectural landmark, and the West Side Market is one of the few remaining municipal markets of its kind in the country. An 18-month, $6.5 million renovation began in August 2000. The 46 tenants and 82 stands in the outdoor fruit and vegetable arcade include families who trace their ethnic roots back to 22 different nationalities. Many of the stands have been operated by the same family for three or four generations, serving customers whose own families have been shopping there just as long. Specialty produce items for many types of cuisine, from pomegranates and star fruit to bean sprouts and green bananas, will be found outside, along with just about any other fresh fruit or vegetable you can imagine. The same huge variety is available inside along the main concourse.

The following list highlights the merchants (with their stand numbers) who offer ethnic products:

**Rhonda Raidel, Pierogi Palace** (E-5), homemade pierogies

**Jerry Czuchraj, Czuchraj Meats** (B-10 & B-6), Eastern European–style cured meats and sausage

**Crepes De Luxe** (C-2) street-style crepes, Slovenian–style cured meats

**Hans Meister, Meister's Meats**, (C-5), German-style cured meats

**Melody Kindt** (C-9), Mexican chorizo sausage

**Dion Tsevdos, Urban Herbs** (C-13), exotic spices, small quantities or bulk

**Michael Mitterholzer** (D-2), Eastern European bakery

**John Bistrick**y (D-11), lamb, goat, Halal meats

**Roberto Rodriquez, Orale** (E-2), prepared Mexican and Puerto Rican specialties

**Angela J. Dohar Szucs** (F-1 & F-2), homemade Hungarian sausage

**Frank Ratschki** (G-3, H-3), bratwurst

**Renee Zaucha** (G-10), German sauerkraut

**Stamatios E. Vasdekis** (E-13), gyros

**Husam Zayed** (Grocery Department #1, 2), Middle Eastern foods

**Hoeun Khin** (E-11), Asian spices, sauces, and condiments

**Judy's Oasis** (A-5), Middle Eastern foods

**Reilly's** (C-11), Irish goodies

**Ohio City Pasta** (E-3)

**Old Country Sausage** (G-8), an international array of sausages

**Sam's International Grocery** (H-13)

**Sopheap Chea** (A-11), prepared Cambodian and southeast Asian specialties.

There is free parking in a lot east of the building. There's information about the market online, including a map and directions for getting there, hours, pictures, a vendor directory with direct phone numbers, and instructions for buying gift certificates, at www.westsidemarket.com.

# INDEXES

## Index by Name *(markets in italic)*

# Index by Location *(markets in italic)*

# Index by Country, Region, or Ethnicity *(markets in italic)*

Asterisk (*) indicates sub-specialty, not main focus of restaurant or market.

# Idea Indexes *(markets in italic)*

Have a special need? Can't decide what you want? Here are some fun suggestions to try when you're not sure where to go. This is by no means a comprehensive list, but it should get you started.

## Added Attractions

*These restaurants are not in big cities, but their locations put them close to interesting and entertaining destinations that can turn a meal into an all-day outing:*

Casablanca, 89
Chez Francois, 160
Ferrante Winery & Ristorante, 100
Hunan by the Falls, 11
Old Prague Restaurant, 137
Russo's, 208
V-Li's Thai Cuisine, 41

## Al Fresco

*Restaurants offering seating in the great outdoors (when the weather obliges):*

Anatolia Cafe, 76
Baricelli Inn, 96
Chez Francois, 160
Donauschwaben German Amer. Cultural Ctr., 164
Ferrante Winery & Ristorante, 100
Harp, 166
Henry's at the Barn, 211
L'Albatros Brasserie and Bar, 161
Lelolai Bakery & Cafe, 183
Lemon Grass Thai Cuisine, 35
Leo's Ristorante, 109
Michaelangelo's, 112
Nighttown, 167
Saravá, 180
SASA Izakaya & Asian Bistro, 26
Sergio's in University Circle, 120

## Around Midnight

*Places where it seems the kitchen almost never closes and you can get anything from a snack to a full meal long after the dinner hour:*

Bo Loong, 8
Corky and Lenny's, 209
Fat Fish Blue, 206
Lancer Steak House, 205
Li Wah, 13
Mardi Gras Lounge & Grill, 90
Nighttown, 167
Savannah, 208

## Bakery/Cafes

*Places to stock up on take-home goodies that also provide tables, chairs, and treats to eat on the premises:*

Caribe Bake Shop, 199
*Casa Dolce Italian Bakery, 125*
*Jasmine Pita Bakery, 80*
*Koko Bakery, 53*
Koko Bakery, 34
Lelolai Bakery & Cafe, 183
*Molisana Italian Foods, 130*
*Ninni's Bakery, 130*
*Perla Homemade Delights, 149*
Presti Bakery, 115
*Stone Oven Bakery Cafe, 132*
*West Side Bakery, 226*
*Wojtilas Bakery, 156*

## Buy in Bulk

*Markets offering various food products in a self-serve setting; purchase as much or as little as you need:*

*Almadina Imports, 81*
*Asia Food Market, 47*
*Cleveland Food Co-op, 221*
*Good Harvest Foods, 50*
*Holyland Imports, 82*
*Koko Bakery, 53*

## By Dawn's Early Light

*Early morning eats for those with the get up and go to get up and go there:*

Athens Restaurant, 88
Cedarland at the Clinic, 67
Corky and Lenny's, 209
Jack's Deli & Restaurant, 210
Koko Bakery, 34
Lelolai Bakery & Cafe, 183
Savannah, 208

## Call the Caterer

*When you want someone else to do your cooking, any restaurants and chefs are happy to oblige:*

Anthony's, 93
Arrabiata's, 95
Bratenahl Kitchen, 181
Caribe Bake Shop, 199
Chef's Choice Meats, 221

Henry's at the Barn, 211
Rachel's Caribbean Cuisine, 182
Savannah, 208
Shuhei Restaurant of Japan, 27
Thai Gourmet, 39

## Cheap Eats, East & Downtown

*Dinner entrees under $10:*

Aladdin's Eatery, 71
Aoeshi Café, 21
Asia Tea House, 42
Dailey's West Indian Food Mart, 181
Garden Cafe , 8
Greek Express, 89
Island Style Jamaican Cuisine, 182
*Koko Bakery, 53*
Koko Bakery, 34
Marie's Restaurant, 139
New Era Cafe, 139
Superior Pho, 46
Sushi 86, 28
Teahouse Noodles, 5
Wonton Gourmet & BBQ, 17

## Cheap Eats, West

*Dinner entrees under $10:*

Aladdin's Eatery, 70
El Taino Restaurant, 193
El Tango Taqueria, 185
La Brasa, 194
La Casa Tazumal, 195
Minh-Anh Vietnamese Restaurant & Market, 43
New Kainan, 17
Thai Hut, 40
Thai Kitchen, 40

## Cheese Choices

*The following stores are good choices if you're looking for some interesting examples of the cheesemaker's art:*

*Aladdin's Baking Company, 81*
*Baricelli Cheese Company, 169*
*Canton Importing Company, 122*
*Chandler and Rudd, 220*
*Dave's Supermarkets, 197*
*Gallucci Italian Food, 128*

Nate's Deli & Restaurant, 75
Phnom Penh Restaurant, 6, 7
Siam Cafe, 45
Szechwan Garden, 16
Taza Lebanese Grill, 69
Teahouse Noodles, 5
Udupi Cafe, 66

## Grocery Shop and Grab a Bite

*Markets with on-site eateries:*

Chef's Choice Meats, 221
Der Braumeister Deli, 170
Mi Pueblo, 199
Miles Farmers Market, 224
Minh-Anh Vietnamese Restaurant & Market, 43
Raj Mahal Indian Foods, 79
West Point Market, 225

## Legal-Ease

*Near the Justice Center*

Flannery's Pub, 166
Johnny's Downtown, 106
Mallorca Restaurant, 121
Osteria, 114
Saigon Restaurant and Bar, 44
Sushi Rock, 28

## Near the Game

*Convenient to Progressive Field and Gund Arena:*

Aladdin's Baking Company, 81
Fat Fish Blue, 206
Flannery's Pub, 166
Ginza Sushi House, 23
Middle East Restaurant, 74
Osteria, 114
Saigon Restaurant and Bar, 44
Sushi Rock, 28

## Out-of-Cleveland Experience

*Servers wear regional dress and/ or decor recreates settings from faraway lands:*

Empress Taytu Ethiopian Restaurant, 58
Frank Sterle's Slovenian Country House, 144
Ginza Sushi House, 23
Jaipur Junction, 63
Mexican Village Restaurante y Cantinas, 188
Mi Pueblo, 190
Shuhei Restaurant of Japan, 27

## Perfect for Parties

*Restaurants with private party rooms or facilities and services suitable for large groups:*

Agostino's Ristorante, 91
Alberini's, 92
Baricelli Inn, 96
Bo Loong, 8
Der Braumeister, 163
Ferrante Winery & Ristorante, 100
Flannery's Pub, 166
Frankie's Italian Cuisine, 101
Henry's at the Barn, 211
Leo's Ristorante, 109
Li Wah, 13
Nighttown, 167

## Quick Lunch

*For those who work in and around downtown, the following places get you seated, served, and back to work in less than an hour:*

Aoeshi Café, 21
Continental Cuisine, 68
Garden Cafe , 8
Ginza Sushi House, 23
Greek Express, 89
Ha-Ahn Korean Bistro, 31
Lelolai Bakery & Cafe, 183
Main Street Continental Grill, 74
Mardi Gras Lounge & Grill, 90
Nate's Deli & Restaurant, 75
Slyman's Deli, 211
Superior Pho, 46
Sushi 86, 28
Teahouse Noodles, 5

## Romance

*Where the atmosphere encourages hand-holding and the whispering of sweet nothings in each other's ears:*

Bucci's, 99
Casablanca, 89
Chez Francois, 160
Guarino's Restaurant, 103
L'Albatros Brasserie and Bar, 161
Mallorca Restaurant, 121
Valerio's Ristorante Cafe & Bar, 119

## A Room With a View

*Location, location, location:*

Bucci's, 99
Casablanca, 89
Chez Francois, 160
Ferrante Winery & Ristorante, 100
Harp, 166
Mallorca Restaurant, 121
Old Prague Restaurant, 137

## Serve Yourself

*Buffets offer a chance to see what each dish looks like before you commit, and to sample freely. A great way to get acquainted with unfamiliar cuisines. Some buffets are open for lunch only, others on specific days of the week. Check listing or call for specific information.*

Cuisine of India, 60
El Charro Restaurante, 184
Heimatland Restaurant, 164
India Garden, 62
La Brasa, 194
Nipa Hut, 18
Raj Mahal Indian Cuisine, 64
Saffron Patch, 65, 66

## Serving Sunday Brunch

Brasa Grill, 179
Bucci's, 99
El Charro Restaurante, 184
Empress Taytu Ethiopian Restaurant, 58
Harp, 166
Johnny Mango, 218
Nighttown, 167

## Side Order of Live Music

Agostino's Ristorante, 91
Fat Fish Blue, 206
Flannery's Pub, 166
Frank Sterle's Slovenian Country House, 144
Harp, 166
Mardi Gras Lounge & Grill, 90
Mexican Village Restaurante y Cantinas, 188
Mi Pueblo, 190
Nighttown, 167
Savannah, 208

## Sophisticated Side

*Restaurants for impressing out-of-towners and entertaining business associates:*

#1 Pho, 42
Akira Hibachi & Sushi, 19
Baricelli Inn, 96
Gavi's, 102
Gusto Ristorante Italiano, 104
L'Albatros Brasserie and Bar, 161
Michaelangelo's, 112
Osteria, 114
Ristorante Giovanni's, 116
Saravá, 180
SASA Izakaya & Asian Bistro, 26

## A Sound Choice

*Close to Severance Hall, these restaurants are used to diners who need to get to the concert hall on time. Reservations, of course, are a must:*

Baricelli Inn, 96
Guarino's Restaurant, 103
L'Albatros Brasserie and Bar, 161
Mi Pueblo, 190
Michaelangelo's, 112
Sergio's in University Circle, 120
Valerio's Ristorante Cafe & Bar, 119

## Take More Than Your Share Home

*These restaurants sell some of their most popular stuff by the pint, the quart, the pound, and the sheet:*

Ali Baba Restaurant, 72
Anthony's, 93
Cedarland at the Clinic, 67
Frankie's Italian Cuisine, 101
Harp, 166
Mi Pueblo, 189
New Era Cafe, 139
Nipa Hut, 18
'Stino da Napoli, 117

## Take the Kids

*Restaurants where the atmosphere is tolerant, the staff accommodating, food includes things kids are sure to eat, and prices won't require a bank loan:*

Frankie's Italian Cuisine, 101
Jimmy Daddona's, 105, 106
Leo's Ristorante, 109
Li Wah, 13
Mamma Santa's, 111
Marcelita's Mexican Restaurant, 187
Mi Pueblo, 189
Sokolowski's University Inn, 144
Vaccaro's Trattoria, 118

## The Show Must Go On . . . But Let's Eat First

*Located near Playhouse Square, and just the right atmosphere for making it a very special occasion:*

Johnny's Downtown, 106
Mallorca Restaurant, 121
Osteria, 114
Saigon Restaurant and Bar, 44

## Wines To Go

Alberini's Cork & More Shoppe, 123
Alesci's of South Euclid, 124
Canton Importing Company, 122
Chandler and Rudd, 220
Chef's Choice Meats, 221
Dioguardi's Specialty Foods, 126
Gallucci Italian Food, 128
Giovanni's Meats & Deli, 129
Molinari's, 113
Pat O'Brien's of Landerwood, 225
West Point Market, 225
Western Fruit Basket and Beverage, 123

# Eat Streets (markets in italic)

Sometimes where you eat and shop is determined by where you are. It's good to know that one street can offer many varied choices:

## Eat Streets—Cedar
Aladdin's Eatery, 71
*Boris's Kosher Meat*, 213
Nighttown, 167
Rachel's Caribbean Cuisine, 182
*Zoss The Swiss Baker*, 175

## Eat Streets—Detroit
Aladdin's Eatery, 70
Frankie's Italian Cuisine, 101
*Halal Meats*, 82
Harp, 166
Helen and Kal's Kitchen, 141
Maria's, 111
Minh-Anh Vietnamese Restaurant & Market, 43
Pearl of the Orient, 14
Savannah, 208
'Stino da Napoli, 117
Szechwan Garden, 16
*Vietnam Market*, 54

## Eat Streets—Lorain
Ali Baba Restaurant, 72
*Almadina Imports*, 81
*Assad Bakery*, 82
*Athens Pastries & Imported Foods*, 122
Der Braumeister, 163
*Der Braumeister Deli*, 170
*Dong Duong Indochina Grocery*, 48
*Farkas Pastry Shoppe*, 150
*Fragapane Bakery & Deli*, 127
*Hansa Import Haus*, 171
*Holyland Imports*, 82
*Jasmine Pita Bakery*, 80
Mi Pueblo, 199
Mi Pueblo, 189
Nuevo Acapulco, 191
Phnom Penh Restaurant, 6
*Saigon Trading USA*, 54
*Supermercado Rico*, 200

## Eat Streets—Madison
El Tango Taqueria, 185
Khiem's Vietnamese Cuisine, 43
Players on Madison, 115
Thai Kitchen, 40
*Tommy's Pastries*, 152

## Eat Streets—Mayfield
*Alesci's of South Euclid*, 124
Anthony's, 93
Arrabiata's, 95
*Corbo's Dolceria*, 126
*Giovanni's Meats & Deli*, 129
*Gorby Grocery Store*, 154
Guarino's Restaurant, 103
*Lakshmi Plaza*, 79
Mamma Santa's, 111
*Oriental Food & Gifts*, 49
Otani, 24
*Presti Bakery*, 131
Presti Bakery, 115
Trattoria Roman Gardens, 117
Valerio's Ristorante Cafe & Bar, 119
*Yeleseyevsky Deli*, 155

## Eat Streets—Payne
*Dave's Supermarkets*, 212
Garden Cafe , 8
*Good Harvest Foods*, 50
Koko Bakery, 34
Li Wah, 13
Seoul Hot Pot, 33
*Tink Holl Food Market*, 50
Wonton Gourmet & BBQ, 17

## Eat Streets—Pearl
Das Schnitzel Haus, 163
*Gaelic Imports*, 174
Goodman's Sandwich Inn, 210
*Jaworski's Meat Market & Deli*, 153
*Kobawoo Oriental Food Market*, 48
*Patel Brothers*, 79
*Samosky Home Bakery*, 154
*Seoul Asian Food*, 53
Tomo, 29

## Eat Streets—Ridge
Agostino's Ristorante, 91
Bovalino's Italian Ristorante, 97
Carrie Cerino's Ristorante, 99
*Casey's Irish Imports*, 173
*Colozza's Cakes & Pastries*, 125
*Dave's Supermarkets*, 197
El Charro Restaurante, 184
*India Food & Spices*, 78
India's Cafe & Kitchen, 62

*Kathy's Kolacke & Pastry Shop*, 148
Little Polish Diner , 143
Luchita's Mexican Restaurant, 187
*Rudy's Strudel & Bakery*, 176
*Sugarland Food Mart*, 49

## Eat Streets—S. Taylor
Cafe Tandoor, 59
*International Foods*, 147
Sun Luck Garden, 15
*Unger's Kosher Bakery & Food Shop*, 215

## Eat Streets—St. Clair
*Asia Food Market*, 47
Asia Tea House, 42
Bo Loong, 8
Empress Taytu Ethiopian Restaurant, 58
Marie's Restaurant, 139
Osteria, 114
Siam Cafe, 45
Slyman's Deli, 211
Tom's Seafood Restaurant, 16

## Eat Streets—Superior
#1 Pho, 42
Ha-Ahn Korean Bistro, 31
*Kim's Oriental Food*, 53
Korea House, 31
Superior Pho, 46

## Eat Streets—W. 25th
Kan Zaman, 73
Kan Zaman, 74
*Lelolai Bakery & Cafe*, 200
Lelolai Bakery & Cafe, 183
*Mediterranean Imported Foods*, 223
Nate's Deli & Restaurant, 75
Phnom Penh Restaurant, 7
*West Side Market*, 226

# Tell me where to go!

Do you know of an authentic ethnic restaurant or market in Greater Cleveland that should have been included in this guide but wasn't? Well, that's what new editions are for! Tell me about your favorite place; if you're the first to suggest it and I add it to the next edition, you'll receive a **free copy** when it's published. There's an link on my Web site ...

## www.ClevelandEthnicEats.com

---

# Free updates!

From time to time I post updated information about the restaurants and markets in this book on my Web site. I also post information of interest to anyone who enjoys Cleveland's great variety of ethnic food. Check it out:

## www.ClevelandEthnicEats.com

— Laura Taxel

**The Toe** / No one played longer for the Browns. Relive the golden era of pro football in this autobiography by Lou "The Toe" Groza. *with Mark Hodermarsky* / $12.95 softcover

**On Being Brown** / Thoughtful and humorous essays and interviews with legendary Browns players ponder what it means to be a true Browns fan. *Scott Huler* / $12.95 softcover

**False Start** / A top sports journalist takes a hard look at the new Browns franchise and tells how it was set up to fail. *Terry Pluto* / $19.95 hardcover

### SPORTS - BASEBALL

**Dealing** / A behind-the-scenes look at the Cleveland Indians front office that tells how and why trades and other deals are made to build the team. *Terry Pluto* / $14.95 softcover

**The Top 20 Moments in Cleveland Sports** Twenty exciting stories recount the most memorable and sensational events in Cleveland sports history. *Bob Dyer* / $14.95 softcover

**Ask Hal** / Answers to fans' most interesting questions about baseball rules from a Hall of Fame sportswriter. *Hal Lebovitz* / $14.95 softcover

**The Curse of Rocky Colavito** / The classic book about the Cleveland Indians' amazing era of futility: 1960-1993. *Terry Pluto* / $14.95 softcover

**Whatever Happened to "Super Joe"?** / Catch up with 45 good old guys from the bad old days of the Cleveland Indians. *Russell Schneider* / $14.95 softcover

**Our Tribe** / A father, a son, and the relationship they shared through their mutual devotion to the Cleveland Indians. *Terry Pluto* / $14.95 softcover

### SPORTS - GENERAL

**The Franchise** / An in-depth look at how the Cleveland Cavaliers were completely rebuilt around superstar LeBron James. *Terry Pluto & Brian Windhorst* / $19.95 hardcover

**Best of Hal Lebovitz** / A collection of great sportswriting from six decades, by the late dean of Cleveland sportswriters. *Hal Lebovitz* / $14.95 softcover

**Curses! Why Cleveland Sports Fans Deserve to Be Miserable** / A collection of a lifetime of tough luck, bad breaks, goofs, and blunders. *Tim Long* / $9.95 softcover

**LeBron James: The Rise of a Star** / From high school hoops to #1 NBA draft pick, an inside look at the life and early career of basketball's hottest young star. *David Lee Morgan Jr.* / $14.95 softcover

**Heroes, Scamps & Good Guys** / 101 profiles of the most colorful characters from Cleveland sports history. Will rekindle memories for any Cleveland sports fan. *Bob Dolgan* / $24.95 hardcover

**The View from Pluto** / Award-winning sportswriter Terry Pluto's best columns about Northeast Ohio sports from 1990–2002. *Terry Pluto* / $14.95 softcover

**Cleveland Golfer's Bible** / All of Greater Cleveland's golf courses and driving ranges described in detail. Essential guide for any golfer. *John H. Tidyman* / $13.95 softcover

**Golf Getaways from Cleveland** / 50 great golf trips just a short car ride from home. Plan easy weekends, business meetings, reunions, other gatherings. *John H. Tidyman* / $14.95 softcover

### CRIME & MYSTERY

**Cleveland Cops** / Sixty cops tell gritty and funny stories about patrolling the streets of Cleveland. *John H. Tidyman* / $14.95 paperback

**Amy: My Search for Her Killer** / Secrets and suspects in the unsolved murder of Amy Mihaljevic. *James Renner* / $24.95 hardcover

**They Died Crawling**
**The Maniac in the Bushes**
**The Corpse in the Cellar**
**The Killer in the Attic**
**Death Ride at Euclid Beach**
Five collections of gripping true tales about notable Cleveland crimes and disasters. Includes photos. *John Stark Bellamy II* / $13.95 softcover (each)

**Women Behaving Badly** / 16 strange-but-true tales of Cleveland's most ferocious female killers. *John Stark Bellamy II* / $24.95 hardcover

**The Milan Jacovich mystery series** / Cleveland's favorite private eye solves tough cases in these 13 popular detective novels. *Les Roberts* / $13.95 (each) softcover

**King of the Holly Hop** / #14 in the popular Milan Jacovich mystery series. *Les Roberts* / $24.95 hardcover

**We'll Always Have Cleveland** / The memoir of mystery novelist Les Roberts, his character Milan Jacovich, and the city of Cleveland. *Les Roberts* / $24.95 hardcover

### AND MUCH MORE . . .

**Truth & Justice for Fun & Profit** / Collected newspaper reporting from 25 years by the *Plain Dealer*'s Michael Heaton. / $24.95 hardcover

**Do I Dare Disturb the Universe?** / A memoir of race and education, this is the story of a girl who grew up and out of the Cleveland projects in the 1960s and '70s. *Charlise Lyles* / $14.95 softcover

**Feagler's Cleveland** The best and most talked about columns from three decades of commentary by Cleveland's top columnist, Dick Feagler. / $13.95 softcover

**Available from your favorite bookseller.** Info at www.grayco.com